25.00

The Origins of Indian Psychology

The Origins of Indian Psychology

N. Ross Reat

ASIAN HUMANITIES PRESS
Berkeley, California

ASIAN HUMANITES PRESS/AHP Paperbacks

Asian Humanities Press offers to the specialist and the general reader alike, the best in new translations of major works and significant original contributions, to enhance our understanding of Asian literature, religions, cultures and thought. "Asian Humanities Press" and "AHP Paperbacks" are trademarks of Jain Publishing Company.

Library of Congress Cataloging-in-Publication Data

Reat, N. Ross, 1951-
The origins of Indian psychology/N. Ross Reat.
p. cm.
Includes bibliographical references and index.
ISBN 0-89581-923-6 (cloth).—ISBN 0-89581-924-4 (pbk.)
1. Vedas. Ṛgveda—Psychology. 2. Upanishads—Psychology. 3. Hinduism—Psychology—History. 4. Buddhism—Psychology—History. 5. Psychology—India—History. I. Title.
BL1112.57.R43 1990
150′.954—dc20

90-48484
CIP

Contents

FOREWORD *vii*

INTRODUCTION 1
Sources and Aims of the Present Study 3

I. MONISM IN THE RG VEDA 9

II. THE VEDIC CONCEPT OF AFTERLIFE 25
Recurrent Natural Phenomena 28
Multiple Identification 30
Hereditary Survival in Offspring 31
The Heavenly Afterlife 38
Possible Latent References to Rebirth 52

III. THE VEDIC CONCEPT OF THE HUMAN BEING 58
A) INDIVIDUAL IDENTITY 63
Tanū 63
Śarīra 69
Rūpa 70
Nāma 74
B) VITAL FACULTIES 79
Jīva 81
Asu 82
Āyu 84
Vayas 89
Breath 91
C) MENTAL ORGANS AND FACULTIES 96
Verbal Roots 99
Citta 101
Manas 107
Hṛd 120
Dhī 129
Kratu 135
Conclusions 141

IV. *YOGA* AND *VEDA* IN THE *UPANIṢADS* 144
Shamanism and *Yoga* 145
Archaic *Yoga* 149
The Development of Rebirth Theories 154
Release and Cosmology in the *Upaniṣads* 166
Soul and Cosmology in the *Upaniṣads* 169

V. UPANIṢADIC PSYCHOLOGY 185
Mind, Speech and Breath 191
Speech and Name 193
Breath and Vitality 197
The Breath Faculties 203
Mind and Consciousness 207
Development and Differentiation of the Faculties 211
The Fifteen Vital, Perceptual and Volitional Faculties 214
The Five Classical Sense Faculties 227
Consciousness and Cosmogony 231
Hṛd 238
Manas 243
Faculties Derived from √*jñā* 247
Citta 251
Hierarchies of Consciousness 254
Early Buddhism and the "Two Soul" Doctrine 271

VI. THE FUNDAMENTALS OF BUDDHIST PSYCHOLOGY 282
Denial of the Soul 288
Vitality 299
The Fundamental Concepts of Buddhist Psychology 301

CONCLUSION 330

SELECT BIBLIOGRAPHY 332

ABBREVIATIONS AND ORIGINAL TEXTS CITED 341

GLOSSARIAL INDEX 345

Acknowledgements

I began the research for this volume under Professor Ninian Smart in 1973 as part of the M.A. and Ph.D. programs at the University of Lancaster. This is my first opportunity to thank him in print for his continuing support and encouragement since that time, and I wish to do so profusely. Much of the research for this work was carried out at the University of Sri Lanka at Peradeniya and at Sanskrit University in Varanasi. In particular, I wish to thank Dr. P.D. Premasiri and Dr. Lily De Silva of the former and my good friend Dr. Jita Sain Negi of the latter. At the time, this research in England, Sri Lanka and India would have been impossible without the financial support of my mother, Genevieve H. Reat. I wish to thank M.K. Jain, the Director of Asian Humanities Press, for his prompt attention to the manuscript during the submission stage. I fondly hope that his considerate and professional attitude toward authors will be rewarded with extravagant financial success for this much needed specialist publishing house. An equally heartfelt curse upon those publishers and reviewers who treat submissions as supplications to be dealt with at their infinite leisure. Finally, thanks to Alec Waskiw, the Wordperfect *guru* of the Prentice Computer Centre, University of Queensland, Australia, for masterminding the typesetting of this volume. This must be one of the largest typesetting projects ever undertaken entirely on a personal computer.

Foreword

Dr. N. Ross Reat is thorough and original in this volume. He sifts the *Ṛg Veda* for all its psychological concepts, and contrasts and compares these ideas with those exhibited in the classical or early *Upaniṣads* and the Pāli canon (especially the *suttas*). He delineates the subtle relationships between them and thereby enriches and modifies Heinrich Zimmer's hypothesis of twin origins of Indian notions — Vedic and non-Vedic. He knocks a final nail into the coffin of those who project key Hindu concepts, other than monism, back into the early hymns. He contrasts the empirical early Buddhist approach to later *Abhidhamma*. All this represents an important contribution to the debates and scholarship concerning ancient Indian thought.

I am proud to have been involved with Dr. Reat's work at Lancaster. He is one of a new generation of fine scholars of religion. I hope this book will stimulate thought about the cosmoses which interacted more than two millennia ago in India.

Ninian Smart

Introduction

Indian philosophy, Hindu and Buddhist, is remarkable for its emphasis upon speculation regarding the nature of consciousness. Starting around 500 B.C. these speculations were systemized into coherent theoretical formulations which justify the term "psychology". Not until the nineteenth century in Europe was the world to see similarly sophisticated treatments of the nature of human consciousness, and most of the modern Western advances on ancient Indian psychology have been in the clinical rather than the theoretical realm. Increasingly, modern psychologists recognize the sophistication of ancient Indian psychology and incorporate various of its aspects into their own theories and even clinical practice.

Several modern works on Indian psychology, most notably those of Jadunath Sinha and Rune Johansson, have rendered classical Indian psychology available to the modern West. This general availability is now such that some introductory psychology textbooks carry chapters on Hindu and Buddhist psychology. Popular works on the subject are numerous in alternative and occult bookshops. Though many of these are best left there on the shelves, they attest the current popularity of Indian psychology in the West.

The present work attempts to deepen existing scholarly understanding of the origins and early development of this remarkable aspect of Indian thought and to contribute to the understanding of the origins of Indian thought in general. With regard to the origins and early development of Indian thought in general, the present work contributes to the school of thought associated primarily with Heinrich Zimmer, which postulates an essentially dual origin of classical Indian thought. The traditional Hindu view is that all properly Indian thought — whether religious or secular, orthodox or heterodox — derives ultimately from a single source: the four *Vedas*, with the *Ṛg Veda* foremost among them. Zimmer's view, now widely but far from universally accepted in the West, is that the Vedic religious tradition, brought into India in the second millennium B.C. by Indo-European invaders, merged with an indigenous Indian tradition. This merger resulted eventually in the classical, orthodox, Hindu religious systems. According to this theory, the various heterodox religious systems — like Jainism, the *Ājīvikas* and Buddhism — represent survivals of the ancient indigenous religious tradition of India. Traditional Hindus, by contrast, regard these heterodox schools of thought as wayward misinterpretations of the revealed wisdom of the *Vedas*.

According to the Zimmer school, the traditional Hindu theory fails to account for what are arguably the three cardinal doctrines of classical Hinduism — the doctrines of 1) the immortal soul, 2) rebirth, and 3) spiritual release — for these beliefs are nowhere apparent in the ancient *Vedas*. According to the traditional Hindu theory, these doctrines are implicit in the *Vedas*, though perhaps not immediately apparent. A great deal of scholarly effort, both ancient and modern, has been expended in Vedic exegesis intended to reveal these supposedly latent doctrines.

The present work participates in this debate at a crucial level. It examines earliest Indian material relevant to the nature of human consciousness. This examination concentrates on the *Ṛg Veda*, the early *Upaniṣads* and the *Pāli Suttas* of Buddhism. It attempts in each case to reconstruct, without reliance upon later commentaries and systematizations, the underlying theories of the nature of human consciousness operating in these ancient texts. Such theories of consciousness impinge directly and obviously upon doctrines of the soul, rebirth and spiritual release. Because these doctrines are so central in Indian religions, there are many commentarial exegeses intended to bring the ancient and venerable scriptures into line with classical, systematic doctrine regarding the nature of human consciousness. As the present work shows, the ancient texts themselves — particularly the *Ṛg Veda* and the *Upaniṣads* — are not nearly as univocal as classical commentaries urge. On the other hand, careful analysis of the texts themselves reveals reasonably coherent psychological theories operating in these ancient scriptures. This is surprising in the case of the *Ṛg Veda*, and particularly surprising for advocates of the Zimmer school of thought.

The present research weighs in heavily on the side of the Zimmer school of dual origins of classical Indian thought. On the other hand, it suggests a larger Vedic contribution to Indian psychology than has heretofore been recognized by modern Western *or* traditional Indian scholars. Though the following is not polemic in nature, it should serve to dispel many of the erroneous interpretations of the ancient scriptures which have arisen over the centuries and which continue to arise as the modern West begins to take cognizance of the wisdom of ancient India.

Sources and Aims of the Present Study

This study of the origins of Indian psychology begins with the *Ṛg Veda,* the most ancient textual material bearing upon the topic in question. The *Ṛg Veda* is of dual importance in this study, first as the earliest expression of certain key psychological concepts, and second as the earliest example of the language in which these ideas and others were expressed and developed over the centuries. The *Ṛg Veda* is not, however, the sole source of Indian religion and philosophy. Therefore this study also involves examination of an equally ancient tradition of knowledge which was non-Vedic in origin, probably indigenous to India, and probably represented most purely in the heterodox schools of Indian thought, most notably Jainism, the *Ājīvikas* and to some extent Buddhism. Certain aspects of this non-Vedic tradition are pervasively influential in most of the so-called orthodox schools of Hindu philosophy as well, though these orthodox schools claim to have been inspired by purely Vedic ideas. In fact, the *Ṛg Veda* itself was partly composed after the migrating Aryans had reached the Indian sub-continent and therefore may not be altogether devoid of non-Vedic influence in its latest hymns.

Given that even the latest hymns of the *Ṛg Veda* — and thus any less ancient Indian textual material — may incorporate non-Vedic material, and since one of the major goals of the present study is to distinguish Vedic from non-Vedic characteristics in Indian psychology, several otherwise important texts will be largely ignored. The *Sāma* and *Yajur Vedas* are not considered because they are for the most part derived from the *Ṛg Veda,* and thus provide little additional Vedic material. More importantly, the *Atharva Veda* and the various *Āraṇyakas* and *Brāhmaṇas* are ignored to a large extent. While these texts contain much that is doubtlessly ancient and purely Vedic, they also contain much that may be non-Vedic in origin and is probably not as old as the most ancient Upaniṣadic material.[1] Moreover, they contain little material that relates to ancient Indian psychological speculations. Of course, the *Ṛg Veda* too contains little psychology, but is of vital importance here because it is the purest repository of the world-view of the ancient Vedic Aryans.

After the *Ṛg Veda,* the ancient *Upaniṣads* are the next oldest texts which this study considers in detail. These contain a wealth of specifically psychological material which reveals the intermingling of Vedic and non-Vedic psychological notions. There are, of course, scores of later *Upaniṣads,* the traditional number being 108, but in the present study, let *"Upaniṣad"* indicate the thirteen principal *Upaniṣads* which comprise the contents of Hume's translation and the bulk of Radhakrishnan's.[2] Of these, the *Maitrī, Kauṣītakī* and *Śvetāśvatara Upaniṣads* in particular appear to contain late, even possibly post-Buddhist material. Even though they use some of the terms of classical philosophy, they are concerned for the most part with genuinely Upaniṣadic ideas and do not appear to be the work of self-conscious systematists.

Shortly after the composition of the earliest *Upaniṣads,* around 500 B.C., the historical Buddha lived. His words, however, were not written down immediately, but retained in the memories of his followers for another 500 years before they were for the first time scratched onto palm leaves on the Island of Sri Lanka. Understandably, there is disagreement as to what the Buddha actually said. Varying accounts of his words were retained in India, where the so-called *Mahāyāna* or "Great Vehicle" came to dominate Buddhist thought. The *Mahāyāna* produced its first written versions of the Buddha-word at about the same time it was written down in Sri

1. Belvalkar and Ranade, *Indian Philosophy,* vol. 2, p. 135.
2. Hume, *The Thirteen Principal Upanishads,* 1931, Radhakrishnan, *The Principal Upaniṣads,* 1953.

Lanka.[3] It is probable, however, that the Sri Lankan *Theravāda* or "Elders' Tradition", by virtue of its isolation from the free flow of philosophical speculation in India, contains the most literal rendition of what the historical Buddha actually said. The archaic, repetitive form of the *Pāli suttas* shows that they are a written record of an established oral tradition, and most of the more sophisticated *Mahāyāna* ideas may be conveniently located in a more archaic form in the *Pāli suttas*.[4]

It should be noted here that at the time of their migration into India and for some time afterward, the Indo-Europeans were almost certainly illiterate. After the demise of the Indus Valley civilization, the first references to writing in India occur in Buddhist *sūtras*, and the earliest surviving examples of writing in India are the inscriptions of the Buddhist emperor Aśoka in about 250 B.C. There is no surviving example of writing in India from the time of the last, still undeciphered, Indus Valley inscriptions, dating about 1,500 B.C., until these Aśokan inscriptions. It is possible, then, that what has been spoken of above as pre-Buddhist literature was not actually written down long, if at all, before the earliest Buddhist literature. Nonetheless, Indologists conventionally rely upon the accuracy of oral tradition in India, and are probably justified in speaking of the chronological order of ancient compositions even in the absence of actual written texts dating from the time of composition.

Other than the three ancient *Vedas*, most of the *Brāhmaṇas* and *Āraṇyakas*, parts of the *Atharva Veda* and parts of the principal *Upaniṣads*, no other texts belonging to the orthodox schools of Indian philosophy may be said with any certainty to record pre-Buddhist thought. Soon after the advent of Buddhism, Indian philosophy, including psychology, enters a period of systematization and consolidation of the several classical schools of thought. The teachings of the historical Buddha, then, are a natural conclusion for this study of the origins of Indian psychology. The principal

---

3. See Conze, *Thirty Years of Buddhist Studies*, p. 124, and *Buddhism*, pp. 123-24.

4. See Thomas, *History of Buddhist Thought*, pp. 261-64; Pande, *Origins of Buddhism*, pp. 1-16.

Upaniṣads are the pivotal texts for this study. They contain at least germinal expressions of most of the important themes in Indian psychology. Some of these themes may be traced convincingly to earlier origins in the *Ṛg Veda,* but many cannot. This situation directs a study of earliest origins in Indian psychology beyond the verifiably ancient *Ṛg Veda* into a consideration of the archaic non-Vedic doctrines of the Jains and *Ājīvikas*. Some of these non-Vedic notions appear to be older than similar ideas found in the *Upaniṣads* and early Buddhist scriptures. The earliest Jain writings are, however, quite late, and the doctrines of the *Ājīvikas,* which school died out completely without leaving its own records, are only available in hostile references to their system in the works of rival schools. Nevertheless, unsatisfactory as this situation is, in order to explain adequately the origins of most of Indian psychology, it is necessary to advance the hypothesis that these schools represent the most ancient discernible form of the non-Vedic tradition mentioned above. Why this is so, and why these schools rather than Buddhism represent the purest form of the postulated non-Vedic tradition will become clearer in the course of this work. First, however, the *Ṛg Veda* demands considerable attention.

The oldest parts of the *Ṛg Veda* speak across four millennia, from an age so remote that we can scarcely hope to recreate a clear picture of it. So enormous was the influence of the Vedic hymns that from a many-centuried span of history, we have no trace of the thought of the Indo-European race other than the six "family books" of the *Ṛg Veda,* its oldest part. Before the beginning of the first millennium B.C., the family books, books two through seven, had been collected from the various traditions maintained by priestly Aryan families and organized in the manner in which we find them today. To that collection, the present eighth and ninth books were added at a slightly later date. Books one and ten were added sometime before 800 B.C., and the *Ṛg Veda* had taken the shape in which we now have it. Thus even a conservative historical estimate locates the composition of the *Ṛg Veda* as extending from 1500 to 800 B.C., making it one of the most ancient, and certainly the most extensive of the ancient religious documents of the human race.

Traditionally, however, the *Ṛg Veda* is considered to be more than ancient. Orthodox Hindus believe the hymns are eternal, revealed to the ancient sages, exactly as they stand, at some unthinkably remote period at the beginning of creation. The *Vedas* were ancient even to the ancients, and as early as the time of Yāska, the first recorded Vedic commentator, circa 500 B.C., there were those who lamented, as modern scholars do, that the hymns were archaic, obscure and mutually contradictory.[5] Yāska himself is highly conjectural in his exegesis of the few hymns he undertook, basing his commentary mostly on etymological grounds. He was often constrained to give several alternative explanations for passages that had become hopelessly obscure even in his time. Even the etymological *Pāda* text, probably pre-dating Yāska, is demonstrably wrong in several instances.[6] Parts of the original meaning of the *Ṛg Veda*, then, had been forgotten even by the time of the most ancient commentators. Modern Vedic scholarship assumes that often we today are better able to determine the original meaning of the *Ṛg Veda* than were its ancient interpreters.

At any rate, long before the *Ṛg Veda* had been written down, the early Upaniṣads had already been composed, and Indian thought had embarked on the course it was to follow until the present day, a course radically different from anything foreshadowed in the *Ṛg Veda*. Nonetheless, the *Ṛg Veda* has remained nominally the primary source of authority in orthodox Indian religious tradition. As a result, it often has been viewed and interpreted through the distorting lens of later and much different thought. The orthodox schools of Hinduism looked to the *Ṛg Veda* for authoritative support, reading into its hymns not only alien interpretations, but even alien subject matter. In fact, however, the two beliefs most obviously expressed in the *Ṛg Veda*, 1) the existence of many gods, and 2) the efficacy of ritual, are denied or seriously subverted in the *Upaniṣads*, which are nevertheless traditionally considered to be derived from the *Vedas*. On the other hand, three of the major Upaniṣadic concepts, 1) the soul as the

---

5. See Macdonnell, *History of Sanskrit Literature*, p. 49; Keith, *Religion and Philosophy*, p. 20. Also *Śābara-bhāṣya* 1.1.32, where even an ancient critic says that the *Veda* is "like the utterance of lunatics and children".

6. See Macdonnell, *History of Sanskrit Literature*, p. 41.

innermost essence of the human being, 2) repeated rebirth, and 3) the possibility of spiritual release *(mokṣa)*, are all lacking in the *Ṛg Veda*, though the pious often claim to find them there. Monism, the fourth major Upaniṣadic characteristic, occurs in a germinal form in a few of the later hymns of the *Ṛg Veda*, and thus appears to be largely a natural outgrowth of Vedic speculations.

Buddhism, which claims to be an independent, non-Vedic system, also makes major doctrines of rebirth and release, while rejecting belief in a soul of any sort. Though early Buddhism also rejects a monistic universal essence, the Buddhist doctrine of release *(nirvāṇa)* is decidedly more universalistic in outlook than the doctrines of release in the non-Vedic Jain and *Ājīvika* systems. This situation suggests that Vedic cosmological monism, which finds its clearest early expression in the *Upaniṣads*, had some effect on the otherwise non-Vedic, Buddhist system of thought, even though the philosophical basis of monism itself was rejected in Buddhism.

These considerations indicate that the doctrinal relationships among the *Ṛg Veda*, the *Upaniṣads* and early Buddhism are complex indeed. In essence, these relationships involve theories of the nature of the individual, of afterlife, of salvation and of cosmology. In the Indian context, each of these issues impinges upon early psychological speculation. Vedic cosmology and its relationship to Upaniṣadic monism is generally well known. Nonetheless this topic is briefly treated in Chapter 1 since it is directly relevant to the Upaniṣadic psychology of *ātman* and indirectly relevant to the Buddhist psychology of *nirvāṇa*. The Vedic concepts of afterlife and salvation are generally understood inadequately, and so are treated in some detail in Chapter 2 in order to differentiate them from apparently similar Upaniṣadic concepts. The Vedic concept of the nature of the human being is scarcely understood at all and extremely difficult to determine. This problem will therefore be treated in minute detail in Chapter 3. Chapters 4 and 5 build upon the preceding material and attempt to reconstruct the development and original nature of ancient Upaniṣadic theories of the nature of consciousness without relying upon later, sectarian exegesis. Finally, Chapter 6 assesses the degree to which this pre-Buddhist fund of psychological knowledge and speculation may have influenced the theoretical psychology of early Buddhism.

Chapter 1

Monism in the *Ṛg Veda*

Upaniṣadic monism is often expressed in psychological terms which equate the soul *(ātman)* with the universal principle *(brahman)*. Buddhist psychology is based on the linguistically opposite doctrine of non-soul *(anātman)*. This study therefore begins with an examination of the development, in the *Ṛg Veda*, of the concept of a monistic absolute. This examination considers the extent to which this absolute was conceived of in psychological terms. In so doing it lays the groundwork for an informed estimate of the extent to which Vedic monism may have influenced subsequent developments in *Upaniṣads* and early Buddhism.

Despite obvious differences, early Buddhism is remarkably similar to certain streams of Upaniṣadic thought with regard to doctrines of individual identity, rebirth, release and ultimate reality. The *Upaniṣads* and Buddhism both assert an ultimate reality in the light of which mundane reality pales to insignificance. Both systems are essentially pessimistic regarding mundane existence, which is seen as inherently unsatisfactory. In both systems, the realization of ultimate reality results in liberation from the vagaries of mundane existence, which, in both systems entails the cessation of rebirth as a finite, self-centered being. In both systems the path leading to the realization of ultimate reality involves morality, meditation and wisdom. In the Upaniṣadic system, however, *ātman* or *brahman* is regarded as the monistic ontological basis of both the universe and the individual psyche, whereas in Buddhism, *nirvāṇa* has no ontological function. Later on this subtle, but important distinction between the early Buddhist and Upaniṣadic concepts of ultimate reality will be examined more closely. First, however, an examination of the nature and development of Vedic monism is necessary from a historical point of view.

Throughout the *Ṛg Veda,* even in the verifiably early family books, which are probably devoid of non-Vedic influence, one encounters a remarkable tendency to elevate whatever deity is being addressed to the position of supreme deity, a tendency called henotheism by Max Müller. The term henotheism, however, suggests the worship of only one god without denying the existence of other gods. In fact, all of the gods in the Vedic pantheon are worshipped on different sacrificial occasions, and several of them are praised as the supreme deity.

Passages revealing this tendency are often of a distinctly anthropomorphic character and the god in question is represented as embracing the universe, holding it in his hand or wearing it as an adornment.

> When thou, O Maghavan (Indra) didst grasp even these two boundless worlds, they were but a handful to thee.
>
> *Ṛg* 3.30.5 (M)

> Him who surpasses heroes in his greatness; the earth and heavens suffice not for his girdles. Indra endues the earth to be his garment, and, God-like, wears the heaven as 'twere a frontlet.
>
> *Ṛg* 1.173.6 (G)

Of Savitṛ it is written:

> Golden, sublime, and easy in their motion, his arms extend unto the bounds of heaven.
>
> *Ṛg* 7.45.2 (G)

A slight modification of the representation of a god as an anthropomorphic titan locates the universe within the deity being praised. Such a twist gives the following verse about Varuṇa more monotheistic mood than the verses which merely ascribe to a particular god a size larger than the universe.

Indeed, the three worlds are embraced within him; he made the golden and revolving sun to shine in the firmament.

Ṛg 7.87.5 (M)

The all-encompassing natures of Aditi and Brāhmaṇaspati are especially interesting because of the survival of these two names in the *Upaniṣads* as terms for the monistic essence of the universe. Aditi appears in the *Bṛhadāraṇyaka Upaniṣad* with her own name, and Brāhmaṇaspati (or Bṛhaspati) is probably the precursor of the Upaniṣadic Brahmā.

Aditi is the sky; Aditi is the air; Aditi is the mother, and father and son; Aditi is all the gods and the five tribes; Aditi is whatever has been born; Aditi is whatever shall be born.

Ṛg 1.89.10 (M)

Thou who in every way supreme in earthly power, rejoicing by thy might and strength hast waxen great. He is the God spread forth in breadth against the Gods: he Brāhmaṇaspati, encompasseth this all.

Ṛg 2.24.11 (G)

Another common Vedic technique of awarding supremacy to one particular god is to convey upon him sovereignty over men and gods.

Thou over all, O Varuṇa, art Sovran, be they Gods, Asura, or be they mortals.

Ṛg 2.27.10 (G)

Agni Vaiṣvanāra, both Earth and Heaven submit them to thy threefold jurisdiction.

Ṛg 7.5.4 (G)

> Him whose high law not Varuṇa nor Indra, not Mitra Aryaman nor Rudra breaketh, nor evil hearted fiends, here for my welfare him I invoke, God Savitar, with worship.
>
> *Ṛg* 2.38.9 (G)

Not only, however, is universal sovereignty attributed to several different gods, but creation itself is said in different passages to be the single-handed feat of various deities.

> Wonderful Mitra propped the heaven and earth apart, and covered and concealed the darkness with his light. He made the two bowls part asunder like two skins. Vaiṣvanāra put forth all his creative power.
>
> *Ṛg* 6.8.3 (G)

> Lord of all wealth, the Asura propped the heavens, and measured out the broad earth's wide expanses. He, King supreme, approached all living creatures. All these are Varuṇa's holy operations.
>
> *Ṛg* 8.42.1 (G)

> Thou, Indra, art the Conqueror: thou gavest splendour to the Sun. Maker of all things (Viṣvakarman), thou art Mighty and All-God.
>
> *Ṛg* 8.87.2 (G)

> Great are the deeds of thee, the great, O Agni; thou by thy power hast spread out earth and heaven.
>
> *Ṛg* 3.6.5 (G)

Thus the earliest books of *Ṛg Veda* reveal a thoroughly polytheistic religion which moves only vaguely in the direction of monotheism by developing the mere concepts of creativity and supremacy and assigning these attributes to several anthropomorphic gods without any apparent hesitation.[1] Books one and ten retain the archaic characteristics of the early family books, but move more positively away from straightforward polytheism. This move, however, is in the direction of impersonal monism rather than monotheism.

Book one is treated separately here, as in all probability it is later than books two through nine, and earlier, in content if not in redaction than the tenth. It is in the first book, if this assumption is correct, that we first find the question posed within Vedic polytheism, "Which god is supreme?". Such a question indicates a concept of creation as the unique emergence of all that exists. This implies that universal creatorship cannot be, as it is generally portrayed in the *Ṛg Veda*, merely another laudatory epithet attached to several gods, but entails a unique first cause from which all else follows.

> 4. Who hath beheld him as he sprang into being, seen how the boneless one supports the bony? Where is the blood of earth, the life, the spirit? Who may approach the man who knows, to ask it?...
>
> 6. I ask, unknowing, those who know, the sages, as one all ignorant for the sake of knowledge. What was that one who in the unborn's image hath stablished and fixed firm these world's six regions?
>
> *Ṛg* 1.164.4-6 (G)

The riddle is a common feature of Vedic poetry, but here, in the famous "Asya-vāmīya" hymn of the sage Dīrghatamas ("Long-darkness"), a series of rhetorical riddles is the motif in which a coherent doctrine of monistic creation is set forth for the first time in the *Ṛg Veda*. In one of the most famous passages of the *Ṛg Veda*, Dīrghatamas says:

1. But see *Ṛg* 5.3.1 & 2, where Agni is said to be Varuṇa, Mitra and Aryaman, suggesting a more monistic concept.

They call him Indra, Mitra, Varuṇa, Agni, and he is heavenly nobly winged Garutmān. To what is one, sages give many a title; they call it Agni, Yama, Mātariśvan.

Ṛg 1.164.46 (G)

The obvious implication of these passages is that the polytheism of the *Vedas* is worship only of the attributes of one absolute being. This idea, by the time of the earliest *Upaniṣads* will have reduced the all-important sacrificial ritual of the *Vedas* to the status of a mere metaphor. The status of the many gods is further diminished in another verse of the same hymn, where not only the creation, but also the continued sustenance of the universe is attributed to this unique principle.

From her (Gaurī, the buffalo) descend in streams the seas of water; thereby the world's four regions have their being. Thence flows the imperishable flood, and thence the universe hath life.

Ṛg 1.164.42 (G)

Thus, in the "Asya-vāmīya" hymn, the sage Dīrghatamas puts forward the idea that the manifold universe is both created and sustained by a unique absolute principle. This represents a distinct philosophical advance over the naive creation hymns of the earlier family books. It is also in this remarkable hymn, not in the later and philosophically more sophisticated tenth book, that the *Ṛg Veda* makes its closest approach to conceiving of this unitary absolute in terms of consciousness, or in Vedāntic terms, conceiving of *brahman* as *cit* (consciousness) as well as *sat* (being). Thus, in this same hymn are some of the earliest verses that connect humans intimately with the absolute and seem to express the possibility of realizing that connection through mystical experience.

20. Two birds with fair wings, knit with bonds of friendship, in the same sheltering tree have found a refuge. One of the twain eats the sweet fig-tree's fruitage; the other eating not regardeth only.

21. Where those fine birds hymn ceaselessly their portion of life eternal, and the sacred synods, there is the universe's mighty keeper, who, wise, hath entered into me the simple.

22. The tree whereon the fine birds eat the sweetness, where they all rest and procreate their offspring, upon its top they say the fig is luscious; none gaineth it who knoweth not the father.

Ṛg 1.164.20-22 (G)

According to Sāyana, the two birds represent the individual soul *(jīvātman)* which eats, i.e. experiences the fruits of *karma,* and the supreme soul *(paramātman)* which is aloof from *saṁsāra,* both living together in the same body, the tree. This classical Vedāntic explanation is doubtful though, in that Veṅkaṭa, following Yāska,[2] says that the two birds represent Aditi and Soma, or the sun and the moon, the tree being the universal tree, a common cosmological motif in Indian symbolism. According to Veṅkaṭa, Aditi, the sun, is the one which eats *(atti).* This etymological explanation finds some support in an Upaniṣadic passage which, by the same pun, also links the deity Aditi to the verb *atti* ("he eats", B.U.1.2.5.). Thus, this may be a rather simple riddle.[3]

Nonetheless, it would seem that the overall intent of this Vedic passage is to state a relationship between "me the simple", the human being, and the absolute principle of the universe. Verse 22, though it may elude precise explanation, almost certainly refers to the possibility of mystical experience of this principle. Nothing in the hymn, however, implies the *identity* of human consciousness and the absolute principle. Dīrghatamas' hymn conceives of the absolute only in terms of being *(sat),* not in terms of consciousness *(cit).*

Nothing else in the *Ṛg Veda* approaches this hymn in context or coherence in expressing a relationship between absolute being and the human being. Even so, it never formulates this relationship in psychological terms. Throughout the *Ṛg Veda,* the human being is

2. *Nirukta* 3.12.

3. This explanation finds further support in Ṛg 10.114.3-5 where one of the "two birds" is obviously the sun or the moon. See also *Ṛg* 10.85.18-19;10.123.6.

defined in terms of the divine, either by his servile relationship to the many gods, or by a relationship of deficient participation in the absolute principle. The Upaniṣadic concept of the absolute as consciousness, on the other hand, seeks to define the absolute in terms of human consciousness, and the human being's relationship to the absolute becomes one of identity rather than deficiency.

The monistic tendency established in Dīrghatamas' hymn is more clearly formulated in a few outstanding hymns of the tenth book. In these hymns, the ancient sages confronted more directly the unsettling mythological and sacrificial implications of a monistic doctrine, but they did not move any closer than Dīrghatamas to Upaniṣadic, psychological monism.

> 1. In the beginning rose Hiraṇyagarbha, born only lord of all created beings. He fixed and holdeth up this earth and heaven. What god shall we adore with our oblation?
> 2. Giver of vital breath, of power and vigour, he whose commandments all the gods acknowledge: the lord of death, whose shade is life immortal. What god shall we adore with our oblation?
>
> *Ṛg* 10.121.1-2 (G)

The question "What god shall we adore with our oblation?" clearly expresses doubt concerning the polytheism of the early *Ṛg Veda*, a doubt which becomes abundantly clear in perhaps the most famous hymn of the *Ṛg Veda*.

> 6. Who verily knows and who can declare it, whence it was born and whence comes this creation? The gods are later than this world's production. Who knows then whence it first came into being?
> 7. He, the first origin of this creation, whether he formed it all or did not form it, (he) whose eye controls this world in highest heaven, he verily knows it, or perhaps he knows not.
>
> *Ṛg* 10.129.6-7 (G)

The first few verses of this same hymn are perhaps the clearest formulation of monism in the *Ṛg Veda*.

> 1. Then was not non-existent nor existent; there was no realm of air, no sky beyond it. What covered in, and where? And what gave shelter? Was water there, unfathomed depth of water?
>
> 2. Death was not then, nor was there aught immortal; no sign was there, the day's and night's divider. That one thing, breathless, breathed by its own nature; apart from it was nothing whatsoever.
>
> 3. Darkness there was; at first concealed in darkness this all was indiscriminated chaos. All that existed then was void and formless; by the great power of warmth *(tapas)* was born that unit.
>
> *Ṛg* 10.129.1-3 (G)

This clear and beautiful postulation of an absolute unity which was cause and apparently the original substance of the entire universe is an important landmark in the development of philosophical thought in India. The fact remains, however, that even in its latest and most sophisticated hymns, the Vedic approach to absolute being is cosmogonically oriented, an orientation which locates the absolute at some inaccessible point in the distant past and stops far short of the Upaniṣadic identification of the universal principle with the essence of the human being.

Various passages describe the exhilarating effects of drinking *soma* as making human beings like the gods in power and majesty. These do not reflect psychological content of Upaniṣadic ilk in Vedic monism, though they may well have provided authoritative referents in Vedic orthodoxy for Upaniṣadic statements such as "I am *brahman*", as for example at B.U. 1.4.10. which refers to *Ṛg* 4.26.1. The follwoing Vedic passage typefies this category of hymn.

> 7. The heavens and earth themselves have not grown equal to one half of me. Have I not drunk of *soma* juice?
>
> 8. I in my grandeur have surpassed the heavens and all this spacious earth. Have I not drunk of *soma* juice?
>
> *Ṛg* 10.119.7-8 (G)

Most of this type of hymn are clearly instances of the poetic device whereby the subject of the poem speaks through the poet. Indeed, the author of this hymn, according to Sāyana, is Indra himself. Even if some of these ecstatic hymns are taken to be the human poet's reaction to an exhilarating drug, statements such as the preceding are most naturally interpreted as hyperbole expressing a euphoric state in which the poet feels like a god. This exhilarated state, even if it is taken to be a sort of human divinity, bears no resemblance to the Upaniṣadic concept of the utterly peaceful and inactive human consciousness which resolves within itself the cosmos without differentiation.

Though the *Ṛg Veda* lacks an overtly psychological orientation in its approach to the absolute, two potentially psychological motifs are employed in two creation hymns of the tenth book. The "Puruṣa Sūkta" declares that the universe originated from a cosmic person, and the "Nāsadīya Sūkta" asserts that desire was the original creative force. These motifs must be borne in mind when evaluating the extent to which Vedic monistic tendencies influenced the Upaniṣadic concept of the absolute as consciousness and the Buddhist cosmology of desire.

The "Puruṣa Sūkta" narrates the creation of the universe by the sacrifice and dismemberment of the cosmic person *(puruṣa)*, who is said to be "all this (universe) what has been and what is to be".[4] The unitary cosmological principle is depicted as a person, a motif reminiscent of the Upaniṣadic identification of the self *(ātman)* with the universal principle *(brahman)*.

> 1. A thousand heads hath Puruṣa, a thousand eyes, a thousand feet. On every side pervading earth he fills a space ten fingers wide.
>
> 2. This Puruṣa is all that yet hath been and all that is to be; the lord of immortality which waxes greater still by food.
>
> 4. With three-fourths Puruṣa went up; one-fourth of him again was here. Thence he strode out to every side over what eats not and what eats.
>
> *Ṛg* 10.90.1-4 (G)

4. *Ṛg* 10.90.2; cp. *Ṛg* 1.89.10.

Though the unique creative principle in this hymn is said to be a person, the thrust of the hymn is to draw a sharp distinction between the divine, the three-fourths that "went up", and the mundane, the one-fourth that encompasses "what eats not and what eats", i.e. inanimate and animate creation. Griffith's translation of verse three is misleading in this respect, and must be considered separately. He renders the third verse as follows:

> So mighty is he in his greatness; yea, greater than this is Puruṣa. All creatures are one-fourth of him, three-fourths eternal life in heaven.
> *Ṛg* 10.90.3 (G)

Muir's translation of the same verse is altogether more accurate.

> Such is his greatness; and Purusha is superior to this. All existing things are a quarter of him, and that which is immortal in the sky is three quarters of him.
> *Ṛg* 10.90.3 (M)

Griffith's translation implies that creatures are composed of one quarter of Puruṣa and three quarters immortality in heaven, but the hymn clearly states that mortal beings, though they share in the primal substance of the universe, do not share in heavenly immortality, the divine three fourths of Puruṣa that "went up".[5] This point is further clarified later in the same hymn:

> 11. When they divided Purusha, into how many parts did they distribute him? What was his mouth? What were his arms? What were called his thighs and feet?

5. Literal translation: "A quarter of him *(pādo'sya)* (is) all beings *(viśvā bhūtāni)*. Three quarters of him *(tripād asya)* (is) immortality *(amṛtam)* in heaven *(divi)*".

12. The Brāhman was his mouth; the Rājanya became his arms; the Viaśya was his thighs; the Śūdra sprang from his feet.

Ṛg 10.90.11-12 (M)

Here the enumeration of the four castes of society obviously refers to the creation of human beings, and from verse six onwards, if Sāyana's interpretation in correct, the hymn deals with the sacrifice and dismemberment of the one-fourth of the original Puruṣa which forms the phenomenal universe. Sāyana's interpretation is based on a paradoxical statement in verse five to the effect that Virāj was born from Puruṣa and Puruṣa was born from Virāj. According to Sāyana, Virāj is in fact the cosmic egg *(brahmāṇḍa).* Sāyana explains this passage along Vedāntic lines, saying that after having produced out of himself this cosmic egg, representing the material substance of the universe, Puruṣa, the animating male principle entered into it and was born again from it in the form of a son, the living, moving universe.[6]

This interpretation, it may be noted, offers a possible explanation for the one-fourth/three-fourths division of Puruṣa. The second Puruṣa, the son, the moving universe, if born from Virāj, the cosmic egg which was half of the original Puruṣa, would be half of the fertilized Virāj. He would be therefore, one-fourth of the original Puruṣa, the quarter which is said to comprise the created universe. Sāyana's explanation however, is doubtful. Yāska, commenting on a similar passage about the reciprocal generation of Aditi and Dakṣa (*Ṛg* 10.72.4.5.), muses: "How can this be possible?" and is content to offer alternative explanations: either they had the same origin, or they were born from each other and derived their substance from each other.[7] It would seem then that Yāska, in the fifth century B.C., was unaware of the Vedāntic interpretationwith which Sāyana explains the reciprocal generation of Virāj and Puruṣa.

At any rate, whatever the correct interpretation of the hymn, the monism of this passage is confined to cosmogony. Though the anthropomorphic metaphor around which the "Puruṣa Sūkta" is built

---

6. See T.U. 2.6.1; Mt.U. 2.6. Cp. *Ṛg* 10.72.4-5.

7. *Nirukta* 11.23.

imbues the hymn with Vedāntic psychological overtones, these overtones are not grounded in the actual text of the hymn. Contrary to the Vedāntic doctrine that human consciousness ultimately encompasses the entire universe, the "Puruṣa Sūkta" sharply delineates the divine and the mundane without relating either to human consciousness. This hymn, then, is not an adequate basis for the Upaniṣadic doctrine of the absolute as consciousness *(cit)*.

Even if one insists upon seeing psychological content in this ancient cosmogony, the resemblance of the central motif of the "Puruṣa Sūkta" to the ancient and apparently non-Vedic, Jain concept of the universe being in the shape of a giant person[8] may indicate non-Vedic influence. Moreover, the delineation of the four *varṇas* or classes (lit. colors) in verse twelve of the same hymn is the earliest recorded reference to the sacred classes of Indian society. This suggests that the Aryans had already come into close contact with the indigenous inhabitants of India when this hymn was composed. The dark skinned Indians, called Dāsas (lit. slaves) in the *Ṛg Veda*, probably comprised the original *śūdra* or peasant class. This and other textual evidence[9] is corroborated by philological evidence of the relative lateness of the "Puruṣa Sūkta" and indeed the entire tenth book of the *Ṛg Veda*.[10] One must therefore be aware of the possibility of non-Vedic influence in the tenth book when one evaluates the extent to which the *Ṛg Veda* may be considered the basis of subsequent Indian thought.

This same consideration must be borne in mind in the examination of the second psychological motif found in the cosmogonic monism of the late hymns, the remarkable statement in the "Nāsadīya Sūkta" that desire was the original motive force behind the creation of the universe from the original unit.

---

8. See Smart, *Doctrine and Argument*, p. 63; Zimmer, *Philosophies of India*, p. 275.

9. In fact the Indian seasons enumerated in verse six may also be an indication of lateness. See Griffith's note and Velankar, *Ṛksūktaśati*, p. 279, n. 6.

10. Macdonell opines without proof that the "Puruṣa Sūkta" is the "latest hymn in the *Ṛg Veda*". *History of Sanskrit Literature*, p. 113.

> 3. In the beginning darkness existed, enveloped in darkness. All this was undistinguishable water. That one which lay void, and wrapped in nothingness, was developed by power of fervour *(tapas)*.
>
> 4. Desire first arose in it, which was the primal germ of mind; (and which) sages, searching with their intellect, have discovered in their heart to be the bond which connects entity with nonentity.
>
> *Ṛg* 10.129.3-4 (M)

Desire *(kāma)* as a cosmogonic force, even more than the *puruṣa* motif of *Ṛg* 10.90, imparts a psychological tone to the present hymn, for the impulse behind the creation of the universe is here said to be a familiar human emotion occurring in the divine mind. This same human desire under a different name *(tṛṣṇa)* is, in Buddhism, said to be the cause of suffering *(duḥkha)*, and thus is, in a way, the Buddhist universal cause. The Buddha was not concerned with the substantial essence of the universe, but rather with the essence of one's experience of the universe, which, he said, is suffering. This suffering is caused by desire, the impulse behind the psychological universe with which the Buddha chose to deal, as opposed to the material universe which the Vedic sages are concerned with explaining.

Several important characteristics, however, make the role of desire in the psychologically oriented Buddhist "cosmology of suffering" strikingly different from the role of desire in the Vedic passage under consideration. First, the universe which is being explained is, in the Buddhist context, *saṁsāra*. This term implies, rather than the physical universe, the ongoing, tedious, unsatisfactory experience of life after life in the form of a limited selfish consciousness. Second, the cause of this "universe" of suffering is individual human desire, rather than a divine parallel. Third, the creation of this psychological universe by desire is not located at some distant, inaccessible point in mythological time, but is continuous, as active in the present moment as ever, and therefore reversible. Suffering may be overcome.

The Upaniṣadic concept of desire as a cosmogonic force shows similarities to and differences from both the Vedic and the Buddhist concepts, as the following passage illustrates.

> 1. In the Beginning this (world) was only the self *(ātman)* in the shape of a person....
>
> 3. He, verily, had no delight. Therefore he who is alone has no delight. He desired *(aicchat)* a second. He caused that self to fall into two parts. From that arose husband and wife.
>
> 10. ***Brahman,*** indeed, was this in the beginning. It knew itself only as "I am ***Brahman***". Therefore it became all. Whoever among the gods became awakened *(pratyabudhyata)* to this, he, indeed, became that. It is the same in the case of seers, same in the case of men. Seeing this, indeed, the seer Vama-deva knew, "I was Manu and the sun too". This is so even now. Whoever knows thus, "I am *Brahman*", becomes this all.
>
> B.U. 1.4.1.-10 (R)

Here, though Vedic mythological elements are prominent, the personal nature of the cosmogonic principle is emphasized. Using a sexual metaphor, the universal principle is pictured as being subject to the same fear and loneliness that plagues the ordinary person. As a result of this principle's desire to escape loneliness, the universe came into being. In the Upaniṣadic context the process of creation remains contemporary in human desire, and is therefore reversible. In the *Upaniṣads,* individual enlightenment, which may be taken as a conquering of desire, is depicted as a return to a pre-creation state of pristine unity, a state which, before the original act of desire, had been the universal situation. In the Upaniṣadic system, individual spiritual attainment is seen as a verification of the speculative monistic doctrine that "all is one". The reversal of the creative process started by desire involves a merging into ontological being. The Upaniṣadic sages may well have learned the concept of cosmogonic monism from the *Vedas,* but Upaniṣadic monism takes on overtly psychological overtones in that the process of creation is seen as an ongoing function of the human mind.

When a few passages of doubtful interpretation are laid aside, it is clear that Vedic monism, unlike Upaniṣadic monism, was primarily concerned with cosmogony, and was ontological rather than psychological in its approach. In accounting for the origin of matter and motion in the universe, the *Ṛg Veda* vacillates even at its most sophisticated level of cosmogonic speculation, between a purely monistic position and a quasi-monistic position. The "Nāsadīya Sūkta" attempts, within the limits of available terms and concepts, to resolve matter and energy to a single source. Some quasi-monistic hymns, however, allow that these two absolutes existed separately in the beginning, or at least do not attempt to explain the origin of the matter upon which the original creative agent exerted itself. Others, like the "Puruṣa Sūkta", do not explain the original agent. This inconsistency seems to reflect a lack of philosophical sophistication rather than divergent views on the nature of creation. The culmination of the *Ṛg Veda's* cosmogonic speculation in the tenth book points toward a monistic concept of a unitary material and efficient cause of the universe. However, this monistic essence of the universe is conceived of in cosmogonic rather than, as in the *Upaniṣads,* psychological terms. In the *Ṛg Veda,* the nature and place of the human being in the universe is considerably less important than it came to be in the *Upaniṣads,* where the human consciousness usurps the position of even the highest gods and comes to be thought of as ultimately identical with the unitary absolute principle of the universe.

Chapter 2

The Vedic Concept of Afterlife and Salvation

This chapter and the following examine the Vedic concept of the nature and potential of the human being. The previous chapter pointed out some of the differences between the Vedic and Upaniṣadic treatments of monism. In the present study, the most important of these differences is that whereas Vedic monism is confined to cosmogony, Upaniṣadic monism extends into the realm of psychology. Though still involved in cosmogony, monism in the *Upaniṣads* becomes an integral part of psychological speculations regarding the essential nature of human consciousness. This psychological monism is also the primary mode of expressing the nature of spiritual release or *mokṣa,* the ultimate potential of the human being. The root of these Upaniṣadic theories, as well as most other Indian psychological notions, is the theory of rebirth.

The *Ṛg Veda* lacks both the concept of rebirth and the notion of mystical release. Scrutiny of the text reveals instead the concept of a single afterlife in heaven or in hell. The concept of the identity strand linking the earthly person with the afterlife entity is a complex affair involving heredity and ritual. There is no indication in the *Ṛg Veda* of the concept of a unitary and essential human soul which inevitably survives death and establishes one's identity in the afterlife. Instead, the person is depicted as a conglomeration of more or less equally important vital and mental faculties, several of which play a role in the afterlife. Thus, the *Ṛg Veda* lacks three of the essential concepts of Upaniṣadic psychology: (1) the concept of a unitary and essential soul or *ātman* which (2) necessarily survives death and is reborn in the normal course of events and which (3) ultimately may be released from the vagaries of rebirth through mystical union with the essence of the universe.

The general Vedic concept of the afterlife is that after death, upon the performance of a proper funeral,[1] one would hopefully enter an exceptionally pleasant paradise,[2] the abode of the ancestors *(pitṛ)*, where one could conceivably live forever.[3] An everlasting afterlife, however, was thought to be contingent upon the continued performance of sustaining rites by one's descendants.[4] The excellence of one's position in the heavenly hierarchy would be determined primarily on the basis of one's ritual activity while alive[5] and to some extent by the ritual activity of descendants on behalf of the deceased.[6] There is some indication that ritual was not thought to be the only requirement for entrance into this paradise. The *Ṛg Veda* implies that the performance of ritual austerity *(tapas)*, heroism in battle, the promotion of sacred rites and great knowledge might also be instrumental in winning a place in the abode of the ancestors.[7] Morality and generosity are encouraged as being of practical expedience in one's earthly life,[8] and there is some indication that such positive social virtues also conduce to a heavenly afterlife.[9] There was also thought to be an exceedingly unpleasant afterlife in an "abyss" of "blind darkness" awaiting the wicked and irreligious after death,[10] but an effective curse might also condemn one to an afterlife in hell.[11] Thus, on the basis of scant information on the Vedic concept of the afterlife, derived mostly from a few funeral hymns in the tenth book, their belief seems to have been that after a single earthly life,

---

1. Normally cremation (*Ṛg* 10.15; 10.16; 10.17), though apparently burial was also practiced (*Ṛg* 10.18.11; 10.15.14).
2. *Ṛg* 9.113.7-11; 1.154.5.
3. *Ṛg* 9.113.11; 1.125.6; 5.4.10; 5.63.2; 7.57.6.
4. See Keith, *Religion and Philosophy*, pp. 425-32. Also *Ṛg* 10.15.6; 10.16.2.
5. *Ṛg* 10.14.8. See Muir's translation, vol. 5, p. 293.
6. *Ṛg* 10.15.1-2, discussed further below.
7. *Ṛg* 10.154.2-5.
8. *Ṛg* 10.117.
9. *Ṛg* 1.125.5; 10.107.
10. *Ṛg* 4.5.5; 9.73.8; 10.103.12.
11. *Ṛg* 10.152.4; 10.103.12.

one enters heaven or hell for ever, the primary criterion being one's ritual activity during the earthly life. The extent to which a moral life was considered to be conducive to a heavenly afterlife is difficult to determine on the basis of the material available in the *Ṛg Veda*. Its priestly concerns naturally tend to emphasize the ritual rather than the moral aspects of securing for oneself a blessed life after death. Regardless of the possible role of morality, it is abundantly clear that proper ritual preparation was thought of as being indispensable, a view contrasting vividly with the predominant Upaniṣadic and Buddhist views of an afterlife determined exclusively by one's moral merit.

An even more striking contrast between the afterlife belief outlined in the *Ṛg Veda* and that of the *Upaniṣads* and Buddhism is the absence in the *Ṛg Veda* of the concept of rebirth, which forms the core of practically all post-Upaniṣadic speculation on the destiny of the individual after death. Clear as this lack of a doctrine of rebirth is, from the time of the *Upaniṣads* there have been those who claim to find references to rebirth in the *Ṛg Veda*. This false attribution probably occurs because of the undisputed position of the *Ṛg Veda* as the supreme authority of Hindu orthodoxy. At any rate, the search for references to rebirth in the *Ṛg Veda* has been going on for 2,500 years now, and is still being pursued by modern scholars.[12] It is perhaps advisable at this point to examine in their proper context all the Vedic passages that have been construed as referring to rebirth as well as some that have not been so construed as referring to rebirth as well as some that have not been so construed but will doubtless be ferreted out sooner or later. Most of these passages may be grouped into four categories according to their actual meanings. References to rebirth have been imagined in Vedic passages which 1) refer to recurrent, personified natural phenomena, 2) are typical Vedic expressions of expansive and multiple identification of one deity with other deities and natural phenomena, 3) refer to hereditary survival in one's offspring and 4) passages which refer to the normal Vedic concept of a single afterlife in heaven.

12. See Keith, *Religion and Philosophy*, pp. 570-571, for a discussion of various attempts to locate rebirth in the *Ṛg Veda*. More recently, Jeanine Miller, *The Vedas,* Rider, London, 1974, pp. 184-5, and note 65 thereto.

Recurrent Natural Phenomena

Vedic passages referring to recurrent natural phenomena are often expressed metaphorically with the adverb *punar*, "again" and the verbal root √*jan* "to be born". Deities which personify such phenomena are said to be born again. This has led many to see in these passages references to the later Indian afterlife theory of rebirth *(punar-janma)*. Significantly, deities who are not associated with recurrent natural phenomena are never said to be born again. This suggests that these references to rebirth are incidental to the construction of poetic metaphors, not indicative of an afterlife theory. In one passage cited by Radhakrishnan[13] the moon[14] is said to be born again in a poetic reference either to its monthly reappearance from its absence on the night of the new moon, or to its nightly reappearance when the sun goes down.

> 18. By their own power these twain in close succession move; they go as playing children round the sacrifice. One (the sun) of the pair beholdeth all existing things; the other (the moon) is born again *(jāyate punaḥ)*.
>
> 19. He, born afresh, is new and new forever, ensign of days he goes before the mornings.[15]
>
> *Ṛg* 10.85.18-19 (G)

A similar passage refers to the dawn, personified as the goddess Uṣas.

---

13. *Principal Upaniṣads*, p. 44, n. 1. Though he admits that no direct reference to rebirth is found in the *Ṛg Veda* he implies that the elements from which the theory was derived are found therein.

14. Radhakrishnan mistakenly says it is Mitra who is born again, giving the passage: *mitro jāyate punaḥ* as occurring at *Ṛg* 10.85.19. The reference is wrong, as is the quotation. Thus, at *Ṛg* 10.85.18 is the line: *anyo* (referring to the moon) *vidadhaj-jāyate punaḥ*.

15. *navonavo bhavati jāyamāno'hnāṁ keturuṣasāmetyagram*, literally, "He becomes new and new, born the banner of days, he goes before the dawn".

Ancient of days, again and again born newly *(punaḥ punar-jāyamānā)*, decking her beauty with the selfsame raiment. The goddess wastes away the life of mortals, like a skilled hunter cutting birds in pieces.

Ṛg 1.92.10 (G)

According to Sāyana, another passage of this sort refers to the seasonal reappearance of the storm gods (Maruts) who, after the violent rainstorms of the monsoon, return to their wombs in the clouds whence they will be born again the next year.

Afterward you again took on, according to (your) power (or will), the embryonic form, assuming sacrificial names.[16]

Ṛg 1.6.4

In similar passages with a slightly different theme, Agni, the fire god is said to be born daily and monthly, which, according to Sāyana, refers to the daily kindling of the sacrificial fire at the *agnihotra* sacrifice, and at the monthly *pitṛyajña* sacrifice for the ancestors.[17]

He springs to life *(jāyate)* each month, each day that passes; so gods have made him their oblation bearer.

Ṛg 10.52.3 (G)

Such metaphorical descriptions of recurrent natural phenomena as being repetitively born do not necessarily indicate that humans too were thought to be reborn in the Vedic context. The assertion, for example, that Agni (fire), when born, devours his parents, the fire-making sticks, does not indicate that humans devour their parents upon birth; nor does the assertion that certain gods, such as Aditi and Dakṣa or Virāj and Puruṣa, may be reciprocally generative indicate that

---

16. *ādādaha svadhāmanu punar garbhatvamerire, dadhānā nāmā yajñiyam.*

17. See also *Ṛg* 10.5.1, where Agni is said to be "born many times" *(bhūrijanmā)*, which according to Sāyana, refers to "many types of birth, at various sacrifices, oblations, etc."

humans may be produced in such a manner. If there were no Vedic theory of afterlife, references to the repetitive births of natural phenomena could provide grounds for the speculation that perhaps humans also were thought to be reborn. The *Ṛg Veda*, however, yields a fairly clear picture of the Vedic concept of afterlife. An examination of this concept, later in this chapter, shows that it has nothing to do with rebirth.

Multiple Identification

In the deceptive light of post-Vedic tradition, the expansive and multiple identification of one deity with other deities and natural phenomena, which is common in the *Ṛg Veda*, is sometimes taken as reference to rebirth. Thus, in a persona poem, Indra speaks through the poet Vāmadeva saying:

> I was aforetime Manu, I was Sūrya: I am the sage Kakṣīvan, the holy singer. Kutsa the son of Ārjuni I master. I am the sapient Ūśanā behold me.[18]
>
> *Ṛg* 4.26.1 (G)

Here, Indra expresses his ubiquitous influence in the affairs of people and the workings of the universe; it is not a reference to rebirth. This hymn is cited in the *Bṛhadāraṇyaka Upaniṣad* and taken there as a Vedic reference to monism of the Vedāntic sort, but not as a reference to rebirth. Contrary to what Keith says,[19] Śaṅkara also takes the hymn as a reference to monism and does not suggest that the words of Vāmadeva refer to rebirth.[20] This Upaniṣadic quotation and the

18. Kakśīvān, Kutsa and Kavi Uśanas are all semi-mythological sages thought of as belonging to the ancient past.

19. Keith, *Religion and Philosophy*, p. 571.

20. "The sage called Vāmadeva, in that state of realization of the identity of the self and *Brahman*, visualised these *Mantras*, 'I was Manu and the Sun', etc., (and these words) refer to its result, identity with all."

explanation of Śaṅkara, however, both alter what was probably the original intent of the Vedic passage by construing this grandiose statement of identity with manu etc. as being a declaration by the mortal Vāmadeva that he had attained *mokṣa* by realizing the identity of the self *(ātman)* and the universal principle *(brahman)*.[21]

A similar pantheistically inclined hymn to Agni, which, out of context might be taken as a reference to rebirth, obviously represents instead the beginnings of the idea of a universal principle.

> He stirs with life in wombs dissimilar in kind, born as a lion or a loudly-bellowing bull.
>
> *Ṛg* 3.2.11 (G)

Other passages of this sort need not be considered individually here, as it is clear that such passages, taken in context as the words of deities, refer to the presence of gods in many different phenomena, and not to the concept of rebirth.[22]

Hereditary Survival in Offspring

The third class of Vedic passages which might be mistakenly construed as referring to rebirth, those referring to genetic continuity between successive generations, surprisingly, have rarely been advanced in support of the argument that belief in rebirth may be found in the *Ṛg Veda*. In many ways these passages represent the strongest evidence in the *Ṛg Veda* of at least a rudimentary form of a rebirth belief. The simplest case of this genetic carry-over is found in the plant kingdom, in which reproduction occurs without apparent sexual contact. In the absence of copulation, Agni (fire) dwelling within plants, is said to be the force behind vegetable reproduction. That Agni dwells within plants is demonstrated by their

---

21. Sāyana also explains the verse this way, but allows the alternative that Indra is the speaker.

22. *Ṛg* 3.53.8; 7.101.3; 9.85.12; 9.64.8; 3.56.3.

inflammability, and it is further postulated in the *Ṛg Veda* that this indwelling fire is also the invisible impregnator of plants.

> Dwelling in old (plants) he is attracted to their offspring, entering newly born *(sadyaḥ jātāsu)* saplings. He makes them (plants) pregnant though they are not fertilized.[23]
>
> *Ṛg* 3.55.5

In this connection it is well to mention the famous cucumber passage, which, though it refers to immortality and not rebirth, is often advanced as an indication of a rebirth belief in the *Ṛg Veda*, presumably because of the similar phrasing of an Upaniṣadic passage which does refer to rebirth.

> As from its stem *(bandhana)* the cucumber, so may I be released *(mukṣīya)* from death, not reft of immortality.
>
> *Ṛg* 7.59.12 (G)

> Just as a mango or a fig or a fruit of the peepul tree releases itself *(pramucyate)* from it bond *(bandhana)* even so this person frees himself *(sampramucya)* from these limbs and returns again as he came to the place from which he started back to a new life.
>
> B.U. 4.3.36 (R)

Oddly, Sāyana does not mention the Upaniṣadic passage in his exposition of this hymn, nor does Śaṅkara mention the Vedic passage in his commentary. It is perhaps obvious to both of them that these similarly worded passages actually do not express similar ideas, for the Vedic passage is a simple poetic simile intended to illustrate the desire for release from death, i.e. for heavenly immortality. If the passage referred to rebirth, the prayer for immortality would be contradictory. What is probably meant is that the sacrificer wishes to be granted immortality in heaven at the end of a full life at a ripe old

23. This translation follows Sāyana's interpretation.

age, just as the fruit of a tree will fall free of its stem when it is ripe.[24]

Parallel to the concept of Agni, dwelling in plants, being born anew in their offspring, is the concept of the father being born again in his son. This belief is the closest thing in the *Ṛg Veda* to a genuine concept of rebirth, but a belief in a hereditary carry-over between father and son is so universally common that its presence in the *Ṛg Veda* establishes nothing. This same belief may be seen in the European tendency to name children after direct blood ancestors.

> He (the pious father) is procreated *(pra + jāyate)* through his progeny *(prajābhir)* according to law *(dharmaṇaspari)*, (whereby) your (Heaven's and Earth's) diverse forms (of beings) are ruled alike.
>
> *Ṛg* 6.70.3

> He is procreated through his progeny according to law *(pra prajābhir jāyate dharmaṇaspari)*, unharmed, he prospers completely.
>
> *Ṛg* 8.27.16

This Vedic belief in the hereditary carry-over of identity, though perhaps occasionally appearing to prefigure a doctrine of rebirth, is recognized explicitly in the *Upaniṣads* as being altogether different from the mechanism of rebirth.

> 1. As is a mighty tree, so, indeed is a man ....
>
> 4. A tree when it is felled springs up from its root in newer form; from what root does a man spring forth when he is cut off by death?
>
> 5. Do not say "from the semen", for that is produced from what is alive. A tree springs also from the seed. After it is dead, it certainly springs again.
>
> B.U. 3.9.28 (R)

Here, the continuity between parent and offspring is recognized as different from the continuity between rebirths. Both men and trees, while living, produce seed from which offspring arise, but they are also both subject to rebirth when they are cut down by death. The tree, in other words, sprouts up from the cut off stump. Nothing, however, in the two Vedic passages cited indicates that their authors were aware of the doctrine of rebirth. Nothing in either passage gives the meaning "born again" or "born anew" as Griffith translates. The evident word play in *pra prajābhirjāyate* — literally "He is procreated by his offspring"[25] — emphasizes the paradoxical nature of being born through the agency of one's children, a concept which preoccupied the Vedic mind.[26]

> The son who is a sage hath comprehended; who knows this rightly is his father's father.
>
> *Ṛg* 1.164.16 (G)

The two hymns cited above offer some insight into the meaning and importance of this idea to the authors of the *Ṛg Veda*. Both of these passages begin identically with: *pra prajābhirjāyate dharmaṇaspari* ("he is procreated by his progeny according to kaw"). This indicates that *dharmaṇaspari* ("according to law")[27] in both cases should be read with *pra prajābhirjāyate*, rather than, as is grammatically feasible in the first passage, read with *yuvoḥ* ("your", dual, i.e. Heaven's and Earth's). In this case, *dharma* probably connotes "duty" as well as "law", suggesting: "He is procreated by his progeny according to (the performance of) ritual duty". This broadened interpretation is in perfect accord with the Vedic belief that the ancestors *(pitṛ)* are fed and maintained in heaven by the sacrificial

---

25. The separable prefix *pra-* should be read with *jāyate*, thus giving prajābhir *prajāyate*.

26. Note also the reciprocal generation of Aditi and Dakśa (*Ṛg* 10.72.4) and of Puruṣa and Virāj (*Ṛg* 10.90.5).

27. See Monier-Williams, p. 591, col. 2.

offerings of their offspring,[28] just as the gods are said to be supported by the offerings of men.[29]

The concept of surviving death through one's offspring is complex and will be examined in some detail in this chapter and parts of the next chapter. A preliminary explanation at this point, however, may help to clarify the immediately following material. The Vedic Aryan was preoccupied with the production of offspring, as frequent prayers for many sons indicate. One of the most important roles of these many offspring was the role they were thought to play in assuring a pleasant afterlife for their parents. The first aspect of this role was to provide a proper funeral, through which the deceased could hope to enter heaven. Once in heaven, the deceased would continue to require sustenance, normally depicted as feeding, which was thought to be provided by one's offspring in the form of the monthly *pitṛyajña* or "ancestral sacrifice". In addition to sustaining the dead ancestor in heaven, the offspring also played an important role by procreating further offspring on earth. The Vedic Aryan imagined that in addition to surviving death in heaven as one of the "ancestors" *(pitṛ)*, he also survived on earth, in some sense, in the form of his descendants. The vedic concept of afterlife, then, involved dual survival in heaven and on earth, both dependant upon the filial piety of one's offspring.

The human parallel to the innate immortality of the gods is possible immortality in the afterlife, contingent upon the faithful performance of supportive rituals by one's descendants and upon their vigor in producing more offspring in the family line. As a result, references to being born and attaining immortality through the agency of one's offspring, in addition to indicating the universal belief that one somehow lives on in one's children, also imply that the father's continued existence in the afterlife depends upon the filial piety of his offspring in performing ritual duties. In the period of the *Brāhmaṇas* the full implications of this type of belief were drawn out, and there

28. See Keith, *Religion and Philosophy*, pp. 425-32. Also *Ṛg* 10.15.6; 10.16.12. See also A.U. 2.1.4. for a reference to this type of belief.

29. See *Ṛg* 10.14.14.

arose the concept of the possibility of death from heaven *(punar-mṛtyu)*, an idea which will be examined further below.

The idea that human immortality depends on the filial piety of succeeding generations is probably also the basis of the next passage to be considered, a passage which Karel Werner makes much of in his arguments to establish the presence of rebirth theory in the *Ṛg Veda.* The following is his translation.[30]

> For at first you bestowed on gods worthy of offerings, immortality, the supreme lot. Then as a gift, Savitṛ, you opened up successive lives *(anūcīnā jīvitā)* for men.
>
> *Ṛg* 4.54.2

The verbal root √*jīv*, and grammatical modifications thereof, is used throughout the *Ṛg Veda* to designate the possession of vitality. It is often found in conjunction with the term *āyu* (life span),[31] the two being conterminal, ideally lasting a hundred years.[32] As nouns, the derivatives of √*jīv* normally refer to "the living", "living beings", although they occasionally designate individual vitality, primarily in the later hymns.[33] The only other use of the identical term, *jīvitā,* is at *Ṛg* 1.113.6, in the context: "different kinds *(visadṛśa)* of creatures *(jīvitā)*" or "different forms of life". In no instance in the *Ṛg Veda* are terms based on √*jīv* used to refer to soul or life principle as is the term *jīva* in post-Vedic philosophy. Instead, these terms invariably refer to simple animation, opposed to sleep[34] and death.[35] These terms designate the simple state of being alive, not an entity. They are, in fact, used almost exactly like the English terms "life, alive", etc. It is,

---

30. Werner, "The Vedic Concept of Human Personality", see Bibliography. See also Jeanine Miller, *The Vedas,* Rider, London, 1974, pp. 184-5, and note 65 thereto.

31. *Ṛg* 1.37.15; 1.44.6; 1.48.10; 1.79.9; 1.89.2; 1.94.4; 8.18.18; 8.18.22; 10.14.14; 10.59.1 & 5.

32. *Ṛg* 3.36.10; 10.18.4; 10.161.4.

33. *Ṛg* 1.48.10; 1.113.16; 1.140.8; 1.164.30; 10.27.4; 10.97.11.

34. *Ṛg* 1.113.16.

35. *Ṛg* 1.140.8; 10.18.3; 10.60.8; 1.91.6.

however, doubtful that the phrase "successive lives" in the *Ṛg Veda* carries the same meaning it does in English, i.e. that of rebirth. There is no other reference in the entire *Ṛg Veda* to indicate that one person could have more than one life. The living, in fact, are said to be strictly separate from the dead.[36]

In the context of what seems to be the general Vedic belief it is more reasonable to take the preceding passage as a reference to successive generations. This is precisely how Sāyana explains the term *anūcīnā*, saying that it means "the succession of father, son, descendants".[37] In the Vedic context, this is the human parallel to divine immortality, the supreme lot. Humans may survive death by proxy in the form of their offspring and may obtain individual immortality in heaven contingent upon filial piety in the performance of rituals of sustenance for deceased ancestors.[38] This survival in the form of one's offspring is clearly the intent of a passage similar to the one under examination, which obviously refers to the ancestors *(pitṛ)* and their offspring.

> 5. They (the ancestors) compassed in their bodies *(tanūṣu)* all existing things, and streamed forth offspring in many successive forms. *(pra asārayata purudha prajā anu).*
>
> 6. In two ways have the sons established in his place the Asura who finds the light, by the third act, as fathers, they have set their heritage on earth, their offspring, as a thread *(tantum)* continuously spun out.
>
> *Ṛg* 10.56.5-6 (G)

As will become clearer below, *tanū,* in verse five, is perhaps better translated here as "form" or "appearance". That is to say, the assertion that the ancestors have encompassed in their *tanvaḥ* all existing things is in fact an assertion that they are archetypal, rather than the

---

36. *Ṛg* 10.18.3.

37. *pitṛputrapautrā ityanukramaḥ.*

38. Several passages mention progeny in connection with derivatives of the root √*jiv: Ṛg* 1.36.6; 3.53.8; 5.78.9; 8.18.18; 8.67.12.

substantial origin of creation. While the English translation "successive" is derived here solely on the basis of the separable prefix *anu-*, the meaning of the passage is nevertheless very similar to that of the passage above, which, viewed through the distorting lens of later tradition, in English translation, and taken out of context may seem to refer to rebirth. The fact is, however, that if rebirth is meant, the phrase *anūcīnā jīvitā* is a clumsy way to state it. Considering that the Vedic Aryans were in no way short on vocabulary or expressive ability, the only reasonable alternative is to construe the passage as a statement in accordance with the general Vedic concept that one lives on after death vicariously in the form of one's offspring, a concept clearly expressed in the following verse.

> As I, remembering thee with grateful spirit, a mortal, call with might on thee immortal, vouchsafe us high renown, O Jātavedas, and may I be immortal by my children *(prajābhis)*.[39]
>
> *Ṛg* 5.4.10 (G)

The Heavenly Afterlife

The most important class of Vedic passages mistakenly taken as referring to rebirth, the class most often cited, are passages which actually do refer to a post-mortem birth of sorts, but a birth into heaven, the world of the ancestors. The identity link through which this transference of the dead person to heaven occurs is the *tanū*, often translated "body", but better translated "form". The term *tanū* is consistently used in the *Ṛg Veda* to refer to an element of personal identity less substantial than the physical body, which is designated by the term *śarīra* or sometimes *rūpa*. Nonetheless, the *tanū* is conceived of as a quasi-physical phenomenon.[40] Other elements of personal identity and vitality are said to be dispersed into the universe upon death, or more precisely, upon performance of the funeral ritual. The funeral apparently was thought to act as a catalyst in the process of

---

39. Cp. *Ṛg* 1.68.8; 1.89.9; 1.136.6; 7.57.6.

40. For a detailed analysis of the use of *tanū* in the *Ṛg Veda,* see chapter III.

re-absorption of the individual's vital forces into their universal counterparts. Thus, in the following series of three verses from a funeral hymn of the tenth book, two things transpire: 1) the dispersion of the vital forces of the deceased into their universal origins, and 2) the transference of personal identity to heaven by means of the *tanū*. As Muir's and Griffith's translations both suffer inaccuracies, they will be compared verse by verse and evaluated on the basis of relevant material from other passages and from the *Ṛg Veda* at large.

> Let his eye go to the sun, his breath *(ātman)* to the wind (vāyu). Go to the sky and to the earth, according to (the) nature (of thy several parts); or go to the waters if that is suitable for thee, enter into the plants with thy members.
>
> *Ṛg* 10.16.3 (M)

Griffith's translation of this same passage misses the sense of dispersion conveyed in the original and imbues the passage with the unwarranted sense of a transmigrating entity.

> The sun receive thine eye, the wind thy spirit, go, as thy merit is, to earth or heaven. Go, if it be thy lot, unto the waters; go, make thine home in plants with all thy members.
>
> *Ṛg* 10.16.3 (G)

Muir's rendering of this verse is, as is often the case, more accurate than Griffith's translation, as a comparison to the original passage will immediately confirm.[41] Several points of translation in this passage, however, are of particular importance with regard to a correct understanding of the verses which follow, and therefore deserve to be considered in some detail. First, nothing in the original text of this verse justifies the use of "his" or "thine",[42] and it would seem that the various vital faculties are being commanded separately to enter sky

---

41. *sūryaṁ cakṣurgacchatu vātamātmā dyaṁ ca gaccha pṛthivīṁ ca dharmanā, apo vā gaccha yadi tatra te hitamoṣadhīsu prati tiṣṭha śarīraiḥ*. (*Ṛg* 10.16.3).

42. Although Sāyana says the dead person's spirit is addressed *(he preta)*.

and earth. The phrase *dyāṁ ca gaccha prtivīṁ ca* certainly means "go to the sky and to the earth". Though *dyāṁ* might be justifiably taken as "to heaven", *svar* is the more common term for the heavenly abode, *dyu* referring more generally to the celestial realm as a spacial phenomenon. Be that as it may, *dyu* and *pṛthivī* are both prescribed as destinations, as in Muir's: "to the sky and to the earth". They clearly are not intended as alternatives, as Griffith's rendition "earth or heaven" wrongly implies.[43]

Second, *dharmaṇā* should probably be taken as "according to (natural) law". The use of *dharma* (masc.) to signify "nature" or "merit" is primarily if not wholly post-Vedic. The Vedic *dharman* (neut.) is derived directly from the verbal root √*dhṛ* (to bear), and means "bearer" or "supporter", thence the usage "natural law", that which supports and maintains the orderly cosmos. Griffith's unwarranted translation would seem to be based on Sāyana's exposition of the passage which, also unjustified, explains *dharmaṇā* as "according to good deeds" *(sukṛtena)*. Both construe the root √*dhr* as expressing the meaning of the root √*kṛ*, though the term *karmaṇā* in the sense of "according to action or deeds" is used elsewhere[44] and would doubtless have been used here if that meaning were intended. Here, *yadi tatra te hitam* probably means literally "if that is ordained of you", *hita* being a past participle of the same root √*dhṛ*, from which *dharmaṇā* is derived. *Oṣadhīṣu prati tiṣṭha śarīraiḥ* means literally "in plants stand separately with bodies", though *śarīra* is used both for the body and in plural for the limbs of the body in other *Ṛg Vedic* passages.[45]

In addition to this strong internal evidence that this passage is to be construed as referring to dispersion of the vital faculties, several other *Ṛg Vedic* passages indicate that dispersion of life faculties was thought to accompany death. In a prayer for lengthened life,[46]

---

43. Although Sāyana says, without justification, that the word *ca* should be taken here in the sense of an alternative *(atra caśabdo vikalpārthe)*.

44. *Ṛg* 8.31.17; 8.39.5; 10.56.6.

45. *Ṛg* 1.32.10; 1.163.11; 6.25.4; 10.16.1; 10.99.8; 10.1136.2. Sāyana takes it as referring here to the "parts of the body" *(śarīravayavaḥ)*.

46. *Ṛg* 10.59.5-7.

apparently intended to overcome a potentially fatal disease, the goddess Asunīti[47] is asked to return the mind *(manas)*, sight *(cakṣu)* and breath *(prāṇa)* of the dying man. Earth, heaven and atmosphere *(antarikṣa)* are asked to return the vital spirit *(asu)*, and Soma is asked for the *tanū* or subtle body.[48] In another prayer to save the life of a dying man, the mind *(manas)* is called back from earth, heaven, the sea, plants, the sun, "from all that lives and moves, from all that is and is to be".[49] Reversal of this process of dispersion is also referred to in another hymn, where the dying man is said to be returned and renewed *(punarnava)* with all his parts *(sarvāṅga)*.[50] References to this type of theory are also found in the *Upaniṣads*,[51] but there the implication is that the dispersed elements are unessential components of the true person *(puruṣa)* which is reborn according to its deeds.

Thus it is clear — on the basis of internal evidence and external corroboration — that *Ṛg* 10.16.3 refers to the dispersion of the individual's life faculties. The next verse in this hymn, however, indicates that some form of individual identity is retained and conveyed to heaven. In this instance, Griffith's translation probably conveys better than Muir's the original meaning of the passage.

> Thy (Agni's) portion is the goat *(ajā)*; with heat consume him; let thy fierce flame, thy glowing splendour, burn him. With thine suspicious forms, O Jātavedas bear this man to the region of the pious.
>
> Ṛg 10.16.4 (G)

---

47. According to Griffith's note *asunīti* is a funeral deity, but in *Ṛg* 10.16.2 he translates the same term as "life that awaits him", while Muir translates "state of vitality". Cp. *Ṛg* 10.15.1 & 14: "world of spirits" (G) "(higher) vitality" (M). Roth thinks it is an epithet of Yama, and Mueller renders it "guide of life". See Muir, vol. 5, p. 297, n. 445.

48. This probably refers to the belief that the moon was an intermediate phase on the journey to heaven, as the *tanū* is that which enters heaven. See Keith, *Religion and Philosophy*, pp. 576, 583. See also *Ṛg* 10.85.5; Ks. U. 1.2 and 2.8; B.U. 6.2.15 & 16.

49. *Ṛg* 10.58.

50. *Ṛg* 10.161.5.

51. See B.U. 3.2.13.

Muir's translation of this passage is substantially the same, except that he translates *ajo bhagas* as "his unborn part". This is also how Sāyana construes the phrase,[52] but if this rendition is correct, this is the only passage in the entire *Ṛg Veda*, where the term *aja* means "unborn individual essence", as the term is sometimes used in the *Upaniṣads*.[53] Normally, *aja* simply means "goat" in the *Ṛg Veda*.[54] Though it occasionally represents the compound *a-ja* ("not born"), this refers in every case to the universal unborn principle,[55] that which, like the three-fourths of Puruṣa which "went up", is not involved in the mundane universe, or at least nor affected by the affairs of the world.

With a proper understanding of these two verses, the reference in the next verse of this hymn to joining a body *(tanū)* is clearly a reference to the normal Vedic afterlife theory, which holds that a person survives in heaven in the form of a subtle body which is maintained by the sacrifices of one's descendants.

> Give up again, Agni, to the Fathers, him who comes offered to thee with oblations. Putting on life *(āyu)*, let him approach (his) remains *(śeṣa)*; let him meet with his body *(tanū)*, O Jātavedas.
>
> *Ṛg* 10.16.5 (M)

Only in the light of Griffith's mistranslation of verse three does the reference in verse five to joining the *tanū* seem to be a deviation from the normal Vedic belief expressed in other verses which invariably refer to joining a subtle body in heaven, the world of the fathers.

---

52. *jananrahitaḥ śarīrendriyādibhāgavyatirikto 'ntarapuruṣalakṣaṁo.*

53. B.U. 4.4.22, 24 & 25.

54. *Ṛg* 1.138.4; 1.162.2 & 4; 1.163.12; 6.55.3,4 & 6; 6.57.3; 6.58.2; 7.103.6; 8.70.15; 9.67.10; 10.90.10; 10.134.6. See also *Ṛg* 2.10.6 where Agni is asked "recognize thy portion (bhaga)" meaning the burnt offering. In *Ṛg* 1.162.3-4 the goat is Puṣan's portion *(puṣṇo bhāgo)*.

55. *Ṛg* 1.67.3; 1.164.6; 5.15.2; 8.41.10; 10.82.6.

> Uniting with a body *(tanū)* be thou welcome, dear to the gods in their sublimest birthplace.
>
> *Ṛg* 10.56.1 (G)

This *tanū*, it seems, in addition to being sustained by the sacrifices of one's descendants, is created or at least strengthened by one's own sacrifices during life on earth.

> Meet with the Fathers, meet with Yama, meet with the (recompense of) the sacrifices thou hast offered in the highest heaven. Throwing off all imperfection again go to thy home. Become united to a body *(tanū)*, and clothed in a shining form.[56]
>
> *Ṛg* 10.14.8 (M)

> Do thou, O self-resplendent god — along with those (Fathers) who, whether they have undergone cremation or not, are gladdened by our oblation — grant us this (higher) vitality *(asunīti)* and a body *(tanū)* according to our desire.[57]
>
> *Ṛg* 10.15.14 (M)

These verses seem to foreshadow the belief expressed in the *Śatapatha Brāhmaṇa* that the highest reward after death is to be born in heaven with a complete tanu, which is created by one's sacrifices during life.

> This sacrifice becomes in the next world the soul *(ātman)* of the sacrificer. The sacrificer who, knowing this, sacrifices with an expiation, is born with his whole body *(sarva tanū)* in the next world.
>
> S.B. 11.1.8.6. (M)

---

56. Cp. *Ṛg* 10.68.11, where the ancestors, apparently with the "shining forms" mentioned here, are said to have "adorned the sky with stars".

57. Griffith translates *kalpayasva* "as thy (Agni's) pleasure wills it". But see *Ṛg* 10.184.1 (which Griffith puts in his appendix, p. 654) *Viṣṇur yonim kalpayatu*, "May Visnu form and mould the womb". (G)

Some have sought a Vedic reference to rebirth in another passage which, in all probability, also refers to a simple afterlife in heaven.[58]

> When Mitra and Varuṇa saw thee quitting the flame of the lightning, that was thy birth; and thou hadst one (other birth), O Vasiṣṭha, when Agastya brought you to the people *(visa).*
>
> Ṛg 7.33.10 (M)

Griffith thinks that only one birth is mentioned here, translating *tatte janmotaikaṁ* as "thy one and only birth was then". This is also a feasible rendition, and in this case, the passage would refer to the miraculous birth of the sage Vasiṣṭha orchestrated by the sage Agastya at a sacrifice.[59] If Muir is right, however, and a second rebirth is intended, the passage would refer to birth in heaven, since Indra is said to be the speaker from verse seven onward.[60] This is how Sāyana construes the passage, taking *viśa* as an ablative form meaning "from (your) previous station (among people)" *(pūrvāvasthānāt),* thus supporting Griffith's phrase: "from thy stock Agastya brought you hither".

Another Vedic passage which probably has nothing whatsoever to do with rebirth or birth in heaven is nonetheless cited in the *Aitareya Upaniṣad*[61] as a Vedic verse referring to the three births of the self. According to the Upaniṣadic theory, the first birth is conception of a child, which takes on part of the identity of its father; the second birth is the actual birth of this child from its mother's womb, and the third birth is the rebirth *(punar jāyate)* of the father when he dies. At

58. See Keith, *Religion and Philosophy,* pp. 570-71; Geldner, *Vedische Studien* vol. 2, p. 142.

59. See verse 13 of the same hymn, where Vasiṣṭha is said to be "born at the sacrifice" (G) & (M). Geldner advances the alternative theory that what is described in this hymn is a political alliance which Agastya forged between Vasiṣṭha and the Tṛtsus. See *Vedic Index* vol. 1, pp. 6-7, 320-22; Geldner *Vedische Studien* vol. 2, pp. 136, 138, 143.

60. Griffith p. 351, note 7.

61. A.U. 2.1.5. See also S.B. 11.2.1.1.

the end of this explanation of the three births of the self, the following Vedic verse, attributed to Vāmadeva, is cited.

> I, as I lay within the womb, considered all generations of these gods in order. A hundred iron fortresses confined me but forth I flew with rapid speed a falcon.
>
> *Ṛg* 4.27.1 (G)

It is not at all certain, however, that even the Upaniṣadic passage refers to rebirth in the phrase *punar jāyate*. In fact, the last verse of the section seems to refer to entrance into heaven, in which case the *Upaniṣad* is propounding a Vedic afterlife theory. If this is so, the period in the womb mentioned in the quoted Vedic verse would refer to the first or embryonic birth; the flying forth like a falcon, would refer to the second birth from the womb, and the Upaniṣadic verse which follows the Vedic citation would be meant to complete the exposition of the doctrine by describing the third birth in heaven.

> He, knowing thus and springing upward, when the body is dissolved, enjoyed all desires in that world of heaven and became immortal, yes, became immortal.
>
> A.U. 2.1.6 (R)

The intent of the Upaniṣadic passage is not, however, clear. The "He" in A.U. 2.1.6 seems to refer to the seer Vāmadeva in the form of a child, whereas it ought to refer to Vāmadeva's father. Śaṅkara explains, however, that "this fact which is stated with regard to another (the father) is implied here (with regard to the son) also; for the father and the son have the same self".[62] Thus, according to Śaṅkara, the death of the father, which will result in his third birth, implies the death and rebirth of his child Vāmadeva also. At any rate, it seems that Vāmadeva, having provided the occasion for his father's first two births, will also undergo these first two births as a father, and eventually die himself, thus accomplishing his third birth. But, as

62. A.U. 2.1.4, *Śaṅkara-bhāṣya*.

we have seen, this third birth seems to be thought of as a heavenly birth in the *Upaniṣad,* which, if this is the case, would be describing a primarily Vedic theory of afterlife.

Śaṅkara, however, explains the Upaniṣadic passage and the Vedic quotation as being references to the standard doctrine of repeated rebirth.[63] This explanation is acceptable, with regard to the *Upaniṣad,* but entirely improbable with regard to the original intent of the Vedic citation. Śaṅkara's assertion that the hundred iron fortresses refer to previous bodies, which confined the seer to *saṁsāra* until he escaped through knowledge of the self, is entirely unwarranted. Sāyana agrees with Śaṅkara's interpretation, but an altogether more convincing exegesis of the Vedic verse is offered by Bloomfield,[64] who says Agni, born within the wombs of clouds, is the speaker of this verse, and in the form of an eagle or falcon, brings Soma to earth, in the form of rain.

Karel Werner[65] cites a touching hymn on the death of a child in support of his view that the doctrine of rebirth is to be found in the *Ṛg Veda,* but here too, nothing indicates that anything other than the normal Vedic afterlife theory is intended.

> I looked reluctantly on him who cherishes those men of old, on him who treads that evil path, and then I yearned for this again.
>
> *Ṛg* 10.135.2 (G)

Even if Griffith's doubtful translation of this obscure passage is correct, and the meaning is that the dead child wishes to return to life on earth,[66] there is no indication that he got his wish. The rest

---

63. A.U. 2.1.5, *Śaṅkara-bhāṣya.* See also *Brahma-sūtra, Śaṅkara-bhāṣya,* 3.4.51.

64. "The Myth of Soma and the Eagle", *Festgruss an Rudolf von Roth,* 1893, pp. 149-155. Also in JAOS, vol. 16, p. 3ff. See Whitney's *Atharva Veda* 6.48.1, and JAOS, vol. 19, p. 11. See also *Ṛg* 9.68.6.

65. In his unpublished paper "The Vedic Concept of Human Personality", see Bibliography.

66. Sāyana's equally doubtful explanation is that the hymn refers to Naciketas, the protagonist in the *Kaṭha Upaniṣad,* who desires the death his father has sentenced him to.

of the hymn describes the cremation of the deceased and his journey to heaven. This journey is metaphorically said to be accomplished in a chariot[67] and a ship.[68]

> Thou mountest, though thou dost not see, O child, the new and wheel-less car Which thou hast fashioned mentally *(manasākr̥ṇoḥ)*, one-poled but turning every way.[69]
>
> Ṛg 10.135.3 (G)

Werner sees in this description a reference to the same type of idea as that found at B.U. 4.4.2-5, where it is said that as someone dies, his vital forces *(prāṇa)* consolidate, and "becoming one, he does not see ... smell ... taste" etc.

> And as a goldsmith, taking a piece of gold turns it into another, newer and more beautiful shape, even so does this self, after having thrown away this body and dispelled its ignorance, make unto himself another, newer and more beautiful shape.
>
> B.U. 4.4.4 (R)

There is, however, not near enough similarity in these two passages to warrant interpreting one on the basis of the other. In the absence of external evidence, the Vedic reference to a wheel-less chariot is most convincingly explained as reference to a vehicle which will carry the deceased to heaven. Though it is relevant to his argument, Werner does not mention a passage in the *Kaṭha Upaniṣad* (1.3.3), to be examined in detail below, in which the individual is likened to a chariot, the various faculties being the driver, reigns, horses etc.[70] Even if all these passages are taken as being related somehow, the fact remains that in the Vedic funeral hymn under examination, every

---

67. In verse 3.

68. In verse 4. See *Ṛg* 7.88.3 where Varuṇa and a sage embark together on a boat.

69. Cp. *Ṛg* 9.75.1 where the sun's car "moves on every side" (G).

70. See *Ṛg* 6.75.6-7; B.U. 4.3.10.

indication is that the chariot bears the deceased to the world of Yama. There is nothing which suggests a doctrine of rebirth.

One passage in the *Bṛhadāraṇyaka Upaniṣad,* in a reference to "the two paths of the gods and ancestors", looks to the *Ṛg Veda* for justification of its rebirth doctrine, but the Upaniṣadic passage itself goes on to show that the Upaniṣadic understanding of these two paths is altogether unfamiliar to the Vedic tradition. In this passage, the brahmin youth Śvetaketu, educated in the traditional manner, approaches the *kṣatriya* king Pravāhaṇa Jaivali and is asked by the king five questions, the last of which relates to the two paths mentioned at *Ṛg* 10.88.15.

> "Do you know the means of access to the path leading to the gods or of the one leading to the fathers? i.e. by doing what the people go to the path of the gods or the path of the fathers? For we have heard even the saying of the seer: 'I have heard of two paths for men, the one that leads to fathers and the one that leads to the gods. By these two all that lives moves on, whatever there is between father (heaven) and mother (earth)'".
>
> "Not a single one of them do I know," said he.[71]
>
> B.U. 6.2.2 (R)

In the rest of the Upaniṣadic passage, it becomes obvious that the path of the fathers *(pitṛyāna)* refers to rebirth, and the path of the gods *(devayāna)* refers to liberation *(mokṣa),* non-return to rebirth in *saṁsāra.* But when Śvetaketu's father Gautama approaches the king for answers to these questions, before explaining the doctrine of rebirth and release, the king hesitates, saying, "This knowledge has never hitherto dwelt with any Brāhmaṇa whatsoever".[72] On this basis alone, it should be obvious that the *Ṛg Veda* passage, composed by members of the priestly caste, was not originally intended as an

71. This Upaniṣadic passage is referred to in the *Bhagavad Gītā* (8.23-28) but without reference to the *Ṛg Veda.* Sāyana takes the *Gītā* passage into account, but ignores the Upaniṣadic citation. Veṅkaṭa notes the *Upaniṣad,* but not the *Gītā.* Both the *Gītā* and the *Upaniṣad* refer to rebirth in these passages.

72. B.U. 6.2.8 (R).

expression of rebirth as opposed to liberation, and was not regarded as such an expression in Upaniṣadic times. The question remains, however, "What does the Vedic passage mean?" Keith, for no obvious reason, says the "two paths" refer to day and night.[73] The passage probably intends, however, the belief mentioned above that innate divine immortality is paralleled in the human sphere by survival of death in the form of one's offspring. It is not clear, why the path of the gods, in the Vedic hymn, is said to be a possible path for mortals. Perhaps what is meant is that some exceptional mortals, like Yama, the first person to die,[74] or the Ṛbhus,[75] are thought to have been raised to the status of gods, i.e. they enjoy immortality not contingent upon the continuation of one's familial line and their good faith in performing rituals of ancestral maintenance.

Yet another passage which might mistakenly be construed as a reference to rebirth, in fact serves to emphasize the strict separation between the status of gods and men.

> None lives, even had he hundred lives *(ātmā)*, beyond the statute of the gods; so am I parted from my friend.
>
> Ṛg 10.33.9 (G)

Griffith's translation of the plural term *ātmā* as "lives" is probably wrong, since the term *āyu* is normally used in the sense "duration of life". Instead, the term *ātman* should probably be taken in the normal Vedic sense of "vital essence", in which case, the meaning would be that even with a hundred times the vital force normally allotted to a human being, one cannot live beyond the time appointed by the gods

---

73. Keith, *Religion and Philosophy*, p. 571. Apparently he refers to Deussen's interpretation *(Philosophy of the Upanishads*, p. 318.) which is based on the supposition that the hymn in question (which he mistakenly labels X.83.15) is "a hymn celebrating Agni in his twofold character as sun by day and fire by night". The hymn states, however, that Agni is three-fold in essence, probably meaning celestial fire, earthly fire and life fire (10.88.8), so Deussen's interpretation is not, as he puts it, "hardly doubtful".

74. *Ṛg* 10.14.2.

75. *Ṛg* 1.161.2; 4.35.3 & 8. See Muir, vol. 5, p. 284.

for his death. This second interpretation is better in accord with the overall nature of the hymn, which is a eulogy of a dead friend, and friends, as we all know, often seem to be too much alive to die. At any rate, the passage certainly does not refer to rebirth, though some might argue on the basis of Griffith's translation that it reflects an awareness of such a doctrine. Given the wording of the phrase, however, such an argument would be unconvincing, since rebirth is never described as a series of souls but as a single soul going through a series of incarnations.

Another passage must be considered as a possible reference to rebirth in the *Ṛg Veda,* primarily because of Radhakrishnan's misleading translation of it in the introduction to his *Principal Upaniṣads,* though others have also seen the possibility of a belief in rebirth expressed in the passage.[76]

> 30. That which hath breath and speed and life and motion lies firmly stablished in the midst of houses. Living, by offerings to the dead he moveth, immortal one, the brother of the mortal. *(anacchaye turagātu jīvamejaddhruvaṁ madhya ā pastyānām, jīvo mṛtasya carati svadhābhiramartyo martyenā sayoniḥ.)*
>
> 38. Back forward goes he, grasped by strength inherent, the immortal born the brother of the mortal. Ceaseless they move in opposite directions; men mark the one and fail to mark the other.*(apāṅ prāṇeti svadhayā gṛbhīto'martyo martyena sayoniḥ, tā śaśvantā viṣūcīnā viyantā nyanyaṁ cikyurna ni cikyuranyam).*
>
> *Ṛg* 1.164.30 & 38 (G)

Given the overall sophistication of this famous hymn of Dīrghatamas, it is possible that these two verses do indeed refer to a body/soul dichotomy, as Sāyana states in his commentary. Griffith, however, conjectures that the first sentence of verse 30 refers to Agni, the second to the moon, and that verse 38 refers to the sun, visible on its daytime journey from east to west, but invisible on its nightly return from the west to the east. This interpretation is not as unreasonable

---

76. See Keith, *Religion and Philosophy,* p. 570. Werner also cites the passage in his unpublished paper "The Vedic Concept of the Human Personality", see Bibliography.

as it first sounds, for Agni is often spoken of as dwelling on the hearth in the houses of people. The moon is often associated with the spirits of the dead, and another passage in the *Ṛg Veda* mentions the visible westward journey of the sun, and its invisible eastward journey back to the point where it rises.[77] Apparently on this or some such basis, Griffith says that the "they" in verse 38 refers to the sun by day and the sun by night, but this is grammatically rather hard to swallow. It is also difficult to believe that two phrases so similarly worded and found in the same hymn refer to totally different things, i.e. the sun and the moon, and to understand why they should be called "brother (*sayoni*, lit. 'of common womb or origin') of the mortal". All things considered, Sāyana's interpretation is thus far the more reasonable, but he goes on to link the verses with rebirth. He refers to a passage in the *Śvetāsvatara Upaniṣad*, which does refer to rebirth, but has no formal similarity to the Vedic verses in question.[78] There is nothing in the original to justify Griffith's inclusion of "born" in verse 38, and, in all, nothing which suggests the doctrine of rebirth in either of these verses. On the contrary, if an individual survival factor is indicated by the term "the immortal" *(amartya)*, then verse 30 contains a clear reference to what has been described as the typical Vedic afterlife belief, i.e. that the surviving factor of a dead person is kept alive by the offerings *(svadhā)* of his descendants.[79]

One more verse needs to be considered here. Though it obviously has absolutely nothing to do with rebirth or afterlife in any form, the juxtaposition in a single verse of words meaning "release and return"

77. *Ṛg* 10.111.7.

78.. S.U. 5.8. Sāyana also refers to C.U. 6.11.3.

79. The term *svadhā* may mean "oblation", "power" or "will". It appears once in both of these verses, and apparently means "oblations" in verse 30, since it occurs in the plural, and "power" in verse 38 where it is in the singular number. Whitney's translation of A.V. 9.10.8, which is almost exactly similar to *Ṛg* 1.164.30, is generally better than Griffith's translation, but he ignores grammar and common sense by using the phrase "the living one moves at the will *(svadhābhis)* of the dead one". Sāyana's interpretation agrees with that of Griffith, assigning two separate meanings to the term in these two verses.

has led some scholars to the conclusion that rebirth and liberation are meant.[80]

> Well knowing have I bound me, horse-like, to the pole; I carry that which bears us on and gives us help. I seek for no release *(vimuca),* no turning back *(āvṛtam punar)* therefrom. May he who knows the way, the leader, guide me straight.
>
> *Ṛg* 5.46.1 (G)

Griffith's translation, in accord with Sāyana's explanation, is doubtless correct, and the verse is a simple reference to dedication to ritual duties.

Possible Latent References to Rebirth

Most of the passages in the *Ṛg Veda* which have been or might be construed as direct references to rebirth have been examined above. In every case they fit more comfortably into the overall scheme of Vedic belief. More plausible than direct references to rebirth is the proposition that the *Ṛg Veda* contains germinal concepts which eventually developed into the classical Indian rebirth theory. The case for latent Vedic origins of the theory of rebirth is argued from two diametrically opposed standpoints. 1) Belief in rebirth was first an element of folk belief in the lower strata of Vedic society which gradually became accepted in more sophisticated circles.[81] 2) The idea of rebirth evolved first as an esoteric doctrine of the priestly elite, was alluded to obscurely in Vedic verses, and finally diffused downward through the social structure to become a popularly held belief.[82]

---

80. Radhakrishnan, *Principal Upaniṣads,* p. 44. Werner "The Vedic Concept of Human Personality", see Bibliography.

81. See Keith, *Religion and Philosophy,* pp. 571-2, 581. Bloomfield, *Religion of the Veda,* pp. 255ff, Deussen, *Philosophy of the Upaniṣads,* p. 316.

82. Werner, "The Vedic Concept of Human Personality", see Bibliography. Cp. Radhakrishnan, *Principal Upaniṣads,* p. 43-4.

The first argument suffers from grave faults, as Keith points out.[83] Not only are the Brāhmaṇic references to beliefs that might be regarded as precursors of a theory of rebirth quite late, but also the type of belief advanced as evidence is widespread and cannot be correlated specifically with belief in rebirth. When it is said in a late Brāhmaṇic text that the ancestors may visit a sacrifice in the forms of birds,[84] what is in fact referred to is transmutation of the dead. Similar beliefs are common, and do not necessarily indicate a theory of rebirth. The Egyptian *Book of the Dead*, for example, contains spells to give a dead person power to assume various forms at will.[85] In the *Ṛg Veda* itself, the gods are said to have the magical power *(māyā)* to take on different forms.[86] There is indication that this type of transmutation was accepted, though despised, as a power accessible to humans as well.[87] Beliefs in the transmutation of the dead or of the living differ in several obvious respects from belief in rebirth. The most obvious of these is that transmutation is normally voluntary, whereas rebirth, at least as the theory developed in India, is thought to function on the basis of moral necessity.

The more plausible second argument for the origins of rebirth in the *Ṛg Veda* hinges on the idea of "re-death" *(punar mṛtyu)* which is first mentioned in the *Brāhmaṇas*.[88] Some argue that since in the *Ṛg Veda*, prayers for immortality are expressed alongside prayers for entrance into heaven, the concept of a possible death from heaven also existed in the time of the ancient hymns.[89] Actually, the only hymn in which a prayer for immortality is combined with a prayer for entrance into heaven does not make a clear distinction between the two

83. Keith, *Religion and Philosophy*, pp. 415-16; 571-72.

84. *Baudhāyana Dharma Sūtra* 2.14.9-10.

85. Chapters 76-89. See also ERE vol. 12, p. 431 and Deussen, *Philosophy of the Upanishads*, p. 316.

86. *Ṛg* 3.53.8. See also *Ṛg* 3.56.3; 7.101.3; 9.85.12; 9.64.8.

87. *Ṛg* 10.100.7; 7.104.17.

88. S.B. 2.3.3.9; 10.1.4.14; 10.2.6.19; 10.4.3.10; 10.5.1.4; 10.6.5.8; 11.4.3.20; 11.5.6.9; 12.9.3.12; T.B. 3.11.8.6; Ks.B. 25.1.

89. Belvalkar and Ranade, *History of Indian Philosophy*, vol. 2, p. 81.

rewards, and in fact suggests that they go hand in hand, heaven being described as the deathless world.

> 7. O Pavamāna, place me in that deathless, undecaying world wherein the light of heaven is set, and everlasting lustre shines. Flow, Indu, flow for Indra's sake.
> 8. Make me immortal in that realm where dwells the king, Vivasvān's son, where is the secret shrine of heaven, where are those waters young and fresh. Flow, Indu, Flow for Indra's sake.
>
> Ṛg 9.113.7-8 (G)

One other verse may be taken as implying that entrance into heaven does not necessarily guarantee immortality.

> Offer to Yama an oblation with butter, and be active. May he grant us to live a long life *(dīrgham āyu)* among the gods.
>
> *Ṛg* 10.14.14 (M)

Neither of these passages, however, explicitly states that being born in heaven is not considered to be commensurate with attaining immortality. The large majority of the Vedic passages relating to heaven and immortality make no distinction between the two.[90]

There are, however, as noted above, ample indications that human immortality was thought of as being contingent upon the performance of sustaining rituals by one's progeny. There are indications that food[91] and wealth[92] will be needed in heaven even as they are on earth. Whether or not the Vedic thinkers actually made a clear doctrinal distinction on this point, it is clear that heaven was thought of as a slightly insecure place. The Brāhmaṇic doctrine of re-death is thus a natural development from concepts found in the most ancient Vedic hymns. Still, there is no indication, even in the *Brāhmaṇas*, that this repetition of death was considered to be multiple or to result in

---

90. *Ṛg* 1.31.7; 1.125.6; 5.55.4; 5.633.2; 7.57.6; 7.59.12; 8.48.3.
91. *Ṛg* 9.113.10.
92. *Ṛg* 1.91.1 & 18.

another life in the mundane sphere. It is more likely that re-death refers to total annihilation of one's identity, which is the subject of the following Vedic curse.

> 10. The fiend, O Agni, who designs to injure the essence of our food kine, steeds, or bodies, may he, the adversary, thief, robber, sink to destruction, both himself and offspring.
>
> 11. May he be swept away, himself and children; may all the three earths press him down beneath them. May his fair glory, O ye gods, be blighted, who in the day or night would fain destroy us.
>
> *Ṛg* 7.104.10-11 (G)

Note that the passage calls for the destruction of both the enemy and his offspring. This is probably because of the concept that one lives on in the form of one's children after death, but possibly also because there would always be the chance of sacrificial redemption of the cursed enemy if his descendants survived. One verse suggests that the status of the ancestors may be enhanced by the offerings of their descendants, although it is not explicitly stated.

> 1. May they ascend, the lowest, highest, midmost, the fathers who deserve a share of soma. May they who have attained the life of spirits *(asu)*, gentle and righteous, aid us when we call them.
>
> 2. Now let us pay this homage to the fathers, to those who passed of old and those who followed, those who have rested in the earthly region *(pārthive rajasi)*, and those who dwell among the mighty races *(suvṛjanāsu vikṣu)*.
>
> *Ṛg* 10.15.1-2 (G)

Almost certainly some sort of hierarchy among the ancestors is stated here, but it is not clear whether *ud iratam* means "may they ascend", as Griffith has it, or simply "let (them) arise", i.e. to participate in the offerings, as Muir translates. At any rate, if it is suggested that the ancestors may be elevated in status by the offerings of their offspring, this change of status is not expressed in terms of dying and being reborn. In fact, it is not expressed clearly here or elsewhere in any terms at all. It is at most an afterthought occurring in one hymn and not a fundamental concept of the Vedic theory of afterlife. The "earthly region" in this passage does not refer to earth *per se*, but to the lower celestial region *(rajas)*, there being six of these regions in all.[93] Sāyana explains *suvṛjanāsu vikṣu* as referring to life in the form of one's progeny, although Griffith may be correct in saying it refers to the gods.

In sum, that there is any reference to the idea of re-death in the *Ṛg Veda* is doubtful, though some such undesirable possibility in the afterlife is vaguely implied. It is also doubtful that the concept of re-death in the *Brāhmaṇas* has anything to do with rebirth. Though the fear of re-death is mentioned in several *Brāhmaṇa* passages,[94] rebirth itself is not mentioned. Re-death in the *Brāhmaṇas* probably represents only the vaguely threatening possibility of total annihilation awaiting those whose descendants neglect to perform the sustaining *pitṛyajña*. Of course, even if reference to rebirth in the *Brāhmaṇas* were demonstrated, these texts are not demonstrably purely Vedic. They are just as likely to have been influenced from outside the Vedic tradition as the Upaniṣadic passages which state clearly the doctrine of rebirth.

This detailed and hopefully not too tedious refutation of the proposition that the *Ṛg Veda* contains a concept of rebirth or the germ of such a concept has been necessary in this study of the origins of Indian psychology. The absence of a Vedic theory of rebirth highlights the difference between the Vedic concept of the ultimate potential of the human being — eternal individual existence in a hedonistic paradise — and the Upaniṣadic concept of supra-personal liberation *(mokṣa)*. The latter concept dominated Indian thought from the time of the earliest *Upaniṣads* onward. Zimmer's theory that the doctrines of souls, rebirth and release *(mokṣa)* are non-Aryan[95] hinges upon the question of the existence of the doctrine of rebirth in the *Ṛg Veda*.

---

93. *Ṛg* 1.164.6. See also 8.88.5. (in Griffith's enumeration 8.77.5). In *Ṛg* 7.87.5 three earthly regions and three heavens are enumerated.

94. See S.B. 2.3.3.9; 10.1.4.14; 10.2.6.19; 10.5.1.4; 10.6.5.8 (cp. B.U. 1.2.7); 11.4.3.20; 11.5.6.9; 12.9.3.12; T.B. 3.11.8.6; Ks.B. 25.1; A.B. 8.25.

95. Zimmer, *Philosophies of India*, p. 280. See Smart, *Doctrine and Argument*, p. 32.

A negative answer to that question establishes that the *Ṛg Veda* lacks concepts of 1) a soul which necessarily survives death, 2) rebirth of this soul on the basis of ethical merit, and 3) the possibility of release from rebirth through mystical union of the soul with the universal absolute. It is clear that the Vedic idea of the nature, destiny and ultimate potential of the human being is altogether different from the ideas expressed in the *Upaniṣads* and early Buddhism. Before turning to these two systems, however, it is necessary to examine the actual Vedic theory of the nature of the human being. This examination proceeds by means of a detailed analysis of psychologically significant terms found scattered throughout the *Ṛg Veda* without any overt systematic theory. Having examined the meanings of psychological terms in the *Ṛg Veda*, it will be possible to gain a more complete understanding of these terms as they are used in the *Upaniṣads* and Buddhism, as well as a clearer understanding of the Vedic theory of the nature of the human being.

Chapter 3

The Vedic Concept of the Human Being

The primary concern of the *Vedas* is with gods and ritual. There is no clear-cut treatment of the nature of the human being, but it is possible to glean from the sacrificial hymns of the *Ṛg Veda* a fairly coherent picture of the Vedic concept of the human being: his place in the universe, and to some extent, his psychological make-up. In the first place, in Vedic thought, human people, though decidedly less important in the universal scheme than divine people, are nonetheless like them. The gods, generally speaking, are conceived of in anthropomorphic terms as having legs and arms, minds and emotions. Earth, moreover, is a reflection of heaven, human actions mirroring those of the gods. The gods, like people, derive their sustenance and personal power from sacrifice and drinking *soma*. In fact, sacrifices offered by humans actually help sustain the gods by supplying them with food, wealth, and *soma* to enliven their spirits and inspire them to heroic deeds.[1]

Not only are humans like gods; they are intimately linked to them, and to the cosmos in general, in origin and essence. The "Puruṣa Sūkta", for example, attributes the origin of the universe, both mundane and divine, to the sacrificial dismemberment of the cosmic person, and though the mundane is sharply distinguished from the divine by the phenomenon of death, part of the original essence of creation is thought to be shared by all. This originally shared essence remains contemporary in two great universal forces, fire and wind, which flow down from their divine sources and infuse the earth and

1. *Ṛg* 3.32.12. See Eliade, *Yoga, Immortality and Freedom* p. 109.

its creatures with life. The god of fire, Agni, is thought of as being manifest wherever there is heat and burning,[2] from the blaze of a wood fire[3] to the warmth of a living body.[4]

> Through various dwellings, through entire existence, spreads manifest, the household light of Agni.
>
> *Ṛg* 2.38.5 (G)

Agni is said to be the progenitor of the human race,[5] indeed, of all that lives.[6] The term *āyu* (life) is an epithet of Agni, who is known as the "living one",[7] and in many passages is called upon as "universal life" *(viśva-āyu)*.[8]

Wind *(vāyu)*, which, like fire, became one of the universal elements in the *Upaniṣads* and Buddhism, was another great link, to the Vedic mind, between people, gods and the universe. The term *ātman*, which attained such great significance in the *Upaniṣads*, meant primarily "breath" in the *Ṛg Veda*, though in later hymns it came to mean "vital spirit". Upon the death of a person the individual *ātman* is said to mingle with the wind.[9] the breath of the gods.[10]

Vedic people saw themselves as being like the gods in origin and essence. They maintained a close bond with the gods by performing ritual acts which simultaneously imitated and sustained their heavenly colleagues. They saw the forces of life within them extending into the world around them and ultimately up to heaven itself.

---

2. *Ṛg* 6.16.17.
3. *Ṛg* 6.12.14.
4. *Ṛg* 6.4.2; 6.9.4.
5. *Ṛg* 1.96.2; 10.53.6.
6. *Ṛg* 3.16.4; 3.2.10-11.
7. *Ṛg* 1.96.2; 6.11.4; 10.20.7.
8. *Ṛg* 6.4.2.
9. *Ṛg* 10.16.3.
10. *Ṛg* 10.168.4.

10. Kinship have I with you, and close alliance, O ye gods, destroyers of our foes.

14. For of one spirit *(manas)* are the gods with mortal man, co-sharers all of gracious gifts.

Ṛg 8.27.10.14 (G)

7. Regard us, Indra, Viṣṇu, here, ye Aśvins and the Marut host, us who are kith and kin to you.

8. Ye bounteous ones, from time of old we here set forth our brotherhood, our kinship in the mother's womb.

Ṛg 8.83.7-8[11] (G)

This original and essential relationship between humans and gods may, moreover, be realized in mystical experience. The nature of this experience with the divine is never clearly described in the *Ṛg Veda*, but there can be little doubt that passages such as the following refer to some sort of divine-human encounter.

> By holy law they kept supporting order, by help of sacrifice, in loftiest heaven, they who attained with born men to the unborn, men seated on that stay, heaven's firm sustainer.
>
> *Ṛg* 5.15.2 (G)

One of the most evocative passages in the *Ṛg Veda*, examined critically above in Chapter 2, a passage from Dīrghatamas' famous "Asya Vāmīya" hymn, bears repetition:

> The tree whereon the fine birds eat the sweetness, where they all rest and procreate their offspring, upon its top they say the fig is luscious; none gaineth it who knoweth not the father.
>
> *Ṛg* 1.164.22 (G)

---

11. In Griffith's enumeration, *Ṛg* 8.72.7-8. See also *Ṛg* 1.164.33; 8-31.12.

Regardless of this mystical connection, the position of the human being in the universe is inherently inferior to that of the gods, not only because humans are subject to death, but also because, while the gods are said to be omniscient, humans suffer the curse of a limited intellect. Dīrghatamas' hymn also contains the clearest formulation in the *Ṛg Veda* of the epistemological limitations of the human mind and the unsatisfactory effects attendant thereon.[12]

> Speech hath been measured out in four divisions, the Brāhmaṇas who have understanding know them. Three kept in close concealment cause no motion; of speech, men speak only the fourth division.
>
> *Ṛg* 1.164.45 (G)

Here, that human beings have obtained only a portion of speech is in fact a statement of their limited conceptual capabilities. The link, in Indian thought, between speech and conceptual ability plays an important role in the proper understanding of the Buddhist technical term "name-and-form" *(nāma-rūpa)*. For now, suffice it to say that in later Indian thought, that which can be conceptually known is that which can be spoken.[13] In this verse, the limited access of humans to speech represents the world's earliest surviving formulation of an epistemological theory.

The inadequacy of speech to deal with the absolute becomes an important doctrine in the *Upaniṣads* and Buddhism. There, it is founded on the premise that words are qualitatively inadequate to capture ultimate truth. In the present Vedic passage, human speech is represented as quantitatively inadequate because it is only a part

---

12. See also *Ṛg* 1.164.4-7; 10.121.10; 10.129.6-7.

13. See *Mīmāṁsādarśana* 1.7.26: *Loke sanniyamātprayoga-saṁnikarṣaḥ syāt.* = "In regard to the ordinary (worldly) things — inasmuch as there is contact (of the thing with the organs of perception) — it is possible for sentences to be composed in usage." (Ganganatha Jha, *Śābara Bhāṣya,* vol. I, Oriental Institute, Baroda, 1973.) See also *Nyāya-bindu* 1.4.5: *Abhilāpa-saṁsarga-yogya-pratibhāsa-pratītiḥ kalpanā.* = "The distinct cognition of a (mental) appearance capable of being associated with a verbal designation is (called) conceptualization." (See Stcherbatsky, *Buddhist Logic,* vol. 2, pp. 19ff.)

of divine speech. The important point here, though, is the recognition of the epistemological limitations of the human mind, an idea more explicitly stated by Dīrghatamas in another verse of this same hymn:

> What thing I truly am I know not clearly; mysterious, fettered in my mind I wander. When the first born of holy law approached me, then of this speech I first obtained a portion.
>
> *Ṛg* 1.164.37 (G)

Humans, having obtained in speech only a portion of holy law, are confused. As a result of limited access to truth, we occupy an uncertain position between the bliss of animal ignorance and the bliss of divine omniscience. The human being alone is tormented by the question, "What am I?", a question which is a primary concern of the *Upaniṣads* and Buddhism.

The formulation of the problem in later Indian philosophy is similar to this Vedic verse, which portrays the human as an inscrutable creature trapped within the tangle of his own mind. But there is no hint in the *Ṛg Veda* of a remedial system whereby one may overcome this situation and conquer the ignorance which fetters the mind. circumscribes the exercise of a truly free will and stunts the development of a complete personality able to take full responsibility for its actions, for its consciousness. The recognition of human ignorance in the *Ṛg Veda* is an admission of inadequacy, encouraging an attitude of submission before the divine rather than the self-sufficient striving for release that one finds in the *Upaniṣads* and Buddhism.

Other than these general observations, there is very little material in the *Ṛg Veda* which might reveal the Vedic concept of the nature and structure of human consciousness. There are however, in the Vedic language as in all languages, many words expressive of the various facets of the mind, but there is no explicit statement in the *Ṛg Veda* of the Vedic theory of the relationship among these various facets in the whole, functioning human consciousness. Therefore, it is necessary to examine these terms as they are found scattered throughout the Vedic hymns in order to formulate some idea of their meaning and to extrapolate some idea of the psychological concepts which underlie them.

The method followed in this examination will be to seek an adequate, comprehensive, conceptual definition of the terms considered rather than merely to enumerate the variety of contexts and meanings in which they occur. One difficulty facing such an approach is that the terms considered are not used precisely in the *Ṛg Veda*. Their meanings often overlap considerably, as would be expected in any non-technical vocabulary. Another difficulty is that in translation it may be necessary to render a single Sanskrit term into several different English words in various contexts. To do so without an adequate awareness of the associations in the mind of the original author — which caused him to use a single word to express apparently different meanings — is to risk a grave misunderstanding of the author's intent. Though it is perhaps somewhat tedious, an examination of Vedic psychological terms in their various contexts and in relation to one another is the only scientific method for determining first, the meanings of the terms, and second, the nature of the Vedic concept of the human being. This concept, though inconsistent and unsystematic, represents the earliest surviving thought on the structure of human consciousness.

The relevant Vedic terms will be examined under three headings: A) terms concerned primarily with individual identity, B) vital faculties, and C) mental faculties. These headings reflect the concerns of later Indian theories regarding the nature of the human being more than they reflect any overt Vedic concern with these specific topics. This procedure, however, facilitates comparison of the largely implicit Vedic material with the more explicit psychological concerns of the *Upaniṣads* and early Buddhism.

A) INDIVIDUAL IDENTITY

Tanū:

On the basis of the foregoing examination of the Vedic theory of the afterlife, it should be clear that in Vedic thought the most essential element of the human being is his individual identity, which resides primarily in the quasi-material *tanū*. In the *Ṛg Veda*, the term *tanū*, much like the term *ātman* and its abbreviated form *tman*, is used often as a reflexive pronoun in the sense of "oneself".[14] In slightly different contexts, the term is used in the sense of "in person" or "personally",[15] and sometimes in the sense "personified" or "embodied".[16] Agni, for example, is said to have a triple *tanū*, which probably refers to his manifestation or embodiment as the sun, lightning, and earthly fire.[17] As noted above in Chapter 3, according to the Vedic theory, the vital and mental faculties of a person — the *ātman*, the *manas*, etc. — are dispersed into the universe upon death, but the *tanū*, the individuating survival factor, is rejoined in heaven.

This Vedic belief, it should be noted, is somewhat contrary to the Upaniṣadic belief that the most essential part of the person is the immaterial and ultimately impersonal soul. Though the *Upaniṣads* are by no means consistently monistic in outlook, the overall import of these scriptures resides in the notion that individuality is but an illusory distinction in the essential unity of the entire cosmos. The *Vedas* played an important part in the development of this monistic idea, but they did not go so far as to resolve individual identity into the monistic principle. Instead they conceived of earthly life as being the functioning of a genuinely personal identity into the monistic principle. Instead they conceived of earthly life as being the functioning of a genuinely personal identity which could continue in an afterlife thought of as being quite similar to this earthly life.

As noted above, the *tanū* is the identity link through which this carry-over into an afterlife was thought to be accomplished. The *tanū* is also involved in the Vedic theory of hereditary survival in the form of one's offspring. In most instances, though, it seems to mean simply "the body". There is no instance in which the term obviously means "appearance" as opposed to "body" or "form" as opposed to

14. *Ṛg* 7.104.10-11; 8.46.15; 10.7.6; 10.8.4; 10.81.5; 10.83.5.

15. *Ṛg* 8.100.1; 10.28.2; 10.120.9.

16. *Ṛg* 10.65.7; 10.66.9.

17. Sāyana is inconsistent in exegesis on this point. In his comment on *Ṛg* 3.20.2, he says that the three *tanū* of Agni are three minor deities, whereas at *Ṛg* 10.107.6 he explains them as I have. See also *Ṛg* 10.88.10 and above, Ch. 2, n. 73.

"substance". In order to reconcile the various implications of the word and its etymological relatives, however, it is necessary to think of *tanū* as implying a sort of subtle body which serves as a template for the physical body without actually being distinct from it. Thus, the most consistently workable translation is probably "form".

The material aspect of the *tanū* is obvious in a charming passage said to be the prayer of a young girl, Apālā by name.

> Make all these grow crops of hair, this cultivated field of ours, my body *(tanū)*, and my father's head.
>
> *Ṛg* 8.91.6[18] (G)

An equally explicit hymn with regard to the materiality of the *tanū* reveals a less charming side of the Vedic Aryan, whom we find in this case hacking a horse to pieces in a gory sacrifice.

> Let not thy dear soul *(ātman)* burn thee as thou comest; let not the hatchet linger in thy body *(tanū)*. Let not a greedy clumsy immolator, missing the joints, mangle thy limbs unduly.
>
> *Ṛg* 1.162.20 (G)

Tanū in other passages, though obviously referring to a primarily physical entity, connotes a subtle body which seems to function more or less as a template for the material body. Passages which mention disease in the *tanū*,[19] and medicine for the *tanū*,[20] in a society not aware of the germ theory of disease, do not necessarily refer to a purely material body, nor do passages in which sin[21] and blessings[22] are spoken of as adhering to the *tanū*. This situation probably

---

18. According to Griffith's enumeration, *Ṛg* 8.80.6.
19. *Ṛg* 10.97.10.
20. *Ṛg* 6.74.3; 10.97.10.
21. *Ṛg* 6.74.3; 7.34.13; 7.86.5.
22. *Ṛg* 1.84.17.

indicates not, as Keith suggests,[23] a materialistic concept of sin, but rather a non-material concept of disease, both of which were thought to affect the quasi-material *tanū*. Passages which speak of performing sex with the *tanū* may also intend a less physical entity than one would expect, particularly given the association of the *tanū* with survival in the form of one's offspring.[24] Passages which mention risking or losing the *tanū* in battle[25] are also amenable to a quasi-physical interpretation of the term particularly when considered in relation to prayers intended to strengthen or transform the nature of the *tanū* and guarantee success in battle.[26] The following verse is a charm addressed to the arrow.

> Avoid us thou whose flight is straight, and let our bodies *(tanū)* be as stone. May Soma kindly speak to us, and Aditi protect us well.
>
> *Ṛg* 6.75.12 (G)

Such charms obviously have no tangible effect on the physical body. They were doubtlessly thought of as fortifying one by rendering an intangible aspect of the body immune to attack. On the basis of such passages, it appears that the *tanū* was thought of as being coextensive with the physical body. It was thought to be susceptible to the influence of magic spells which could, by operating on the subtle *tanū*, render the physical body safe from harm.

The immaterial aspect of the *tanū* is even more obvious in passages which assert that communion with the gods and entrance into heaven after death are accomplished through the agency of the *tanū*. In one such passage, the poet expresses the desire to join Varuṇa by means of the *tanū*.[27] Several passages, as noted above in Chapter 2, state that one meets the *tanū* in heaven after the death and cremation or burial

---

23. Keith, *Religion and Philosophy*, p. 245.
24. *Ṛg* 10.10.7 & 12; 10.95.5; 10.85.27.
25. *Ṛg* 4.24.3; 6.75.1; 10.4.6; 10.128.5; 10.154.3.
26. See also *Ṛg* 7.95.3; 2.17.2; 2.36.5.
27. *Ṛg* 7.86.2.

of the earthly body,[28] though it should be noted that one passage states that the *tanū* decays in 100 years, considered to be the optimum extent of human life.[29]

Tanū as the survival factor by means of which one exists in heaven after death, is related to several terms deriving from the verbal root √*tan*. These denote the offspring, the family line. The root √*tan* means primarily "to spread or extend", but is also used in the sense "to weave, to spin out" (as thread), and finally "to propagate", i.e. to extend or spin out a family line.[30] This suggests that the term *tanū* implies "that by which one's family line is maintained and extended".[31]

> Give us, where heroes exert their bodies *(tanū)* in the battle, the protection that our fathers loved. To us *(tanve,* lit. "to our forms") and to our family line *(tane)* give refuge; keep afar all unobserved hostility.
>
> *Ṛg* 6.46.12

> Or ne'er may we, O wondrous strong, enjoy another's solemn feast, ourselves *(tanū),* our sons *(śeṣas),* or progeny *(tanas).*
>
> *Ṛg* 5.70.4 (G)

That these derivatives of √*tan* do not denote simply "children" or "sons" as Griffith often translates, is clear in a number of passages which differentiate between immediate offspring *(śeṣa, tuca,* or *toka)* and the family line *(tan, tana,* or *tanas)*[32] It should be noted also that the term *tanaya*, which is used often in conjunction with the term *toka*

---

28. *Ṛg* 10.14.8; 10.15.4; 10.16.5; 10.65.1 & 2.

29. *Ṛg* 1.89.9.

30. Thus, *tanti* means "thread". and *tantu* may mean "thread" or "propagator of a family line", while *tantra,* in addition to its mystical connotation, may simply refer to propagation.

31. Other passages use the reflexive pronoun *tman,* instead of *tanū,* in conjunction with derivatives of √*tan,* to mean "oneself and one's offspring". See *Ṛg* 1.114.6; 1.183.3.

32. *Ṛg* 1.114.6; 5.70.4; 8.18.18.

(children), should probably be translated as an adjective modifying *toka* and meaning "propagating or belonging to a family". Thus, the common phrase *tokas tanaya* probably means "children of our line" or "children who propagate the family line", rather than, as Griffith translates, "children and progeny" or "seed and offspring".[33]

Two passages, one of which has already been examined above with reference to the Vedic afterlife theory,[34] explicitly state the relationship between the *tanū* and survival of death in the form of one's offspring. It will be remembered that in the passage quoted above, the ancestors *(pitṛ)* are said to have encompassed within their bodies *(tanū)* all things, and to have "streamed forth" *(pra asārayanta)* progeny *(prajā)*. These progeny in turn, as fathers, maintain the family line "as a thread continuously spun out" *(tantumātatam)*. The term *tantu* (thread), derived from √*tan*, may also mean, in later Sanskrit, "one who propagates a family" or "a line of descendants".[35] The past participle *tata* is also derived from √*tan*. Thus, this passage demonstrates clearly the etymological connection between *tanū* meaning "body" and other derivatives of the root √*tan*, which refer to descendants. It is, in fact, indicative of the Vedic concept of an actual identity carry-over, via the *tanū*, from parents to offspring. The family line *(tantu)* is propagated *(tata)* from out of and by means of the *tanū*.

Griffith mistranslates the second important passage relevant to the relationship between the *tanū* and offspring, presumably under the influence of a misplaced sense of sexual propriety. The passage should probably be translated:

> Sperm commingled, non-fools, desiring it, are born by their own potency in the bodies *(tanū)* of their offspring.[36]
>
> *Ṛg* 1.68.8

---

33. *Ṛg* 3.53.18; 4.24.3; 6.25.4; 8.9.11.

34. *Ṛg* 10.56.5-6.

35. See Monier-Williams and A.B. 7.17.

36. *icchanta reto mithastanūṣu saṁ janata svairdakṣairamurāḥ.*

The precise meaning of the passage is doubtful, but it is clear that one's identity, which somehow crosses over into one's offspring, is enshrined in the *tanū*.

Śarīra:

The term *śarīra*, on the other hand, is in the *Ṛg Veda* used exclusively in the sense of the physical body.[37] In the plural, the term sometimes refers to the limbs of the body,[38] in which case it is synonymous with the term *aṅga* (limb or part). There is one instance in which *śarīra* in the plural might be taken as referring to non-material parts or constituents of the individual, but it probably means simply "bodies", as suggested above in Chapter 3.[39] The seven references cited in the preceding footnotes are the only occurrences of the term *śarīra* in the *Ṛg Veda*, which serves to emphasize that the term *tanū*, even though it carries connotations of a non-material entity, is in fact the most common term for simply "body" in the *Ṛg Veda*. Still, a verse in the "Keśin Hymn" demonstrates the purely physical nature of the *śarīra*.

> Transported with our munihood[40] we have pressed into the winds. You therefore, mortal men, behold our natural bodies *(śarīra)* and no more.
>
> *Ṛg* 10.136.3 (G)

This may be contrasted to the use of *tanū* to denote the intangible body of the dawn.

---

37. *Ṛg* 1.32.10; 1.163.11; 10.16.3; 10.136.3.

38. *Ṛg* 6.25.4; 10.99.8; 10.16.3. *Ṛg* 10.16.3 may refer simply to "bodies" in the plural, although Sāyana explains it as: *śarīrāvayavaiḥ* = "by parts of the body".

39. The term *aṅga* denotes the non-material constituents of the individual at *Ṛg* 10.161.5.

40. *Muni* = "a sage". Four of the six occurrences of the term in the *Ṛg Veda* are in this hymn (*Ṛg* 10.136.2, 3, 4 & 5), where it seems to connote inspiration or ecstasy. The other occurrences (*Ṛg* 7.56.8; 8.17.14) provide little insight into its intended meaning, which may differ from classical Sanskrit.

> Fair as a bride embellished by her mother thou showest forth thy form *(tanū)* that all may see it.
>
> *Ṛg* 1.123.11 (G)

Rūpa:

Another synonym of *tanū* and *śarīra* is *rūpa*, which term in later Sanskrit, came to be commonly used in the sense of "body". This usage is, however, rare in the *Ṛg Veda*,[41] and in these few passages, it is not certain that *rūpa* should be understood as "body". The most explicit usage of this kind occurs in a very late hymn, which Griffith banishes to an appendix.

> May Viṣṇu form and mould the womb, may Tvaṣṭar duly shape the forms *(rūpa)*, Prajāpati infuse the stream and Dhātar lay the germ for thee.
>
> *Ṛg* 10.184.1 (G)

Normally in the *Ṛg Veda*, *rūpa* denotes visible form in general, and in almost every case the term may be understood as referring to "appearance" rather than, as *śarīra* and *tanū*, to the individual body. While *śarīra* is never specifically distinguished from *tanū* in the *Ṛg Veda*, two verses provide some hint as to the difference between *tanū* and *rūpa* by juxtaposing the two terms.

> Deck out thy body *(tanū)* with the fairest colours *(rūpa)*, with golden splendour of the sun adorn it.
>
> *Ṛg* 10.112.3 (G)

---

41. See also *Ṛg* 1.71.10, where it is said that old age impairs the *rūpa;* and *Ṛg* 2.13.3, where the forms *(rūpa)*, of animals apparently, are dismembered and distributed at a sacrifice.

Though *rūpa* may refer to color in some passages, and in some cases is associated with specific colors,[42] it is clear from other contexts that color is only one of the characteristics of *rūpa*, the most general characteristic of which is visibility. Thus, in the above passage, the *tanū* of Indra, his quasi-physical "embodiment", is to be decorated, i.e. made visibly manifest, with various visible characteristics. *Rūpa* is never spoken of as being felt, but it is often spoken of with specific reference to verbs of seeing,[43] even as being an essential condition of visibility.

> In the sky's lap the sun this form *(rūpa)* assumeth that Varuṇa and Mitra may behold it.
>
> *Ṛg* 1.115.5 (G)

In most cases "appearance" would be an appropriate translation of *rūpa*,[44] which is often said to be dazzling or beautiful, and in some cases, seems to denote beauty itself.[45] When the *rūpa* is not seen, it is an oddity, an occasion for wonder. This situation occurs only twice in the *Ṛg Veda*, both times with reference to the wind, the *rūpa* of which is invisible, though its effects may be seen.[46]

The second passage in which *rūpa* and *tanū* are juxtaposed employs a common metaphor in which the *rūpa* is spoken of as being worn or assumed, as a costume.[47]

---

42. White: *Ṛg* 9.74.7; 10.21.3. Red: *Ṛg* 1.114.5; 7.97.6; 8.101.3. Black: *Ṛg* 10.21.3 Yellow: *Ṛg* 10.96.3. *Rūpa* is also spoken of as radiant: *Ṛg* 1.114.5; 9.65.18; 9.71.8.

43. *Ṛg* 1.108.5; 1.115.5; 1.163.7; 5.52.11; 6.47.18; 9.85.12; 10.136.4; 10.139.3.

44. *Ṛg* 1.114.5; 4.11.1; 9.16.6; 9.25.4; 9.65.18; 9.71.8; 9.95.15; 10.85.1.

45. *Ṛg* 4.11.1; 9.16.6; 10.62.5.

46. *Ṛg* 1.164.44; 10.168.4.

47. See also *Ṛg* 1.115.5; 1.160.2; 1.164.9; 2.13.3; 7.55.1; 9.71.8; 9.74.7; 9.34.4; 10.85.35; 10.112.3.

> Maghavan weareth every shape *(rūpaṁrūpam)* at pleasure, effecting magic changes *(māyā)* in his body *(tanū)*.
>
> *Ṛg* 3.53.8 (G)

Note here the characteristically Vedic usage of the term māyā as "magical transformation" rather than as "illusion", which is how the term is used in classical Indian philosophy. As shown above, the *tanū* is particularly susceptible to magical operations, which may, for example, fortify it for battle. This passage seems to suggest that another way in which magical operations may work upon the *tanū* is to alter its appearance or *rūpa*. Thus, it appears that the *tanū* remains essentially the same but that certain of its characteristics, such as appearance or vulnerability, may be changed through the agency of magic. In this connection, it is interesting to note the role of *māyā* in the following passage where it is said to operate directly upon the *rūpa*.

> In every figure *(rūpaṁrūpam)* he hath been the model *(pratirūpa);* this is the only form *(rūpa)* for us to look on. Indra moves multiform *(pururūpa)* by his illusions *(māyā),* for his bay steeds are yoked, ten times a hundred.
>
> *Ṛg* 6.47.18 (G)

When, as in the above passage, *māyā* is said to operate upon appearance, the meaning of the term comes surprisingly close to the Vedāntic usage of *māyā* as "illusion". This entire passage is surprisingly monistic in flavor. It is, in fact, quoted at B.U. 2.5.19 with a monistic explanation suggesting that a single, unchanging entity, *brahman* or Indra, appears to be diverse in the manifested universe by the process of *māyā*.[48] This passage, in which Indra is said to be the model *(pratirūpa)* of the universe, should doubtlessly be compared to the famous verse in the "Asya Vāmīya" hymn where it is in the image or form *(rūpa)* of the unborn principle *(aja)* that the

---

48. Cp. K.U. 2.2.9.

universe is fashioned.[49] Another passage of this type exhorts warriors to march forward taking the irresistible advance of fire as their model, the phrase being "in the form of fire" *(agnirūpa)*.[50] In each of these passages, the term *rūpa* seems to imply the existence of a more essential entity, a model, as it were, of which the *rūpa* is a visible approximation, a form or an appearance. *Rūpa*, then, denotes nonessential, changeable characteristics, primarily visible characteristics, which "refer back", as the word *pratirūpa* suggests, to a prototype.

In the *Upaniṣads*, however, the term *rūpa* came to designate a much more personal or individual phenomenon than it does in the *Ṛg Veda*. It was thought of as that which, in conjunction with the name *(nāma)*, imparts individuality to discrete objects. Thus, in the *Upaniṣads*, the manifold universe is said to have been precipitated from original homogeneity by means of names and forms *(nāmarūpa)*.[51] In this cosmological context, it is useful to consider the use in the *Ṛg Veda* of the phrase *viśva-rūpa*, which departs in some contexts from the normal Vedic sense of the term *rūpa* and seems to denote form as an element of identity. In many contexts, *viśvarūpa* means simply "all kinds of", or perhaps "of all colors", as in plants[52] or horses[53] of every form or color. Otherwise, as would be expected on the basis of the passages cited above, where *rūpa* means appearance, the phrase *viśvarūpa* may indicate all forms of an essentially single entity which is variable in appearance, for example Soma[54] or the universal cow.[55] In the majority of contexts, however, the phrase *viśvarūpa* seems to indicate the universal set of all individual forms *(rūpa)*. Thus, it is said that Tvaṣṭṛ made all forms;[56]

49. *Ṛg* 1.164.6.
50. *Ṛg* 10.84.1.
51. B.U. 1.4.7.
52. *Ṛg* 10.88.10.
53. *Ṛg* 10.70.2.
54. *Ṛg* 9.85.12.
55. *Ṛg* 1.164.9.
56. *Ṛg* 1.188.9.

Vastoṣpati enters all forms;[57] Soma flows to and encompasses all forms;[58] and the Keśin *muni*[59] and Savitṛ[60] are said to look upon all forms. Such passages almost certainly indicate omnipresence or omniscience, being present in or knowing all of the individual forms *(rūpa)* in the universe. In most cases the term *rūpa*, in the *Ṛg Veda*, seems to refer to the variable appearance or form of something single. In a few passages, however, the term *viśvarūpa* seems to mean, not all forms of something, but the totality of individual entities. *Rūpa* is never spoken of specifically as an element of individual identity in the *Ṛg Veda*. In later texts, in conjunction with *nāma* (name), *rūpa* became an essential constituent of individuality, both of persons and things.

Nāma:

The last element of individual identity to be considered is the name, *nāma*, which in the *Ṛg Veda*, as in Indian thought in general, is considered an essential, innate characteristic rather than a mere designation. Buddhist linguistic philosophy denies this general Indian notion, but in early Buddhist literature, the term *nāma* denotes a great deal more than merely "name". In the early Buddhist context, as shown below in Chapter 4, the term *nāma*, when associated with the term *rūpa*, designates the conceptual content of one's experience of an object *(rūpa)*. The association of *nāma* with *rūpa* is rare and of little importance in the *Ṛg Veda*. The few contexts in which the terms are used together are nonetheless worth examining because of the importance of the Buddhist technical term *nāma-rūpa*, and the importance of the same term in the *Upaniṣads*. There, in contrast to the Buddhist term, *nāma-rūpa* denotes the two aspects of any discrete entity's identity, namely its form *(rūpa)* and its innate name *(nāma)*, which imparts genuine individuality to the form.

57. *Ṛg* 7.55.1.

58. *Ṛg* 9.64.8; 9.111.1.

59. *Ṛg* 10.136.4.

60. *Ṛg* 10.139.3.

The two terms occur together in only four passages in the *Ṛg Veda*. In two of these, the juxtaposition seems insignificant.[61] In two passages, however, the terms are deliberately used together.

> Invoked by us bring hither, Jātavedas, the Maruts all under their names *(nāma)* and figures *(rūpa)*.
>
> *Ṛg* 5.43.10 (G)

> 10. Whether as wanderers from the way or speeders on or to the path, under these names *(nāma)* the spreading band tend well the sacrifice for me.
>
> 11. To this the heroes well attend, well do their teams attend to this. Visible are their varied forms *(rūpa)*. Behold, they are Pārāvatas.
>
> *Ṛg* 5.52.10-11 (G)

In both of these passages, particularly the first, the association of *nāma* with *rūpa* is specific, the implication being that the names identify the forms by a one-to-one correspondence with them. These passages may be another instance, in addition to the phrase *viśva-rūpa*, of a deviation from the common Vedic usage of *rūpa*, a deviation which comes close to the Upaniṣadic usage of *rūpa* as an element of individual identity. It is not clear above whether each Marut has his own form and name, or if each of them has various names and forms. At any rate, the one-to-one correspondence between names and forms is clear enough. In the second passage, the primary intent of verse eleven, in which the term *rūpa* occurs, seems to be to indicate that the Maruts are literally present at the sacrifice, and supposedly visible. This may be the intent of the first passage as well, though in the absence of similar passages for comparison, the precise meaning of these juxtapositions of *nāma* and *rūpa* is impossible to determine. Also noteworthy in this connection is the direct association in one passage of *nāma* and *tanū*, it being said that the Aśvins have been born with their own names and forms *(tanū)*.[62]

---

61. *Ṛg* 8.41.5; 10.169.2. See also *Ṛg* 10.84.1 & 5.

62. *Ṛg* 1.181.4.

At any rate, the role of the name in Vedic ritual is abundantly clear. In the first of the above passages, the Maruts are to be brought by their names *(nāmabhiḥ)* because it is by knowing the names of the gods that the sacrificer gains the power to summon them to the sacrificer gains the power to summon them to the sacrifice and thereby press their powers into the service of his ends. The name is not a mere designation, but an essential element of one's identity, and knowledge of the name empowers one with influence upon the bearer of that name. Knowledge of the gods' names is an important quality of the sage,[63] their names being secret *(guhya)*, not known by all.[64]It is also essential that hymns bear the names of gods,[65] not only because the names afford access to the gods, but also because in bestowing names on the gods, one enhances their majesty.[66] This is no doubt related to the concept that one wins names by heroic deeds, as for instance when Indra is said to have earned the name Vṛtra-slayer by killing the dragon Vṛtra.[67] Thus, the name reveals one's nature, and in some cases nāma is virtually synonymous with "individual nature".[68] In all cases, knowledge of the name connotes knowledge of the nature. One may bear more than one name, which is particularly likely if one is a god, but the connection of the name with one's individual nature and identity is not lessened by this situation. Obeisance is paid[69] and praise sung[70] to the names of gods. It is thought significant that Soma, having been crushed to juice from the plant, reaches the filter bearing his name, i.e. his personal power and identity.[71] Agni is said to take

---

63. *Ṛg* 1.156.3; 5.5.10; 10.5.2; 10.45.2; 10.82.3.

64. *Ṛg* 5.3.2; 9.95.2; 9.96.15; 10.45.2; 10.55.1 & 2. See also *Ṛg* 1.84.15, where *amanvata nāma* = "mystic name" (G).

65. *Ṛg* 8.80.9; 9.99.4; 10.63.2; 10.64.1.

66. *Ṛg* 5.3.10; 9.75.1. See also *Ṛg* 10.61.14.

67. *Ṛg* 10.74.6. See also *Ṛg* 9.75.1.

68. *Ṛg* 1.123.9 & 12; 10.28.12; 10.73.6; 10.97.9.

69. *Ṛg* 10.63.2.

70. *Ṛg* 7.57.6; 10.84.5.

71. *Ṛg* 9.92.2. Cp. *Ṛg* 9.14.4 and 9.78.1, where it is said that the *tanū* of Soma, but not the name, is left in the strainer used to purify the drug.

on a name after his metaphorical birth from the fire-making sticks.[72] This is to say that the blaze reveals the nature of fire. As a universal principle, fire is latently present in all phenomena, but it only becomes manifest in a specific, individual instance of burning to which the name fire *(agni)* may be attached.

This essential connection between the name and the individual identity makes knowledge of one's name, in the hands of others, a potential instrument of one's weal or woe, depending upon the intent with which the supernatural susceptibility of the name is used. Thus, the priest sends the sacrificer's name to heaven,[73] and telling forth someone's name not only has the effect to making him famous,[74] but also the effect of preserving his identity in the remembrance of his name.

> 7. He in his might, with name *(nāma)* that lives forever, hath far surpassed all human generations. ...
> 8. Stranger to guile, who never was false or faithless, bearing a name that may be well remembered.
>
> *Ṛg* 6.18.7 (G)

In another verse, Indra is said to have been established among the gods through the agency of the name.[75] Apparently out of a wish to avoid inducing some such immortality, in one passage a neglected wife refuses to speak her rival's name.[76] This may also be the intent of a verse in which the destruction of the enemy's name is called for,[77] but it may also refer to the possibility of wrecking magical malevolence by means of the name. This latter possibility is clearly implied in a verse praising Indra for not having revealed the Aryans'

---

72. *Ṛg* 10.115.2. See *Ṛg* 1.123.12.
73. *Ṛg* 5.44.8.
74. *Ṛg* 10.69.5.
75. *Ṛg* 10.49.2.
76. *Ṛg* 10.145.4. See *Ṛg* 1.3.10, where "Vṛtra's nameless *(ninya)* body *(śarīra)*" apparently refers to annihilation of the identity.
77. *Ṛg* 10.23.2.

name to their foes.[78] In several passages, knowing the names of cows apparently gives one the power to attain them,[79] cattle being an important commodity in the Aryan economic system.

The intimate connection between the name and individual identity, which, in the *Ṛg Veda,* is based on the supposed magical potency of the name, was, in the *Upaniṣads,* abstracted philosophically into a cosmological concept, for, as mentioned above, the *nāma,* in conjunction with the *rūpa,* was that which was thought of as imparting individuality to discrete objects.

> At that time this (universe) was undifferentiated. It became differentiated by name and form *(nāma-rūpa)* (so that it is said) he has such a name, such a shape.[80]
>
> B.U. 1.4.7 (R)

It is this individuality which blinds one, it is said, to realization of one's essential unity with the unitary principle of the universe, the *brahman* or *ātman,* or, as it is expressed in the following passage, the *puruṣa.*

> Just as the flowing rivers disappear in the ocean casting off name and shape *(nāma-rūpa),* even so the knower, freed from name and] shape, attains to the divine person *(puruṣa),* higher than the high.[81]
>
> Mu.U. 3.2.8 (R)

The concept expressed by the phrase *nāma-rūpa* was further abstracted in Buddhist writings which rejected the idea of innate identity. Though the last passage makes it clear that the Upaniṣadic sages considered this so-called individuality to be ultimately illusory, it was nonetheless thought of in cosmological terms. The *nāma* was

---

78. *Ṛg* 10.49.3.

79. *Ṛg* 4.1.16; 7.87.4; 9.87.3; 10.68.7.

80. See also B.U. 1.6.4; C.U. 6.3.2-3; 8.14.1.

81. Cp. P.U. 6.5.

thought to be the individuating factor, belonging inherently to the object *(rūpa)* from the time of creation. In the early Buddhist context, the *nāma* refers to a set of subjective thought constructions which one associates with the so-called objective forms *(rūpa)* that one experiences, thereby projecting upon them an imagined independent existence. Since this point has been often misunderstood, a detailed discussion of *nāma-rūpa* in early Buddhism is better postponed until the last chapter, where it will be examined in its proper context.

B) VITAL FACULTIES

The terms discussed thus far deal with the concept of individual identity and its perpetuation after death. In the Vedic context, individual identity is expressed primarily with recourse to the term *tanū*, and to some extent, to the term *nāma*. Around this nucleus of individual identity, several vital and mental faculties are thought to cluster during one's lifetime. Upon death, these faculties are said to disperse and rejoin the macrocosmic sources from which they derive. They are only temporarily individualized in a microcosmic entity. Correspondences between the macrocosmic universe and the microcosmic individual are not as exhaustively listed in the *Ṛg Veda* as they are in the *Upaniṣads*, but the concept is clearly revealed in the "Puruṣa Sūkta".

> The moon was gendered from his mind *(manas)*, and from his eye the sun had birth; Indra and Agni from his mouth were born, and Vāyu (the wind god) from his breath *(ātman)*.
>
> *Ṛg* 10.90.13 (G)

Here, the various universal vital forces are conceived of as being derived from the sacrificial dispersion of the original, unitary principle of creation, which is represented as a person *(puruṣa)*. The universe is regarded as being alive, like a person. Individual people derive their vital faculties from universal sources, and upon death, these faculties are reabsorbed into the universe at large.

> Let his eye go to the sun, his breath *(ātman)* to the wind *(vāyu)*. Go to the sky and to the earth, according to (the) nature (of thy several parts); or go to the waters[82] if that is suitable for thee, enter into the plants with all thy members.
>
> *Ṛg* 10.16.3 (M)

Several passages, as noted above in Chapter 3, are designed to save a person from death by summoning his various vital faculties back from the universal sources into which they have begun to disperse as death approaches.[83] Thus, most of the various vital and mental faculties to be discussed below are not, strictly speaking, individual, personal phenomena. They belong to a person only for the duration of life, on loan as it were from the living universe. This general concept, it must be stressed, does not attain the status of a doctrine in the *Ṛg Veda*. It is never precisely formulated, nor are the hymns consistent in their approach to the nature of the human being. There are instances of vital faculties accompanying the *tanū* in heaven, and instances in which vital or mental faculties seem to be confined to mundane life. The overall tendency in the *Ṛg Veda*, however, is to associate mundane and supra-mundane individuality with the tanu. Around this nucleus of individuality, various universal life forces are thought to become individualized temporarily to make up a complete, living human being.

The most striking characteristics of the human being are life and consciousness. As broad, general categories, these are referred to in the *Ṛg Veda* with derivatives of the verbal roots √*jīv* (to live) and √*cit* (to think, to perceive). The hymns are not entirely consistent in distinguishing vital faculties from mental faculties, but these two roots provide a convenient division under which the human faculties mentioned in *Ṛg Veda* may be considered. Thus, the terms *āyu, asu, vayas, prāṇa,* and *ātman* will be considered with reference to vitality and the terms *manas, hṛd, dhī,* and *kratu* with reference to consciousness.

---

82. See *Ṛg* 10.169.1, where the waters are said to be rich in life *(jīva)*.

83. *Ṛg* 10.57; 10.58; 10.59; 10.60; 10.158.2; 10.161.5.

Jīva:

The verbal root √*jīv*, and its grammatical modifications, as noted above, are used in the *Ṛg Veda* to denote life in general. As nouns, they usually refer to living beings in general. In the few cases where they are used with reference to a single individual, they refer to life or vitality in general, and not, as in later Indian literature, to an individual vital faculty or life principle.[84] The root √*jīv* occasionally occurs in an adjectival sense meaning simply "alive", but in the majority of cases it occurs in a verbal form The derivatives of the root √*jīv* not only denote life as opposed to death,[85] but also activity as opposed to sleep.[86]

> Dawn, at her rising, urges forth the living *(jīvam);* him who is dead she wakes not from his slumber.
>
> *Ṛg* 1.113.8 (G)

Derivatives of √*jīv* are often used in conjunction with terms which do denote vital faculties. In most of these cases, it is clear that the presence of the various life faculties is a necessary condition for life, represented by derivatives of √*jīv*, to continue. These derivatives of √*jīv* occur most frequently in conjunction with the term *āyu*, which normally denotes "life duration". In most of these passages, the sacrificer asks that the *āyu* be extended, strengthened or retained so that he may continue to live *(√jīv)*.[87] The terms *ātman* and *prāṇa*,

84. For nominal instances of √*jiv* which might be taken as referring to an individual entity, see: *Ṛg* 1.113.6; 1.164.30 *(jīvaḥ)*. *Ṛg* 10.97.11; 10.36.8 (*jīva*-compound). *Ṛg* 1.140.8; 10.57.5 *(jīvam)*. *Ṛg* 10.19.6 *(jīvabhiḥ)*. *Ṛg* 8.8.23; 10.18.4 *(jīvebhyaḥ)*. These may be compared to the following nominal forms which obviously refer to life in general or to "the living": *Ṛg* 1.68.2; 5.44.5; 5.78.9 *(jīvaḥ)*. *Ṛg* 1.31.15; 10.80.4; 1.149.2; 10.30.14; 10.169.1 (*jīva*-compound). *Ṛg* 1.113.8; 4.51.5; 7.77.1 *(jīvam)*. *Ṛg* 7.32.26; 10.18.3; 10.36.9; 10.37.7 & 8 *(jīvaḥ)*.

85. *Ṛg* 1.91.6; 1.140.6; 7.32.26; 10.18.3; 10.60.7-10; 10.97.11; 10.137.1.

86. *Ṛg* 1.113.16; 7.77.1. See also *Ṛg* 1.164.30; 1.36.30; 1.36.14.

87. *Ṛg* 1.44.6; 1.89.2; 1.94.4; 8.18.18 & 22; 10.14.14; 10.18.6; 10.59.1 & 5; 10.85.39; 10.144.5; 10.161.4.

both of which are connected with the breath, also occur as conditions necessary for the continuation of life.[88] Only in a concentrated group of three hymns in the tenth book, is *manas* (mind) said to be a condition for life.[89] In one of these passages, there is an interesting listing of several vital and mental faculties with reference to the desire that they not be dispersed into the universe, and that life *(√jīv)* may thereby continue.

> 5. O Asunīti, keep the mind *(manas)* within us, and extend the life *(āyu)* that we may live *(jīvātave)*. ...
> 6. Give us our sight again, O Asunīti, give us again our breath *(prāṇa)* and our enjoyment. ...
> 7. May Earth restore to us our vitality *(asu)*; may heaven, the sky and the mid-air restore it.
>
> *Ṛg* 10.59.5-7

Asu:

In addition to verse seven above, the term *asu* (vitality) occurs twice again in conjunction with *√jīv*.[90] In neither instance is *asu* specifically stated to be a condition for life as expressed by a derivative of *√jīv*. Nonetheless, the relationship of *asu* to the state of vitality designated by *√jīv* is obvious, in that *asu*, like *√jīv* is represented as being opposed to both sleep and death. In a hymn to Dawn, the rise from slumber which she induces is represented as the return of life and vitality.

> Arise! Life *(jīva)* and vitality *(asu)* have come to us, darkness has departed; light approaches.
>
> *Ṛg* 1.113.16

88. *Ṛg* 10.33.9; 1.48.10.

89. *Ṛg* 10.57.4-5; 10.58.1-2; 10.59.5; 10.60.8-10.

90. *Ṛg* 1.113.16; 1.140.8.

Asu and *jīva* are opposed to death in a metaphorical passage in which Agni, the fire god, is said to revive the flames, personified as long-haired maidens, which lie dead or asleep in the firewood.

> Dead, the long-haired maidens chatter to him and rise up again for the living one *(āyave)*. Releasing them of their decrepitude, he comes chanting, producing vitality *(asu)* and undissipated life *(jīva)*.
>
> *Ṛg* 1.140.8

It is also noteworthy that in some passages *asu* is apparently thought to accompany the *tanū* in the afterlife. The two dogs of Yama, messengers of death, are said to take possession of the vitality *(asu-tṛpa)*, presumably to take it to the next world, and are begged to restore it "that we may see the sunlight", i.e. continue to live.[91] This idea is inconsistent with the passage quoted above (*Ṛg* 10.59.7) in which the *asu* is represented as going to earth, sky and mid-air upon death. In a funeral hymn in the tenth book, however, the departed ancestors *(pitṛ)* are specifically said to have gone to or attained life *(asum īyuḥ)*[92] Thus, *asu* (vitality) is frequently though inconsistently associated with the afterlife. This association is probably responsible for the name of the funeral deity, Asunīti, mentioned in four hymns of the tenth book.[93] Of the various interpretations of this name which Muir notes,[94] Müller's "guide of life" is probably the best, in that this deity was probably thought of as guiding *(√nī)* the vitality *(asu)* to heaven. The term *asu* is probably also the basis of the word *asura*, which initially meant "spiritual, incorporeal life" but came to be used to denote "a ghost or spirit", and finally became a proper name

---

91. *Ṛg* 10.14.12. There is little doubt that this is the correct interpretation of *asutṛpa* in this context. Both the *Pāda* text and Sāyana construe the compound as *asu* + *√tṛp*. Griffith, however, seems to read *a-sutṛpa* in his translation "insatiate".

92. *Ṛg* 10.15.1.

93. *Ṛg* 10.12.4; 10.15.15; 10.16.2; 10.59.5 & 6.

94. Muir, vol. 5, p. 297, n. 445.

indicating a particular class of supernatural beings thought to be the opponents of the gods.

The term *asu*, then, seems to denote mere vitality. In comparison to the vital faculties which will be examined below, *asu* is not associated with personal power *(bala)* as is *ātman;* nor, as *vayas*, is it associated with will power *(kratu)* or inspiration *(kavi)* nor as *āyu*, is it associated with the primary mental faculties *manas* (mind) and *hṛd* (heart).

On the basis of the admittedly insufficient evidence in the *Ṛg Veda*, it appears that *asu* is the subtlest and most passive of the vital faculties. It is the faculty farthest removed from the actual process of living and least susceptible to adventitious influence. The *asu* is never pictured as doing anything, nor, generally speaking, may anything be done to it. The inevitable exception to this observation is a curse to make the niggard's *asu* decay.[95] It survives death, and there is some indication that, like *āyu*, it is thought of as accompanying the *tanū* in heaven rather than being dispersed into the universe with the other vital faculties. Again though, inconsistencies may be noted.[96]

Āyu:

Next on a descending scale of subtlety and passivity would be *āyu*. *Āyu* is a curious term to the modern Western mind. It designates the duration of one's life conceived of as an entity and a vital faculty. The most common context in which the term occurs is in prayers that *āyu* be lengthened so that one may live *(√jīv)* longer, the optimum extent of human life being a hundred years.[97] In contrast to *asu*, *āyu* is specifically said to be a direct condition for the continuation of active life *(jīva)*.[98] The fact that the state of the *āyu* may be influenced also serves to distinguish it from *asu*. Normally, this influence is pictured as lengthening, usually expressed by the verbal root *√tṛ*, which literally means "to cross over or accomplish". The

95. *Ṛg* 1.182.3.

96. *Ṛg* 10.59.7, quoted above.

97. *Ṛg* 1.89.9; 3.35.10; 10.18.4; 10.161.4.

98. See references in note 88 above.

wish expressed is that the *āyu* be fully accomplished, that the sacrificer may live a hundred years. The *āyu* is also spoken of as being influenced from without by being shortened,[99] strengthened,[100] destroyed,[101] and moulded.[102] Regardless of these influences upon the *āyu*, however, the effect of passing time on it is inexorable, an effect hauntingly portrayed in a hymn to the dawn.

> Ancient of days, again and again born newly, decking her beauty with the self-same raiment, the goddess wastes away the life *(āyu)* of mortals, like a skilled hunter cutting birds in pieces.
>
> *Ṛg* 1.92.10 (G)

By contrast, the *āyu* of the gods are said not to be subject to decay,[103] this being an expression of immortality. The god most often associated with *āyu* is Agni, the terms *āyu, āyava* and especially *viśva-āyu* being epithets of the fire god.[104] The presence of Agni in all life, which has been noted above, is represented primarily by his association with the *āyu* of all creatures. In one passage, Agni is said to be the "one life" or "unifying life" *(eka-āyu)*.[105] In another, he is called the "pillar of life" *(āyoḥ skambha)*.[106] The conterminal association between *āyu* and *jīva* noted above is borne out in the similar usage of *āyu* and *jīva* to denote life in general, living beings.[107] In many instances the term *viśva-āyu* occurs in this sense, though in a few cases it means "the

99. *Ṛg* 3.49.2; 7.1.24.

100. *Ṛg* 3.62.15.

101. *Ṛg* 10.161.2.

102. *Ṛg* 10.18.5.

103. *Ṛg* 1.84.16; 10.45.8; 10.51.7.

104. Indra (*Ṛg* 5.34.5), Soma (*Ṛg* 9.23.2 & 4; 9.64.17; 9.107.14), and Sarasvati (*Ṛg* 5.49.7) also bear epithets based on *āyu*.

105. *Ṛg* 1.31.5.

106. *Ṛg* 10.5.6.

107. *Ṛg* 4.4.7; 7.104.5; 9.66.19; 10.53.3.

full extent of life",[108] in which case it is synonymous with *sarva-āyu*.[109]

Again like √*jīv*, and in this case like *asu*, *āyu* is associated with wakefulness and activity as opposed to sleep. The goddess Dawn, who, in the passage quoted above is said to waste away the *āyu*, is also said to give new *āyu*, i.e. to invigorate sleeping creatures.

> Giving fresh life *(navyam āyu)* when she hath hid the darkness, this Dawn hath wakened there with new-born lustre.
>
> *Ṛg* 7.80.2 (G)

The goddess Sasarparī, who according to Sāyana represents Vak, the goddess of speech, is also said to give new life, although this is apparently in relation to a famine.[110]

The principal distinction between *āyu* and other vital faculties, then, is the association of *āyu* with the duration of life. However, the term does not denote primarily a time span, but is pictured as a true vital faculty, the potency of which is lessened by the passing of time. To be young is to be in the beginning of life *(pūrva-āyuni)*.[111] *Āyu*, more than *asu*, is manifest in the actual phenomenon of living, and the natural lessening of vitality in an aging person would be thought of as the visible result of the deterioration of *āyu*. As would be expected on the basis of this observation, *āyu* is represented as being related to other components of the individual more often than *asu*.

The (earthly) *tanū* is also said to be subject to decay in a hundred years, and like the *āyu*, is subject to calamity which may curtail its natural duration. It is *āyu*, however, which imparts life to the *tanū*. A natural death at the end of a hundred years, or a premature death, are both primarily results of the natural deterioration or adventitious curtailment of *āyu*, the continuation of which is the immediate condition for the vitality of the *tanū*.

---

108. *Ṛg* 8.31.8; 10.85.42.

109. *Ṛg* 10.161.5.

110. *Ṛg* 3.53.15-16.

111. *Ṛg* 9.100.1; 10.5.7.

> A hundred autumns stand before us, O ye gods, within whose space ye bring our bodies *(tanū)* to decay; within whose space our sons become fathers in turn. Break ye not in the middle our course of fleeting life *(āyur-gantoḥ* = lit. "life in the middle of (its) course".
>
> *Ṛg* 1.89.9 (G)

Āyu is also that which invigorates the heavenly aspect of the *tanū*, although, as noted above, the asu also seems to play a part in heavenly life after death.

> Again, O Agni, to the fathers send him who, offered in thee, goes with our oblations. Wearing life *(āyur-vasān)* let him increase his offspring. Let him join a body *(saṁ gacchatāṁ tanvā)*, Jātavedas.[112]
>
> *Ṛg* 10.16.5

In one passage, *āyu* is said to be like breath *(āyur na prāṇa)*,[113] which apparently indicates that these two vital faculties were considered to be of equal importance. Elsewhere, however, it is suggested that *āyu* is dependent upon *vayas*, which, therefore, may have been thought of as a more essential life force than *āyu*.

> Like gold to look on, far he shone refulgent, beaming imperishable life *(āyu)* for glory. Agni by vital powers *(vayobhiḥ)* became immortal when his prolific father Dayus begat him.
>
> *Ṛg* 10.45.8 (G)

Elsewhere again, *vayas*, which is more characteristically found in the singular number, seems to be represented as being on an equal footing with *āyu*.

---

112. The bracketed Sanskrit phrases indicate where I have modified Griffith's translation.

113. *Ṛg* 1.66.1. Cp. Ks.U. 3.2.

> Through this *(soma?)*[114] came life force *(vayas)*, through this, lengthened life *(āyu)* to live, and relations.
>
> *Ṛg* 10.144.5

Griffith's translation, without grammatical justification, suggests that here too, *āyu* is represented as dependent upon *vayas*.

> Through this came vital power which lengthens out our days, and kinship through its help awoke.
>
> *Ṛg* 10.144.5 (G)

Regardless of this point of translation, there can be no doubt that in the following verse, *kratu* (mental power) is represented as being basic to both *vayas* and *āyu*. *Kratu*, as will be seen below, is often associated with *soma*, which seems to be the agent through which vayas and *āyu* are reinforced in the previous verse.

> Through mental power *(kratu)* (there is) life force *(vayas)* and lengthened life *(āyu)*, O Sukratu (Indra). From us, by mental power this *(soma)* is pressed our.[115]
>
> *Ṛg* 10.144.6

It is also implied that *manas* (mind)[116] and *hṛd* (heart)[117] are thought of as fundamental conditions for the continuation of *āyu*. Thus, it is clear that the vital faculties do not operate in isolation from the mental faculties, though the relationship between them is vaguely and inconsistently expressed in the *Ṛg Veda*.

---

114. See *Ṛg* 6.40.4, where Indra's *vayas* is said to be increased by *soma*.

115. Griffith, of course, reiterates his interpretation of the previous verse: "Wisdom, most sapient one, brings force that lengthens life. May wisdom bring juice to us."

116. *Ṛg* 10.59.5.

117. *Ṛg* 10.186.1.

Vayas:

Vayas, on a descending scale of subtlety, is represented as being less subtle than *asu* and *āyu*, though there is reason to believe that it was considered a more essential life force than either of these. In many contexts, *vayas* may be rendered convincingly in translation as "food", which is how Sāyana often explains the term,[118] even in passages where it is inappropriate to the context.[119] *Vayas*, of course, actually means food in the later language, but Sāyana was no doubt aware that its usage in the *Ṛg Veda* did not correspond to its usage in his day. One should probably understand Sāyana's explanation of *vayas* as food *(anna)* with reference to the Upaniṣadic concept of the threefold nature of food.

> Food, when eaten, becomes threefold; its coarsest portion becomes the feces, its middle (portion) flesh and its subtlest (portion) mind *(manas)*.
> C.U. 6.5.1 (R)

It is clear that *vayas* represents power, but in various contexts it may be taken as physical power, vital power or mental power. The possession of *vayas* is often associated with heroism in battle,[120] and most prayers which seek to affect the *vayas* ask for strengthening *(√vṛdh)*[121] The association of *vayas* with life has been noted above in what seems to be its role as the foundation of *āyu*. In some passages, however, *vayas* is apparently used in the same sense as *āyu*, as in a prayer asking for *vayas* "so that we may live" *(jīvase)*.[122] In one hymn, *vayas* as vital power and as mental power occurs in successive verses.

> 1. The Ṛbhus for their parents made life *(vayas)* young again, and fashioned for the calf a mother by its side.

---

118. *Ṛg* 1.127.8; 1.136.2; 1.178.2; 1.183.4; 2.23.10.

119. *Ṛg* 1.111.2; 6.45.2; 10.45.8.

120. *Ṛg* 1.151.9; 2.3.9; 2.4.9; 2.13.11; 5.55.1; 7.58.3.

121. *Ṛg* 3.51.6; 5.5.6; 5.15.5; 5.54.2; 8.60.11.

122. *Ṛg* 9.86.38.

2. For sacrifice make us active vital power *(vayas)* for skill (dakṣa) and wisdom *(kratu)*, food *(iṣam)* with noble progeny.

Ṛg 1.111.1-2 (G)

Sāyana explains the first instance of *vayas* by offering the synonym *āyu*, and the second he explains as "food in the form of an oblation" *(havir-lakṣanam-annam)*. Sāyana's intent in this latter explanation is uncertain, but the association of *vayas* with mental phenomena is clear. Here again, an inconsistency in the representation of this relationship will be noted in that above, in *Ṛg* 10.144.6, *kratu* seems to be the basis of *vayas*. At any rate, that there is some relationship between the two faculties is clear, as is some relationship between poetic inspiration *(kavi)* and *vayas*.[123]

The precise role of *vayas* in the Vedic concept of the human being, unfortunately, cannot be more accurately determined. The vague picture that emerges from the foregoing observations is that the Vedic concept of the basis of human life is surprisingly materialistic when considered in relation to later Indian psychology. The association of *vayas* with food is beyond doubt. Though "food" is obviously not an adequate translation of *vayas*, *vayas* may be conceived of as that vigor of body and mind which is present in a well-fed person, but absent in a malnourished person.[124] In almost every case, *vayas* is pictured as something obtained as opposed to an inherent faculty. Nonetheless if a hierarchy may be established among the vital faculties on the basis of the scant information available, *vayas* would seem to be the most fundamental.

In summary, it appears that the Vedic Aryan saw life pragmatically, as a phenomenon based on nutrition. The universe itself is alive, but individual vitality is maintained only by funneling the life forces in the universe at large into the individual. This is the case even in the afterlife, where the ancestors' *tanū* are thought to be maintained by ritually feeding them by means of the ancestral sacrifice *(pitṛyajña)*. It is true even of the gods, who are represented as being, like humans,

---

123. *Ṛg* 2.4.9; 9.9.1. See also *Ṛg* 6.6.7.

124. See C.U. 6.7.

dependent upon a continued supply of nourishment. Individuality seems to have been thought of as a precious and fragile possession, wrested from the universe at large, and retained only by continuous effort in localizing the universal vital forces around oneself. The most important mechanism through which this funneling process was thought to be accomplished was the sacrificial ritual.

The similarity between these Vedic concepts and certain later Upaniṣadic concepts is immediately obvious, as is the difference. In the *Upaniṣads* too, individual identity is often seen as deriving from the universe at large, specifically from the unitary universal principle *(brahman)*, but in the *Upaniṣads* this individuality was thought of as a curse. The ultimate spiritual goal was, rather than to maintain the individuality, to merge it with the universal principle upon which it was thought to be founded. The possibility of this merger is expressed in the doctrine that the *ātman* (soul) is identical to *brahman* (the universal principle). In the *Ṛg Veda* too the term *ātman* has universal connections, but in a sense that is far removed from this Upaniṣadic idea. In the *Ṛg Veda ātman* is directly associated with the phenomenon of breath.

Breath:

Prāṇa, and the similar term *ana*, both derived from the verbal root √*an*, "to breathe", denote breath as a physical phenomenon.[125] Breathing, however, appears to be regarded as the functioning of an entity, so that in a prayer for renewed life, Asunīti is begged to return the *prāṇa*.[126] Another passage expresses the wish that the *prāṇa* should abandon an enemy.[127] Like the other vital faculties, *prāṇa* connotes primarily life. It is, in fact, equated with *āyu* in one passage.[128] In another, in the form *ana*, it is represented as the criterion whereby the inanimate may be distinguished from the animate.[129] Again, like the

---

125. *Ṛg* 10.189.2.

126. *Ṛg* 10.59.6.

127. *Ṛg* 3.53.21.

128. *Ṛg* 1.66.1.

129. *Ṛg* 10.120.2.

other vital faculties examined so far, *prāṇa* also connotes wakefulness[130] and activity,[131] as opposed to sleep and inertia. Macrocosmically, it corresponds to the wind.[132]

The term *vāta* came to designate a "vital air" or "subtle breath" in later Indian thought, but in the *Ṛg Veda* it seems to denote simply meteorological wind. The term merits consideration here, though, because it is identified with *ātman* in three passages. In one, the wind *(vāta)* is said to be the *ātman* of Varuṇa,[133]and in another, *vāta* is said to be the *ātman* of the Aśvins.[134] The third passage *Ṛg* 1.34.7. is obscure. Griffith translates the phrase, addressed to the Aśvins, *ātmeva vātaḥ svasarāni gacchatam,* as "come, like vital air to bodies". This translation expresses the intent of Sāyana's vague explanation, construing *vāta* as a vital faculty, but does not account for all of the words in the original passage. The literal meaning of the text, considering the numerous other contexts in which *vāta* obviously means wind, is probably more accurately rendered as "come to our homes (in the form of) wind (which is) like (your) *ātman*". Wind under the name of *vāyu* is said to be the *ātman* of the gods.[135] The *ātman* of a dead person, as noted above, is said to disperse into the wind *(vāta)* upon the performance of the cremation ritual.[136] In the *Ṛg Veda, vāta* means simply wind, it became an important vitalistic term in later Indian literature, but it is of importance in the *Ṛg Veda* primarily because, as meteorological wind it is linked to the term *ātman,* the microcosmic manifestation of wind.

In Vedic passages in which *ātman* is represented as being related to the wind, the most obvious translation would be simply "breath". Like *prāṇa, ātman* is represented as a vital faculty which, on a

---

130. *Ṛg* 1.48.10; 10.121.3.

131. *Ṛg* 1.101.5.

132. *Ṛg* 10.90.14. See also *Ṛg* 10.125.8.

133. *Ṛg* 7.87.2.

134. *Ṛg* 10.92.13. Griffith's translation, based on Sāyana, is misleading, rendering the single word *ātman* as "breath of all".

135. *Ṛg* 10.168.4.

136. *Ṛg* 10.16.3.

macrocosmic scale, corresponds to wind. In other Vedic contexts, however, it is clear that the term *ātman* represents a more complex psychological concept than does *prāṇa*. Nonetheless, the fundamental connection of *ātman* with respiration is beyond doubt, a situation which suggests translation of the Vedic term *ātman* with the English "spirit" because of the etymological connections of spirit with breath.

Just as the possession of *prāṇa* distinguishes the animate from the inanimate, so the term *ātman-vant* ("having spirit") apparently means "animated, living" when applied to normally inanimate objects, like boats and clouds.[137] In passages which describe Soma as the "spirit of the sacrifice" *(ātma-yajñasya),*[138] the term should probably again be taken as implying an animating principle rather than in the Vedāntic sense as "essence of the sacrifice". *Ātman,* like *vāyas,* is associated with food, food being the source of *ātman.*[139] One interesting passage in this connection seems to imply that the *ātman* is more essential than the *tanū,* for it is said, "Spirit *(ātman)* is food *(pitu),* body *(tanū)* is raiment *(vāsa)*".[140] This passage should probably be understood, however, as descriptive of the natures of *tanū* and *ātman* rather than indicating a hierarchical relationship between the two terms.

In addition to the vitalistic function of *ātman,* a few passages imply a more psychological connotation of the term. One passage indicates that *ātman* is a source of joy,[141] another identifies is as a source of torment.[142] Yet another passage represents *ātman* as a repository of strength *(balam).*[143] These, however, are not typical usages of the term *ātman,* which, it is clear, denotes primarily a subtle form of breath which functions as an individual vital faculty. The dependence of the *ātman* upon food indicates that it was not conceived of in Upaniṣadic

---

137. *Ṛg* 1.116.3; 1.182.5; 9.74.4.

138. *Ṛg* 9.2.10.

139. *Ṛg* 10.107.7.

140. *Ṛg* 8.3.24.

141. *Ṛg* 1.73.2.

142. *Ṛg* 1.162.20.

143. *Ṛg* 9.113.1. Note that the verbal root √*bal,* from which *bala* is derived, may also mean "to breathe".

terms as the imperishable innermost essence of the individual. This point becomes even clearer in a passage in which the priest, by means of medicinal herbs, seeks to restore the *ātman* of a dying man.[144]

Two passages which contain the phrase *ātmā jagatas-tasthuṣaś-ca,* "the spirit of (all) that moves and stands".[145] These suggest the concept of a universal spirit which encompasses all individual spirits, but this concept is still far removed from the Vedāntic idea of the innermost individual essence being ultimately identical to the unitary essence of the universe. In the *Ṛg Veda,* the *ātman* is merely one of several vital faculties, standing on a more or less equal footing with the others. The term *āyu,* it will be remembered, also has universal connections in the *Ṛg Veda,* usually with reference to the god Agni, who is often said to be "universal life" *(viśva-āyu).* It is not difficult to see, however, why the term *ātman,* out of all the vital faculties mentioned above, was chosen in later writings for expansion into a term denoting the innermost essence of human life and consciousness, and ultimately the unitary essence of the entire universe. The *tanū,* which, in the *Ṛg Veda,* was considered the most essential element of individual identity, was a term too much associated with corporeal individuality to denote a comprehensive universal principle. Moreover, its association with the Vedic theory of afterlife probably explains why, in later Indian psychological literature, the term *tanū* never attained the status of a technical term, since the Vedic theory was superseded by the conflicting theory of repetitive rebirth. The term *āyu,* which does have universal implications in the *Ṛg Veda,* is too much associated with finite duration to denote an everlasting entity. The term *ātman,* however, is amenable to expansion into a word denoting "individual *cum* universal essence" and the correspondence between breath and wind is a particularly evocative symbol for the correspondence of individual essence to universal essence. The *Upaniṣads* are not entirely consistent in expressing this monistic connection, and in some cases

144. *Ṛg* 10.97.4 & 8.

145. *Ṛg* 1.115.5, where the sun is said to be this universal spirit,"the *ātman* of all that moves and stands", and *Ṛg* 7.101.6, where Puṣan is said to contain this *ātman* within himself.

the term *ātman* seems to denote a purely individual, reincarnating entity.[146] Still, *ātman* is also a particularly apt choice to denote individual essence, even without universal connotations, because of its common Vedic usage in the abbreviated form *tman* in a wide range of reflexive senses ranging from "oneself" as in "know oneself",[147] "turn oneself to a task",[148] to "one's own possession",[149] "one's own power",[150] "own nature",[151] "in person",[152] and "by one's own choice, freely, spontaneously".[153] The term *tman* is far more common than *tanū* in the reflexive sense, and again, does not suffer the disadvantage of being associated with the Vedic afterlife theory. Thus, though the development in meaning of the term *ātman* from its Vedic usage to its Upaniṣadic usage is natural, it must be remembered that development did occur, and that reading the Upaniṣadic *ātman* retrospectively into the Vedic *ātman* distorts the meaning of the Vedic texts. Even in the Vedic passages which imply a universalized concept of *ātman*, its primary Vedic sense, a vital faculty, should be emphasized. The universal *ātman* of the *Ṛg Veda* refers to the life force, the spirit if you will, of the universe, which is conceived of as a living being.

It is interesting that while several of the vital faculties, namely *āyu*, *asu*, and *ātman*, have universal connotations, none of the mental faculties mentioned in the *Ṛg Veda* are applied to the universe at large. The universe lives, but apparently is not conscious, further indication than the Vedic sages did not arrive at a concept of psychological monism of Upaniṣadic ilk. The vitalistic orientation of Vedic speculations relating to the nature of the human being does, however, have an effect upon Upaniṣadic psychology. Conceptually, the *Upaniṣads*, on the whole, stress consciousness rather than vitality

---

146. B.U. 4.4.3-4; C.U. 8.12.1. Cp. S.B. 10.5.1.4.

147. *Ṛg* 10.176.3.

148. *Ṛg* 1.183.3.

149. *Ṛg* 4.41.6.

150. *Ṛg* 1.79.6; 1.139.10; 10.64.6.

151. *Ṛg* 8.94.8.

152. *Ṛg* 10.171.1.

153. *Ṛg* 1.151.6; 4.4.9; 8.6.8.

as the essence of the human being, but they are not, as is often assumed, consistent in this orientation. Many Upaniṣadic passages represent vitality as the monistic essence of the human being and the universe. Vitalistic terminology, most notably the terms *ātman* and *prāṇa*, is often retained even in Upaniṣadic passages which obviously advance a psychological theory of the nature of the human being. The *Ṛg Veda* contains scattered references to several mental faculties which also appear in Upaniṣadic psychological material, but as the following section shows, the roles and relationships of these faculties in the *Ṛg Veda* are quite different from those found in the *Upaniṣads*.

C) MENTAL ORGANS AND FACULTIES

Whereas the Buddhist and Upaniṣadic treatments of human consciousness tend to arrange the various mental faculties in ascending layers, there is no real tendency in this direction in the *Ṛg Veda*. Instead, the *Ṛg Veda* deals with different types of consciousness rather than different levels of consciousness. Psychological terminology in these ancient hymns is imprecise, and the characteristics of these various types of consciousness overlap considerably. Nevertheless, this section differentiates between mental organs on the one hand and mental faculties on the other. The mental organs considered are *manas* (mind) and *hṛd* (heart), and the mental faculties are *citta* (thought), *dhi* (mental vision) and *kratu* (mental power).

Even the distinction between organs and faculties is somewhat artificial, there being insufficient precision in the usage of the terms to justify even such a broad division. The distinction here is based on two considerations. First, *manas* and *hṛd*, much more often than the other terms mentioned, are depicted as loci or agents of mental activity. Second, an overview of the passages of psychological import in the *Ṛg Veda* leaves the impression that *manas* and *hṛd* are thought of as being innate in any given human being. The so-called faculties, on the other hand, seem to be thought of as the functioning of these two organs. These faculties are not necessarily innate, at least not in their full potency, but must be developed, stimulated, increased, etc.

In relation to this distinction between organ and faculty, it may be useful to note at this point that the *manas* is depicted as the immediate agent of each of the mental processes to be examined, with the exception of *kratu* (mental power. *Kratu* is depicted, however, as indirectly dependent upon the *manas* in a few passages.[154] Otherwise, *manas* is said to perform the processes indicated by the verbal roots √*cit*,[155] √*dhi*,[156] and its own verbal root √*man*.[157] The heart *(hṛd)*, on the other hand, is depicted only as performing the process denoted by √*man*.[158] Although the heart is the locus of *dhi* (mental vision)[159] and *kratu* (mental power),[160] the association of the verbal root √*cit* with *hṛd* is indirect and infrequent.[161] The term *hṛd*, however, is infrequent in the *Ṛg Veda*, and it is difficult to evaluate its relationship to *manas* and the faculties on the basis of the very few passages in which they are mentioned together. Nevertheless, in the Vedic context *hṛd* plays an essential role in human consciousness. This in conjunction with the fact that it is the only one of the terms examined which does not have a corresponding verbal form, dictates that if a distinction be drawn between mental organs and faculties, the *hṛd* must be labelled an organ. The following passage provides an illustration of the distinction between organs and faculties.

> The thoughtful *(vipaścitaḥ)* perceive *(paśyanti)* with heart *(hṛd)* and mind *(manas)* the bird adourned with the magic *(māyā)* of an *Asura* (a class of heavenly being).
>
> *Ṛg* 1.177.1

Here, *manas* an *hṛd* are represented as agents of the mental faculty of perception, which is represented by the root √*paś* (to see). This mental perception is, however, apparently available only to "the

---

154. *Ṛg* 6.9.5; 10.57.2.

155. *Ṛg* 8.13.20 *(mano cetati);* 10.183.1 *(manasā cekitānam).*

156. *Ṛg* 10.181.3; 10.183.2 *(manasā didhyānam).*

157. *Ṛg* 7.4.8 *(manasā mantavai).*

158. *Ṛg* 5.4.10 (hṛdā manyamana); 5.56.2 *(hṛdā manyasa).*

159. *Ṛg* 1.61.2; 10.64.2.

160. *Ṛg* 5.85.2; 10.64.2.

161. *Ṛg* 7.33.9; 10.103.12.

thoughtful" *(vipaścita)*. The term *vipaścita* is composed of the roots √*vip* (to vibrate, quiver) and √*cit* (to think); or alternatively from the prefix *vi-* and the verbal roots √*pas* and √*cit*, i.e. "insightful in thought".[162] Thus, the thought process *(citta)* is a mental faculty, and the degree to which this faculty is developed indicates the effectiveness of the organs *hṛd* and *manas*, the agents of the mental process. Here, the thought process *(citta)* is represented as being insightful or vibrant. The faculty denoted by √*cit* is highly developed, and as a result, *hṛd* and *manas* can "see". Presumably, if these faculties were not so developed, a lesser person, though having the organs *hṛd* and *manas*, could not see the magical bird.

The root √*cit* and its derivatives, as used in the *Ṛg Veda*, represent in the most general way the activity of the essential mental organs *manas* and *hṛd*, while the terms *dhī* and *kratu* represent more specific activities of these basic organs. It bears repeating, however, that a distinction between mental organs and faculties is not consistently observed or even recognized in the *Ṛg Veda*, where one finds such phrases as *dhiyā cetati* (thinks with mental vision)[163] and *cetasā cetayate* (thinks with thought),[164] as well as many more examples that tend to blur this distinction. This twofold division is proposed here solely as an attempt to differentiate broadly between terms which are otherwise difficult to separate.

The following analysis, though based on this twofold distinction, organ and faculty, begins with an overview of the most important verbal roots in ancient Indian psychology as they are used in the *Ṛg Veda*. Of these, √*cit* and √*man* are by far the most important with regard to vedic psychology. It is therefore convenient to treat first their derivatives *citta* (a faculty) and *manas* (an organ) before moving on to the less common terms *hṛd* (an organ) and *dhī* and *kratu* (faculties). In this way, the analysis moves from very general to more specific concepts.

---

162. See Monier-Williams, p. 972, col. 3 under √*vip*.
163. *Ṛg* 3.11.3.
164. *Ṛg* 9.86.42.

Verbal Roots:

The most important verbal roots denoting mental processes in the *Ṛg Veda* are √*cit*, √*man*, √*jñā*, √*vid*, and √*dhī*. Of these, √*cit* is the most general in meaning, so general in fact, that it refers simply to the functioning of any of the mental organs and faculties. The most common nouns derived from this verbal root, *citta*, *citti* and *cetas*, are for all intents and purposes synonymous, and refer very generally to "thought" or in some cases "mind". Nouns and verbs derived from the root √*cit* are so broad in meaning as to be capable of being substituted for virtually any of the more precise terms for mental organs and faculties. The verbal root √*man* and its derivatives are almost as broad in meaning as the derivatives of √*cit*. Generally speaking, they imply more specifically than √cit the process of intellectual cogitation. Other than this very vague and inconsistent distinction, the derivatives of √*cit* and √*man*, in the *Ṛg Veda*, are practically indistinguishable in meaning. Verbal forms of √*cit*, however, are more common than nominal forms, while the opposite is true of derivatives of √*man*. It is probably best therefore to translate nominal forms of √*cit* with "thought", and the term *manas* with "mind". Such translation construes *manas* as a mental organ and *citta* etc. as mental faculties, even tough admittedly there is no clear distinction between these terms in actual usage in the *Ṛg Veda*. This, at any rate, is the distinction between these terms in later Indian psychology, particularly in Buddhism, where *citta* represents consciousness in general while *manas* refers to mind as the mental sense organ.

On the other hand, the later Indian, particularly Buddhist, technical terms *vedanā* (feelings) *samjñā* (perception) and *vijñāna* (consciousness) are scarcely similar in meaning at all to their Vedic counterparts. In the *Ṛg Veda*, the roots √*jñā* and √*vid* are practically interchangeable, meaning "to know, understand, be acquainted with". They imply knowledge of or familiarity with an objective fact or circumstance rather than the process of cogitation, which is associated more with the roots √*cit* and √*man*, especially √*man*. The root √*vid*, however, is sometimes used in the sense "to find",[165] or even "to obtain",[166] where √*jñā* would be inappropriate. This may be a vague point of similarity between the usage of the root √*vid* in the *Ṛg Veda* and the later, particularly Buddhist usage of the term *vedanā*, derived from √*vid*, to denote mere hedonistic feelings without conceptualization. As used in the *Ṛg Veda*, neither √*jñā* nor √*vid* are the source of any nouns with independent psychological importance, terms like *vijñāna*, *samjñā* or *vedanā*. The term *vedanā* in the *Ṛg Veda* normally means "possessions, wealth", i.e. that which one has found or obtained.[167] Normally, the prefix *vi-* plus the root √*jñā* conveys no different meaning, or at most a slightly more intensive meaning, than the root √*jñā* by itself.[168] In some cases, the word thus formed seems to imply discrimination or discernment[169] as opposed to knowledge, which makes this compound vaguely similar to the Buddhist and Upaniṣadic use of *vijñāna* as a technical term denoting consciousness. In the *Ṛg Veda*, *sam-* plus √*jñā* in most cases seems to mean "one-minded, accordant, in agreement".[170] In the early Buddhist *sūtras*, the term *samjñā* refers to the mental faculty of perception, the faculty which constructs meaningful experience out of what has been felt hedonistically and non-conceptually by the faculty of *vedanā*. In the *Upaniṣads*, the term *samjñā* is infrequent, but usually appears to be associated with the functioning of *manas*, and as a psychological term appears to be more or less similar in meaning to its Buddhist counterpart. Of these verbal roots, only the derivatives of √*cit*, √*man* and √*dhī* will be examined in the present chapter, since the others, though important in later Indian psychology, are of little psychological import in the *Ṛg Veda*.

---

165. *Ṛg* 1.67.2; 5.46.1; 10.53.3; 10.107.4; 10.161.4.

166. *Ṛg* 1.143.4; 5.67.3.

167. *Ṛg* 1.33.15; 1.176.4; 4.30.13; 7.32.7; 10.34.4.

168. *Ṛg* 1.164.5, 16, 36; 5.49.2; 10.2.2; 10.77.1; 10.107.2 & 7.

169. *Ṛg* 1.69.2; 3.39.7; 7.104.12.

170. *Ṛg* 1.72.5; 7.76.5; 7.104.12; 10.30.6; 10.191.2.

Citta:

The verbal root √*cit*,[171] being the psychological term applicable to the broadest range of contexts, is a good point of departure in an inquiry into the Vedic concept of human consciousness. The derivatives of √*cit* in the *Ṛg Veda*, like the term *citta* in Buddhism, refer in the broadest way possible to mental processes whether perceptive, intellectual, emotional or imaginative. It is, then, the most general of the mental faculties.

The association of derivatives of √*cit* with vision is in some cases quite literal, as when Agni is said to be observant *(cetiṣṭham)* with the eyes *(akṣabhir)*,[172] or in a wartime curse in which the wish is expressed that the perception *(citta)* of those foes who stand watch be destroyed.[173] In other contexts, the term *citta* seems to mean simply "visible", as in the phrase *citta-garbha*, which Griffith translates "visibly pregnant".[174] In still other cases, derivatives of √*cit* refer to mental perception, as when it is said that Mitra and Varuṇa perceive *(cikyatuḥ)* even with their eyes closed,[175] or where it is said with relation to a riddle that those who have eyes, obviously mental eyes, can see while the blind do not perceive *(na vicetad andhaḥ)*,[176] or again where it is asked, "who discerns *(ciketa)* the workings of Mitra and Varuṇa?"[177] Relevant also to the use of derivatives of √*cit* used to denote vision, particularly mental vision, is the association in several

---

171. There is no point in distinguishing between derivatives of √*cit* and those of the related verbal root √*ci*, which are often indistinguishable, and have the same meanings with reference to consciousness. See Gonda, *Vision*, pp. 56-57; 99-100.

172. *Ṛg* 10.21.7. Gonda suggests, as the general meaning of the root √*cit:* "perceiving, being attentive, distinguishing, observing, taking notice of." See *Vision*, p. 99, and note 174 below.

173. *Ṛg* 10.128.6.

174. See *Vision*, pp. 99-100, where Gonda suggests "appearing, becoming conspicuous" as an additional meaning of √*cit*, citing as examples: *Ṛg* 1.113.4; 7.67.2; 7.78.4; 1.92.12; 8.56.5; 6.12.3; 10.3.4; 5.59.3; 10.91.5.

175. *Ṛg* 8.25.9.

176. *Ṛg* 1.164.16.

177. *Ṛg* 1.152.3. See also *Ṛg* 10.177.1.

passages of √*cit* with √*dhī*,[178] which term, as shown below, denotes visualization in the *Ṛg Veda*.

Related to both the intellectual and the emotional functions of √*cit* is the property of motion which is often associated with this root. Thus, when it is said that thought *(citta)* is as swift as wind,[179] its intellectual or perceptive properties are probably intended. In other contexts, derivatives based on √*cit* are said to be moved by an external force, as when the sacrifice stirs the thought *(cetana)*.[180] These derivatives are also said to be the moving force which incites various gods to action, as when Soma[181] and Agni[182] are said to be moved or stirred into action by the thought of the sacrificer. In these contexts, the implication of motion seems to be emotional more than intellectual.

The intellectual connotation of derivatives of √*cit* is predominant in the majority of the instances of their occurrence, but it is rarely entirely separable from the implication of perception which in most cases is also conveyed. The intellectual connotation is obviously predominant in the phrase "to solve *(āciketam)* a riddle",[183] or when it is said that the citta may be deluded *(pratilobhayati)*,[184] or that Soma grasps all things with thought *(cetasā)*.[185] But where it is said that Vak, the goddess of speech, spoke words that are incomprehensible *(avicetanāni)*,[186] it is not so easy to separate the intellectual connotation from the perceptual. The compound could conceivably imply "unmanifest or imperceptible" words. This is again the case in a passage stating that what the Dawn knows *(yac-ciketa)*

---

178. *Ṛg* 1.67.5; 1.68.3; 1.159.1; 1.164.36; 3.11.2; 8.34.19; 10.183.2.
179. *Ṛg* 1.163.11.
180. *Ṛg* 8.13.18; 8.92.21.
181. *Ṛg* 9.16.4.
182. *Ṛg* 8.44.19.
183. *Ṛg* 10.28.5.
184. *Ṛg* 10.103.12.
185. *Ṛg* 9.20.3.
186. *Ṛg* 8.100.10.

is true *(satya)* not false *(mogha)*,[187] which could just as easily mean, "what she perceives is accurate, not mistaken".

The intellectual connotation of these derivatives is again evident, though not exclusive, in several compounds which denote some sort of development or excellence of the faculty of thought or perception, as in the term *vipaścita*[188] meaning "wise or insightful", or *sucetas* (thoughtful),[189] *gambīira-cetas* (deep thoughted),[190] *praceta* (wise).[191] These terms are matched by terms indicating deficiency in the faculty of thought or perception, terms such as *apracetas* (foolish, ignorant),[192] *dabhracetas* (weak-minded),[193] or *acit* (foolish, thoughtless, a fool).[194]

The emotional connotation of derivatives of √*cit* is most evident in passages of the type already pointed out above where the thought is said to be moved or stirred by worship and sacrifice. There is also note emotional content in passages such as the one where Atri is said to "think with a friendly mind" *(ciketati ... sumnena cetasā)*,[195] or in another beautiful hymn to Dawn:

> Youthful and unrestrained she cometh forward; she hath turned thoughts *(acikitat)* to sun and fire and worship.
>
> *Ṛg* 7.80.2 (G)

There may be further indication of an emotional connotation of these derivatives in passages in which they are associated with the heart

187. *Ṛg* 10.55.6.

188. *Ṛg* 1.164.36; 8.43.19; 10.177.1.

189. *Ṛg* 1.61.10; 4.36.2; 7.60.6.

190. *Ṛg* 8.8.2.

191. *Ṛg* 8.100.16.

192. *Ṛg* 9.98.11.

193. *Ṛg* 8.101.16.

194. *Ṛg* 7.86.7; 7.104.1. See *Ṛg* 4.54.3; 7.86.6; 7.89.5 for the related terms *acitta* and *acitti*.

195. *Ṛg* 5.73.6.

(hṛd),[196] though the heart, like the *manas*, is depicted as an organ of thought and perception as well as emotion.

Far more frequent than the association of terms derived from √*cit* with the *hṛd* (heart), is the association of these terms with the *manas* (mind). The *manas* is often depicted as the agent of the process of thought as represented by derivatives of √*cit*, as in the phrases *manasā cekitānam*, "thinking or perceiving with the mind",[197] or *mano cetati*, "the mind thinks".[198] In other contexts, a derivative of √*cit* may qualify the mind in an adjectival sense, as in the phrase *cikitvin-manas*, "thoughtful or perceptive mind".[199] In still other contexts, derivatives of √*cit* are apparently indicative of a faculty or process which is independent of the *manas* but parallel to it, as in the phrase "accordant *(sam jānate)* in mind *(manasā)* and thought *(cikitre)*".[200] In a similar context the assembled worshipers are said to be joined in mind *(samānam manas)* and thought *(saha citta)*.[201] In yet another context, the *manas* and "excellent thought" *(sucetas)* are said to be the source of the creation of a miraculous chariot by the Ṛbhus.[202]

Derivatives of √*cit* in many cases carry also the connotation of morality, which in these passages is depicted as following upon a correct perception or understanding of the universal order, the *ṛta* or *dharma*. Thus, it is said that through thoughtlessness or lack of perception, through negligence *(acitti)* one breaks the law *(dharma)* of Varuṇa.[203] This same negligence *(acitti)*, it is said, causes sin[204] and leads one astray with wine, dice and anger.[205] This same gambling drunkard, the victim of *acitti*, is labeled a fool *(acit)*, which term thus

196. *Ṛg* 7.33.9; 10.83.5; 10.103.12; 10.177.1; 10.191.3-4.
197. *Ṛg* 10.183.1.
198. *Ṛg* 8.13.20.
199. *Ṛg* 5.22.3; 8.95.5.
200. *Ṛg* 10.30.6.
201. *Ṛg* 10.101.3.
202. *Ṛg* 4.36.2.
203. *Ṛg* 4.36.2.
204. *Ṛg* 7.89.5.
205. *Ṛg* 7.86.6.

carries the connotation of lack of moral as well as intellectual development, and it is through the agency of Varuṇa, the ethical god, that this fool may be made wise *(acetayat)*, i.e. awakened to or made to perceive the ethical law of the universe.[206] This moral connotation must also be understood in a passage calling for the annihilation of fools *(acit)*,[207] who presumably are roughly equivalent to the evil-minded *(huras-cit)*.[208] It is because of *citti* (intelligence) that Indra is said to drive away the sinner.[209] Agni, it is said, distinguishes between sense and folly, and apparently rewards the sensible.

> May he who knows *(vidvān)* distinguish *(vicinavat)* sense *(citti)* and folly *(acitti)*, like straight and crooked backs of horses. Lead us, O god, to wealth and noble offspring; keep penury afar and grant us plenty.
>
> *Ṛg* 4.2.11 (G)

Thus derivatives of √*cit* connote both perception of fact and intellectual ability. The effectiveness of this faculty is judged with reference to objective truth and good, which are functions of the underlying moral law of the universe, as when Agni is said to be truthful *(satya)* because he is a knower of law *(ṛta-cit)*.[210] The moral desirability of knowledge or perception of this universal law is, it would seem, paralleled by an attendant practical advantage.

> Indra, bestow on us the best of treasures, the spirit *(citti)* of ability and fortune; increase of riches, safety of our bodies, charm of sweet speech, and days of pleasant weather.
>
> *Ṛg* 2.21.6 (G)

---

206. *Ṛg* 7.86.7.

207. *Ṛg* 7.104.1.

208. *Ṛg* 1.42.3; 9.89.11.

209. *Ṛg* 8.79.4 in Griffith's enumeration.

210. *Ṛg* 1.145.5.

In another passage, this perception or knowledge is said to accompany fame and splendor as gifts to mortals from Agni,[211] and elsewhere it is suggested that if this *citta* is deluded *(pratilobhayanti)* it will lead to one's downfall.[212]

Thus, in the wide range of applications of the verbal root √*cit*, there emerges from the obscure hymns of the *Ṛg Veda*, an ethical concept of the highest order. Namely: knowledge and perception of the order of the universe necessarily leads to moral behavior, which brings in its wake the blessings of the gods in this very life. This knowledge or perceptiveness is the greatest treasure, and all other treasures follow upon it automatically.

Before moving on to an examination of the more specific mental organs and faculties, one more aspect of the general term √*cit* bears mentioning, the creative aspect. This creativity is not confined to artistic composition, as when it is said that the hymn springs from the thoughtful mind *(cikitvin-manas)*.[213] It may also refer to the idea of spontaneous creation of an entity, as in a hymn stating that the gods created fire with *citti*,[214] or as noted above where the Ṛbhus are said to have created a miraculous chariot by means of "excellent thought" *(sucetas)* and mind *(manas)*.[215]

The association of *dhī* with √*cit* and the general association of mental "vision" with the intellect, which has already been noted above, is probably the most important key to understanding this creative aspect of thought as represented by the general term √*cit*. As will become clearer in the examination of *dhī* in a following section, creation of a mental image of an object was considered tantamount to the creation of the object itself for ritual purposes of offerings to the gods. Since commerce with the gods was thought to be a give and take affair, the gods were thought to return gifts to humans by means of the creative power of their mental vision. The following point will

---

211. *Ṛg* 5.7.9.

212. *Ṛg* 10.103.12.

213. *Ṛg* 8.95.5.

214. *Ṛg* 3.2.3.

215. *Ṛg* 4.36.2.

also be examined in greater detail below, but at present, for the sake of complete coverage of the term √*cit*, the association of √*cit* with the term *kratu*, "will or mental power", should be noted. *Kratu* is sometimes represented as the faculty which performs the process of thought, as in the phrase, "think with the mental power" *(kratvā cetati)*.[216] Sometimes derivatives of √*cit* may qualify the term *kratu* as in the phrase "wise *(cetistha)* with mental power *(kratu)*".[217] As will be seen below, *kratu* also plays an important role in the creative aspect of mind, in that it is conceived of as the motive force which actualizes the creation of objects visualized in the creative imagination.

By way of summary; the derivatives of the verbal root √*cit* occur in relation to all of the mental organs and faculties which will be considered in the remainder of this chapter. They cover such a wide range of meanings and connotations that it may be said that these derivatives denote the functioning of any one of the several mental organs and faculties mentioned in the *Ṛg Veda*. Used with the term *manas*, √*cit* indicates mental perception or intellectual thought. With *hṛd* (heart) it refers to emotional or intuitive thought. With √*dhī* it refers to imaginative, visionary thought. With *kratu* it refers to volitional thought. It is this broad, general nature of √*cit* and its derivatives that constitutes the most distinctive characteristic of this family of terms. Similarly it is this applicability to all mental processes that sets the important term *citta* apart from other terms designating the mind in later Indian thought, particularly in Buddhist psychology.

Manas:

The term *manas*, like *citta*, derives from a verbal root, the root √*man*. As nouns, the words *manas* and *citta* are practically synonymous in the *Ṛg Veda*. The verbal forms of √*man*, however, carry a decidedly more intellectual connotation than derivatives of √*cit* or even the term *manas* itself. Though not adequate in all cases,

---

216. *Ṛg* 1.128.4.

217. *Ṛg* 1.65.5. See also *Ṛg* 6.5.3; 7.3.10.

the English "to consider" is an attractive translation for verbal forms of √*man* because it corresponds to the two most prominent verbal meanings of this root. These are: (1) to ponder or cogitate upon, as in the phrase to consider a plan",[218] and (2) to evaluate, judge, deem, as in the phrase "to consider wealth sufficient".[219] In some cases, however, the visual, imaginative implication is also present in this verb, as with the root √*cit*.[220] To draw too sharp a distinction between these two roots would lead to misunderstandings. Two common nominal derivatives of √*man*, namely *mati* and *maniṣa*, seem to denote primarily inspired, visual thought in the *Ṛg Veda*, and are used in contexts very similar to the term *dhī* (mental vision).[221] These terms will therefore be considered below in the discussion of *dhī*.

As a noun, the *manas* (mind), more than any other term in the *Ṛg Veda*, is represented as being the locus or agent of mental activity. On this basis, it will be dealt with here, along with the heart *(hṛd)*, as a mental organ as opposed to *citta* and its etymological relatives, which have been labeled as a mental faculty, along with *dhī* and *kratu*. The function of *manas* itself, when it is not represented merely as the agent of one of the mental faculties, is distinguished from the general term *citta* and relatives by being less specifically associated with intellect and imagination. *Manas* is associated more with the emotions and particularly the essential character of the person. Unlike the verbal forms of √*man*, *manas* seldom refers to abstract intellectual thought, which it may be noted, is represented mainly by the verbal roots √*man*, √*jñā*, and √*vid* without being associated with any specific mental organ or faculty. Like the intellectual connotations, the moral connotations of *manas* are also less pronounced than those of the derivatives of √*cit*, but again, not altogether absent. On the other hand, the creative function of *manas* is more pronounced than that of the derivatives of √*cit*, and it is apparently for this reason that *manas* is extremely important in sacrifice.

---

218. *Ṛg* 10.12.8. See also *Ṛg* 1.159.2 & 5; 5.48.1; 5.50.5; 10.12.6.

219. *Ṛg* 10.34.13. See also *Ṛg* 5.39.2; 6.30.2.

220. *Ṛg* 5.6.1; 5.35.8.

221. See Gonda, *Vision*, pp. 13, 47, 51ff, 57, 70, 109.

As one might expect, having noted the emotional orientation of *manas* clearly expressed in the "Nāsadīya" hymn — where it is said that desire *(kama)* is the original seed of *manas*[222] — the most common function of *manas* in the *Ṛg Veda* is its function as the locus of a wide range of emotions. These may be grouped into the following general categories: desire,[223] fear and disturbance, anxiety,[224] love, devotion, adoration,[225] anger, rage, hatred,[226] joy and pleasure,[227] generosity and kindness.[228] In several of these passages, the heart *(hṛd)* is represented as a co-experiencer, along with *manas*, of these emotions.[229]

No doubt related to its function as the primary locus of emotions is the frequent portrayal of the manas as the repository of the individual's personality and character traits. A frequent epithet indicating character is the term "hero-minded" *(nṛmanas)*.[230] Several passages contain phrases in which the manas is depicted as the seat of various types of good and bad character,[231] and it is in this sense too that the moral facet of manas finds expression, mostly in the phrase *satya-manas* (truthful mind).[232] Some are even said to have a god-like mind *(deva-manas)*.[233] It is probably also in this connection that one should understand the function noted above of manas as a semi-vital faculty, implored not to desert the dying man so that his

222. *Ṛg* 10.129.4.

223. *Ṛg* 1.164.27; 2.32.2; 3.31.9; 4.1.15; 6.46.10; 10.129.4; 10.147.2.

224. *Ṛg* 1.121.6; 5.36.3; 9.77.2; 10.11.2.

225. *Ṛg* 1.61.2; 1.77.2; 1.93.8; 1.182.5; 2.3.3; 3.14.5; 4.24.6; 6.40.3; 7.100.1; 10.10.3, 13, 14; 10.145.6.

226. *Ṛg* 4.27.3; 7.20.6; 7.67.7; 10.95.1; 10.103.10.

227. *Ṛg* 1.31.13; 1.36.2; 1.55.7; 1.157.6; 3.1.21; 3.35.8; 3.54.22; 4.10.3; 5.39.3; 6.63.1; 10.51.5; 10.53.12; 10.70.4; 10.85.44; 10.117.2.

228. *Ṛg* 1.73.10; 4.37.2; 6.21.4; 6.63.4; 6.75.8; 7.33.14; 7.98.2; 8.48.7; 8.71.3; 8.82.3; 10.20.1; 10.25.1; 10.50.7; 10.116.2.

229. *Ṛg* 1.61.2; 1.73.10; 4.37.2; 8.71.3; 8.82.3.

230. *Ṛg* 1.51.5 & 10; 1.167.5; 10.45.1 & 3.

231. *Ṛg* 1.52.12; 1.63.4; 1.54.3; 2.23.12; 3.38.2; 4.22.6; 5.44.7; 7.104.8; 10.103.9.

232. *Ṛg* 1.73.2; 7.90.5; 10.67.8.

233. *Ṛg* 1.91.23; 1.164.18.

life might continue.[234] *Manas*, then, is an even more essential element of the human being than the term "mental organ" might suggest. It is portrayed as the basis of one's emotional life, and therefore one's character and temperament. A further extension of this tendency to see *manas* as a deep-seated source of one's most intimate feelings, probably accounts for the use of the term to denote the basis of life itself. It should be remembered, however, that the apparent use of *manas* as a vital faculty is confined to a late series of four consecutive hymns in the tenth book.[235]

Again, more than any other mental organ or faculty, *manas* is represented as being creative, a function which it retains throughout the history of Indian thought. In the famous "Nāsadīya Sūkta", a hymn to creation examined above, it is implied that the *manas* of the original universal principle was the motive force behind creation out of chaos. In another passage, the Ṛbhus, mortals who, by virtue of their supreme artistry, were granted the status of gods, are said to have performed the miraculous deed of extracting a cow (apparently living) from out of its hide by means of *manas*.[236] More to the point is a verse stating obliquely that wherever the power of Agni's mind is applied, fire will be produced.

> Wherever your mind *(manas)* applies (its) supreme power, there you make a seat (for yourself)
>
> *Ṛg* 6.16.17

The creative power of the *manas* is most clearly revealed in the term *manas-maya*, "mind-made". In the form *manomaya*, this phrase is of great psychological importance in the *Upaniṣads*, where it is the name of one of the subtle layers of the soul.[237] The term is also used to describe the universal principles *ātman*[238] and *brahman*,[239] as well

234. *Ṛg* 10.57.3-6; 10.58.1-10; 10.59.5; 10.60.7-9.

235. See note 234, above.

236. *Ṛg* 3.60.2.

237. T.U. 2.3-5; 2.8.

238. B.U. 1.3.5; 4.4.5.

as the individual soul *(puruṣa)*,[240] Oddly, the Vedic sense of the phrase — i.e. "made by mind" rather than "made of mind" as in these Upaniṣadic passages — is more faithfully retained in Buddhist literature. There, the *mano-maya-kāya*[241] is a miraculous body made and projected by the mind of one who has developed super-normal psychic powers. In the Vedic context, chariots are especially often mentioned as being created by *manas*.

> Clean, as thou wentest, were thy wheels; wind was the axle fastened there. Surya (the sun), proceeding to her lord, mounted a spirit-fashioned *(manasmaya)* car ..
>
> *Ṛg* 10.85.12 (G)

These "mind-made chariots" not only denote the vehicles of gods, as in the above passage,[242] but also indicate the vehicles by which sacrificial offerings are conveyed to the gods,[243] and the vehicles which convey the deceased to the next world.[244] So common is this association between *manas* and chariot, that in later literature the term *mano-ratha* (mind-chariot) came to denote any wish, fantasy or illusion.

As suggested by the predominantly sacrificial roles of the "mind-made chariots" of the *Ṛg Veda*, the creative power of *manas* is particularly important in the context of the sacrifice. Messages, goods and services were thought to be exchanged between gods and humans via the medium of imaginative visualization. In addition to chariots, hymns and prayers are sometimes said to be made by the mind,[245] or

---

239. C.U. 3.14.2; 4.4.5.

240. B.U. 5.6.1; T.U. 1.6.1.

241. D1: 17, 34, 77, 186; M1: 410; S4: 71; A1: 24; A3: 122, 192; A4: 235; A5: 60. See Buddhaghosa's definition of *manomaya* at Vsm. 405.

242. See also *Ṛg* 3.31.5; 4.36.2.

243. *Ṛg* 1.94.1; 7.64.4; 10.114.6.

244. *Ṛg* 10.135.3.

245. *Ṛg* 1.94.1.

sometimes by the mind and heart *(hṛd)* together,[246] and *manas* is often said to be the agent which performs the sacrifice.[247] In fact, the term *mantra*, which means, in the Vedic context, a hymn or incantation, is derived from the verbal root √*man*.

Gaining the aid and blessings of the gods was not, then, thought of as the result of merely performing mechanically the proper ritual. It involved also visualization of the sacrificial offering and of the prayers themselves, a point which will become clearer in the examination of the term √*dhī* below. This visualization or "mentalization" of the sacrifice and prayers apparently was thought of as making earthly products and language accessible and acceptable to the gods. The *manas*, then, in the sacrificial context, is represented as being something like a television transmitter which transforms the scene in the studio into a subtle form which may be sent to a distant place and received there. Lacking electronic communication with which to compare this process, the Vedic Aryans conceived of it as a sort of mental pony express operating between gods and humans, thus the association between *manas* and the chariot.

Also related to the vehicular connections of the creative power of *manas* in the sacrificial context, is the frequent association of *manas* with the verbal root √*yuj*, "to yoke". This connection which is doubtlessly relevant to the origins of the use of the term *yoga* to denote a spiritual discipline. In this context, it would appear that *manas* is thought of as being the motive force behind the sacrificial communication between heaven and earth, or at least as some sort of essential link in this communication. The precise meaning of the common term *mano-yuja* is not clear, but several examples of its occurrence will make the general intent obvious.

> O Indra, caster of the stone, thou helpest him who praises thee. From sacrifice I send thee a mind-yoked hymn *(dhiyaṁ manoyuja)*
>
> *Ṛg* 8.13.26 (G)

---

246. *Ṛg* 1.61.2; 1.171.2.

247. *Ṛg* 1.76.1; 1.157.6; 10.5.3; 10.20.2; 10.47.4; 10.63.7.

It would seem here that *dhī*, literally a vision rather than a hymn — a hymn transformed into a vision — is yoked to *manas* as a cart to a horse, *manas* being the motive force. This would seem to be the most obvious intent of another passage which states that the priests "yoke the mind and yoke the visions" *(yuñjate mana uta yuñjate dhiyo)*,[248] i.e. that the two are yoked together so that the motive power of the mind may carry the visualization of the hymn to heaven. In other cases, however, the horses of gods, which obviously represent the motive force of their transportation, are said to be *manoyuja*,[249] which would in this case seem to mean "yoked by mind" rather than "yoked to mind" as in the previous passages. Be that as it may, the process of communication implied by this "mind-yoking" is said to operate in both directions, from humans to gods and from gods to humans.

> Let the swift steeds who carry thee, thought-yoked *(manoyuja)* and dropping holy oil, bring the gods to the *soma* draught.
>
> *Ṛg* 1.14.6 (G)

In a similar verse, the same term is used with reference to the horses of the Aśvins which bring them to the sacrifice so that they may drink.[250] In other verses, the yoking is specifically said to be done "by the mind", which appears in the instrumental case *(manasā)*, rather than "to the mind".[251] Thus, the overall intent of the compound *manoyuja* is probably "made mobile or functional by the mind". This is almost certainly the meaning of a verse in which Soma is asked to release or pour forth the vision *(dhī)* that is mind-yoked, as thunder releases and causes to pour fourth the rain.[252]

---

248. *Ṛg* 5.81.1.
249. *Ṛg* 1.14.6; 5.75.5.
250. *Ṛg* 5.75.6.
251. *Ṛg* 2.40.3; 7.69.2;
252. *Ṛg* 9.100.3. See Gonda, *Vision*, p. 75.

The role of *manas* in the sacrificial process is not limited, however, to transportation of the vision *(dhī)*. In several passages, *manas* is represented as the mental organ responsible for the mystical vision of the seer. In addition to its function as the mobilizer of visions, in various passages manas is represented as the agent of verbal forms of the verbal root √*dhī*,[253] the locus of visions denoted by nominal forms of √dhi,[254] and the organ through the development of which one may become "visionary" *(dhīra)*.[255]

Aside from creativity, *manas* is represented as being generally capable of causing results, as when the priests are said to have driven forth the dawn with *manas*.[256] This effective power is sometimes more akin to persuasion, as when the gods are said to be provoked into action by *manas*,[257] or when it is said that their hearts *(hṛd)* are touched by hymns spoken by the mind *(manasā vacya)*.[258] That persuasion is not the full extent of the mind's power is obvious in a passage stating that curses from the manas pierce the hearts *(hṛd)* of demons.[259]

It is this powerful aspect of *manas* which, no doubt, accounts for its frequent association with *kratu*, "mental power",[260] *Kratu*, more specifically than *manas*, represents will or volition. In some passages, the *manas* itself is depicted as a willful faculty, as when it is said that the reigns of a chariot declare the *manas*, i.e. the will or intent, of the driver.[261] In other passages, *manas* is mentioned in conjunction with

253. *Ṛg* 7.90.5; 10.181.3; 10.183.2; 4.33.9.

254. *Ṛg* 1.61.2; 1.164.36; 7.64.4; 8.102.22.

255. *Ṛg* 1.64.1; 10.71.2; 10.82.1.

256. *Ṛg* 3.31.5.

257. *Ṛg* 10.37.12.

258. *Ṛg* 10.47.7.

259. *Ṛg* 10.87.13.

260. In addition to the passages cited below, see *Ṛg* 7.90.5; 10.25.1.

261. *Ṛg* 6.75.6-7. See also *Ṛg* 6.16.43 and 10.27.5, where *manas* and the verbal form *manasye* seem to indicate volition. Cp. K.U. 1.3.3.

kratu as being productive of some desirable result such as wealth,[262] or protection.[263]

The functions of *manas* and *kratu* are distinguished in an unfortunately sexist passage stating that since the *manas* of a woman is without discipline, the feminine *kratu* is of little weight, i.e. incapable of bringing about results. Sexism aside, the association of mental discipline, i.e. concentration, with mental power is a marked feature of Buddhism, and indeed all Indian systems involving yogic techniques of mental training, it being on the basis of mental concentration that the various psychic powers are said to evolve.

As noted above, the visual connotations of the term *manas* are less pronounced than those of the derivatives of √*cit*. There is nonetheless a distinct and important visual aspect of the *manas*. It has been noted above that those who are endowed with thoughtfulness, who have become *vipaścita*, see *(paśyanti)* the sun-bird with the *manas* and the heart *(hṛd)*.[264] Another passage which apparently refers to the sun depicted as a bird, also names *manas* as the agent of the process of supra-normal seeing denoted by the verbal root √paś.[265]

> One of these birds hath passed into the sea of air; thence he looks round and views this universal world. With simple heart *(manas)* I have beheld him from anear; his mother kisses him and he returns her kisses.
>
> *Ṛg* 10.114.4 (G)

In these verses, the metaphorical representation of the sun as a bird apparently indicates that some mystical aspect of the sun as seen rather than the star itself. That the sight of the mind is a supra-normal vision is abundantly clear in the following passage, in which one may also note the distinction between the verb √*man* and the mental organ

262. *Ṛg* 10.31.2.
263. *Ṛg* 1.73.2.
264. *Ṛg* 10.177.1.
265. *Ṛg* 10.114.4.

manas, which is less associated with intellectual thought than its verbal root.

> So by this knowledge men were raised to *ṛsis*, when ancient sacrifice sprang up, our fathers. With the mind's eye *(manasā cakṣasā)* I think *(manye)* that I behold *(paśyan)* them who first performed this sacrificial worship.
>
> *Ṛg* 10.130.6 (G)

Another passage makes even clearer the distinction between the sight of the eye *(cakṣu)* and the sight of the mind, representing the two forms of vision with different verbs and assigning to them different objects, or rather different aspects of the same object, a horse.

> 6. From afar I recognized *(ajānām)* your spirit *(ātman)* with (my) mind *(manasā)*, a bird flying below heaven. ...
> 7. Here, I saw *(apaśyām)* your supreme form *(rūpa)*. ...
>
> *Ṛg* 1.163.6-7

The spirit *(ātman)*, the essential nature of the horse, is known *(√jñā)* by the *manas* even at a distance, i.e. when the horse is not physically present, while the literally visible form *(rūpa)* is seen *(√paś)* only when the horse is present in the range of vision.

Another interesting passage relevant to this visual aspect of *manas* is a verse depicting a nightmare as the "master of the mind" *(manasas pati)*,[266] which would seem to indicate that *manas* is thought of as the mental organ which perceives dreams. In the light of the foregoing, it is probable that Griffith's translation of *Ṛg* 3.38.6 is wrong,[267] and that the intended meaning of the second half of the verse is another instance of the *manas* as an organ of supra-normal perception.

---

266. *Ṛg* 10.164.1.

267. *apaśyam-atra manasā jaganvānvrate gandharvān api vayu-keśān.* "There saw I, going thither in the spirit Gandharvas in this course with wind-blown tresses." (G)

> Here, in the (fulfillment of my) vow *(vrate)*, with (my) mind *(manas)* I saw the wind-haired Gandharvas in motion.
>
> *Ṛg* 3.38.6

Clearly, the common term *manojave*, "mind-swift",[268] implies an intellectual quickness of mind. Nonetheless the primary sense of the qualities of motion and swiftness as applied to the *manas* should probably be thought of as indicative of imaginative quickness in conjuring up mental perceptions or vision. It appears that the Vedic sages thought of the mind as functioning primarily by means of perceptions rather than intellectual concepts. They did, however, distinguish between sensual perceptions and mental perceptions, as in the following passage.

> Unequal in the quickness of their spirit *(manojavesu)* are friends endowed alike with eyes and hearing
>
> *Ṛg* 10.71.7 (G)

Though here *manojava* represents a quality of the mind, in most instances, the term is an adjective meaning "as swift as mind", mind being, it is said, "the swiftest of flying things".[269]

> 5. A firm light hath been set for men to look on; among all things that fly the mind *(manas)* is swiftest. ...
>
> 6. Mine ears unclose to hear, mine eye to see him (Agni); the light that harbours in my spirit *(hṛd)* broadens. Far roams my mind *(vi me manaś-carati)* whose thoughts *(ādhī)* are in the distance. What shall I speak,what shall I now imagine *(maniṣye)?*
>
> *Ṛg* 6.9.5-6 (G)

---

268. *Ṛg* 1.23.2; 1.71.9; 1.163.9; 1.181.2 & 3; 1.183.1; 1.186.5; 5.77.3; 6.22.6; 6.62.3; 6.63.7; 7.68.3; 10.39.12; 10.61.3; 10.81.7; 10.112.2.

269. *Ṛg* 6.9.5.

The swiftness of the mind is no doubt related to the role of *manas* in the Vedic sacrifice as the mobilizer of the visualizations *(dhī)* which are to be transported to heaven. Thus, the Aśvins are said to carry the visualizations *(dhī)* of the sacrificer with horses that are as swift as mind *(manojava)*.[270] The swiftness and mobility of the mind, so movingly expressed in the previous passage, immediately call to mind the Buddhist characterization of the mind as a fantastically swift phenomenon. In the Buddhist context, however, the mobility of the mind is an undesirable quality which the sage must subdue, as the following passage indicates

> 35. The mind *(citta)* is hard to check, swift, flits wherever it listeth; to control it is good. A controlled mind is conducive to happiness.
>
> 36. The mind is very hard to perceive, extremely subtle, flits wherever it listeth. Let the wise person guard it; a guarded mind is conducive to happiness.
>
> 37. Faring far, wandering alone, bodiless, lying in a cave, is the mind. Those who subdue it are freed from the bond of Māra.[271]
>
> Dhp. #35-37

This swiftness of mind, in the Vedic and to some extent the Buddhist contexts, indicates a different concept than what probably comes to the mind of a modern reader confronted with this term. It does not represent quickness in coming to intellectual conclusions, but rather imaginative quickness in perceiving mental images. This is not to say, of course, that the process of thought itself was different in Vedic times than today, but merely that in Vedic times the thought process seems to have been conceived of in different terms, primarily visual and emotional terms.

After having gone through all of these various connotations, implications and associations of the term *manas*, none will fail to agree that the *Ṛg Veda* portrays the mind as a fantastically complex

---

270. *Ṛg* 6.62.3.

271. Translation by Nārada Mahā Thera, *The Dhammapada*, Maha Bodhi Society, Calcutta, 1970.

phenomenon. The following charm designed to ward off bad dreams is emphatic in this regard.

> 1. Avaunt, thou master of the mind *(manasas-pate)*! Depart, and vanish far away. Look on destruction far from hence. The live man's mind *(manas)* is manifold.
>
> 2. A happy boon do men elect, a mighty boon they obtain. Bliss with Vaivasvata they see. The live man's mind seeks many a place.
>
> *Ṛg* 10.164.1-2 (G)

The last three verses of the *Ṛg Veda* provide a good review of the terms considered so far. These verses provide one of the largest groupings of psychological terms in the entire work. They also offer some further insight into the Vedic concept of the nature of the human consciousness and its relation to sacrificial ritual, as well as an entrance into the examination of *hṛd* (heart) which will be the next mental organ to be considered.

> 2. Come together, speak together, let your minds *(manāṁsi)* accord together *(saṁ ... jānatām)*, as the ancient gods (who) sit down accordant *(samjānānā)* to their share.
>
> 3. The hymn *(mantra)* is common, common the assembly, common the mind *(manas)*, united the thought *(citta)* of these. I sing *(mantraye)* your common hymn *(mantra)*, with your common oblation I sacrifice.
>
> 4. Common your resolve, common your hearts *(hṛd)*, common be your mind *(manas)*, as (when) you are happily together.
>
> *Ṛg* 10.191.2-4

With reference to the theme of mental discipline as being conducive to mental power, noted in the sexist passage above, the present passage extends the concept of concentration and makes it a communal desideratum in order to maximize the power of the sacrifice. Not only is the individual expected to discipline thought and funnel mental energy into the sacrificial ritual, but apparently, the success of the sacrifice depends also upon the simultaneous, collective, coordinated mental concentration of all present. This collective coordination is represented primarily as the establishment of a common *manas*. This explains to some extent the use of derivatives of √*man* to denote the hymn and the singing of the hymn, which are respectively the (mentally) visual and the audible representations of the single-mindedness of all present at the sacrifice. Conversely, the singing of the hymn and its visualization by all present would serve to evoke the single-mindedness necessary to render the power of the ritual sufficient to move the gods to action on behalf of the sacrificers. On the one hand, the hymn is created by the power of *manas;* on the other hand it serves to channel the power of *manas* into an effective ritual visualization.

The singing of the hymn, also denoted by a derivative of √*man*, obviously denotes more than a mere verbalization of a ritual formula. It indicates as well as concentrated mental recitation, which seems to involve primarily the visualization of the contents of the hymn and the accompanying sacrifice. In this whole process, *manas* obviously plays the key role. In the last verse of the above hymn, the last verse of the *Ṛg Veda* in fact, the heart *(hṛd)* is represented as being a partner of the *manas* in this process, and the Vedic sages sign off from the early years of the first millennium B.C. with the timeless injunction that people should harmonize their hearts and minds. The next task in this study of the Vedic concept of human consciousness is an examination of the term *hṛd*, a mental organ similar in many ways to *manas*, but nonetheless distinguishable from it.

Hṛd:

The coordination of heart *(hṛd)* and mind *(manas)* is a fairly common theme in the *Ṛg Veda*, occurring most often in the context of the sacrifice. Prayers are said to be fashioned with the heart and mind,[272] visions *(dhī)* polished, i.e. clarified, by heart and mind,[273] and libations purified, i.e. made fit for the gods, probably by being visualized, in heart and mind.[274] Moreover, prayers etc. which are

---

272. *Ṛg* 1.171.2.
273. *Ṛg* 1.61.2.
274. *Ṛg* 4.58.6.

conceived, clarified and purified in the hearts and minds of humans are said to satisfy and please the hearts and minds of gods.[275] The ritual, then, seems to be thought of as some sort of communication between the hearts and minds of humans and those of the gods. The respective roles of these two mental organs in the sacrificial process will be clarified by recalling a passage quoted above with reference to the distinction between sensual perception and mental perception and considering it in the context of the verses which follow it.

> 7. Colleagues *(sakhāya)* having (similar) eyes and ears are (nevertheless) unequal in swiftness of mind *(manojavesu)*. Some are like (deficient pools) reaching the mouth or armpit, others look like pools fit for bathing.[276]
> 8. In (regard to) that which is fashioned by the heart *(hṛd)*, in the swiftness of mind *(manaso javesu)*, colleagues sacrifice together. Here, indeed, some, the worthy Brāhmaṇas, by (virtue of their) wisdom (vedyābhiḥ) leave you and wander *(vi caranti)*.
>
> *Ṛg* 10.71.7-8

Yāska[277] and Sāyana, in their explanations of these verses, propose an interesting and perhaps not completely unfounded etymological definition for *sakhāya*, literally "friend". They say that the term intends "those having common perceptions" *(samānakhyāna)*. At any rate, in this context, "that which is fashioned by the heart" obviously refers to the hymn *(mantra)*. The "swiftness of mind" which serves to distinguish the adequate sacrificers from the inadequate seems to refer to the ability to actualize or communicate to the gods the intent of the hymn. The adequate leave behind the impotent worshiper, the one who fails to participate in the communal mind and heart which the last

275. *Ṛg* 1.73.10; 4.37.2; 8.82.3 (= 8.71.3 in Griffith's enumeration).

276. The precise meaning of the second *pāda* is not clear. Sāyana, following Yāska (*Nirukta* 13.13), suggests the translation I adopt, saying that armpit-level water represents those with little wisdom, and mouth-level represents those with middling wisdom, while "pools fit for bathing" *(hradā-iva-snātvāḥ)* represent the truly wise. Whatever the literal translation, the sense of the passage is obviously that some are deficient in knowledge and some adequate.

277. *Nirukta,* 13.13.

hymn of the *Ṛg Veda* enjoins as being conducive to a successful sacrifice. The role of the verbal root √*car* (to move) in the above passage becomes clearer in the next verse of the same hymn.

> Those who do not move *(caranti)* back and forth are not Brāhmaṇas, are not performers of liberation. Having approached speech with sin, they spin out the thread (of sacrifice) *(tantraṁ tanvate)* in ignorance *(aprajñayaḥ),* like (mere) weavers.
>
> *Ṛg* 10.71.9

Here, movement as represented by the root √*car,* seems to indicate some form of communication with the gods. It is the mind, apparently by virtue of its swiftness, which is represented as being primarily responsible for this "movement" between earth and heaven. This same mobile, communicative function of *manas,* again denoted by the root √*car,* occurs in the following passage, which also serves to clarify the distinct role of the heart *(hṛd)* in the sacrificial process.

> 5. A steady light is set for to see. Mind *(manas)* is the swiftest *(javiṣṭham)* of flying things. All the gods, single-minded *(samanas),* with one intention *(saketa),* move well toward a single purpose *(ekaṁ kratum).*
>
> 6. Opened is my ear, my eye, and this light set in (my) heart *(hṛd).* (Opened also is) my mind *(manas);* it wanders *(carati),* visions (ādhīḥ) in the distance. What shall I say, what imagine *(maniṣye)?*
>
> *Ṛg* 6.9.5-6

In both this passage and *Ṛg* 10.71.8, the heart *(hṛd)* seems to be thought of as the primary locus of the inspiration of the worshiper, represented here by light. It is the central basis of the religious impulse, which is conceptualized in a visualization and transported to heaven by the powerful, mobile *manas.* Here again, as in the last hymn of the *Ṛg Veda,* the coordination of several minds is thought to increase the effectiveness of the ritual. In the following passage as well, the term *sakhāya* probably indicates that the collective mind of the sacrificial community communicates the needs of the worshipers, represented by children, to the heart of Indra, who is supposed to be the speaker.

> When the lovers of holy law *(ṛta)* ascended to me sitting alone on the dear (sky's) summit, the mind *(manas)* spoke to my heart *(hṛd)*, colleagues *(sakhāya)* with children, crying out.
>
> *Ṛg* 8.100.5

The impression left by these passages — i.e. that the heart is thought of as being a more intimate, more essential organ of human consciousness than the *manas* — is in general borne out in the rest of the *Ṛg Veda*, though as always, inconsistencies do crop up. Several passages represent the heart as the locus or agent of terms derived from the root √*man*,[278] although as mentioned above, the verbal forms of √*man* do not have much in common with the noun *manas*. The terms *mati* and *manīṣa* (denoting a mental perception), which are similar to *dhī* (a vision), in several passages are said to originate in or by the agency of the heart.[279] The *mantra* (hymn) which is a verbalization of these mental perceptions and visions is also said to be fashioned in or by the heart in several verses.[280]

It is difficult to say more about the relationship of the heart and mind as conceived in the *Ṛg Veda*. The two terms do not often occur together in these ancient and obscure hymns. The two terms as they are found scattered throughout the *Ṛg Veda* are to a large extent interchangeable.[281] The heart, like the mind, is portrayed as the locus and agent not only of derivatives of √*man* and √*cit*,[282] but also of

278. *Ṛg* 5.4.10 *(hṛdā manyamana)*; 5.56.2 *(hṛdā manyasa)*. See next two notes for nominal derivatives.

279. *Ṛg* 1.105.15; 3.26.8; 3.39.1; 8.76.8; 10.91.14; 10.119.5; 10.129.4.

280. *Ṛg* 1.60.3; 1.67.4; 2.35.2; 3.39.1. See also Gonda, *Vision*, pp. 277-78.

281. In his discussion of *hṛd*, Gonda proposes several definitions, each of which could just as well apply to *manas:* "The heart is the organ by means of which one comes into touch with the gods ... with which one is able to see what is denied to the physical eye." (*Vision*, p. 276) "It is in, or by, the heart that the visions are fashioned into words." (*Vision*, p. 278).

282. *Ṛg* 7.33.9. See also *Ṛg* 10.103.12; 10.177.1.

kratu (mental power),[283] and of *dhī* (vision).[284] Like *manas*, the heart is characterized as being endowed with mystical vision,[285] and the heart is represented as the seat of an assortment of emotions very similar to those associated with the mind: desire,[286] fear,[287] love,[288] kindness and generosity,[289] joy,[290] and dejection.[291]

The intellectual connotations of the term *hṛd* are vague and confined primarily to its role as the agent of verbal derivatives of √*man*. This has been dealt with above, but in this specific connection two interesting passages suggest that the heart was thought to function as an intellectual organ, although again, it is difficult to separate intellect from mental perception in these verses. In the famous "Nāsadīya Sūkta", the sages are said to have discovered within their hearts the relationship between being and non-being.[292] Elsewhere it is said that with the perceptions *(praketa)* of their heart the sages penetrate into *(abhi saṁ caranti)* the thousand-branched mystery.[293] The heart shares with *manas* the capacity for creativity, though the creativity of the heart seems to be confined to hymns and prayers etc. in the context of sacrifice.[294]

Even though the heart, in different contexts, shares practically all of the characteristics of *manas* and the other mental faculties, it stands apart from these terms in that it is so frequently portrayed as the most

---

283. *Ṛg* 5.85.2; 10.64.2.

284. *Ṛg* 1.61.2; 1.146.4; 3.26.8; 10.64.2.

285. *Ṛg* 7.33.9; 10.123.6; 10.177.1.

286. *Ṛg* 10.11.6; 10.40.12; 10.123.6; 10.151.4.

287. *Ṛg* 1.32.14; 2.29.6; 5.44.9; 6.53.8; 9.53.2; 10.103.12.

288. *Ṛg* 1.43.1; 5.11.5; 6.53.6; 10.10.13; 10.91.3, and notably 10.95.15, where it is claimed by a rejected lover that the hearts of women are like the hearts of hyenas.

289. *Ṛg* 8.20.18.

290. *Ṛg* 1.73.10; 7.98.2; 7.101.5; 8.43.31; 8.82.3; 9.72.7; 10.186.1.

291. *Ṛg* 10.34.9; 10.84.7; 10.95.17.

292. *Ṛg* 10.129.4.

293. *Ṛg* 7.33.9.

294. *Ṛg* 1.60.3; 1.61.2; 1.67.1; 1.71.2; 2.35.2; 3.39.1; 4.58.6; 6.16.47; 8.76.8; 10.91.4.

essential seat of one's character and consciousness. Thus, it is said of Agni,

> He only is the sea *(samudra)*, holder of treasures; born many a time he views *(vi-caste)* the hearts *(hṛdaḥ)* within us.[295]
>
> *Ṛg* 10.5.1 (G)

The role of the heart as the primary seat of consciousness is most vividly revealed in the frequent association of the heart with *soma*, an intoxicating, probably hallucinogenic[296] drug ingested in the course of some Vedic rituals. The powerful psychotropic effects of *soma* are frequently described in the *Ṛg Veda*.

> 5. As a wright bends a chariot seat, so round my heart *(hṛd)* I bend the hymn *(mati)*. Have I not drunk of *soma* juice?
>
> 6. Not as a mote within the eye count the five tribes of men with me. Have I not drunk of *soma* juice?
>
> 7. The heavens and earth themselves have not grown equal to one half of me. Have I not drunk of soma juice?
>
> *Ṛg* 10.119.5-7 (G)

In many verses, the drug *soma* is said to enter the heart[297] and exert its profoundly moving influence upon the heart.[298] The heart is, in fact, portrayed as the primary locus of operation of *soma*.

---

295. See Gonda's discussion in *Vision*, p. 281 on the relationship of the heart and the ocean. Cp. *Ṛg* 8.18.15.

296. See R. Gordon Wasson, *Soma: The Divine Mushroom of Immortality*, Harcourt Brace and Jovanovich, New York, 1971, a somewhat overdrawn but nonetheless convincing attempt to identify *soma* with the hallucinogenic *Amanita mascaria* mushroom.

297. *Ṛg* 1.91.13; 1.168.3; 1.179.5; 3.42.8; 8.48.4 & 12; 9.60.3; 9.70.9; 9.84.4; 9.86.19; 9.108.16; 10.32.9; 10.97.18.

298. *Ṛg* 8.48.4; 8.79.8; 9.8.3; 9.72.7; 10.25.2.

4. Absorbed into the heart, be sweet, O Indu, as a kind father to his son, O Soma, as a wise friend to friend *(sakheva sakhye),* do thou wise ruler, O Soma lengthen out our days for living.

5. These glorious drops that give me freedom have I drunk. Closely they knit my joints as straps secure a car. Let them protect my foot from slipping on the way, yea, let the drops I drink preserve me from disease.

6. Make me shine bright like fire produced by friction; give us a clearer sight *(cakṣu)* and make us better, for in carouse (*made,* lit. "in exhilaration") I think of thee, O Soma. Shall I, as a rich man, attain to comfort?

7. May we enjoy with an enlivened spirit *(manas)* the juice thou givest, like ancestral riches. O Soma, king, prolong thou our existence as Surya makes the shining days grow longer.

Ṛg 8.48.4-7 (G)

It should not be necessary to emphasize that the intoxicating effects of *soma* were not thought of as a frivolous diversion by the Vedic sages. They were considered conducive to spiritual enlightenment, insight and even mundane blessings. In the above translation, Griffith's depiction of the *soma* rite as a drinking bout is reprehensible. The psychotropic effects of *soma* are represented as being so powerful as to be potentially terrifying, as in the following passage in which the deity Soma is begged, as it were, not to cause a bad trip.

7. Gracious, displaying tender love, unconquered, gentle in thy thoughts *(kratu)* be sweet, O Soma, to our heart *(hṛd).*

8. O Soma, terrify us not; strike us not with alarm, O king. Wound not our heart *(hṛd)* with dazzling flame.

Ṛg 8.79.7-8 (G)[299]

Even independently of the effects of *soma,* the heart is represented as being the locus of spiritual light. In the passage quoted above, "a steady light" is said to have opened out or dawned within the heart.

---

299. In Griffith's enumeration, *Ṛg* 8.68.7-8.

On the basis of this light, the *manas* becomes active *(carati)* in the ritual process.[300] Elsewhere, Indra is said to chase darkness from the heart,[301] and Agni, "the sun of men", is said to dwell within the hearts of visionary *(dhīrāsa)* sages.[302] Agni himself is said to hold within his heart a mental image *(mati)* in the form of light.

> Because he had, with three strainers, clarified the hymn of praise, tracing with (in) the heart the 'thought' *(mati)*, the light *(jyoti)*, he has made himself, according to his own nature, the highest gem; then he beheld heaven and earth.[303]
>
> *Ṛg* 3.26.8

In relation to this passage, Gonda notes that the manual purification of *soma* by straining the juice through a sieve is paralleled subjectively by the purification of clarification of the worshiper's visions in the heart and their transformation into the ritually effective hymn.[304]

Finally, it is noteworthy that only one passage in the *Ṛg Veda* seems to employ the term *hṛd* with reference to the heart as a biological organ.[305] The heart is nonetheless thought of as a vital organ to a much greater extent than the *manas*, which, as noted above, is represented as a vital organ only in a concentration of four hymns in the tenth book.[306] In the following hymn, Agni is addressed in his aspect as the power of life.

---

300. *Ṛg* 6.9.5-6.

301. *Ṛg* 5.31.9.

302. *Ṛg* 1.146.4.

303. Gonda, *Vision*, p. 279.

304. Gonda, *Vision* pp. 278-82.

305. *Ṛg* 10.163.3, but this still may not be the beating heart.

306. Hymns 57-60.

> The universe depends upon thy power and might within the sea *(samudra),*[307] within the heart *(hṛd),* within all life *(āyus).*
>
> *Ṛg* 4.58.11 (G)

The heart as an organ of vitality is obviously intended in several passages which speak of disease as residing in the heart,[308] and probably in passages which speak of curses directed against the hearts of enemies.[309] The implication in both cases is that an affliction of the heart will affect the entire being on both the vital and mental fronts.

This central, essential nature of the heart is again evident in numerous passages which pictures hymns and rites as moving or touching the hearts of gods.[310] It is the heart, more than any other organ or faculty, which is associated with both emotions and life itself. In the following passage, the effect of the rite upon the heart of Agni is likened to the visceral effect of sexual love.

> This newest eulogy will I speak forth to him the ancient one who loves it. May he hear our voice. May it come near his heart and make it stir with love, as a fond matron clings about her lord.
>
> *Ṛg* 10.91.13 (G)

The hearts of the gods are represented as being susceptible to entreaty as well as seduction as in the following verse where the hymns are likened to envoys.[311]

---

307. On the relationship of the ocean to the heart, see Gonda, *Vision,* p. 281.

308. *Ṛg* 1.50.11; 1.122.9; 8.48.4; 10.163.3.

309. *Ṛg* 6.53.5 & 7; 10.87.4 & 13; 10.103.2.

310. *Ṛg* 1.16.7; 4.10.1; 4.37.2; 4.41.1; 4.43.1; 7.86.8; 7.101.5; 10.47.7; 10.91.13; 10.119.5.

311. Cp. *Ṛg* 8.100.5, quoted above, where the collective mind of the sacrificial community *(sakhāya)* speaks to the heart of Indra.

> My lauds, like envoys, craving loving kindness, go forth *(caranti)* to Indra with their strong entreaty, moving his heart *(hṛdispṛśa)* and uttered by my spirit *(manas);* vouchsafe us mighty and resplendent riches.
>
> *Ṛg* 10.47.7 (G)

To say that the *hṛd* is central is largely a truism. As Gonda notes, in Sanskrit *hṛd* practically means "center or middle", even "bowels".[312] Thus, though it may be said for the sake of making a distinction that *hṛd* is a more central or essential organ than *manas*, it is never suggested in the *Ṛg Veda* that the *manas* operates at the beck and call of the *hṛd*. Nor is there any specific relationship between the actions of *hṛd* and those of *manas*. They have only slightly different functions, but not interdependent functions as do the various faculties in the post-Vedic theory of a layered consciousness. Nonetheless, Gonda is probably right in asserting that the *hṛd* of the *Ṛg Veda* is a concept related to the *hṛd* of the *Upaniṣads*, and even possibly the *hṛd* which appears with psychological importance in the Pāli *Abhidhamma*.[313]

Dhī:

The visionary function of the human mind has been noted as an aspect of each of the mental organs and faculties examined thus far, but the terms most specifically representative of this function are the derivatives of the verbal root √*dhī*, primarily the nouns *dhī* and *dhīti*. Jan Gonda's exhaustive examination of these terms in *The Vision of the Vedic Poets* renders further detailed contextual analysis unnecessary, and a few sentences here will suffice to summarize his findings and incorporate them into the present scheme.

Gonda's well-considered, albeit vague and somewhat inconsistent conclusions with regard to the meaning of the *dhī* family of terms are for the most part accepted here. The primary reservation is that Gonda fails to distinguish between vision as a phenomenon, "a

312. Gonda, *Vision*, p. 282.

313. Ibid. pp. 283-88.

vision", and vision as a mental faculty. Thus, in one place he suggests that *dhī* is:

> "the exceptional and supranormal faculty, proper to 'seers', of 'seeing', in the mind, things, causes, connections as they really are, the faculty of acquiring sudden knowledge of the truth, of the functions and influence of the divine powers, of man's relations to them etc. etc. It is this 'vision' which they attempt to give shape, to put into words, to develop into intelligible speech, to 'translate' into stanzas and 'hymns' of liturgical value".[314]

Later, he says that *dhī* is "a flash of divine omniscience striking the human mind and the normal sphere of human thought".[315] Though Gonda devotes a separate chapter to the noun *dhīti,* it is not clear how he means to distinguish it from *dhī,* or whether he considers either or both of these terms to mean "vision" as a faculty, or "a vision" as a phenomenon.

A careful examination of the Vedic passages cites in his chapters on *dhī* and *dhīti* confirms that these two nouns refer indistinguishably to "a vision" rather than to the mental faculty which perceives vision. Gonda himself points out that these visions are often represented as being bestowed upon receptive people by the gods.[316] Moreover, both terms frequently occur in the plural where this would be inappropriate if they were to be thought of as referring to a mental faculty in an individual. In fact, Gonda's theory of the role of *dhī* in the sacrifice hinges upon interpreting *dhī* as "a vision".

Before moving on to a closer examination of this point, however, it is necessary to pause for a moment with Gonda's definitions. Though probably a bit overdrawn, they no doubt reflect the great importance that the Vedic seers themselves placed upon their visions. In the present analytical study of psychological terms in the *Ṛg Veda,* there is no basis upon which to evaluate the truth value of these visions, which Gonda implies is very great indeed. The Vedic sages

---

314. Ibid. pp. 68-69.

315. Ibid. p. 130.

316. Ibid. pp. 69-94. See the discussion of the phrase *dhiyam* √*dhā,* "to bestow a vision", on pp. 87ff.

certainly thought that their visions were real and accurate. Most of the philosophizing in the above definitions, however, appears to be Gonda's own, based on concepts and concerns that are later than genuine Vedic thought. There is, for example, little indication in the *Ṛg Veda* that the Vedic Aryan was concerned with seeing things "as they really are". Such an ambition presupposes a critical attitude toward overt sensual experience, and there is very little evidence of such an attitude in the *Ṛg Veda*. Instead *dhī*, a mental vision, was thought to extend rather than to override normal sensual perception.

Gonda notes, in fact, that the verbal root √*dhī* may denote simple vision, as in the phrase "as far as men see *(dīdhyānāh)* with the eye *(cakṣasā)*".[317] In other cases, however, it obviously refers to mental seeing, and is, in fact, in one verse, used interchangeably with the root √*cit*,[318] the mental and visual connotations of which have been examined above.

> 1. I saw you thinking with the mind *(apaśyaṁ tva manasā cekitānam)*. ...
> 2. I saw you having visions with the mind *(apaśyaṁ tva manasā dīdhyānam)*.
>
> *Ṛg* 10.183.1-2

As the above verse suggests, in most cases when the verbal root √*dhī* and its derivatives are associated specifically with a mental faculty, *manas* is usually the faculty which performs the action denoted by √*dhī*.[319]

It is fairly clear that all of the nominal derivatives of *dhī* represent the occurrence of a mental image of some sort, and that these visions, at least in their advanced, ritually effective form, occur only in exceptionally gifted individuals. As noted above, the *manas* is considered to be the most important agent or locus of these visions.[320]

---

317. Ibid. p. 202, citing *Ṛg* 7.91.4. See also *Ṛg* 7.33.5; 5.40.5.

318. Ibid. p. 207, and on √*cit*, pp. 99ff.

319. *Ṛg* 1.71.5; 1.139.2; 1.163.12; 4.33.9; 10.18.3.

320. *Ṛg* 1.139.2; 3.60.2; 5.81.1; 7.64.4; 7.90.5; 8.102.22; 9.100.3; 10.71.2.

The heart *(hṛd)* too is sometimes represented as the agent of visions,[321] but most often it is mentioned in this context in conjunction with *manas* as a partner in the perception and refinement of a vision.[322] Apparently, one becomes capable of experiencing *dhī* by virtue of the development of these two mental organs, particularly *manas*. This development, as we have seen is denoted primarily by means of various derivatives of the verbal root √*cit*, which refers to mental activity in general.

It was noted above that verbal derivatives of √*dhī* and √*cit* in some cases indicate similar and apparently interchangeable functions of the *manas*. In the majority of instances where these two roots occur together, however, highly developed thought, indicated by terms like *vipaścita*,[323] *pracetas*,[324] or *cikitvin-manas*[325] — all derived from √*cit* — is represented as being a prerequisite condition for the experience of *dhī*. Strictly speaking, then, *dhī* is not a mental faculty, but a phenomenon occurring in minds with well developed faculties. Its relevance in the study of Vedic psychology is not so much as an indication of the nature of human consciousness as it is an indication of the potential of the mind. The ability to perceive mental visions is represented in the *Ṛg Veda* as a function of the special development of the normal mental organs and faculties examined thus far, namely thought *(citta)*, mind *(manas)*, and heart *(hṛd)*.

Admittedly, some passages do seem to represent *dhī* as a mental faculty like *citta* (thought) or *kratu* (will). Usually such passages may be as comfortably translated or even more comfortably translated by adhering to the more circumscribed definition of *dhī* as "a vision", the phenomenon of a mental image. Two examples follow. The phrase *dhiyā* cetati[326] might immediately seem to mean "thinks with the mental faculty of vision", if it is construed as analogous to the phrase

---

321. *Ṛg* 10.64.2.
322. *Ṛg* 1.61.2; 2.20.1; 6.9.6.
323. *Ṛg* 1.164.36; 9.22.3.
324. *Ṛg* 1.159.1.
325. *Ṛg* 8.98.5.
326. *Ṛg* 3.11.3.

manasā cetati, "thinks with the mind". However, a translation more in line with the usual meaning of *dhī* would be "thinks or is mentally active with a vision".

The second passage to be considered is: *apaśyāma hiraṇyayam dhībhiś cana manasā svebhir akṣabhih somasya svebhir akṣabhiḥ.*[327] Gonda translates: "we saw something golden with our power of vision — in whatever way (that is) — with our mind, through our own eyes, through eyes proper to Soma".[328] The translation suggested by the present interpretation of *dhī* would be: "we saw something golden through our vision, by the mind, with our won eyes, with Soma's own eyes". In this case, the latter translation is not only more accurate grammatically, since *dhībhis* is a plural form, but it also has the virtue of preserving the lack of parallelism between *manasā* and *dhībhis* in the original. If the terms had been intended as parallel phrases indicating analogous faculties, as Gonda construes them they would probably occur in the same number.

Gonda's interpretation of the role of *dhī* in the sacrifice also depends upon understanding *dhī* as meaning "a vision". Gonda notes that the gods, having great facility in the realm of *dhī*, are thought to aid humans in achieving visions, and may even bestow vision upon their favorites. The mere experience of a vision, however, is only the first step. Once apprehended, the vision, in order to be of lasting value, must be cast into a liturgical hymn which, when chanted, has the power to recall and evoke the original vision again and again.[329] The vision thus evoked in liturgical hymn chanting was thought to have power to influence the gods and procure for humans the objects of their desires, from wealth to victory in battle to long life and a large family.[330] This bringing of the vision to fruition in the attainment of some human goal is most commonly represented by the phrase

---

327. *Ṛg* 1.139.2.
328. Gonda, *Vision*, p. 69.
329. Ibid. pp. 106-130.
330. Ibid. pp. 123-69.

dhiyam √*sādh*, "to accomplish the vision", in the sense of putting it to use rather than realizing or attaining its specific contents.[331]

Gonda notes that "the close connection of *dhītiḥ* and *kratuḥ* is worth noticing"[332] without mentioning the similar connection between *dhī* and *kratu*, and without explaining why this connection is important. His intent seems to be that *kratu* is instrumental in the process of bringing a vision to fruition. Rather than the standard translation "will", Gonda understands *kratu* as "effective mental power or intelligence, mental energy and determination, which enables its possessor to have solutions to preponderantly practical difficulties".[333] That *kratu* means "mental power" more than merely "will" is accepted here, but the second part of Gonda's definition regarding "practical difficulties" has little basis in the actual usage of the term. His suggestion elsewhere of the translation "resourcefulness or inventiveness"[334] is also without support in actual usage.

The function of *kratu* in developing or bringing visions to fruition is indicated most clearly in a passage where little else is clear.

> He, the first seer of the great ones, by (their) mental powers *(kratubhir)* consecrated *(ānaje);* father Manu consecrated visions *(dhiya ānaje)* which are a door to the gods.
>
> *Ṛg* 8.63.1

Another passage speaks of "mental powers *(kratavaḥ)* and visions *(dhītayaḥ)* functioning with mental power *(kratūyanti)* in hearts *(hṛtsu).*"[335] In another, the vision *(dhīti)* is said to reach Agni by means of *kratu*.[336] The role of *kratu* in actualizing visions is borne out in the general function of this mental faculty in channeling and

331. Ibid. pp. 131-33.

332. Ibid. p. 183.

333. Ibid. p. 183.

334. Ibid. p. 111.

335. *Ṛg* 10.64.2.

336. *Ṛg* 4.5.7.

making effective any of the mind's imagining.[337] Further clarification of the term *dhī* requires a consideration of the term *kratu* and its role in actualizing visions.

Kratu:

The term *kratu* in the *Upaniṣads* and later Indian literature in general indicates volition or will. For the purposes of Vedic translation this standard meaning is somewhat misleading. Gonda proposes replacing the standard translation "will" with something like "inventiveness or resourcefulness",[338] unfortunate suggestions which correspond to the actual Vedic usage of the term *kratu* even less than the standard translation "will". Apparently, Gonda is thinking in terms of the largely accurate definition quoted above, "effective mental power or intelligence, mental energy and determination",[339] That this mental power implies resourcefulness in overcoming practical difficulties,[340] however, misses the mark entirely. *Kratu* is conceived as a self-actualizing mental power, more like the "power of positive thinking". The translation adopted here will be "mental power", and the rest of this section will be an attempt to note the various connotations of the term *kratu* and relate them to this central concept.

In several Vedic passage, *kratu* is obviously used in the sense of "will".[341] In various passages it is said that the *kratu* of the father is obeyed by his son,[342] that the gods obey Varuṇa's *kratu,*[343] and that Indra is submissive to his wife's *kratu,*[344] though it is said elsewhere,

---

337. See Gonda, *Vision,* pp. 72, 111, 183-84 for discussions on *kratu*. See also *Ṛg* 7.90.5; 9.86.13; 10.8.7.

338. Gonda, *Vision,* p. 111.

339. Ibid. p. 183.

340. Ibid. p. 183.

341. In addition to the passages in the next four notes, see *Ṛg* 5.29.5; 6.9.5; 8.61.4; 8.66.4; 10.83.5.

342. *Ṛg* 1.68.5.

343. *Ṛg* 4.42.2.

344. *Ṛg* 10.159.2.

as noted above, that a woman's *kratu* has little weight.[345] Volition, however, is only an aspect of the more central meaning of the term *kratu*. In some ambiguous contexts *kratu* may or may not indicate simple will power, as when the *kratu* of Bṛhaspati is said to be as strong as a wild beast,[346] or when the great *kratu* of Indra is said to be irresistible.[347] In other contexts *kratu* appears to indicate the brute psychological force associated with aggressive machismo, as when it is said that the gods yield to Indra by virtue of his manly might *(vīrya)* and his *kratu*. Here *kratu* seems to represent the mental attitude of a fierce warrior.[348] The role of *kratu* as sheer force is more explicit in the following passage in which Indra is said to be *vṛṣa-kratu*, literally "having the mental power of a macho male".

> May the strong *(vṛṣa)* heaven make thee the strong *(vṛṣa)* wax stronger. Strong *(vṛṣa)* thou art borne by thy two strong *(vṛṣa)* bay horses. So, fair of cheek, with mighty *(vṛṣa)* chariot, mighty *(vṛṣa)*, uphold us, strong-willed *(vṛṣa-kratu)*, thunder-armed in battle.
>
> *Ṛg* 5.36.5 (G)

The basis meaning of the term *kratu* may well be an assertive mental attitude. This meaning is overshadowed in the *Ṛg Veda*, however, by the more frequent use of the word to denote a mental power which is generally instrumental in gaining one's ends, whether or not the attainment of these ends depends on the outcome of some sort of strife. This, no doubt, is the meaning which Gonda intends to convey with "inventiveness or resourcefulness". In this sense, however, the term has a much more magical implication than either Gonda's suggestions or the more acceptable translations "will power or determination" would suggest. Often it is through the *kratu* of the gods that human and divine ends are attained.[349] In these contexts, the

345. *Ṛg* 8.33.17.

346. *Ṛg* 1.190.3.

347. *Ṛg* 8.66.10.

348. *Ṛg* 8.62.7.

349. *Ṛg* 6.5.3; 6.7.2; 6.16.26; 8.19.29; 9.4.3-6; 10.83.5.

term might be taken as the self-actualizing will of the gods. In several instances, however, it is this same self-actualizing *kratu* in humans, often bestowed upon them by gods, which is said to be conducive to the attainment of one's goals.[350] it is primarily in this sense that *kratu* plays an important role in the ritual. "Mental power" is an important possession of the visionary poet and the hymn singer,[351] apparently because, as in the following verse, *kratu* is instrumental in rendering the vision into an effective communication to the gods.

> Indeed, may the purifying vision *(dhīti)*, by means of mental power *(kratu)*, reach him (Agni), the universal, at once.
>
> *Ṛg* 4.5.7

Why the vision is said to be purifying *(punati)* becomes clearer in the light of the following passage, in which it is said to purify or clarify the *kratu*. Gonda translates:

> 10. Here goes, in proper time, a vision *(dhītiḥ)*, rather new, worshipping, dear to many, it is realized in the phenomenal world *(mimīta)*...
>
> 11. The new-born child of the act of worship *(garbho jayñasya)* who is devoted to the gods (tries to reach the gods), clarifies *(punita)* the (seer's) inventiveness *(kratu)* uninterruptedly.[352]
>
> *Ṛg* 8.12.10-11

I would suggest "mental power" for *kratu* in verse eleven, and would prefer "womb or embryo of sacrifice" for *garbho yajñasya*, but the general meaning is clear enough. The vision, which is doubtlessly identified with the "embryo of sacrifice", purifies or clarifies the *kratu*,[353] and is, in some sense realized *(mimīta)*. Gonda suggests that this realization refers to the development of the initial vision into a

---

350. *Ṛg* 10.25.4; 10.57.4; 10.144.6.

351. *Ṛg* 1.1.5; 1.151.2; 9.9.1; 9.25.5; 10.100.11-12.

352. Gonda, *Vision*, pp. 182-83.

353. See *Ṛg* 8.13.1 and 8.93.6 for other instances of purifying the *kratu*.

complete hymn. It could just as well refer to the realization of the sacrificial request as a blessing granted to humans by the gods, for, as noted below, the *kratu*, both divine and human, plays an important part in actualizing the contents of the sacrifice and the gods' intentions. It is by virtue of his *kratu* that Agni is said to be the "charioteer of blessings",[354] and through the *kratu* and *dhī* of Indra that *soma* flows between heaven and earth.[355] The sun, in another passage, is said to have been created by the *kratu* of the gods.[356]

Thus, there seems to be a reciprocal relationship between the vision *(dhī)* and the *kratu*. The vision clarifies or purifies the *kratu*, and the *kratu* helps make the vision effective. *Kratu*, particularly in the sacrificial context in which it is most often found, should be thought of specifically as that type of mental power which is based upon concentration, single-mindedness and determination, as noted above, something like the proverbial "power of positive thinking". Visions *(dhī* and *dhīti)* purify this mental power by giving it something to concentrate upon, and *kratu*, in turn, serves to energize the vision and transform it into an effective ritual force. It must be emphasized, however, that this transformation is accomplished not by mundane means, as Gonda's translations "inventiveness" or "resourcefulness" suggest, but through numinous, magical channels.

"Inventiveness" and "resourcefulness" would be better reserved for the term *dakṣa*. This term is often used in conjunction with *kratu*, and seems to denote a more mundane faculty specifically involved with the execution or actualization of the intentions which are enshrined in the *kratu*. Thus, it is said in the *Śatapatha Brāhmaṇa*, "When a man wishes, 'May I do that; may I have that', that is *kratu*. When he attains it, that is dakṣa."[357] Most of the passages which mention these two terms together do not distinguish *kratu* from *dakṣa*, both being represented as qualities which are in an unspecified way advantageous

354. *Ṛg* 6.5.3. See also *Ṛg* 8.19.29, where wealth is gained through the agency of Agni's *kratu*.

355. *Ṛg* 9.86.13.

356. *Ṛg* 7.76.1. See also *Ṛg* 6.71.1, where Savitṛ is the creator of life and is called *sukratu*.

357. S.B. 4.1.4.1. See Keith, *Religion and Philosophy*, p. 484.

to the attainment of one's ends.[358] The following passage, however, which does distinguish the two terms, fits the definitions given in the *Śatapatha Brāhmaṇa*, although it does not contain conclusive support for them.

> He must converse (and agree) with his own *kratu* and must gain, with his *manas*, *dakṣa*, which is conducive to welfare.[359]
>
> *Ṛg* 10.31.2

It is clear, at any rate, that *kratu* is in some sense instrumental in the attainment of human ends, probably as the power of single-mindedness. On the one hand, it sets in motion *dakṣa*, practical skill or resourcefulness directed toward the attainment of these ends. On the other hand, it energizes the visions *(dhī)* and puts these to work in the magical, numinous realm for the attainment of the same goals. Thus, unlike *dhī*, *kratu* is best conceived of as a mental faculty based on a special mode of functioning of the more basic mental organs *hṛd* and *manas*. One characteristic of this special mode of functioning, as mentioned above, seems to be concentration. This notion finds direct support in two passages which suggest that the unified *kratu* of the gods apparently has enhanced power.

> United in thought *(sacita)*, united in thinking *(sacetas)* those (gods), by the stimulation of the god Savitṛ, participate *(sacante)* in the *kratu*.
>
> *Ṛg* 10.64.7

> All the gods, united in mind *(samanas)*, united in intention *(saketa)* move well toward a single *kratu*.
>
> *Ṛg* 6.9.5

---

358. *Ṛg* 7.62.1; 9.100.5; 9.102.2 & 10; 10.25.1; 10.57.4; 10.91.3.

359. The translation follows that offered in *Vision*, p. 184, but the Sanskrit terms have been substituted where Gonda's translations would have been confusing in the present context.

Other than the particular association of concentration with a powerful *kratu*, the term is generally associated with a vigorous, active mind. *Kratu* is often associated with derivatives of the verbal root √*cit*, which denote general mental activity. *Kratu*, like the ability to perceive visions, is associated with excellent or highly active thought as denoted by the root √*cit*. Thus, the phrase *kratvā cetati*[360] probably means "is mentally active with the faculty of will power". The phrase *kratvā cetiṣṭho*,[361] probably means: "most mentally active with the *kratu*"; and the phrase *api kratum sucetasam vatema*:[362] "may we attain (or comprehend) the *kratu* characterized by excellent mental activity".

Kratu is normally represented as being located in the heart *(hṛd)* and performed by the mind *(manas)*.[363] Indeed, if any distinction may be made between these two so-called "organs", it is, as the following examples suggest, that the heart is primarily a locus of various forms of mental activity, while the mind is primarily an agent. In a hymn already discussed, which is intended to revive a dying person, the *manas* is begged to return so that the dying man may once again have *kratu* and *dakṣa*, and that he may live.

> May your *manas* return to you for mental power *(kratu)* and skill *(dakṣa)* so that you may live, so that you may long behold the sun.
>
> *Ṛg* 10.57.4

The next passage too, though less directly, suggests that *manas* is somehow basic to *kratu* and *dakṣa*.

360. *Ṛg* 1.128.4.

361. *Ṛg* 1.65.10.

362. *Ṛg* 7.3.10. See also *Ṛg* 10.83.5.

363. In addition to the passages quoted below, see *Ṛg* 6.9.5; 10.31.2.

> Send us a good and happy mind, send energy *(dakṣa)* and mental power *(kratu).*
>
> *Ṛg* 10.25.1 (G)

Two passages explicitly state that the locus of *kratu* is the heart *(hṛd).* One says that Varuṇa set the *kratu* in the heart as he set fire in water and the sun in the sky.[364] The other passage, already discussed above, says that *kratu* and *dhī,* located in hearts *(hṛtsu)* exert themselves, this activity being indicated by a verbal form of the noun *kratu (kratūyanti).*[365]

Conclusions:

On the basis of the foregoing analysis of psychological terms in the *Ṛg Veda,* only the broadest of conclusions are justified, most of them negative with regard to the origins of classical Indian psychology. *Hṛd* and *manas* are the most basic and essential psychological phenomena mentioned in the *Ṛg Veda.* For this reason, it seems reasonable to label them "organs" so as to distinguish them from the less essential "faculties", *citta* and *kratu.* General mental activity is designated by the verbal root √*cit* and its derivatives. None of these words, even nominal forms, can be specifically associated with any particular form of mental activity or experience.

Indeed, throughout the *Ṛg Veda,* intellectual mental functions are not clearly distinguished from perceptual functions. Regarding perception itself, all that can be said is that it is recognized as a means of knowledge,[366] as the following passage.

---

364. *Ṛg* 5.85.2.

365. *Ṛg* 10.64.2. See Gonda, *Vision,* p. 183.

366. The bare germ of a self-conscious concept of inference may be seen in a passage in which it is noted that the effects of the wind are seen, but not its form *(rūpa),* which suggests that the wind is known by inference from perceiving its effects (*Ṛg* 1.164.1).

> Who knows that earliest day whereof thou speakest? Who hath beheld *(dadarśa)* it? Who can here declare it?
>
> *Ṛg* 10.10.6 (G)

Sensual perception is to some extent distinguished from mental perceptiveness, as in the following passages from a hymn to the goddess Vak, speech personified.

> 4. One man hath ne'er seen Vak, and yet he seeth. One man hath hearing but hath never heard her. ...
>
> 7. Unequal in the quickness of their spirit *(manas)* are friends endowed alike with eyes and hearing.
>
> *Ṛg* 10.71.4-7 (G)

Mental activity as denoted by √*cit* and its derivatives is usually represented as merely an extension of perception.

To summarize, thought, in the *Ṛg Veda,* is represented as primarily a perceptual phenomenon. Generally speaking, its locus is the heart *(hṛd),* and the agent or instrument of thought is the *manas*. Derivatives of the verbal root √*cit* denote simply mental activity in general, and this primarily perceptual mental faculty may be applied to the achievement of ends by being channeled through the mental faculty *kratu,* "mental power". These faculties function primarily in the context of ritual to encode the contents of the sacrificer's vision *(dhī)* into an effective message and transmit this message to the gods, who, it is hoped, will help the sacrificer to actualize his desires.

Roughly speaking, the entire human psychological complex, as represented in the *Ṛg Veda,* may be conceived in terms of electronic communications. In such a model, *hṛd* would be the transmitting room, *manas* the transmitter itself, and derivatives of √*cit* would be the various forms of current and electrical activity in the transmitter. *Kratu* would be the antenna, which focuses and directs the signal, and *dhī* would be the message sent, hopefully to be received by the gods. Ultimately, the power source for all this would be the sacrificial ritual.

The scant psychological material to be gleaned from these ancient hymns points to and outlines a vague set of beliefs primarily relevant to the supernatural mechanism of the sacrifice. This, of course, is not surprising, since the *Ṛg Veda* is, after all, a hymnal. Not only, however, is a systematic approach to psychology as such lacking in the *Ṛg Veda*. Vedic psychological terms, when isolated from their liturgical context do not reveal even an unstated concern with human psychology. What material there is of true psychological insight is confined to a random scattering of folksy observations which are incidental to the main Vedic corpus. As the following chapters show, certain aspects of Vedic thought are of significant influence in the development of later Indian psychology. The *Ṛg Veda* alone, however, does not account for the proliferation of sophisticated theoretical psychology in the *Upaniṣads*, Buddhism, and later Indian thought in general. In particular, Upaniṣadic and Buddhist psychological concepts seem to have been worked out on the basis of a synthesis of two world-views, one Vedic, the other non-Vedic, or more specifically, yogic.

Chapter 4

Yoga and *Veda* in the *Upaniṣads*

The previous chapters have consisted of a detailed examination of the ancient hymns of the *Ṛg Veda* with reference to the origins of psychological speculation in India. On the one hand, this has been an attempt to show as accurately as possible the actual Vedic position on matters relevant to the question of the nature of human consciousness. On the other hand, the foregoing shows that Vedic psychological speculation is not only an extremely small seed, but also a seed of the wrong variety to account for the luxuriant growth of psychological speculation in post-Vedic India. From the *Upaniṣads* onward, psychological speculation is based on premises and concerns fundamentally different from those of the Vedic texts.

The only psychologically significant theory of post-Vedic Indian philosophy which can be convincingly traced back to the *Ṛg Veda* is the idea of monism. Chapter 1, demonstrated, however, that incipient Vedic monism was almost entirely cosmological in orientation. It showed little tendency or potential to move toward the psychological, consciousness-orientated monism which is so eloquently expressed in even the earliest *Upaniṣads*. Chapter 2 showed that the Vedic afterlife theory lacks a concept of rebirth, and Chapter 3 showed that the *Ṛg Veda* lacks any theory of the nature of human consciousness other than scattered and disconnected references to a limited set of ill-defined concepts which are primarily of relevance to the theory of sacrifice.

It should be clear by this point that none of the various Vedic psychological concepts correspond to a simple, necessarily immortal soul standing at the base of human life and consciousness. Instead, a contingent immortality was thought to be possible with reference to a complex concept of a post-mortem identity perpetuated through the hereditary and sacrificial aspects of the *tanū*. *Tanū* as a technical term is abandoned in post-Vedic Indian thought, whether orthodox or heterodox. Those Vedic terms which do come to represent the ubiquitous concept of the soul are pressed into the service of representing concepts alien to the original Vedic context of these terms. *Puruṣa*, for example, meant only "person" in the *Ṛg Veda*. *Jīva* referred to life in general, and *ātman* was a relatively rare Vedic term denoting a subtle form of breath. None of these terms which later came to be applied to the essential, individual soul were associated with the Vedic theory of the survival of one's identity after death. *Ātman*, in particular, is specifically said to disperse into the wind when one dies, and the Vedic theory of afterlife is usually stated with specific reference to the *tanū*, and occasionally to *asu* and *āyu*.

In short, the foregoing chapters offer negative evidence in support of the theory associated primarily with Heinrich Zimmer which holds that several essential characteristics of Indian philosophy are non-Vedic, and in fact, non-Indo-European in origin. The most important of these characteristics are the interrelated theories of individual souls, rebirth and release. All three of these theories must be understood in the overarching context of yogic practice, whereby the *soul* may be *released* from the trials of repeated *rebirth*. It is to this archaic theory of *yoga* in its various forms that one must look for the origins of much of Indian psychology.

Shamanism and *Yoga*:

Several attempts have been made to locate the origins of *yoga* in the *Ṛg Veda*. It is well known that the *Ṛg Veda* contains references to certain shamanistic practices centering around the concept of *tapas* ("mystical heat") and the ingestion of the drug *soma*, and that these bear some resemblance to the practice of *yoga*. Shamanism and ecstatic mysticism are, however, universal elements in human religious experience, and all instances of their occurrence must necessarily resemble each other to some extent. It would be a misuse of the more specific term *yoga* to apply it to shamanistic or mystical practices which are not geared specifically toward the *release* of the *soul* from *rebirth*. It is in the context of these three beliefs that the term *yoga* acquires its specific meaning and its specifically Indian context. All instances of yoga in post-Vedic India, and these are not necessarily confined to the classical Yoga school, involve these three characteristics, the primary characteristics which distinguish Vedic from non-Vedic in the history of ideas in India.

It must be admitted that, properly speaking, Buddhists may be said to practice *yoga* even though they do not accept existence of a soul, one of the essential characteristics in the above definition. The Buddhist position, however, represents a self-conscious discarding of some of the philosophical baggage of the general *yoga* complex without changing the destination, namely release from rebirth. It may be noted as well that even some of the materialist (Carvaka) schools seem to have accepted the immediate hedonistic or practical utility of *yoga* practice while rejecting all of the essential elements proposed here,[1] much in the same way that modern day executives are encouraged to engage in certain varieties of yogic practices without necessarily buying into the traditional belief structure.

Nevertheless, such instances may legitimately be called *yoga* because they can be demonstrated to have developed out of the typical Indian *yoga* practice described above, while rejecting or simply ignoring the theoretical concepts which underlie the practical discipline. The alleged Vedic references to *yoga,* however, do not satisfy the criteria of either conceptual similarity or derivation, and may not properly be called instances of *yoga*. Briefly, there are three classes of Vedic hymns in which the origins of Indian yoga have been mistakenly seen: (1) hymns dealing with the ritual ingestion of the drug *soma,* (2) Hymns dealing with *tapas* ("mystical heat"), and (3) the single "Keśin Hymn" in Book Ten[2] which describes the attributes and feats of a "long-haired" *(keśin)* shaman. All of these Vedic examples, however, resemble Indian *yoga* only insofar as any examples of shamanisic mysticism must necessarily resemble *yoga*.

---

1. See *Brahmājala-sutta,* D1: 34-36, where the seven types of annihilationists may entertain concepts of a soul and may undergo yogic discipline sufficient to attain the eighth *jhāna,* although they all agree that the soul perishes inevitably and completely when the body dies.

2. *Ṛg* 10.136.

That the yogic techniques of fasting, breath control, postures and in some cases asceticism alter the brain chemistry in a manner roughly analogous to the ingestion of intoxicating drugs cannot be denied.[3] But to propose, as does the mycologist R. Gordon Wasson, that yogic practice developed as a replacement for the hallucinogenic *soma* is a speculation without any basis other than the fertile imagination of an enthusiastic mycophile.[4] The exhilarated ecstasies of the soma eater have nothing in common with the serene meditation of the yogin, and the *soma* eater's boast of universal sovereignty is altogether different from the *yogin's* claim to have transcended the universe.

Chauncy Blair's thorough analysis of the concept of *tapas* in the *Ṛg Veda* demonstrates vividly that *tapas*, or "mystical heat" is, in its fundamental and original conception, a purely shamanistic phenomenon.[5] He notes that, of a total of twenty-one instances in the *Ṛg Veda* of significant derivatives of the verbal root √*tap* (to heat), only six occur before the tenth book. Of these six instances, four refer to "magical heat" used as a weapon against enemies and demons, while two are confined to the context of ritual.[6] In fact, all derivatives of √*tap* which occur before *Ṛg* 10.87 are used in one of these senses.[7] It is only in verses 10.109 and after that *tapas* denotes the special power of the sage which is both conducive to the attainment of heaven[8] and in some sense creative,[9] *tapas* being that which in one verse is said to be the creative principle of the universe.[10] Thus, it is clear, as Blair concludes, that the meaning and application of the term *tapas* has changed in later hymns from the original, basic meaning

3. R.E.L. Masters and Jean Houston, *The Varieties of Psychedelic Experience*, Holt Rinehart and Winston, New York, 1966, pp. 247-49.

4. R.G. Wasson, Soma: *The Divine Mushroom of Immortality*, Harcourt Brace and Jovanovich, New York, 1971, p. 70.

5. Chauncy Blair, *Heat in the Ṛg and Atharva Vedas*, American Oriental Society, New Haven, 1961.

6. Blair, *Heat*, Ch. 12.

7. Ibid. Ch. 12.

8. Ibid. Ch. 12. See *Ṛg* 10.109.4; 10.154.2.

9. Ibid. Ch. 12. See *Ṛg* 10.154.5; 10.181.3.

10. *Ṛg* 10.129.4.

found in the earlier passages. It should be noted as well that the term is used more often in the later hymns of the *Ṛg Veda.* All of this supports Eliade's theory that *tapas,* though originally an example of the typical shamanistic practice of "creative sweating", was later emphasized by representatives of the Vedic tradition for the purpose of "the assimilation of yogic techniques to orthodox Brāhmaṇic methods", and that this assimilation represents "the homologization of extra-Brāhmaṇic and even extra-Aryan religious values".[11] Furthermore, Eliade notes that the "interiorization" of the Vedic sacrifice, which is begun in the *Brāhmaṇas* and emphasized in the *Upaniṣads,* is a further concession of the Vedic tradition to an increasingly influential non-Vedic tradition based on contemplative yogic techniques rather than upon ritual.[12] These concessions, it will be noted, seem to have begun in the latest hymns of the *Ṛg Veda* itself.

Finally, the protagonist of the famous "Keśin Hymn" (*Ṛg* 10.136) is, in the same vein, recognized by Eliade as "an ecstatic who only vaguely resembles the yogin". The *keśin* may well be an example of the mysterious ascetic *vratyas* who appear in the *Atharva Veda,* but, as Eliade notes, it is by no means clear whether the *keśin* and the *vratyas* are representatives of the Indo-European population or of an indigenous, pre-Aryan Indian population.[13] Thus, the case that can be made for the development of Indian *yoga* from these few vague concepts found in the *Ṛg Veda* is extremely weak. An equal or better argument can be advanced in favor of the theory that many of these Vedic concepts, if they have any relationship to *yoga* at all, derive from contact with non-Vedic thought. Thus, not only is the conceptual framework of *yoga* absent in the *Ṛg Veda,* but also the supposedly *yoga*-like shamanism described in the ancient hymns bears little actual resemblance to the phenomenon of *yoga.* The doctrines of souls, rebirth and release, however, are fundamental in most of the non-Vedic heterodox schools. Indeed, their doctrines cannot be imagined without this yogic triad of beliefs.

---

11. M. Eliade, *Yoga, Immortality and Freedom,* pp. 106-111.
12. Ibid. pp. 111-114.
13. Ibid. pp. 101-105.

Archaic *Yoga:*

The evidence for the extremely ancient status of certain of these non-Vedic schools, particularly Jainism, has been thoroughly stated, and even over-stated by Heinrich Zimmer. He cites sociological evidence, such as the absence of considerations of caste in the fundamental structures of these systems, as well as historico-mythological evidence based on clan names and the reputed geographical origins of various legendary and semi-historical personages in the schools.[14] The most persuasive evidence, however, is that the verifiably ancient Buddhist texts mention various thriving schools, most notably Jainism and Ājīvikism, whose leaders claim to be conservative heirs of even more ancient doctrines independent of Vedic influence. There is no reason to discount this information at face value. The doctrines of these heterodox schools cannot be traced back to Vedic concerns. In addition, they provide a convincing source for the several essentially non-Vedic doctrines which appear unexpectedly in the *Upaniṣads* without Vedic antecedents. These doctrines of souls, rebirth and release centered around yogic practice, have been overwhelmingly dominant in Indian thought since the time of the *Upaniṣads*.

It is arguable, though not perhaps demonstrable, that this religious tradition was not only non-vedic, but non-Aryan as well, that is to say, indigenous to India.[15] The argument in favor of this indigenous tradition admittedly has very little hope of ever being conclusively verified. An analogous situation would be to attempt to unravel the origins of Christianity on the basis of Columbus' Bible. Nonetheless, it is a speculation worth making. If it is true — and it is at present more likely than any rival speculation — then the hitherto mute voice of an independent wellspring of human thought identifies itself, however feebly, across the ages, and credits the Indian sub-continent

14. Heinrich Zimmer, *Philosophies of India,* pp. 59-60, 218-225.

15. Ibid. p. 60, ed. note 23.

with the birth of one of the most influential religious traditions ever conceived by the human race.

Difficulties abound in reconstructing the archaic doctrines of ancient Jainism and Ājīvikism. At any rate, it is clear that they are based on the conviction that there is an inner, essential, individual soul which undergoes rebirth, and may attain release, a conviction which encourages the practice of introspective *yoga*. In short, all of the major characteristics of Indian philosophy which are lacking in the ancient *Vedas* may be accounted for with reference to ancient, coherent, self-contained, non-Vedic systems.

The most ancient surviving form of this tradition is probably the heterodox, non-Vedic Jain religion, the doctrinal basis of Jainism, though relatively late in its earliest recorded forms, harks back to an archaic world-view of doubtlessly great antiquity. The ancient Jain cosmology pictures the universe as being in the form of a giant person,[16] which is to say basically that it has a top and a bottom. There is no evidence in Jainism of any attempt to inquire into the origin of this universe. The transmigration, ascent and ultimate liberation of individual souls, was thought to occur within the context of the given cosmos, and the status of the soul at any particular stage of development was related to its vertical position within this given cosmos.

According to classical Jainism, individual souls are said to be finite in extent, though they expand to fill whatever body they may inhabit. They are everlasting, though not eternal, for they are changed in the course of their transmigration from body to body. Infinite numbers of these souls exist in a primitive state of bare animation in the lower reaches of the cosmos. These primitive souls constitute an inexhaustible fund of beings who, in the middle region of the cosmos, undergo repeated birth and death until they become individually liberated. The liberated soul rises to the top of the cosmos where it exists forever deathless, omniscient and blissful.

16. Ibid. p. 275. Smart, *Doctrine and Argument*, p. 63. Jacobi, "Jain Cosmology", ERE, vol. 4, p. 161.

The tendency of souls to rise is innate, but they are weighed down through the agency of their actions *(karma)*. Actions accrue to the soul a very subtle defiling matter that prevents it from rising. When this karmic matter is removed from the soul by the practice of strict moral discipline and ascetic sensual restraint, it naturally rises to the top of the universe where in a state of liberation it lives forever blissful and omniscient.

When a liberated soul leaves *saṁsāra* in this manner, another of the innumerable primitive souls in the lower cosmos enters into the realm of karmic transmigration. It begins its transmigratory journey with life as one of the so-called material elements, which are conceived of as very primitive living beings. Eventually it will pass through reincarnations as mineral, vegetable and animal life. A being's level in the hierarchy of *saṁsāra* is indicated by the number of senses it possesses. The primitive souls in the bottom of the cosmos have no senses at all, the material atoms of earth, water, fire and air have only the sense of touch, they can actually feel pressure. Air molecules, for instance, are hurt by violent movements, so that even quick motions are strictly speaking violations of the Jain principle of non-violence. Lower animals, worms, etc., have the senses of touch and taste, and so on up to the higher animals with the five senses. Human beings, gods and the tortured denizens of the hells have all five senses plus mind *(manas)*.

The liberated souls at the top of the universe, however, have no sense faculties, and do not perceive or think, though they are said to be omniscient, i.e. directly aware of reality as it is without the intervention of the senses and mind.[17] Thus, the soul undergoes the odd process of first struggling to acquire the full array of five senses and mind, and then to free itself from their influence and thereby effectively lose them again. But through this process, the soul attains

---

17. Ibid. p. 260. See *Tattvārtha-sūtra,* Ch. 10, on the liberated soul, and 1.30, where omniscience is defined as "cognition which grasps all the aspects of even a single object (and thus) can grasp all aspects of all objects".

perfection by undergoing an actual transformation.[18] The soul is everlasting but not eternal.

The doctrines of the Ājīvikas are known to modern scholarship only through hostile references to the system of the literature of rival schools. Thanks to the patient efforts of A.L. Basham, who extracted "every possible hint from the material available" we have at our disposal a "faint outline" of the ancient doctrine of the mysterious Ājīvikas.[19] Basically, their presuppositions seem to have been very similar to those of the Jains. The universe is a given. Though it is said to have existed through the enormous time spans so characteristic of Indian mythology,[20] there is no hint of speculation regarding its origin.[21] Innumerable individual souls are assumed. Like Jain souls, they are finite in size, though they are extremely large, said to extend, in the form of an aura, for 500 *yojanas,* over a thousand miles. Like the Jains, the Ājīvikas held that the soul transmigrates through numerous rebirths, changes in the process, and is finally liberated from the suffering of *saṁsāra.*

In the Ājīvika system, however, every detail of the soul's experience is rigidly predetermined including its inevitable liberation at the end of 8,400,000 *mahākalpas* (great ages) of transmigration.[22] As in Jainism, this liberation entails a cessation of rebirth and thereby release from the suffering of *saṁsāra.* The Ājīvika system, however conceives of release as an absolute extinction of the soul. According to a classical Ājīvika simile, the soul is like a ball of string unraveling in *saṁsāra* until it inevitably reaches its end. One's actions do not cause a better or worse birth, they are only of one's position in the hierarchy of the universe. Asceticism, for example, is not the cause of liberation, but only a symptom indicating that the completion of one's 8,400,000 *mahākalpas* is coming up soon.

---

18. See *Pramāṇanaya-tattvāloka* 7.56: *caitanya-svarūpah paraṇāmī kartā sakṣadbhoktā.* See M.L. Metha, *Jaina Philosophy,* p. 95.
19. A.L. Basham, *History and Doctrines of the Ājīvikas,* Luzac, London, 1951.
20. Basham, *Ājīvikas,* p. 253.
21. Ibid. p. 240.
22. Ibid. p. 225.

Despite the decidedly amoral tone of the Ājīvika theory of transmigration, it resembles the Jain theory in that both assume a changing soul. The soul of the Ājīvika system is limited in lifespan. The Jain soul is everlasting. Nonetheless, both systems agree that the soul evolves in the course of its transmigratory journey from a state of bondage to a state of liberation. The importance of the concept of the evolution of the soul from an original state of bondage to a final state of release becomes important in distinguishing the liberation doctrines of the heterodox schools of Indian philosophy from those of the *Upaniṣads* and related orthodox schools of classical Hinduism.

Though these orthodox schools accepted souls, rebirth and release, they conceived of liberation as the realization of the pre-existing, innate purity of the soul. That is to say that in line with their Vedic orthodoxy they conceived of liberation in terms of a cosmological model in which the state of release is thought of as a return to an original state of purity, analogous to the state of cosmic purity which existed before the universe was created. The distinctively non-Vedic concept of the evolving, changing soul, on the other hand, is less cosmological in orientation. In Jainism and Ājīvikism, liberation is conceived of as an individual attainment achieved, or arrived at as the case may be, in the context of the given universe.

In the *Upaniṣads* the universe is not taken for granted, but is assumed to be the result of the creative activity of the unitary cosmogonic principle postulated in the *Vedas*. The *Upaniṣads* also contain much that is obviously not Vedic material, but probably originates instead in the beliefs of non-Vedic systems of thought such as the archaic Jain and Ājīvika systems outlined above.

The *Upaniṣads* are the earliest surviving texts which propound the non-Vedic concepts of: 1) a soul which necessarily survives death as the basis of individual identity, 2) the repeated transmigration of the soul, and 3) release of the soul from transmigration as the *summum bonum*. On the other hand, there is a Vedic trend in the Upaniṣadic doctrine of the soul, rebirth and release. The *Upaniṣads* are concerned with resolving Vedic questions about the origin and nature of the universe. On the basis of Vedic speculations, some Upaniṣadic passages hold that yogic release is not only a realization and participation in the essential nature of the soul, but also a realization and participation in the essential nature of the universe. In such passages the soul is regarded as an ultimate or the ultimate cosmological principle, and yogic psychology is thus bound up with Vedic cosmology.

A large part of the impetus behind the original Upaniṣadic syntheses of these concepts must have been a desire to maintain inherited Vedic cosmological doctrines against the onslaught of the persuasive, practical and no doubt popular yogic teachings. The nature of yogic meditation may have been an equally important factor. Yogic *samādhi* reveals unity and changelessness at the root of human consciousness, and a passive, utterly subjective state in the light of which the manifold, changing universe seems, if not positively illusory, at most insignificant. The equation of this state with the Vedic concept of the universal principle may be an attempt to verbalize the indescribable yogic experience by resorting to the evocative images of ancient mythology.

At any rate, the outcome of the Upaniṣadic synthesis was a genuine transformation of both Vedic and non-Vedic thought. This synthesis was influential not only in almost all subsequent orthodox psychological thought, and probably in heterodox psychology as well, Buddhism in particular. Let us proceed now to an examination of the development of some of the Upaniṣadic treatments of rebirth, release and the soul to see how this synthesis was worked out in the ancient texts themselves.

The Development of Rebirth Theories in the *Upaniṣads:*

The Vedic theory of afterlife outlined above in Chapter 2 is not completely abandoned in the *Upaniṣads*, though in most cases reference to the Vedic theory are vestigial remnants incorporated into some form of rebirth theory. The *Upaniṣads* carry on enthusiastically with the Vedic practice of proposing correspondences between the individual's vital and mental faculties and the elements of the universe. The following passage even suggests the Vedic theory of the dispersion at death of these faculties into their universal counterparts.[23] In this passage the pupil Ārthabhāga asks, citing an extended list of correspondences:

> When the speech (voice) of this dead person enters into fire, the breath into air, the eye into the sun, the mind into the moon, hearing into the quarters, the self *(ātman)* into the ether *(ākaśa),* the hairs of the body into the herbs, the hairs on the head into the trees and the blood and the semen are deposited in water, what then becomes of this person *(puruṣa)*?
>
> B.U. 3.2.13 (R)

The question is essentially Vedic, but the sage Yajñāvalkya goes on to answer with the non-Vedic doctrine conditioned by *karma.*

> 'Ārthabhāga, my dear, take my hand. We two alone shall know of this, this is not for us two (to speak of) in public.' The two went away and deliberated. What they said was *karman* and what they praised was *karman.* Verily one becomes good by good action *(karma),* bad by bad action.
>
> B.U. 3.2.13 (R)

Yajñāvalkya's secrecy has been taken as an indication that early in the Upaniṣadic period the doctrine of rebirth was considered a dangerously unorthodox belief. By and large, though, rebirth is the predominant afterlife theory in the *Upaniṣads.* The *Upaniṣads* allude to both of the Vedic modes of survival of death, but such allusions usually occur in the course of propounding typically Upaniṣadic theories of rebirth and release. It will be remembered that according to the Vedic theory of afterlife, which centers around the concept of the *tanū,* there are two modes of survival after death: 1) in heaven, where one creates for himself a *tanū* by means of ritual acts while alive, and 2) on earth in the form of one's offspring, an aspect of

---

23. Cp. *Ṛg* 10.16.3; 10.59.5-7; 10.58; 10.161.5. Cp. *Īśa* U. 17.

one's *tanū*, who must continue to maintain the deceased ancestor's heavenly tanu by performing further rituals.

At one point in a protracted discourse on the nature of *brahman*, Yajñāvalkya, perhaps in order to demonstrate his competence as a priest, states that death may be overcome by performing a certain type of ritual.[24] Such ritual performance supposedly would result in a heavenly afterlife along Vedic lines, but it becomes clear in the course of his teaching that Yajñāvalkya considers yogic release to be the only final escape from death.[25]

More to the point is a comparison of the Naciketas stories in the *Katha Upaniṣad* and the *Taittirīya Brāhmaṇa.* In both accounts, Naciketas' second wish, granted by Yama the king of the realm of the dead, is to know the exact procedure of the ritual that will secure for its performer an afterlife in heaven.[26] In the *Taittirīya Brāhmaṇa*, Naciketas' third wish is to learn how to gain freedom from *punar mṛtyu* (re-death).[27] In the Upaniṣadic version his third wish is to know whether or not one exists after having attained yogic release.[28] This has the effect of relegating the attainment of heaven through ritual, the second wish, to a secondary level of importance. The implication of the *Upaniṣad* is that attainment of heaven is not final salvation, a common assertion in the *Upaniṣads*.

The Vedic theory of survival in heaven and in one's offspring is elaborated upon in the *Aitareya Upaniṣad* in a passage already considered above in Chapter 2. As noted there, it is possible that the entire second section of this *Upaniṣad*, which deals with the three births of the soul (conception, birth, and heavenly birth) contains no

---

24. B.U. 3.1.3.

25. B.U. 3.9.26-28.

26. K.U. 1.1.12-19.

27. *Punar-mṛtyu*, "death again (from heaven)". See T.B. 3.11.8 and Keith, *Religion and Philosophy*, pp. 440-41.

28. K.U. 1.1.20. Though *prete* means only "with regard to one who has departed", there is little doubt that the reference is to liberation rather than mere death, since Naciketas has already asked how to attain an afterlife in heaven, and since the explanation given by Yama involves the practice of *yoga* (K.U. 1.2.12) and discovery of the true soul (K.U. 1.3.15).

reference to rebirth, and is entirely an exposition of the Vedic afterlife theory. In this passage, heavenly immortality, the third birth of the soul, is apparently presented as the *summum bonum* of human existence. Other portions of this *Upaniṣad* imply a monistic concept of release, though the universal principle is often spoken of theistically as Brahmā. At any rate, the first two births in this passage, the conception and physical birth of one's child, refer to survival in the form of one's offspring, who are expected to perform, on behalf of the father, "meritorious rituals" *(puṇyebhyaḥ karmabhyaḥ)*, or less likely, "pious deeds", as Radhakrinan translates:

> He (the son) who is one self of his (father) is made his substitute for (performing) pious deeds. Then the other self of his (father's) having accomplished his work, having reached his age, departs. So departing hence, he is,indeed, born again. That is the third birth.
>
> A.U. 2.4 (R)

Here, the third birth, whereby the father is born again *(punar jāyate)*, could refer to rebirth, but the third birth is described as birth into an immortal heavenly life.

> He, knowing thus and springing upward, when the body is dissolved, enjoyed all desires in that world of heaven and became immortal, yea, became (immortal).
>
> A.U. 2.6 (R)

Be that as it may, on the whole, the second Vedic mode of survival, survival in the form of one's offspring, is taken more seriously in the *Upaniṣads* than heavenly survival. In the *Kauṣītakī Upaniṣad*, the son is said to be the *ātman* of his father,[29] and later in the same passage this theme is elaborated upon in a description of the *pitā-putrīyam* or "father-son ceremony", to be performed when the father is on his death bed. In this ceremony the father's vital and mental faculties, along with his *karma*, pleasure, pain and procreation,

29. Ks.U. 2.11.

are ritually transferred to the son.[30] A similar ceremony is described in the *Bṛhadāraṁyaka Upaniṣad,* where it is said:

> When a man thinks that he is about to depart, he says to his son, 'You are *Brahman,* you are the sacrifice and you are the world.' ... Being thus the all, let him (the son) preserve me from (the ties of) this world, thus, (the father thinks) ... When one who knows this departs from this world, he enters into his son together with his breaths. Whatever wrong has been done by him, his son frees him from it all, therefore he is called a son. By his son a father stands firm in this world.
>
> B.U. 1.5.17 (R)

In general, hereditary survival in the for of one's offspring retains more independent importance in the *Upaniṣads* than does heavenly survival. Overall, the *Upaniṣads* degrade the Vedic heavenly mode of survival in the world of the ancestors to a possibly pleasant but insecure situation from which one is certain to undergo "death again" *(punar-mṛtyu).* In the *Brāhmaṇas* there is no clear concept of what happens after this *punar-mṛtyu,* which is presented there as a vague threat against one who neglects his ritual duties. Several Upaniṣadic passages speculate that death from the world of the ancestors, which is inevitable, results in birth again in the mundane sphere.

> 9. The immature, living manifoldly in ignorance, think 'we have accomplished our aim'. Since those who perform rituals do not understand (the truth) because of attachment, therefore they sink down, wretched, when their worlds (i.e. the fruits of their merits) are exhausted.
>
> 10. These deluded men, regarding sacrifices and works of merits as most important, do not know any other good. Having enjoyed in the high place of heaven won by good deeds, they enter again this world or a still lower one.
>
> Mu.U. 1.2.9-10 (R)

---

30. Ks.U. 2.15.

Thus, one Upaniṣadic rebirth theory, combining elements of both Vedic and yogic afterlife theories, pictures rebirth as a cyclical process alternating between this world, the human world *(manuṣya-loka)* and the Vedic ancestral world *(pitṛ-loka)*. A third possibility, gained through wisdom, is the divine world *(deva-loka)*, in most cases a metaphorical reference to yogic release. Similar passages in the *Bṛhadāraṇyaka* and *Chāndogya Upaniṣads*, deal extensively with this cyclical process of rebirth.[31] Both passages present an account of the "five fires" and the two alternative paths after death: the divine path *(deva-yāna)* and the path of the ancestors *(pitṛ-yāna)*.[32] Both the "five fires doctrine" and the "two paths doctrine" converge upon the cremation ceremony, which is depicted as a sacrifice.

> They carry him to (be offered in) fire. His fire itself becomes the fire, fuel the fuel, smoke the smoke flame the flame coals the coals, sparks the sparks. In this fire the gods offer a person *(puruṣa)*. Out of this offering the person, having the colour of light, arises.
>
> B.U. 6.2.14 (R)

In order to understand the present passage fully, it must be remembered that in the Vedic sacrificial context, fire is thought to both consume and transform that which it burns. Mundane offerings, burned in the sacrificial fire are thought to be transformed into a form accessible to the gods. The burned offerings become, in fact, the sustenance of the gods. Agni, the god of fire, is thought of as the messenger or oblation bearer of the gods, since fire serves as the intermediary between the mundane and divine spheres. Similarly, the cremation fire in the above passage transforms the deceased, the offering as it were, into a purified essence acceptable to the gods. In the *Upaniṣad*, however, this purified essence is the soul (*puruṣa*, lit. "person"). Alluding to Vedic sacrificial theory, this soul, like any

---

31. B.U. 6.2.9-16 and C.U. 5.4.10. Less extensive versions of the same occur at C.U. 4.15.5; Ks.U. 1.2.3; and P.U. 1.9.10.

32. These two paths are mentioned at *Ṛg* 10.88.5, but apparently refer to a different belief. Cp. *Ṛg* 1.72.7.

other offering, is said to become food for the gods. To this end, it enters the path of the ancestors, a desirable fate in the *Vedas*, but here a rather gruesome alternative.

> But those who by sacrificial offerings, charity and austerity conquer the worlds, they pass into the smoke (of the cremation fire), from the smoke into the night, from the night into the half-month of the waning moon, from the half-month of the waning moon into the six months during which the sun travels southward, from these months into the world of the fathers *(pitṛ-loka)*, from the world of the fathers into the moon. Reaching the moon they become food. There the gods, as they say to king Soma, increase, decrease, even so feed upon them there.
>
> B.U. 6.2.16 (R)

It will be remembered that in the Vedic context the gods, like humans, are thought to perform sacrifices, and are thought to be sustained by the sacrifices of humans. Similarly, in this Upaniṣadic passage, the gods, sustained by the offerings of humans, in this case the souls of the deceased, perform the heavenly fire sacrifice. Their offering is faith *(śraddhā)*, which, apparently along with the human souls they have eaten, is transformed in the heavenly fire into *soma*. This is the first of the five great sacrificial fires, the fire of "that world".

> Yonder world, Gautama, is (sacrificial) fire. The sun itself is its fuel, the rays its smoke; the day the flame, the quarters the coals, the intermediate quarters the sparks. In this fire the gods offer faith. Out of that offering King Soma arises.
>
> B.U. 6.2.9 (R)

Soma, a plant god, in the Vedic context is thought to be brought from heaven to the earth by rain. For this reason, the second great fire in the Upaniṣadic passage is the fire of Parjanya the rain god. In it the offering, *soma*, along with the souls that it now contains, is transformed into rain.

> Parjanya (the god of rain), Gautama, is fire. The year itself is its fuel, the clouds its smoke, the lightning the flame, the thunder-bolt the coals, the thundering the sparks. In this fire the gods offer the king Soma. Out of that offering rain arises.
>
> B.U. 6.2.10 (R)

This rain, the essence of *soma,* divine food, falls upon the earth carrying the souls of the deceased, and is there transformed into vegetation in the third great sacrificial fire, the fire of "this world".

> This world, verily, Gautama, is fire. The earth itself is its fuel, fire the smoke, night the flame, the moon the coals, the stars the sparks. In this fire the gods offer rain. Out of that offering food arises.
>
> B.U. 6.2.11 (R)

When these food plants, containing souls, are eaten, they are offered in the fourth sacrificial fire, the "man-fire", the digestive fire, and are transformed into semen.

> The person (man) verily, Gautama, is fire. The open mouth itself is its fuel, vital breath *(prāṇa)* the smoke, speech the flame, the eye the coals, the ear the sparks. In this fire the gods offer food. Out of that offering semen arises.
>
> B.U. 6.2.12 (R)

This semen, offered in the "woman fire", the fifth great sacrificial fire, the sexual fire, is transformed into a person *(puruṣa)* in the *Bṛhadāraṇyaka* version, or an embryo *(garbha)* in the *Chāndogya* version.

> The woman, verily, Gautama, is fire. The sexual organ itself is its fuel; the hairs the smoke, the vulva the flame, when one inserts, the coals; the pleasurable feelings the sparks. In this fire, the gods offer semen. Out of that offering a person arises. He lives as long as he lives. Then when he dies, they carry him to (be offered in) fire.
>
> B.U. 6.2.13-14 (R)

Returning to B.U. 6.2.16, it is clear that the "path of the ancestors", the path of the reincarnating soul, is in fact a journey through the five fires.

> When that (being food) passes away from them, they pass forth into this space, from space into air, from air into rain, from rain into the earth. Reaching the earth they become food. Again, they are offered in the fire of man. Thence they are born in the fire of woman with a view to going to other worlds. Thus do they rotate.
>
> B.U. 6.2.16 (R)

Those who do not find such prospects in the afterlife particularly appalling should take note of the *Chāndogya Upaniṣad's* version of the two paths. The *Chāndogya* observes that, obviously, an animal rather than a person might eat the plant containing one's soul, in which case, one would be reborn as an animal.[33]

In the Upaniṣadic context, the world of the ancestors is not even a potentially immortal condition as it is in the Vedic context. Instead, it is a strictly temporary stage in the endless revolving of the soul through the universal fire. The similarity of this idea to the Jain notion of the transmigration of the soul through mineral, vegetable and animal life is striking, though possibly coincidental. At any rate, the Upaniṣadic cyclical theory of rebirth simultaneously preserves and transforms several Vedic concepts in a synthesis with the non-Vedic belief in rebirth.

The perpetual consumption of the transmigrating soul by the gods and the universal fire is a common mode of expression for Upaniṣadic pessimism regarding mundane life. Early in the *Bṛhadāraṇyaka Upaniṣad* it is said that death or hunger, which are equivalent, created the universe as food for himself.[34] Later in the same *Upaniṣad*, death is equated with fire, the universal consumer.

---

33. C.U. 5.10.6-7.

34. B.U. 1.2.1-5.

'Yajñāvalkya', said he, 'since everything here is food for death, what, pray, is that divinity for whom death is food?' 'Fire, verily, is death. It is the food of water. He (who knows this) overcomes further death *(punar-mṛtyu)*.'

B.U. 3.2.10 (R)

It is seemingly a paradox that this same universal fire which is equated with death, is also equated with life.

This fire which is here within a person is the Vaiśvanāra (the universal fire) by means of which the food that is eaten is cooked (digested). It is the sound thereof that one hears by covering the ears thus. When one is about to depart (from this life) one does not hear this sound.

B.U. 5.9.1 (R)

Only the ignorant person, however, fails to perceive that the digestive fire consuming food within him is only an aspect of the universal fire in which he himself is consumed as the food of the living universe.

Thus, the Vedic doctrine that the gods are sustained by sacrifice is subtly transformed in the *Upaniṣads*. The *Vedas* assert that ritual is vital in maintaining the cosmic order. The *Upaniṣads*, by and large, condemn ritual as an inadequate mode of spirituality whereby human beings are kept in ignorance of their true divine nature, and thereby continue to serve the gods by remaining within their food chain.[35]

Whoever knows thus, 'I am *Brahman*, becomes this all. Even the gods cannot prevent his becoming thus, for he becomes their self. So whoever worships another divinity (than his self) thinking that he is one and *(Brahman)* another, he knows not. He is like an animal to the gods. Even if one animal is taken away, it causes displeasure, what should one say of many (animals)? Therefore it is not pleasing to those (gods) that men should know this.

B.U. 1.4.10 (R)

---

35. See also B.U. 4.4.6; Mu. U. 1.2.10.

Needless to say, the Vedic doctrine of ritual as a means of attaining salvation is seriously undermined by the cyclical rebirth theory, even though it preserves certain Vedic characteristics. The *Chāndogya* version of the cyclical rebirth theory specifies morality as the criterion which determines one's fate. In the future life conduct in this life will result in a favorable rebirth, which will follow after a cyclical celestial interlude.

> Those whose conduct here has been good will quickly attain a good birth (literally womb), the birth of a Brahmin, the birth of a Kṣatriya or the birth of a Vaisya. But those whose conduct here has been evil, will quickly attain an evil birth, the birth of a dog, the birth of a hog, or the birth of a Candala.
>
> C.U. 5.10.7 (R)

Other passages expounding cyclical rebirth suggest that one's reward or punishment for actions in this life consist of a longer or shorter stay in the heavenly world before being born again in the mundane world.[36]

> Exhausting the results of whatever works he did in this world, he comes again from that world, to this world for (fresh) work.
>
> B.U. 4.4.6 (R)

The cyclical theory de-emphasizes but retains Vedic concerns with the influence of ritual upon the afterlife. A second form of rebirth theory found in the *Upaniṣads* does away with the role of ritual altogether. For want of a better term, this may be called the linear theory of rebirth. According to this theory the soul transmigrates directly, without a repetitive celestial interlude, to another body, the excellence of which is determined solely by the moral quality of one's actions. The following passage graphically depicts the direct transition of the soul to another body.

---

36. See again B.U. 4.4.6; Mu.U. 1.2.10.

> Just as a leech (or caterpillar) when it has come to the end of a blade of grass, after having made another approach (to another blade) draws itself together towards it, so does this self *(ātman)*, after having thrown away this body, and dispelled ignorance, after having another approach (to another body) draw itself together (for making the transition to another body).
>
> B.U. 4.4.3 (R)

A later verse in the same passage indicates that not only actions, but also desires and intentions play a role in determining one's destiny after death.

> Others, however, say that a person consists of desires. As is his desire so is his will; as is his will, so the deed he does, whatever deed he does, that he attains.
>
> B.U. 4.4.5 (R)

This passage shows a striking resemblance to Buddhist ideas about *karma* and rebirth, in that here *karma* (action) is only a symptom of the deeper psychological tendencies which actually determine one's fate in *saṁsāra*.

In neither the *Upaniṣads* nor Buddhism, however, is a pleasant rebirth particularly to be desired in itself. It should not be imagined that the designation linear is meant to imply that this type of rebirth is conceived of in the *Upaniṣads* as a mode of progress toward the *summum bonum*. The ultimate goal, like the mechanism of rebirth, is conceived of in different ways in the *Upaniṣads*. The texts are unanimous, however, in the opinion that knowledge, not goodness, is the criterion for ultimate salvation, the complete cessation of rebirth forever. Preoccupation with merit may even be a severe disadvantage with respect to attaining release.

> These deluded men, regarding sacrifices and works of merits as most important, do not know any other good. Having enjoyed in the high place of heaven won by good deeds, they enter again this world or a still lower one.
>
> Mu.U. 1.2.10 (R)

This is an important point of distinction between the linear rebirth theories of archaic Jainism or Ājīvikism and the linear theory of the *Upaniṣads*. In the Ājīvika theory, the soul progresses along a predetermined course until it reaches its inevitable extinction. The Jains, even in the classical system, conceive of the soul as progressing toward the top of the universe as the various karmic defilements which prevent it from rising are "burned off" by severe ascetic practices and the extreme observance of non-violence. Knowledge, in the Jain theory of salvation, plays a secondary role to morality and asceticism, and is thought to evolve naturally as the soul is unburdened of its *karma*. On this point, the doctrines of Buddhism are closer to those of the *Upaniṣads* than they are to those of the heterodox traditions. In both the *Upaniṣads* and Buddhism, some form of wisdom, rather than morality, is the ultimate criterion of salvation.

Release and Cosmology in the *Upaniṣads*:

The *Upaniṣads* are unanimous regarding the primacy of wisdom in attaining release, and in all cases this saving knowledge involves a radical departure from the transmigratory path of rituals and works. The nature of this saving knowledge, however, is characterized in several different ways. Normally it is mystical knowledge of the unity of the soul and the universal principle, but in some cases it is knowledge of a theistic god[37] or even knowledge of the esoteric meaning of certain rituals or doctrines.[38]

As might be expected, the precise nature of release is itself not consistently described in the *Upaniṣads*. The various concepts of final liberation fall into two broad categories: 1) concepts similar to the archaic Jain idea, where release is the attainment of a permanent heavenly existence by an individual soul, and 2) concepts more in line with Vedic cosmological concerns, in which release is not only a cessation of rebirth, but also a revelation of the origin and nature of

37. S.U. 2.15; 5.13-14; 6.13.

38. A.U. 3.6; C.U. 5.24.1-4; C.U. 5.10.10; 10.1; B.U. 6.2.15.

the cosmos and a return to the original principle underlying creation. Let us deal briefly with the first category, as it is of far less importance in the general scheme of the *Upaniṣads* than the second.

In the previously examined passage propounding cyclical theory of rebirth, release is depicted as a simple ascent *via* the divine path *(deva-yāna)* to a permanent heaven called the world of Brahmā. Thus, when the liberated person is laid on the funeral pyre:

> Those who know this as such and those too who meditate with faith in the forest on the truth, pass into the light, from the light into the day, from the day into the half-month of the waxing moon, from the half-month of the waxing moon into the six months during which the sun travels northward, from these months into the world of the gods, from the world of the gods into the sun, from the sun into the lightning (fire). Then a person consisting (born) of mind goes to those regions of lightning and leads them to the worlds of Brahmā. In those worlds of Brahmā they live for long periods. Of these there is no return.
>
> B.U. 6.2.15 (R)

This concept of heavenly release is not limited to the cyclical rebirth theory, and in addition to the world of Brahmā,[39] the heavenly region is also called simply "heaven" *(svarga)*,[40] the "divine world" *(deva-loka)*[41] or even left unnamed.[42] Some passages of this category are overtly theistic and the knowledge required for release is knowledge of a personified god.[43] Some descriptions of release in a heavenly realm may be metaphorical treatments of monistic or quasi-monistic material.[44] Other Upaniṣadic passages refer to a simple concept of release of the soul very similar to the Jain notion of ascent to the top

---

39. B.U. 4.3.32-3; 4.4.23; 6.2.15; C.U. 5.10.2; 8.3; 8.12.6; P.U. 1.16; 5.5.

40. *Kena* U. 4.9; B.U. 4.4.8; K.U. 1.1.13.

41. B.U. 1.5.3.

42. C.U. 8.6.5-6; B.U. 5.10.

43. S.U. 3.7; 5.13-14; 6.13; Mu.U. 3.1.2-3, where self and lord *(Īśa)* are distinguished.

44. See B.U. 4.1; 4.3.32-3; 4.4.6; 4.4.23-5; 5.15. C.U. 3.12.7-9 compared to C.U. 3.6-11. Ks.U. 1.6 compared to Ks.U. 1.2-3. See also C.U. 4.15.5; 8.3; 8.13-14.

of the given universe. Of course, Vedic mythological notions are often retained in such treatments.

We may note in passing that Buddhism, though denying the soul, contains a similar notion with regard to the "non-returner" *(anāgāmin)*. Upon death the non-returner is reborn in the "pure abodes" *(suddhāvāsa)*, which guarantees his eventual attainment of *nirvāṇa* without returning from that world to the mundane sphere.[45] Similarly, in the *Upaniṣads* those who pass into the light of the cremation fire are said not to return from the worlds of Brahma.[46] In these Upaniṣadic passages, however, heavenly rebirth seems to be thought of as the *summum bonum* rather than an intermediate stage before ultimate release as in the Buddhist theory of the non-returner.

Some Upaniṣadic passages, on the other hand, take a critical attitude toward the possibility of attaining permanent heavenly release while retaining individual identity.[47] These passages seem to foreshadow Śaṅkara's view that a heavenly release, such as that described as the culmination of the divine path in the *Bṛhadāraṇyaka Upaniṣad*, may be called permanent only in the sense that it may last until the end of the present world cycle.[48] Other passages which may originally have been intended to refer to a similar heavenly immortality are interpreted by Śaṅkara as being metaphorical treatments of monistic release,[49] and again, several Upaniṣadic passages foreshadow Śaṅkara's interpretation.

Perhaps the clearest example of this is the description in the *Kauṣītakī Upaniṣad* of the path to the world of Brahmā. As in the mythological description of the two paths after death, the moon is depicted as the door to heaven or rebirth. But here, the moon poses a question to the deceased: "Who are you?" A wrong answer results in rebirth, but the correct answer, "I am you", wins entry into the divine path. Reaching the world of Brahmā by this path, after having

---

45. See *Puggala Paññatti*, para. 42-46 (PTS).

46. As at B.U. 6.2.15: *teṣām na punar āvṛttiḥ*.

47. C.U. 8.1.6; K.U. 1.2.10.

48. See Śaṅkara's commentary on B.U. 6.2.15; K.U. 1.1.13; 1.2.10.

49. See Śaṅkara's commentary on B.U. 4.3.32; 4.4.23; 4.4.8; *Kena* U. 4.9.

met several of the gods and been garlanded by nymphs, the deceased finds Brahmā reclining on a couch an is asked again, "Who are you?" He should answer:

> I am season, I am connected with the seasons. From space as the source I am produced as the seed for a wife, as the light of the year, as the self of every single being. You are the self of every single being. What you are, that am I.
>
> Ks.U. 1.6 (R)

Thus, some Upaniṣadic passages seem content to adopt a basically Jain theory of release as the simple ascent of the individual soul to a heavenly realm which is presided over, in the Upaniṣadic context, by the deity Brahmā. This tendency represents a synthesis of the archaic yogic notion of the rebirth and release of the soul and the Vedic mythology of heaven. There is, however, evidence in the *Upaniṣads* themselves of dissatisfaction with this concept. The result is a tendency to represent heavenly salvation as a metaphorical expression of the monistic unity of the essence of the individual with the essence of the cosmos, an idea which neither the Vedic nor the non-Vedic antecedents of the *Upaniṣads* can adequately account for alone. Thus, an examination of the second category of concepts of release in the *Upaniṣads* — in which release represents monistic union with the universal principle — necessitates an examination of the expansion in the *Upaniṣads* of the non-Vedic concept of the individual soul into a cosmological principle.

Soul and Cosmology in the *Upaniṣads:*

In the Indian context, the concept of individual identity inhering in an immortal soul which necessarily survives death is traced to its earliest form in ancient, non-Vedic systems such as Jainism. Similarly simple concepts of the soul, more or less independent of cosmological concerns, also occur in several Upaniṣadic passages. Some of the rebirth passages cited above, in which an individual soul transmigrates from body to body and may attain release within the context of the given cosmos, are examples of such a concept. Even Yajñāvlkya's famous discourse to Janaka of Videha,[50] — in which he expounds upon the soul *(ātman)* as the "person *(puruṣa)* made of awareness *(vijñāna)* among the breaths *(prāṇa)*, the light in the heart" — contains little that suggests a universalistic interpretation of the soul. Of course, other passages attributed to Yajñāvalkya are explicitly monistic.

Interestingly, the fact that the discourse to Janaka lacks any overt universalism, and is at the same time a penetrating treatment of the nature and scope of individual consciousness, brings it to the brink of solipsism. In the following passage from that discourse, the universe is not given, but rather is presented as a projection by the soul in the state of dreaming:

> There are no chariots there, nor animals to be yoked to them, no roads, but he creates (projects for himself) chariots, animals to be yoked to them and roads. ... He, indeed is the agent (maker or creator).
>
> B.U. 4.3.10 (R)

The implication is that the soul which creates the dream world may also create the waking world. Indeed no specific ontological distinction is drawn between the two worlds of waking and dreaming.

> After having tasted enjoyment in this state of deep sleep ... dream ... waking, after having roamed about and seen good and evil, he returns again as he came to the place from which he started to the state of dream.
>
> B.U. 4.3.15-17 (R)

Later in this section, a haunting repetition of the description of the transition between these three states of consciousness is applied to the transition between rebirths.

50. B.U. 4.3.

> When this (body) gets to thinness, whether he gets to thinness through old age or disease, just as a mango or a fig or a fruit of the peepul tree releases itself from its bond (gets detached from its stalk), even so this person frees himself from these limbs and returns again as he came to the place from which he started back to (new) life.
>
> B.U. 4.3.36 (R)

Indeed, in the section immediately following the above passages, one of the descriptions of the mechanism of rebirth assigns a creative function to the soul that is reminiscent of the creative capabilities of the dreaming soul.

> And as a goldsmith, taking a piece of gold turns it into another, newer and more beautiful shape, even so does this self, after having thrown away this body and dispelled its ignorance, make unto himself another, newer and more beautiful shape like that of the fathers or of the *gandharvas*, or of the gods or of Prajāpati or of Brahmā or of other beings.
>
> B.U. 4.4.4 (R)

It is noteworthy too, in this group of passages, that the reabsorption of the sense faculties into the soul is also described in similar terms with reference to deep sleep and death, both of which are portrayed as unconscious states from which the soul eventually emerges unharmed. Thus, when a person goes to sleep, it is said:

> Verily, when there (in the state of deep sleep) he does not see, he is, verily seeing, though he does not see, for there is no cessation of the seeing of a seer, because of the imperishability (of the seer). there is not, however, a second, nothing else separate from him that he could see.
>
> B.U. 4.3.23 (R)

At the point of death, a similar retraction of the senses it is said to occur.

> He is becoming one, he does not see ... smell ... taste ... speak ... hear ... think ... touch ... know, they say. ... And when he thus departs, life departs after him.
>
> B.U. 4.4.2 (R)

The eventual re-projection of the sense faculties after the intermediate states of deep sleep or death is represented in the *Upaniṣads* as being tantamount to re-creation of the universe. In the preceding passages, which do not specify that the soul concerned is universal, creation of the universe in the dreaming and waking states is tantamount to solipsism.

Normally it is clearer than it is in the preceding passages that it is the universal, monistic aspect of the soul that is the ultimate source of the psychological projection of the universe through the senses.[51] In every case, though, the individual is thought to have an actual role in the creation and maintenance of the universe by virtue of the ultimate equality of the cosmic essence and the individual soul. Thus, as the afterlife and soteriological concerns of the yogic and Vedic traditions are combined in the *Upaniṣads,* so are their respective doctrines of the soul and the cosmos combined. "That one", the monistic principle of the *Vedas,* is equated with the individual soul of the yogic tradition. This identity, moreover, is said to be realized in the state of yogic release. The ultimate essence of the universe is thus equated with the ultimate essence of the individual, and the yogic realization of the true nature of the soul, resulting in release, is held to be a participation in and verification of a monistic cosmological doctrine inherited from the *Vedas.*

---

51. Other references to sleep and dreaming are obviously employed to teach the implications of monism. See C.U. 6.8; 8.10-12; P.U. 4; Ks.U. 3.3; 4.15; 4.19, and in particular, the entire Ma.U., all of which deals with sleep and dream, and which adds a fourth state, said to be higher than deep sleep, and equated with monistic release.

> That which is the subtle essence (the root of all) this whole world has for its self *(ātman)*. That is the true. That is the self. That art thou, Śvetaketu.
>
> C.U. 6.8.7 (R)

> On this there is the following verse: 'When all the desires that dwell in the heart are cast away, then does the mortal become immortal, then he attains *Brahman* here (in this very body).' Just as the slough of a snake lies on an anthill, dead, cast off, even so lies this body. But this disembodied, immortal life *(prāṇa)* is *Brahman* only, is light indeed, Your Majesty.
>
> B.U. 4.4.7 (R)

Vedic monism was mostly concerned with cosmogony. The monistic unity of the universe was confined to that time "in the beginning" when all was one and as yet undifferentiated. Vedic monism was a search for a unitary material and efficient cause of the universe, Upaniṣadic monism became an inquiry into the psychological creation of the universe by the universal self, the world soul, which is not only analogous to the individual soul, but actually identical to it. A cosmic analogy of desire as a cosmogonic force occurs at *Ṛg* 10.129. In the *Upaniṣads,* though, human desire itself, along with ignorance, is held directly responsible for the "creation" of the universe. The continued sustenance of the universe is also thought to be a result of the perpetuation of human psychological shortcomings.

As one would expect, a universe viewed in such a way is regarded pessimistically as a fundamentally unsatisfactory state of affairs. Just as ignorance and desire are defilements of the soul, so is the existential universe thought to be a defilement of the universal soul. Since the individual and universal soul are held to be ultimately identical, however, it is thought that one may, by dispelling human ignorance and desire, in effect reverse the cosmogonic process and return to the original state of purity and unity that existed "in the beginning". At this point it is useful to examine more closely this Upaniṣadic psychological cosmogony and its reversal in the attainment of release.

1. In the beginning this (world) was only the self, in the shape of a person. Looking around he saw nothing else than the self. He first said, 'I am'. Therefore arose the name of I. Therefore, even to this day when one is addressed he says first 'This is I' and then speaks whatever other name he may have. ...

3. He, verily, had no delight. Therefore he who is alone has no delight. He desired a second. He became as large as a woman and a man in close embrace. He caused that self to fall into two parts. From that arose husband and wife. Therefore, as Yajñāvalkya used to say, this (body) is one half of oneself, like one of the two halves of a split pea. Therefore this space is filled by a wife. He became united with her. From that human beings were produced.

4. She thought, 'How can he united with me after having produced me from himself? Well, let me hide myself'. She became a cow ... mare ... she-ass ... she-goat ... ewe, the other became a bull ... stallion ... he-ass ... he-goat ... ram and was united with her and from that ... he produced everything whatever exists in pairs, down to the ants.

B.U. 1.4.1-4 (R)

In this, the mythological section of the present account of creation, it should be noted that at every point, care is taken to link the universal self with the individual self. One's consciousness of self is identified with the original, universal self-consciousness. One's sexual urge is identified with the original desire for a second, and as a result of that desire, creation occurred then just as it does now, sexually. The preceding account is, however, quite obviously a metaphorical treatment of a theme which is in essence psychological. The psychological nature of the present cosmogony is more explicit in the following passage, a continuation of the previous passage, which states more directly the identity of the universal soul and the individual soul. Moreover, the following passage presents that identity as being more than merely an identity of origin. It is a real, contemporary identity which may be realized at any time if certain spiritual requirements are fulfilled.

7. At that time this (universe) was undifferentiated. It became differentiated by name and form *(nāma-rūpa)* (so that it is said) he

has such a name, such a shape. Therefore even today this (universe) is differentiated by name and shape *(nāma-rūpa)* (so that it is said) he has such a name, such a shape. He (the self) entered in here even to the tips of the nails, as a razor is (hidden) in the razor-case, or as fire in the fire-source. Him they see not for (as seen) he is incomplete, when breathing he is called the vital force *(prāṇa)*, when speaking voice, when seeing the eye, when hearing the ear, when thinking the mind *(manas)*. These are merely the names of his acts. He who meditates on one or another of them (aspects) he does not know for he is incomplete, with one or another of these (characteristics). The self is to be meditated upon for in it all these become one. This self is the foot-trace of all this, for by it one knows all this, just as one can find again by footprints (what was lost). He who knows this finds fame and praise. ...

9. They say, since men think that, by the knowledge of *Brahman*, they become all, what, pray, was it that *Brahman* knew by which it became all?

10. *Brahman*, indeed, was this in the beginning. It knew itself only as 'I am *Brahman*'. Therefore it became all. ... This is so even now. Whoever knows thus, 'I am *Brahman*,' becomes this all. ...

15. One should meditate only on the self as his (true) world. The work of him who meditates on the self alone as his world is not exhausted for, out of that very self he creates whatsoever he desires.

17. In the beginning this (world) was just the self, one only. He desired, 'Would that I had a wife, then I may have offspring. Would that I had wealth, then I would perform rites'. ... Therefore, to this day, a man who is single desires, 'Would that I had a wife, etc.' So long as he does not obtain each one of these, he thinks himself to be incomplete.

B.U. 1.4.7-17 (R)

In Vedic cosmogony, the postulated universal principle was pressed to account for both the material and the efficient causes of creation. Given this duality of creative force and material upon which to exert itself, it was thought that the origin of the present manifold universe would be adequately explained. In the present Upaniṣadic passage, however, the situation is somewhat different in that the original duality, characterized as sexual in verse three,[52] is approached psychologically in verse seven as "name and form".[53]

Even in the *Ṛg Veda,* name *(nāma)* was more than a mere verbal designation; it was one of the components of individual identity.[54] In the *Vedas, rūpa* meant primarily "visible characteristics" or even "color", and generally did not connote substance or individuality as the term "form" might suggest. In the present passage, then, the cosmogonic differentiation of the monistic universal principle by name-and-form does not indicate the operation of its force aspect upon its material aspect. Instead, *nāma-rūpa* indicates the illusory distinction created by the assignment of names to appearances. Thus in verse seven, the true, unitary reality of the self is not seen. Only its apparent activities, its forms, are given names, so that its true nature remains unknown. This ignorance, which creates multiplicity by assigning names to forms, is depicted in verse seventeen as being reinforced by desire, the objects of which are precisely these illusory distinctions in the innately complete self. And so the vicious cycle goes on until, by knowledge and the cessation of desire, which are also mutually supporting, one is able to stop the creative process. By implication, the creative process remains contemporary in the human mind.

The psychological nature of the creative duality may be clarified by an examination of the various metaphors, in addition to name and form, with which the concept is approached. The mythological male-female dichotomy has been noted above.[55] In several passages this sexual imagery is applied to mind *(manas)* and speech *(vak),* mind being male and speech female.[56] In a late passage in the *Śataptha Brāhmaṇa,* mind is directly equated with form, and speech with name.

---

52. See *Ṛg* 10.90.5, where it is said: "From him Virāj was born, and from Virāj, Puruṣa", referring to reciprocal generation. See also *Ṛg* 10.72.4: "Dakṣa sprang from Aditi, and Aditi from Dakṣa". Cp. B.U. 2.2.3.

53. See also C.U. 6.2-4; 8.14.

54. Cp. B.U. 3.2.12.

55. See also B.U. 1.2.4; 1.5.7 & 12.

56. See B.U. 1.2.4; 1.4.17; 1.5.7.

> Now, when he makes the libation to mind — form being mind, inasmuch as it is by mind that one knows, 'This is form' — he thereby obtains form; and when he makes the libation to speech — name being speech, inasmuch as it is by speech that he seizes (mentions) the name; — as far as there are form and name, so far, indeed extends this whole (universe); all this he obtains.
>
> S.B. 11.2.3.6 (SBE)

In the *Upaniṣads,* eye, an agent of the *manas,* is said to be the source and perceiver of forms, while the source and perceiver of names is still speech,[57] also regarded as a "sensual" agent of the mind.[58] There will be occasion in the next chapter to examine further the development of the concepts of mental and sensual faculties. For now, suffice it to say that in several passages the fundamental sensual pair is mind and speech, which correspond roughly with form and name,[59] male and female.

In a similar vein, the fundamental duality is presented in an even more overtly psychological form in which the mythological male-female imagery is abandoned and the two aspects of the monistic principle are characterized as perceiver and perceived,[60] internal *(antara)* and external *(bāhya),* i.e. subject and object,[61] or eater and food,[62] food being the object and the eater the subject. Though these two sets of creative dualities are not specifically coordinated in the texts themselves, a table of correspondences may be set up as follows. In this table, a + sign indicates a fundamental duality, and arrows indicate an evolutionary correspondence, horizontal arrows showing

57. See B.U. 1.6.1-2; 3.2.3 & 5. Cp. C.U. 5.18.2.

58. See B.U. 1.5.3; C.U. 3.18.2.

59. Cp. B.U. 2.2.3, where the head contains all forms *(viśva-rūpa).* Other texts pair speech with breath *(prāṇa)* (B.U. 6.4.20; C.U. 1.1.5). Elsewhere breath is the child of mind and speech (B.U. 1.2.4; 1.5.7 & 12; 1.4.17); *ātman* consists of mind, speech and breath (B.U. 1.5.3); and breath is superior to speech and mind (B.U. 6.8.7-13; C.U. 4.3.3; 5.1.1-16).

60. B.U. 1.4.14; 3.2.3-9; 4.3.23-30.

61. B.U. 2.5.19; 4.3.21; C.U. 4.12.7-8.

62. B.U. 1.2.5; 1.2.17; 1.4.6; 1.5.1; 3.8.8; 5.18.1; T.U. 3.7; 3.10.5.

cosmogonic correspondence and vertical arrows indicating psychological correspondence.

male	→	mind (or eye)	→	form
+		+		+
female	→	speech	→	name
		↓		↓
		perceiver	+	perceived
		↓		↓
		subject	+	object
		↓		↓
		eater	+	food

These correspondences are not so extensively drawn out in the *Upaniṣads,* the horizontal (cosmogonic) and vertical (psychological) parts of the table being more or less independent in actual usage. The ideas are related nonetheless. Consciousness and object are said to be mutually interdependent for the maintenance of individuality of any sort. In other words, cosmogony cannot proceed until both the subjective and objective elements of creation have evolved from the original duality (male/female, mind/speech, form/name). The clearest statement of this interdependence is found in the *Kauṣītakī Upaniṣad,* in a passage which is probably late and may even betray Buddhist influence.

> For truly, if there were no elements of being (name, form, odor, etc.), there would be no elements of intelligence (speech, eye, smell, etc.). Verily, if there would be no elements of intelligence, there would be no elements of being. For truly from either alone, no appearance *(rūpa)* whatsoever would be effected.
>
> Ks.U. 3.8 (H)

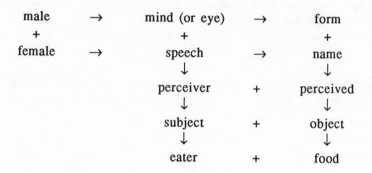

Thus, unlike Vedic cosmology, which explained the manifold universe as being the result of force acting upon matter, the Upaniṣadic cosmology employs the concept of subject operating on object and *vice versa*. Furthermore, creation in the *Vedas* was regarded as a good thing, whereas the *Upaniṣads* view it pessimistically as the occasion for suffering in a potentially endless round of rebirths. Release from rebirth may be gained only by resolving within the soul the creative duality and, as it were, reversing cosmogony. In the *Upaniṣads*, this resolution may be represented as a collapsing of the above table of correspondences.

> Just as the flowing rivers disappear in the ocean casting off name and shape *(nāma-rūpa)*, even so the knower, freed from name and shape, attains to the divine person, higher than the high.
>
> Mu.U. 3.2.8 (R)

> For where there is duality as it were, there one sees the other, one smells the other, one tastes the other, one speaks to the other, one hears the other, one thinks of the other, one touches the other, one knows the other. But where everything has become just one's own self, by what and whom should one speak ... hear ... think ... touch ... know? By what should one know him by whom all this is known? That self is (to be described as) not this, not this *(neti, neti)*.
>
> B.U. 4.5.15 (R)

In the synthetic psychological cosmogony of the *Upaniṣads*, the innermost essence of the individual, the soul or self, is the unitary cause of creation, and that is bad. The soul or self is also the focal point of the resolution of the apparently manifold universe back into its essential unity, and that is good. On the other hand, the soul is said to undergo within this universe suffering and transmigration, which is bad. But is may also attain release from transmigration and suffering, and that, of course, is good. Creation and resolution of the cosmos are fundamentally Vedic concern. Rebirth and release are originally the concerns of the non-Vedic *yoga* tradition. In the synthetic Upaniṣadic philosophy, all these concerns center around the nature of the soul, which given the nature of monism, must account for both the "good" and the "bad", or in a word, the eternal and changeable aspects of existence. Witness the confusion that may result from this overburdening of the concept of the soul:

> I know this undecaying, ancient ((primeval) self of all, present in everything on account of infinity. Of whom they declare, there is stoppage of birth. The expounders of *Brahman* proclaim him to be eternal.
>
> S.U. 3.21 (R)

Here, the soul *(ātman)* is universal and eternal on the one hand, but on the other hand it is this same soul which is to be released from the bondage of rebirth. In other words, the soul is both universal and individual. In some passages, these apparently contradictory aspects of the soul are intentionally juxtaposed in order to convey the inexpressibility of ultimate reality.

> This is my self within the heart, smaller than a grain of rice, than a barley corn, than a mustard seed, than a grain of millet or than the kernel of a grain of millet. This is my self within the heart, greater than the earth, greater than the atmosphere, greater than the sky, greater than these worlds.
>
> C.U. 3.14.3 (R)

In the end, however, it was thought necessary to impose conceptual consistency upon the Upaniṣadic teachings. These apparently contradictory attributes of the soul are reconciled in both the Advaita Vedānta system and the Sāṁkhya-Yoga system by adopting the expedient of declaring that there are actually two souls. One of these — the *liṅga-śarīra, jīvātman,* etc. — is active, involved in the world, transmigrating, and ultimately illusory. The other is aloof, inactive, unchanging and eternal: the *puruṣa* of Sāṁkhya-Yoga or the *paramātman* of Advaita Vedānta. There is little evidence that a genuine, individual and eternal *puruṣa* of Sāṁkhya ilk is to be found in the *Upaniṣads.*[63] There are, however, a number of proto-Sāṁkhya

63. Though Anima Sen Gupta has published two volumes, *Chāndogya Upaniṣad: Sāṁkhya Point of View* and *Katha Upaniṣad: Sāṁkhya Point of View,* M. Sen Publishing Co. Kanpur, which propose an exegesis of these *Upaniṣads* according to Sāṁkhya doctrines.

passages,[64] and the strict *puruṣa-prakṛti* dualism of the classical system is probably proposed as an answer to the present conceptual problem regarding the dual nature of the soul as individual and universal. The two soul doctrine of Advaita Vedānta, which addresses this same problem, is anticipated in various passages in the *Upaniṣads* themselves.

In the Advaita Vedānta system, the released soul is said to realize its essential identity with the unitary principle of the universe, which only appears to be diverse because of illusion *(māya)*. Śaṅkara compares this process to the reflection of the sun in a puddle "returning" to the sun when the water dries up.[65] In the Sāṁkhya-Yoga system, the liberated soul *(puruṣa)* realizes that it is individual and absolutely separate from matter *(prakṛti)*, and by nature perfectly calm, aloof, blissful, inactive and eternal. Matter, which evolves only in the presence of the *puruṣa*, is also stilled when the soul attains liberation.

Classical Sāṁkhya, retains the non-Vedic concept of a plurality of individual souls, but it is nonetheless cosmological in orientation. In the first place, in the classical system the soul *(puruṣa)* is eternal. It stands outside time and is absolutely changeless. It is an observer only, absolutely inactive; although it is individual, it is omnipresent. More importantly, as in the Advaita Vedānta system, the soul, strictly speaking, does not transmigrate. It merely observes the transmigration of certain mental aspects of *prakṛti*. The transmigratory self is an epiphenomenon of matter. In the last analysis, both the subject and the object evolve out of *prakṛti* solely for the sake of the enlightenment of the *puruṣa*, and both subject and object cease when the *puruṣa* realizes its own innate purity. In the classical Sāṁkhya system,

---

64. See K.U. 1.3.10-11 and 2.3.7-8, where several of the Sāṁkhya *tattvas* are named. S.U. 6 mentions Sāṁkhya and Yoga by name (vs. 13) and speaks of *pradhāna*, a synonym of *prakṛti* (vs. 10), the *guṇas* (vs. 4) and contrasts the *kṣetrajñā* and *pradhāna* (vs. 16), but there is little doubt that the passage expresses the doctrine of an all-embracing creator god rather than the strict duality of Sāṁkhya.

65. See Śaṅkara's commentary on P.U. 4.9.

however, this evolution and cessation of the universe takes place with reference to an individual *puruṣa*.

Śaṅkara's system is one step closer to Vedic concerns in that it denies the individuality of the soul. For Śaṅkara the *ātman* is, in effect, a subjectivized Hirānyagarbha which accounts for the entire cosmos. Both Śaṅkara and Sāṁkhya borrow from the Vedic and the non-Vedic traditions. Essentially, both classical systems integrate Vedic cosmogonic concerns with the non-Vedic theory of the soul. Moreover, the borrowed doctrine of yogic release is advanced, in the orthodox context, as a verification of essentially Vedic cosmological speculations.

In this complex tangle of origins, the position of Buddhism, fundamentally a heterodox yogic system, is not what might be immediately expected. In several surprising ways, Buddhism shares the concerns of the orthodox systems. Buddhism accepts the doctrine of rebirth, but due to its denial of the individual soul, there can be no transmigrating entity. This situation is roughly analogous to the situation in Sāṁkhya or Advaita Vedānta, where the transmigrating entity is ultimately illusory. Unlike these orthodox systems, however, Buddhism denied any entity — individual or universal — standing behind the process of rebirth. Though denying the soul, Buddhism accepts the yogic concept of liberation in its doctrine of *nirvāṇa*. Realization of *nirvāṇa* is regarded as final verification of the doctrine of no soul, ironically the antithesis of the doctrine said to be verified by yogic experience in the Sāṁkhya and Advaita Vedānta systems.

Because there is no soul in Buddhism, *nirvāṇa* cannot be like the Jain or Sāṁkhya concepts of the eternal survival of an individual entity; nor can it be like the Ājīvika concept of the extinction of an individual entity; nor can it be like the Advaita concept of merging with a universal entity. Thus, due to its no-soul doctrine, with regard to the question of the nature of release, Buddhism is as much cut off from its heterodox sister traditions as it is from orthodox system of philosophy.

This would seem to be the result of its having made use of, and having further transformed, the Upaniṣadic synthesis of Vedic and non-Vedic material. Of course, the Buddha need not have been directly aware of the *Upaniṣads* in order to have been influenced by ideas that are first expressed in them. The point is that such ideas were current at the time of the Buddha, and cannot be adequately explained as being developments entirely within either orthodox or heterodox thought.

The Buddha's denial of the soul may also have been influenced by the heterodox materialist schools (Carvaka or Lokayata) which flourished in his time. These schools left no texts and survive only in the hostile references of their opponents. According to these sources, the ancient Indian materialists either denied the soul altogether or asserted that the soul perished with the body.[66] In any case, the materialists denied rebirth or afterlife in any form. In some ways, the Ājīvikas propounded a doctrine of delayed materialism, in that they held that the soul inevitably would perish after an extremely long but nonetheless finite period of transmigration. In the ancient Indian context, both the Carvakas and the Ājīvikas regarded the final extinction of the soul as tantamount to liberation from the trials of mundane existence.

Such notions are in some ways similar to the Buddhist concept of *nirvāṇa*. Both are concepts of liberation without individual survival or merging with a universal essence. Buddhist *nirvāṇa*, however, aside from not representing the extinction of an entity, is in no sense inevitable, but is the result of tremendous effort.

On the other hand, Buddhist *nirvāṇa* is also similar in some ways to salvation in the orthodox systems of Sāṁkhya or Advaita Vedānta. In all three systems the immediate requirement for release is knowledge of the nature of reality rather than, as in the Jain system, an ascetic "burning up" of karmic impurities. Furthermore the Buddhists, concept of *nirvāṇa* has cosmological overtones which resemble Upaniṣadic notions. According to early Buddhism knowledge of the nature of reality is attainable through introspection. Successful introspection reveals that in each individual's case, the universe he experiences whether it exists or not, unfolds because of his own psychological activity. In the deluded person, this psychological activity is a manifestation of ignorance and desire, the two points at

66. See D1: 34-6.

which the chain of dependent origination *(paṭiccasamuppāda)* may be broken. Such Buddhist concepts are remarkably similar to the contemporary, reversible cosmogonies of Sāṁkhya and Advaita Vedānta. The following chapters examine some more specific points of similarity between Buddhist psychology and the synthetic speculations of the *Upaniṣads*. In many cases, early Buddhism seems to have availed itself of psychological concepts similar to those which appear to have been laboriously worked out in the *Upaniṣads* in the course of synthesizing Vedic and non-Vedic material.

Buddhism, from its very inception, stands astride an array of diverse, pre-Buddhist speculations. It survives more successfully than any single system of Indian philosophy on a bare minimum of conceptual intake from these antecedent speculations. Aside from his alleged spiritual excellence, the historical Buddha exhibited remarkable religious genius in his acute sensitivity to both the problems and the insight of the religious traditions of his time. The Buddha's system of thought, though highly original in many ways, also appears to have taken into account both the successes and the failures of religious and philosophical thought current at his time. This fund of thought, particularly rich in the area of psychological theory, represented many centuries of cumulative human experience funneled together from a remarkably wide range of sources.

Not in spite of, but because of their internal inconsistency, the *Upaniṣads* are an invaluable repository of the fund of cumulative human knowledge available at this pivotal point in the history of India and of the human race as a whole. In this regard, psychological speculations recorded in the *Upaniṣads* are of particular importance. These speculations record, however vaguely, the intellectual state of flux which resolved into the most sophisticated assessments of human consciousness the world would see for some two thousand years.

Chapter 5

Upaniṣadic Psychology

In the foregoing attempt to unravel the Vedic concept of the nature of the human being, the method employed was to try to discern the intent of several psychological terms by examining the contexts in which they are employed. What emerged from this examination was a fairly consistent, if rather vague picture of the natures and functions of various organs and faculties of the individual human being. The *Upaniṣads,* by contrast, present more explicit but widely varying concepts of what comprises the human being. The meanings of the psychological terms themselves are easier to ascertain in the *Upaniṣads* than they were in the *Ṛg Veda,* and in most cases where Upaniṣadic terms are similar to Vedic terms, their relationship to antecedent Vedic terms is clear. Many new terms appear in the *Upaniṣads,* however, Upaniṣadic psychology is even further complicated by a tendency to arrange and rearrange this enhanced list of the faculties of the individual into a welter of schemes and hierarchies which will be the primary subject matter of the present chapter.

Whereas individual identity was a rather complex matter in the *Ṛg Veda,* in the *Upaniṣads* the doctrine of the soul provides a relatively simple concept of human identity. This Upaniṣadic teaching appears to represent an appropriation of the even simpler yogic concept of the soul current among the Jains and Ājīvikas. Though perhaps somewhat unsophisticated, the Jain and Ājīvika doctrines of the soul functioned admirably to explain both personal identity and the mechanism of rebirth. The Upaniṣadic concept is complicated somewhat by the notion that this soul is also the monistic principle of the universe. Consideration of this complication may be postponed until the end of this chapter. Regardless of the metaphysical problems which plague the Upaniṣadic concept of the soul, psychologically speaking it provides a clear reference point around which the various vital and mental faculties may be arranged. Upaniṣadic terminology concerning the soul, however, is confused. This confusion is probably the result of a gradual shift in the *Upaniṣads* away from the vitalistic, Vedic notion of the human being, and toward the more psychological yogic concept. As a result of this gradual shift, conflicting vitalistic and psychological concepts of the soul are recorded side by side without apparent hesitation.

The term *tanū*, which represents the nearest approach to a concept of individuality in the Vedic context, is practically abandoned in the *Upaniṣads*, where *tanū* is more or less synonymous with *rūpa*, meaning "form or appearance".[1] The individual, immortal soul in which personal identity inheres is usually designated by one of the three terms *ātman*, *puruṣa* and *prāṇa*.[2] Due to the incorporation of Vedic monism into the theory of the soul, each of these terms may also denote the universal principle. None of these terms, however, not even *ātman*, always has universal connotations. *Ātman*, for example, sometimes seems to mean "body". Śaṅkara, often unjustifiably, interprets *ātman* as body whenever it suits his purposes, as often it does give some of the vitalistic characterizations of the soul in the *Upaniṣads*. In the following passage he is possibly correct in so interpreting the last instance of the term, since the five desires seem to be paralleled by the five parts of the person, leaving the original, universal *ātman* equated with *manas*.

> In the beginning this (world) was just the self *(ātman)*, the only. He desired, 'would that I had a wife, then I may have offspring. Would that I had wealth, then I would perform rites.'... Therefore, to this day, a man who is single desires, 'would that I had a wife', etc. ... So long as he does not obtain each one of these, he thinks himself to be incomplete. Now his completeness (is as follows), mind *(manas)* truly is his self *(ātman)*, speech is his wife, breath *(prāṇa)* is his offspring,

1. *Tanū* only occurs in ten verses in the thirteen principal *Upaniṣads:* K.U. 2.23; Mu.U. 3.2.3; S.U. 3.5; 5.14; Mt.U. 4.6; 5.2; 6.5; 6.6; 6.13; P.U. 2.12.

2. *Ātman:* C.U. 8.12.1; 4.4.1; 4.4.3-4; etc. *Puruṣa:* B.U. 4.3.46; 6.2.14; P.U. 4.9; etc. *Prāṇa:* P.U. 2.7; 3.3; etc.

the eye is his human wealth ... the ear his divine wealth ... the body *(ātman)*, indeed, is his work, for with it he performs (ritual) work *(karma)*.

B.U. 1.4.17 (R)

Even *brahman* is not always strictly universal in meaning. In the following passage it refers to the common origin of a limited group of similar things rather than to the universe as a whole.

Verily, this (world) is a triad of name *(nāma)*, shape *(rūpa)* and work *(karma)*. Of names, speech ... of shapes, eye ... of works, the body *(ātman)* is the source, for from it all works *(karma)* arise. It is their common feature, for it is common to all works. It is their *brahman*, for it sustains *(bibharti)* all works. These three together are one, this self *(ātman)*; the self, though one, is this triad. This is the immortal veiled by the real. Breath *(prāṇa)*, verily, is the immortal, name and shape are the real. By them breath is veiled.

B.U. 1.6.1-3 (R)

The preceding passage also contains an example of the ambiguous use of *ātman*, as well as an example of the use of *prāṇa* as a universal principle. *Prāṇa* and *puruṣa* commonly connote individuality more than universality, but each of these three terms — *ātman*, *puruṣa* and *prāṇa* — as well as *brahman*, may be applied to the universal principle,[3] and all four of them, along with other, less common terms,[4] are used synonymously with reference to the identical essence of the individual and the universe. In Vedic psychology, life and consciousness were considered to be the primary characteristics of the individual human being. In Upaniṣadic psychology, they are the primary characteristics of the soul, but in the *Upaniṣads* another aspect of the soul receives considerable attention as well. This is the aspect of volitional activity, which relates to the idea that the soul

---

3. *Ātman:* B.U. 1.5.15; 2.1.20; 2.4.12-14; 2.5.19; 3.5.1; 3.7.16; 4.4.5; C.U. 3.14; 5.18.1; 6.8; 7.25; 7.26; Ma.U. 2; P.U. 3.3; etc. *Puruṣa:* B.U. 1.4.1; 3.9.10; 2.5.14; P.U. 6.6; Mu.U. 1.1.13; 2.1.2; 2.1.10; etc. *Prāṇa:* B.U. 3.9.9; 5.13.2; 6.1.1 & 13; C.U. 3.15.4; 5.1.1; Ks.U. 2.1; 3.8; Mt.U. 1.7; etc. *Brahman:* B.U. 4.4.18; C.U. 3.12.7-9; etc.

4. Such as *antaryāmin:* B.U. 3.7.1-3; Ma.U. 6 *kṣetrajñā:* Mt.U. 2.5; 5.2.

created the universe, but is based primarily on the incorporation of the idea of *karma* and rebirth into Upaniṣadic psychology. Thus, in the *Upaniṣads,* the soul is not only said to be characterized (*-maya,* lit. made) by life *(prāṇa,* lit. breath) and consciousness *(manas, vijñāna, prajñā),* but is also said to have an active, volitional aspect.[5]

> That self is, indeed *Brahman,* characterized by consciousness *(vijñāna),* mind *(manas),* breath *(prāṇa),* sight, hearing, earth, water, wind, space, heat, non-heat, desire, non-desire, anger, non-anger, dharma, *adharma,* everything; so that it is said, "made of this, made of that". As one does, as one behaves, so he becomes. The doer of good becomes good; the doer of bad becomes bad. Good occurs by good action, bad by bad.
>
> B.U. 4.4.5

It is interesting that in the context of ancient Jainism, the preceding would imply that the soul is quite literally *karma-maya*, in that *karma* in the ancient Jain system was understood as a subtle material adhering to the soul. This ancient Jain concept may perhaps seem rather crude, but it does have the virtue of explaining clearly how the doer is thought to be affected by his deeds. Because of the ultimately universal nature of the soul such clarity is possible in the Upaniṣadic context. The search for the ultimate agent, under different names,[6] is long, confused, and ultimately unsuccessful in the *Upaniṣads.* In the last analysis the only tenable position, given the doctrine of monism, is that the soul as ultimate doer is not really a doer. It only seems to act because of the ultimately illusory actions of an imaginary entity, the individual self. Though illusory, the individual self is nonetheless ontologically grounded in the ultimate, non-doing doer.

> Verily, this self, the seers declare, wanders here on earth in every body (from body to body) unaffected, as it seems, by the light or the dark

---

5. See also B.U. 1.6.3 for volitional aspect associated with the term *karma.* Note also the volitional aspect of the soul as described by *kratu:* C.U. 3.14.1; and *kāma:* B.U. 3.9.11; Mt.U. 6.30. Cp. K.U. 1.2.11; C.U. 8.1.5; T.U. 2.6.1; Mu.U. 3.2.

6. *Kartṛ:* Mt.U. 2.3; S.U. 5.7. *Kārayitṛ:* Mt.U. 3.2-3; 2.3-5; S.U. 1.6; *Kena* U. 1.1; C.U. 8.1.15; B.U. 4.4.22. *Antaryāmin:* Ma.U. 6; B.U. 3.7.1-23; Mt.U. 6.22, 25, 29 & 36.

> fruits of action. On account of this unmanifestness, subtility, imperceptibility, ungraspability, freedom from self-sense, (the self) is unabiding and a doer only in seeming, truly is not a doer, he is abiding.
>
> Mt. U. 2.7 (R)

Such problems are perhaps most obvious in the Upaniṣadic context with reference to the volitional characteristics of the soul, but they also arise with reference to the vital and mental characteristics of a soul imagined to be at once individual and universal. Put simply, that which is eternal cannot change, and therefore cannot act or be affected by actions. An eternal entity cannot in any meaningful sense of the terms be said to live or be conscious, since these involve change. In the end, though it is not consistently recognized in the *Upaniṣads*, the individual *cum* universal soul can only be characterized as *neti, neti*, "not this, not that".[7] This leaves Upaniṣadic psychology to deal only with its apparent, though ultimately illusory characteristics: consciousness, life and volitional activity.

Eventually these three apparent characteristics of the soul gave rise to the three groups of five faculties that became standard in orthodox philosophy: 1) the faculties of consciousness *(jñāna-indriya* or *buddhi-indriya)*. 2) the faculties of action *(karma-indriya)* and 3) the five vital faculties or breaths *(prāṇa)*. These vital breaths are not to be confused with a common set of sensual faculties also called *prāṇas*. In the present analysis these sensual faculties will be called "breath faculties" for the sake of clarity.

It would be tempting to speculate that these various faculties of the soul were borrowed, along with the soul idea itself, from a non-Vedic source, but as far as can be judged from the extant literature, the Upaniṣadic enumeration of faculties of the soul evolved gradually out of largely Vedic concerns. Given their propensity for psychological speculation, the *Upaniṣads* are remarkably inconsistent in their various enumerations of the faculties of the soul. This seems to indicate a gradual process of working out a coherent doctrine over time, rather than a wholesale borrowing from an existing tradition.

---

7. B.U. 2.3.6; 3.9.26; 2.4; 4.4.22; 4.15.5.

Somewhat surprisingly, upon analysis it appears that the starting point for this process was the Vedic theory of correspondences between aspects of the microcosmic individual and macrocosmic, natural phenomena. From this unlikely starting point, the Upaniṣadic sages appear to have identified — for the first time in recorded history — the five empirical senses: sight, hearing, smell, taste and touch. This identification of the five senses appears to be a part of the Upaniṣadic shift from a vitalistic to a psychological concept of human identity.

Chapter 3 examined several Vedic psychological faculties which were made to correspond to certain natural phenomena. The clearest of these correspondences in the *Ṛg Veda* are the relationships of the eye to the sun and the *ātman* (spirit, breath-soul) to the wind. The *Brāhmaṇas* and *Upaniṣads* exhibit a proliferation of such correspondences apparently limited only by the fertile imaginations of the priests and sages. These expansive tables of correspondences may include such "faculties" as head, bladder, feet, hair, skin, navel, semen, etc., which are made to correspond to various natural phenomena such as sky, sun, moon, water, plants, etc.[8] There is little consistency in most of this, and the associations appear in most cases to be random, or at best based on superficial resemblances. These extensive lists of correspondences between the macrocosm and the microcosmic person are perhaps interesting as archaic attempts to impose order on the bewildering array of phenomena which occur in human experience, but in the end this approach proved to be a dead end. Many of the microcosmic elements in these lists of correspondences, however, were eventually reworked into a more satisfying map of the individual. This reworking resulted from the incorporation of the concept of the soul as a central reference point, and eventually resulted in a psychological rather than a vitalistic concept of the essence of the human being.

The largely random universal correspondences often remained in Upaniṣadic material, but the parts and faculties of the individual gradually came to be more purposefully selected and arranged with the express goal of illuminating the nature of the soul, which was

---

8. See C.U. 5.11-23; A.U. 1.1.4.

thought to stand at the core of every human being. In other words, the orientation of the analysis of the individual became subjective, the ultimate subject, the soul, providing the reference of analysis rather than the universe. The aspects of the individual chosen for analysis came to represent, rather than parts or characteristics of a biological organism, faculties of a psychological entity. These were the faculties whereby the soul was thought to interact with its environment, even if ultimately that environment was thought to be illusory. Throughout this process of change, vitalistic terminology — terms such as *ātman* and *prāṇa* — continued to be used to denote the essence of the human being, but these terms came to be increasingly psychological in implication. Because vitalistic and psychological concepts of the individual co-exist in the *Upaniṣads*, careful analysis is required in order to perceive this shift or to arrive at an accurate interpretation of much important Upaniṣadic material.

Mind, Speech and Breath:

The most common set of faculties of the soul enumerated in the *Upaniṣads* are not selected on the basis of empirical observation or introspection. Instead, they are derived from Vedic categories. This set of five faculties includes: breath *(prāṇa)*, mind *(manas)*, speech *(vak)*, eye and ear. By virtue of their continued association with universal phenomena — normally wind *(vāyu)*, moon, fire, sun, and the directional quarters *(diś)* — these five faculties are sometimes called divinities *(devata)*.[9] More commonly, by means of a rationale to be examined presently, they are known as the "breath faculties" *(prāṇa)*. Of these, the most essential are the triad of mind, speech and breath.

In many ways, this archaic triad is cosmological rather than psychological. Mind and speech, as shown above, are fundamental aspects of the cosmogonic duality. They are often represented as a

9. See also B.U. 1.3.10; 1.5.15-20; Ks.U. 1.6; 2.3; 2.14; 4.20.

sexual pair, and in some passages, their sexual union is said to produce breath, the third member of the triad.[10]

> 11. Of this speech, the earth is the body, its light form is this (terrestrial) fire. As far as speech extends, so far extends the earth, so far (extends) this fire.
>
> 12. Now of this mind, heaven is the body and its light form is that sun. As far as the mind extends, so far extends the heaven, so far (extends) that sun. These two entered into union and from that was born breath. He is Indra (the supreme lord). He is without rival. Verily, a second person is a rival. He who knows this has no rival.[11]
>
> B.U. 1.5.11-12 (R)

"These two" indicates speech and mind, along with the various other correspondences indicated. Oddly, the offspring of this sexual union, breath, is presented here as being the supreme member of the triad. This is probably because, according to Upaniṣadic logic, the parents are dual, but the offspring is a unity comprising the essence of both. Sexual motifs are employed in other Upaniṣadic creation passages as well, for example, death as the cosmogonic principle is said to have brought about the sexual union of mind and speech to create the universe as food for himself.[12] The previous chapter quotes an account at B.U. 1.4.1-4 of the creation of various life forms by the incestuous activity of the male and female parts of the universal *ātman*. This same passage, at verse 7, recognizes that such procreative activity is mirrored by the functions of mind and speech as cosmogonic principles. These two psychological principles are every bit as changeable as the two cosmogonic principles described in the passage in question. Whatever speech utters, the mind is capable of assuming that form and procreating as it were, by producing a proliferation of conceptual/verbal constructs. In Upaniṣadic terms, such constructs are known as *nāma-rūpa*, "names and forms", a concept which will be discussed in detail in the following section of this chapter. This same idea is approached from another angle in a passage

10. See also B.U. 1.5.7; 1.4.7.

11. Cp. B.U. 1.4.2.

12. B.U. 1.2.4.

where speech, mind and breath, are said to correspond respectively to the known *(vijñāta)*, the knowable and the unknown. Speech represents what is known, mind what is knowable and breath what is unknown, probably referring to ultimate reality, the essential, universal soul.[13] Thus, speech and mind as cosmological *cum* psychological principles cooperate in actualizing in a manifold way the potential of reality, but they are powerless to conceptualize its essence, the universal soul, which is beyond the scope of words or thought. Still spoken of in vitalistic terms as breath, in such passages, the soul takes on psychological significance as the union of mind and speech. Mind and speech come to represent faculties of the soul. As cosmogonic principles, they represent the means whereby the universal soul creates the universe. At the individual level, they represent the means whereby the individual projects the illusory, manifold universe as in a dream.

Speech and Name:

The inclusion of speech in this essential triad, and its identification with "the known", may seem odd to the modern reader. Its inclusion apparently arose out of Vedic concerns with the magical efficacy of Vedic rituals. In the context of the Vedic hymns, speech was regarded as being capable of producing concrete effects in this world. In the *Upaniṣads*, speech as a faculty of the soul is shifted around in the various lists of hierarchies of human faculties to suit the point being made. Its inclusion, however, was more or less compulsory due to its importance in the Vedic scheme of things. In the *Vedas*, speech was a goddess, all encompassing by virtue of the fact that everything has a name. From Vedic times name *(nāma)* is an important constituent of individuality. In early Brahmanic and Upaniṣadic mythological *cum* psychological cosmogonies name, along with form *(rūpa)*, plays a crucial role in the creation of the manifold universe. The cosmological origin of individuality through name-and-form is reflected in the make-up of the existential person in that speech and mind in the

---

13. B.U. 1.5.8-10.

Upaniṣads are said to be the individual faculties co-responsible for perceiving the names and forms which constitute the apparent individuality of entities.[14] Mind " or sometimes eye " represents perceptual consciousness in general, mind in one passage being called the divine eye.[15] Speech, however, is also often treated as a perceptual faculty, the faculty which perceives the names of the forms perceived by mind or the eye. Retaining the Vedic attitude toward language, the Upaniṣadic sages do not regard names as mere conventional designations of things. Instead, names are believed to be inherent properties of the things they designate. To exist as an entity is to have both a form accessible to perception and a name accessible to the faculty of speech. The name which a thing bears corresponds to the concept which the thing engenders in consciousness. In the Upaniṣadic context, where the universe is usually represented as an illusory projection of consciousness, the name which a thing bears is every bit as constituative of its reality as the form the thing takes.

In the duality mind-and-speech, mind is the faculty primarily responsible for apprehending form. Speech is the faculty which apprehends Names, the underlying conceptual/verbal order among the multitude of forms encountered in the universe. Thus, speech is praised at one point as the basis of true and false, right and wrong.[16] Even when differentiation is said to be illusory, speech is held responsible in part for the mistakenly perceived individuality, as in a famous passage attributed to Uddālaka:[17]

> Just as, my dear, by one clod of clay all that is made of clay becomes known, the modification being only a name *(nāma)* arising from speech while the truth is that it is just clay.
>
> C.U. 6.1.4 (R)

In the Indian context, this "modification arising from speech" means something quite different from the immediate impression that

---

14. S.B. 11.2.3.6. Cp. C.U. 8.12.5.
15. C.U. 8.12.5.
16. C.U. 7.2.1.
17. See also C.U. 6.1.5-6; 6.4.1-4; B.U. 4.4.21.

the English translation probably gives to most modern readers. In the *Upaniṣads*, speech is considered a genuine faculty of perception rather than a learned set of random associations between words and things.[18] What Uddalaka probably means is that speech is the actual perceptual basis of mistaken knowledge, just as the eye or ear may be mistaken in perceiving manyness. He does not mean that individuality is just a "way of speaking". Consider the following passage in this connection.

> Verily, by speech, Your Majesty, a friend is recognized *(prajñāyate)*. By speech alone, Your Majesty, the *Ṛg Veda*, the *Yajur Veda*, the *Sāma Veda*, the *Atharvāṅgirasa*, history, ancient lore, arts, the *Upaniṣads*, verses, aphorisms, explanations, commentaries, (the effects of) sacrifices, oblations, food and drink, this world and the other and all beings are known.
>
> B.U. 4.1.2 (R)

Belief in the independent existence of the name or word was, of course, an important doctrine for those who maintained the eternality and infallibility of the Vedic scriptures. The independent existence of the word *(śabda)* became and remained a fundamental doctrine of the Mīmāṁsā school. The *Upaniṣads* contain a prototype of one of the classical Mīmāṁsā arguments to establish the eternality of the word, an argument advanced primarily against the Buddhists who held that speech is based on mere convention.[19]

> Whatever word *(śabda)* there is, is speech. It determines an end *(antam,* a conclusion or an object), but it is not (determined).
>
> B.U. 1.5.3

The idea here is that the concept of, "a cow", for example cannot be created by pointing to all cows and saying "cow", because the hearer could just as well assume that the speaker meant "horns" or "tail". Instead, the Mīmāṁsakas, and apparently the author of the preceding, hold that the verbal ideal must precede its various referents.[20] In other

---

18. See also B.U. 4.1.2.

19. See also B.U. 4.5.12; 2.4.11; 4.1.2.

20. See *Mīmāṁsā Darśana* 1.1.6.19, *Śābara Bhāṣya*.

words, the name of a thing is equally important or even more important than its form in determining the nature of that thing.

This same idea is reflected in the passage quoted above which equates speech with "the known". That same passage equates the breath with "the unknown", thus indicating its supremacy over speech and mind. This supremacy is emphasized by the characterization of breath as the child of mind and speech. These several themes are brought together explicitly in the following passage. In this passage eye substitutes for mind, representing perceptual consciousness in general. The soul *(ātman)* is identified with breath and naively characterized as the agent of *karma*. In such circumstances, Śaṅkara routinely interprets the active, *karma*-producing *ātman* as "body", though such passages actually almost certainly indicate a more primitive concept of the soul operating in many Upaniṣadic passages.

> 1. Verily, this (world) is a triad: name *(nāma)*, form *(rūpa)* and action *(karma)*. Of these, speech is the source *(uktha)* of names, for from it all names arise. It is their *sāma*, for it is uniform *(sāma)* in all names. It is their *brahman*, for it bears *(bibharti)* all names.
>
> 2. Now, eye is the source of forms, for from it all forms arise. It is their *sāma*. ...
>
> 3. Now, of actions, the soul *(ātman)* is the source, for from it all actions arise. It is their *sāma*. ... This triad is a unity, the soul. The unitary soul is this triad. This is the immortal adorned by the true. Breath is the immortal, name and form are the true. By them, this breath is adorned *(channa)*.
>
> B.U. 1.6.1-3

This entire passage is a complex pun based on the concept of the universe as a ritual utterance. Thus, *uktha*, translated "source", means literally "utterance". Sama, meaning "uniform" is related to sāma, a type of hymn, and *brahman* obviously suggests the older meaning "prayer" as well as "universal principle". *Channa*, "(seductively) adorned", implies verbal adornment, and in particular the metrical adornment of the Vedic hymns *(chandas)*. The universe is depicted as a sacrificial ritual in which sacred words (names) actually participate in and constitute part of the reality of the forms we perceive around us. It appears then that several essentially Vedic notions, rather peculiar notions to the modern mind, account for the frequent

Upaniṣadic inclusion of speech as one of the essential faculties of the soul. These Vedic notions also account for the important cosmological role of names, in conjunction with forms, in accounting for the orderly differentiation of discrete entities in the universe.

Breath and Vitality:

The supremacy of breath over mind and speech in the essential triad of faculties of the soul is a recurrent theme in the *Upaniṣads*. It amounts to a vitalistic definition of the soul, whereby the conscious characteristics of the individual are represented as deriving from the more essential characteristic of vitality. The Upaniṣadic concern with the vital principle of the soul, eventually superseded by concern with the psychological principle of the soul, appears to derive from Vedic themes. In the *Ṛg Veda*, the individual is said to derive existence from the universe by consuming food. In the Vedic scheme *vayas* is the vital faculty deriving most directly from this nourishment. Even after death, should one be fortunate enough to attain a heavenly body *(tanū)*, it was thought necessary to nourish it with "food" provided in the sustaining rite, or ancestral sacrifice (pitṛ-yajña) performed by one's offspring. Naturally, that aspect of the *tanū* which survived in one's offspring also had to be maintained by food. This dependence upon food was transformed in the *Upaniṣads* into a metaphor for the motive behind creation. This motive, desire for food, is said to infect the mechanism of the universe, which functions by the perpetual consumption of beings in the universal fire.

Of course, beings are consumers as well as consumed. One of the most archaic attempts to locate the point of identity between the universal and the individual, a point presupposed by monism, was to identify the consumer in oneself with the universal consumer. Thus the method behind the seeming madness of the following:

> With that speech, with that self *(ātman)* he brought forth all this whatsoever exists here. ... Whatever he brought forth, that he resolved to eat. Verily, because he eats *(attīti)* everything, therefore the *aditi-*

> nature of Aditi. He who knows thus the *aditi*-nature of Aditi becomes an eater of everything here, and everything becomes food for him.
>
> B.U. 1.2.5 (R)

Elsewhere, this common, consuming essence of both the universe and the individual is identified with the universal fire. It is this universal fire which one hears upon covering one's ears, cooking the food one has eaten.[21] Individually, it is the digestive fire. Its heat is the warmth of the body. Breath, which always accompanies heat in a living organism, was also thought of as primarily a digestive force. The scientific insight behind these concepts is remarkable in such an early age. Digestion is recognized for what it is: the oxidation of food. This burning is recognized as involving three things, fuel (food), heat and air (breath).

In this vein, *brahman,* which encompasses everything, may be represented as the duality of breath and food,[22] a duality which ultimately represents life and matter, life being that which transforms matter into consciousness.

> Prajāpati, desirous of offspring, verily performed *tapas*. Heated by that *tapas,* he caused a (sexual) pair to arise, matter *(rayi)* and breath, (thinking) "These two will produce many kinds of offspring for me".
>
> P.U. 1.4

In other words, the digestive vital breath will consume matter and organize it into organic bodies which may support consciousness. Such theories appear to derive directly from the Vedic theory that the universe is ingested as food for the *tanū.*

This theme is elaborated upon considerably in the *Chāndogya Upaniṣad* in an interesting sequence of passages in which rudimentary scientific observation is brought to bear upon an essentially Vedic cosmogony. The correspondences between the cosmos and the individual are proposed with the express purpose of establishing the essential nature of the soul. This attempt begins with an abstract

---

21. C.U. 3.13.7-8.

22. See also B.U. 3.9.8; C.U. 4.3.7; Mt. U. 6.1; 6.9-15.

statement of the ancient Vedic mythological cosmogony according to which the universal principle, by performing *tapas* (heat-producing austerity), sweated, thus producing the universal waters from which the material universe was fashioned.[23]

> 1. In the beginning, my dear, this was Being *(sat)* alone, one only without a second. ...
> 3. It thought, "may I be many, may I procreate". It sent forth heat *(tejas)*. That heat thought, "May I be many, may I procreate". It sent forth water. Therefore, whenever a person grieves or perspires, water is produced from the heat.
> 4. That water thought, "May I be many; may I procreate". It sent forth food. Therefore, whenever it rains anywhere, there comes to be abundant food. Thus is food, for eating born from that (water).
>
> C.U. 6.2.1-4

Somewhat artificially, mind, breath and speech are made to correspond to these three cosmic evolutes — heat, water and food — which obviously resemble the three *guṇas* of *prakṛti* in the Sāṁkhya system.

> 1. Food when eaten becomes threefold; its coarsest portion becomes the faeces; its middle (portion) flesh and its subtlest (portion) mind.
> 2. Water when drunk becomes threefold ... its subtlest (portion) the breath.
> 3. Heat when eaten becomes threefold ... its subtlest (portion) speech.
> 4. Thus, my dear, mind consists of food, breath consists of water and speech con-sists of heat.
>
> C.U. 6.5.1-4 (R)

The correspondences offered here are subsequently justified on the empirical basis that it may be observed that if a person ceases to eat for fifteen days, but drinks only water, he will continue to breathe, but will not be able to think. When he eats again, it is observed that, on the basis of the digestive activity of the breath, his mind will begin

---

23. See *Ṛg* 10.129.2-4, but cp. a slightly different account at B.U. 1.2.1-2.

to function again, will "blaze up" like a coal covered with straw.[24] The dependence of mind upon food is thus established empirically. This same discourse also teaches that food, in turn, depends on water, water upon heat, and heat upon being, a theory based on the cosmogonic order of appearance of these principles. Moreover, the priority of breath over mind on the individual level is also empirically justified, for as long as there is breath, when solid food is eaten it will be digested and transformed into mind. In other words, one's psychological existence depends upon the continuation of one's vitality.

In this same passage, breath is said to depend on its cosmic counterpart, water, just as mind depends upon food. Presumably, this indicates that if one were deprived of water as well as food, one would stop breathing and die. Because of the lingering presence of heat, the body would remain warm for a short time. In this same passage it is said that when death does occur, the cosmogonic emanation outlined above (being to heat to water to food) is reversed on the individual level when mind (from food) merges into breath (from water), which merges into heat, which merges into being, or, as it is stated in the *Upaniṣad,* into the "highest divinity".[25] Upaniṣadic cosmology thus appears to be verified by observing death, whereupon one first ceases thinking, then stops breathing and finally ceases to be warm. The correspondence of speech to heat is conveniently ignored at this point in the passage.

The present instruction culminates with the famous statement, *tat tvam asi,* which in context is a vitalistic approach to the identity of the individual essence and the universal essence.

> Verily, indeed, this body dies when deprived of the living self *(jīva);* the living self does not die. That which is the subtle essence this whole world has for its self *(ātman).* That is the true. That is the self. That art thou *(tat tvam asi),* Śvetaketu.
>
> C.U. 6.11.3 (R)

24. C.U. 6.7.

25. C.U. 6.8.6.

Here, it appears that *jīva* (lit. life) is identified with the ultimate universal principle *(ātman)* and not, as in some later passages, the conditioned, transmigrating, strictly individual soul.[26]

Thus, in some Upaniṣadic passages, vitality as symptomatized by breath and heat is held to be the essence of the individual by virtue of the observable fact that the continued functioning of consciousness depends upon the presence of these vital faculties. These deathbed observations are further supported with the observation that in sleep too, the mind ceases to function while breath, and presumably heat, continue to be present.

> 1. Learn from me, my dear, the true nature of sleep. When a person here sleeps, as it is called, then, my dear, he has reached pure being. ...
>
> 2. Just as a bird tied by a string, after flying in various directions without finding a resting-place elsewhere settles down (at last) at the place where it is bound, so also the mind, my dear, after flying in various directions without finding a resting-place elsewhere settles down in breath, for the mind, my dear, is bound to breath.
>
> C.U. 6.8.1-2 (R)

Following this passage, again, the dependence of mind on food, food on water, water on heat and heat on being is reiterated, as is the vitalistic mergence of the faculties at death.[27] In these passages, the supremacy of breath and heat among the individual faculties is proposed on the basis of the observable dependence of consciousness on vitality. In good scientific form, it is explained with the theory that breath, as a digestive force, is essential in the transformation of food into consciousness, which is thus represented as an epiphenomenon of vitality and matter. Though the preceding passages suggest a reality or essence of existence beyond mere vitality as symptomatized by breath and heat, several passages are content to equate breath directly

---

26. Cp. C.U. 6.3.2.

27. Radhakrishnan, though apparently following Śaṅkara, is obviously wrong in interpolating "body" into C.U.1 6.8.3, since mind, throughout the passage, is said to be dependent upon food.

with the absolute principle.[28] Breath is more common in this role than is heat, but either may appear, as the following passage makes clear.

> Just as the slough of a snake lies on an anthill, dead, cast off, even so lies this body. But this disembodied, immortal breath is indeed *brahman*, is heat.
>
> B.U. 1.4.7

The apparent superiority of heat over breath in several passages in the sixth section of the *Chāndogya Upaniṣad* may relate to the observation that a dying person remains warm longer than he breathes, though this observation is not specifically recorded. It may also be explained by the cosmogonic role of heat noted at the outset of the speculations in the sixth section of the *Chāndogya Upaniṣad.*[29] Here, however, heat is a universal as opposed to an individual principle in the list of principles enumerated. At any rate, the merging of breath into heat is clear. The correspondence between individual speech and universal heat at C.U. 6.5.3, however, in the sections closing is ignored account of the mergence of the faculties at death, when, apparently on empirical grounds, speech is said to merge into mind.

> Also, my dear, the relatives gather around a sick (dying) person and ask, 'Do you know me? Do you know me?' So long as his speech is not merged in mind, mind in breath, breath is heat and heat in the highest divinity, so long he knows (them).
>
> C.U. 6.15.1

All of this obscures the precise role of heat in this group of passages, although elsewhere too, heat, as the universal fire *(vaiśvanāra,* "pertaining to all men", an epithet of Agni) is characterized as the individual *cum* universal essence.[30] One passage even suggests that heat is the basis of dream consciousness.[31]

---

28. B.U. 1.3.21; 3.9.9; Mt. U. 1.1; Mu.U. 3.1.4. Cp. B.U. 2.1.20; 2.3.1; 3.3.2.
29. C.U. 6.2.3.
30. C.U. 5.11.2, 4, 6; 5.12.1; etc. See Jacob, *Concordance,* p. 897.
31. Ma.U. 4.

At any rate, the search for an essential vital faculty of the individual is also one form of the search for a route by which the individual may be identified with the monistic principle of the universe. Though the mythological, cosmogonic status of heat was convenient for such purposes, breath was without a doubt the primary vital faculty in the *Upaniṣads*. Its digestive role may be taken as implying a subsuming of the less important vital faculty, heat.

The Breath Faculties:

The supremacy of breath among the faculties of the soul is maintained even in the preliminary stages of a more thorough inquiry into the nature of consciousness which eventually supersedes the vitalistic speculations examined above. In fact, vitalistic terminology is never completely abandoned, even when vitalistic concepts have waned in the shifting Upaniṣadic characterization of the human being. Thus, the most common Upaniṣadic enumeration of the faculties of the soul is arrived at by the introduction of eye and ear, or sight and hearing, to the more archaic triad of mind, speech and breath. Eye and ear, it may be noted, are the only sensual faculties specifically mentioned as such in the *Ṛg Veda*.[32] In the *Upaniṣads*, they are usually construed as extensions of the mind, though in some versions of the five breath faculties they seem to be represented, along with mind and speech, as independent and equal faculties subordinate only to breath. These five faculties do not appear, then, to be a scientific attempt to define the faculties of the human being. Instead, they seem to be a distillation, based on incipient empiricism, from earlier, more extensive and random lists of correspondences between the individual and elements of the universe at large. Due to their original context, these five faculties, as noted above, are sometimes called "divinities". More commonly they are called "breaths" *(prāṇa)*, presumably because, initially at any rate, they were considered secondary characteristics of an essentially vitalistic soul. These faculties will be

32. See *Ṛg* 10.71.4 & 7.

called "breath faculties" below in order to distinguish them from the five "vital breaths", which are also called collectively *prāṇa*.

This vitalistic terminology is explained mythologically in the texts themselves by reference to the well-known "dispute of the breath faculties" *(prāṇa-saṁvāda)*. An early version of this dispute occurs in the *Jaimani Upaniṣad Brāhmaṇa*, in which six divinities — fire, wind, sun, breath, food and speech — each advance their respective claims to supremacy. In the end all agree that each is indispensable.[33] Similar disputes between speech and mind occur even in such ancient texts as the *Taittirīya Samhita*,[34] as well as in a few *Brāhmaṇa* passages,[35] where the disagreement is over who will carry the oblation to the gods. Mind is judged the more essential ritual force, as the foregoing analysis in Chapter 3 of the role of *manas* in the sacrifice would suggest. In the Upaniṣadic versions of the dispute,[36] however, breath is judged to be the most important faculty on the basis of the essentially empirical observation that mind, speech, sight or hearing may cease,[37] and the individual, though deficient, will go on living, whereas if breath ceases, all of the other faculties must cease also.

> One lives deprived of speech, for we see the dumb. One lives deprived of eye, for we see the blind. One lives deprived of ear, for we see the deaf. One lives deprived of mind, for we see the fool. One lives deprived of arms; one lives deprived of legs; for thus we see. Thus it is the breath alone, this intelligent soul *(prajñātman)*, which grasps the body and causes it to rise.
>
> Ks.U. 3.3

A variation on the dispute of the breath faculties occurs in a few passages wherein the gods *(deva)* and demons *(asura)* clash over the superintendency of the universe. The gods eventually win the struggle

---

33. J.U.B. 4.11-13. See Belvalkar and Ranade, *Indian Philosophy*, vol. 2, p. 147.

34. T.S. 2.5.11. See Belvalkar and Ranade, *Indian Philosophy*, vol. 2, p. 70.

35. S.B. 1.4.1.8; J.U.B. 1.13.1.

36. See B.U. 1.5.21; 6.1.7-14; C.U. 5.1.7-15; Ks.U. 2.14; 3.2; P.U. 2.4.

37. Some versions include other "faculties" or "divinities" as well, such as semen, wind, fire, water, earth, hands, feet. See B.U. 4.1.3; P.U. 2.2-5; Ks.U. 3.3.

by means of the ritual chanting performed by each of the breath faculties. The demons, however, retaliate successfully against these ritual weapons by piercing each faculty with evil, except, that is, for breath, which proves impervious to evil and is thus the instrument of the demons' demise.[38] The supremacy of breath consists not only of being immune to evil — such as thinking, speaking, hearing or seeing what is evil — but also of being deathless, evil and death being deemed essentially equivalent.[39] Thus, in several passages, breath is said to be the essence of life and is identified directly with that which is reborn.[40] Elsewhere, however, the superiority of breath among the faculties of the soul is explained by reference to the Vedic correspondences between the individual and the cosmos, in which breath *(prāṇa* or *ātman)* is said to correspond on the universal scale with wind *(vāyu)*. In the *Upaniṣads,* both breath and wind are often said to be the supreme divinity in the universe,[41] and often this superiority is said to derive from the fact that they absorb other, secondary divinities into themselves.[42]

> 1. Wind *(vāyu)* verily is the absorbent, for when fire goes out, it goes into wind. When the sun sets, it goes into wind. When the moon sets, it goes into wind.
>
> 2. When water dries up, it goes into wind. Wind, indeed, absorbs them all: thus (is the teaching) with regard to divinities *(adhidaivata,* i.e. macrocosmically).
>
> 3. Now, with reference to oneself *(adhyātman,* i.e. microcosmically), breath, indeed is the absorbent. When one sleeps, into breath go speech, sight, hearing and mind. Breath, indeed, absorbs them all.
>
> C.U. 4.3.1-3

38. B.U. 1.3; C.U. 1.2.
39. B.U. 1.3.11; 1.5.21.
40. C.U. 6.1.3; 1.2.9; 7.15.1-3; P.U. 2.6-7; 3.7-9; B.U. 1.5.21; 4.4.1-2; Ks.U. 3.3 Cp. B.U. 1.5.17.
41.. P.U. 2.11; K.U. 3.2.2-3; *Īsa* U. 17; B.U. 1.5.22-23; 2.3.3-5; 3.2.7; C.U. 3.16.
42. See also P.U. 3.2.12-13; C.U. 5.1.15; 6.8.2; Ks.U. 2.12-13.

Aside from its supposed absorptive qualities, the superior position of breath among the faculties is most often based entirely on its vital function. That which supports life and that which survives death are assumed to be identical and to be the essence of human existence. This preoccupation with vitalistic immortality suggests that the desire to identify the reincarnating soul with the vital principle of the universe is in some sense a replacement for the Vedic quest for immortality in heaven. The concept of a living universe was also a feature of Vedic thought. To some extent Upaniṣadic vitalism is reminiscent of the correspondences noted in the *Ṛg Veda* between certain elements of the living individual and certain elements of the living universe. Most notably in the *Ṛg Veda,* wind *(vāyu)* is thought of as the universal breath *(prāṇa* or *ātman),* and fire *(agni)* is often called "universal life" *(viśva-āyu).* Similarly in the *Upaniṣads,* breath and heat, the two major vital forces in the individual, also have universal connotations. Many of the elements of Upaniṣadic vitalism are, in fact, probably attributable to antecedent Vedic notions.

In the *Upaniṣads,* though, even in basically vitalistic passages, correspondences of the individual to the universe occur along a converging course rather than as a simple set of parallels. This reflects, no doubt, the introduction of the concept of the soul into Vedic theories of the nature of the individual. The Vedic sages were content to point out correspondences between certain aspects of the individual and certain universal phenomena. The Upaniṣadic sages seek to reduce human consciousness and vitality to a single essence, often a vital essence such as breath or heat. This essence, they often maintain, is also the ultimate source and focus of convergence of the universal counterparts of the individual faculties. Thus, the individual is not pictured as deriving his vitality from the universe, as in Vedic speculations. Instead, in the Upaniṣadic context, both the universe and the individual are said to emanate from and be re-absorbed into a single, common essence, which is identified with the soul. This is the fundamental Upaniṣadic insight: that the essence of the individual and the essence of the universe are identical. Whatever is the essential nature of the individual is also the essential nature of the universe. The balance of this chapter shows that this insight remained operative in Upaniṣadic thought despite significant changes in the concept of the essential nature of the human being. In general, the changes to be examined represent a shift from a vitalistic to a psychological concept of the essence of the human being, the soul.

Mind and Consciousness:

The major, though not the final shift in the Upaniṣadic perspective on the human being was an increasing tendency to regard consciousness rather than vitality as the essence of the individual and the universe. The empiricism in some of the ancient vitalistic speculations examined above is impressive to the modern mind. In the end, though, the Upaniṣadic inquiry into the essential nature of the soul and its relationship to the postulated universal principle was most fruitfully pursued along the avenue of the analysis of consciousness. This psychological analysis also involves empirical observation of a different sort, namely introspective observation of the functioning of human consciousness, as well as deductive reasoning based on the admittedly questionable intuition that "all is one". The initial stages of this shift in perspective, though not well defined, are probably best approached by noting a tendency in some passages to promote mind to a position superior to speech and breath in the ancient cosmogonic *cum* psychological triad.

In the *Ṛg Veda,* even when the mind was brought into the cosmogonic picture in the "Nāsadīya Sūkta", the primal entity, "that one" *(tad ekam)* remained primarily a vital entity. Though "breathless" *(avāta,* lit. windless), it "breathed by its own inherent nature" *(svadhayā,* i.e. spontaneously). By performing *tapas,* it got warm, another characteristic of vitality. Then it was born, i.e. became existent. Only then did desire *(kama)* arise, presumably desire for food, which is said to be the seed *(reta,* lit. semen) of mind *(manas).*[43] In the *Upaniṣads,* alongside the primarily Vedic notion of vitalistic monism, there appears a tendency to regard consciousness as the monistic principle of the universe and the individual. In the end, the psychological notion won out over the vitalistic.

---

43. *Ṛg* 10.129.

It is not always easy to separate the psychological from the vitalistic point of view. Even teachings attributed to a single sage often appear to be a conglomeration of various and often contradictory theories. Nonetheless, it seems reasonable to suppose that the impetus behind the increasing emphasis upon the conscious characteristics of the soul stemmed primarily from two considerations, both of which relate to the synthetic Upaniṣadic intuition that the soul is the essence of the universe. First, the concept of a universal mind lent itself more readily to a truly monistic doctrine of creation, and second, a clearer path to union with the universal principle lay in the possibility of refinement and transformation of human consciousness by yogic meditation.

With regard to creation, the identity of the soul and the universal principle was postulated from the start in the *Upaniṣads*. The nature of the soul, however, remained open to question. In general, the *Upaniṣads* reveal a drift from vitalistic to psychological concepts of the soul, and developments in the area of psychology were accompanied by corresponding developments in the area of cosmology. Early vitalistic theories of the nature of the soul were accompanied by vitalistic notions of the universe. Cosmological concerns, however, also exerted an influence upon theories of the individual, and vitalism is a poor vehicle for monism. It leaves unexplained the origin of the material stuff which life organizes around itself into a living organism.

Not only the exigencies of monism, but also the status of yogic practice must have played a key role in the ascendency of the psychological soul theory. Though one hears much of the respiratory feats of *yogins, yoga* is fundamentally an exploration and transformation of consciousness. Breath control is only a technique sometimes employed toward the attainment of this end. Yogic experience, then, also suggested the supremacy of the conscious aspects of the soul and at the same time provided a ready tool for the exploration of that consciousness.

It would probably be a mistake to view the transition from a vitalistic concept of the soul to a psychological concept as having taken place at a well defined period in the composition of the *Upaniṣads*. Even archaic creation theories often made use of the imagery of consciousness to explain the monistic origin of the universe. Nonetheless, a clear-cut concept of an essentially conscious soul seems to be a relatively later development than that of the vitalistic soul. It is clear, at any rate, that the concept of consciousness as the essence of the individual and the universe is basic to many of the developments in Upaniṣadic psychology which will be examined in the balance of this chapter.

The first indications of a transition from vitalism to psychology are instances of the promotion of *manas* to a rank above the other breath faculties and even above breath itself. This is perhaps the intention behind passages which represent speech and breath — rather than speech and mind — as the original sexual pair. In this case, mind is the offspring, the implication being that mind is the unitary essence of speech and breath, i.e. that speech and breath are aspects of consciousness.[44]

> One should meditate on speech as a milch cow. She has four udders which are the sounds *svāhā, vaṣaṭ, hanta* and *svadhā*. The gods live on two of her udders, the sounds *svāhā* and *vaṣaṭ;* men on the sound *hanta,* and the fathers on the sound *svadhā*. The vital breath *(prāṇa)* is her bull, and mind *(manas)* the calf.
>
> B.U. 5.8 (R)

The implication that speech, with her four udders is the source of food is borne out elsewhere, as, for example where it is said:

> With that speech, with that self he brought forth all this whatsoever exists here. ... Whatever he brought forth that he resolved to eat.
>
> B.U. 1.2.5 (R)

Versions of the mind-speech-breath triad which characterize breath as the offspring — i.e. the union of the other two — are essentially vitalistic. In such versions, food, which is identified with matter in general, is created by speech, is in fact a manifestation of speech. Breath, in its digestive mode, consumes this food and thereby sustains consciousness, which is thus an epiphenomenon of vitality. The foregoing rearrangement of the triad — with mind in the central

44. See C.U. 1.1.5-6; B.U. 6.4.20.

position of offspring — implies that life (i.e. breath) and the matter (i.e. food) upon which it lives, are both derivatives of consciousness. A subsequent passage in the same section of the *Bṛhadāraṇyaka Upaniṣad* states this more explicitly.

> "*Brahman* is food" say some. This is not so, for, verily, food becomes putrid without breath. "*Brahman* is breath" say some. This is not so, for breath dries up without food. But these two divinities, having become united, reach the supreme.
>
> B.U. 5.12

The supremacy of *manas* and its identity with the essence of the individual and the universe is yet more explicit in several other passages. In the well known "Śāndilya Vidyā", the soul *(ātman)*, residing in the heart, is characterized as *mano-mayaḥ prāṇa-śarīro bha-rūpa satya-saṁkalpa*, "made of mind, (with) breath (for a) body, the form (or appearance) of light, true conceptioned".[45] Here, the essence of the soul is consciousness. Life, represented by breath, is its vehicle, its body, just as the material body is the vehicle of life. Elsewhere, *manas* is specifically identified with *brahman*,[46] as well as *ātman*,[47] and is said to be the divine eye *(daivam cakṣa)* of the soul *(ātman)*, an epithet obviously intended to confer upon *manas* the supreme rank among the faculties of the soul.[48] The theory that during sleep the sense faculties are absorbed into breath is occasionally replaced with the theory that they are absorbed into *manas*, and breath is demoted to the lowly role of night watchman, while consciousness absorbs the perceptual faculties and may venture forth in a dream.

> 2. As all the rays of the setting sun become one in this circle of light and as they spread forth when it rises again and again, even so does all this become one in the supreme god, the mind *(manas)*. Therefore, there (in sleep) the person hears not, sees not, smells not,

---

45. C.U. 3.14.2-3; Mt.U. 2.6; 2.2.8. Cp. B.U. 5.6; T.U. 1.6.

46. C.U. 3.18.1-2. Cp. B.U. 4.1.2-7.

47. B.U. 1.4.7.

48. C.U. 8.12.4-5.

tastes not, touches not, speaks not, takes not, rejoices not, emits not, moves not. (then) they say, he sleeps.

3. The fire of breath alone remains awake in this city.

P.U. 4.2-3

Guarding his low nest with the vital breath, the immortal moves out of the nest. That immortal one goes wherever he likes, the golden person, the lonely bird.

B.U. 4.3.12 (R)

Development and Differentiation of the Faculties:

Along with the tendency to rank mind *(manas)* above breath, one may note also a tendency to promote *manas* to a station above the other "breath faculties". In most treatments of these faculties, even while breath retains its supreme position, *manas* begins to dominate the other faculties. In the archaic "dispute of the breath faculties", these faculties were depicted as peers of *manas*, subordinate only to breath. The subordination of speech to mind occurs even in ancient Vedic texts on the basis of their respective roles in the ritual, and even in these ancient texts empirical evidence of a sort was cited in justification of this ranking.

Speech and mind disputed. "I will bear the offering to the gods", Speech said. "I (will bear it) to the gods", said mind. They went to question Prajāpati. He, Prajāpati, said to her, "Thou art the messenger of mind, for what one thinks of in the mind, one utters in speech".[49]

T.S. 2.5.11

The subordination of eye and ear to mind in the *Upaniṣads* is also supported by observational evidence and the admirable reasoning of the following:[50]

49. From Belvalkar and Ranade, *Indian Philosophy*, vol. 2, p. 70. Cp. S.B. 1.4.1.8; J.U.B. 1.13.1.

50. Cp. Ks.U. 3.7.

> Three he made for himself. Mind, speech, breath, these he made for himself. (They say) my mind was elsewhere, I did not see it, my mind was elsewhere, I did not hear. It is with the mind that one sees. It is with the mind that one hears.
>
> B.U. 1.5.3 (R)

Of the two empirical senses thus subordinated to mind, eye naturally enough takes precedence over ear. In later literature sight alone often represents sensual perception in general. This superiority of sight over hearing in the *Upaniṣads* probably relates to the eye's initial role as an extension of *manas* with the specific capacity of perceiving form *(rūpa)*, mind being called "the divine eye".[51] Speech was the faculty responsible for the perception of the other half of a given thing's identity, the name *(nāma)*. The early appearance of ear as the second empirical sense faculty must relate to its capacity to perceive the word *(śabda)*. Word, uttered by speech, is the mundane manifestation of the eternal name *(nāma)*.

The twofold function of speech as both the perceiver of *nāma* and the speaker of *śabda* will be more closely examined later in this section. First, it is important to note that *śabda*, the perceptual object of ear, is on a secondary level of reality, whereas *rūpa*, the eye's object, is a primary reality, as is *nāma*, the supposed perceptual object of speech. Thus, it is observed, again on empirical rather than mythological or dogmatic grounds, that the ear is inferior as a sense faculty to the eye.

> Verily, truth is sight; for, verily, truth is sight. Therefore, if now, the two persons come disputing, one saying, 'I saw,' and the other 'I heard', we should trust the one who says, 'I saw'.
>
> B.U. 5.14.4 (R)

The eye appears in practically all lists of faculties in the *Upaniṣads*, but the ear is occasionally omitted. Ear may be omitted even from the more or less standard list of the five breath faculties when only four

51. C.U. 8.12.15. See S.B. 11.2.3.6.

adhyātmika (microcosmic, individual) correspondences are needed.[52] However, speech rather than ear may also be omitted in such a situation.[53] This may indicate increasing concern with the actual psychology of the human being and the nature of perception rather than with ancient mythological correspondences.

The process by which the faculty of smell was added to the five essential "breath faculties" as a fourth subordinate to *manas* is also fairly clear. In some forms of the dispute of the breath faculties, two forms of breath appear, the breath in the nose and the breath in the mouth. The breath in the nose, in this case, is merely another sense faculty, the faculty of smell. The breath in the mouth is declared to be the supreme, digestive breath, the basis of life. The empirical justification for the location of the vital breath in the mouth is that one's mouth falls open when one dies, and, of course, that one eats food with the mouth.[54] Later, as concern with the empirical senses grew, the faculty of smell, or rather in most cases its organ the nose, displaced breath altogether from the list of sense faculties. The resulting list includes eye, nose, speech, ear and mind, which as the "divine eye" is obviously intended to be the supreme faculty.[55]

The two breaths — the breath in the mouth and the breath in the nose, also characterized as the in-breath *(prāṇa)* and the out-breath *(apāna)*[56] — were removed from the sphere of sensual activity and began to appear independently in purely vitalistic lists of three breaths,[57] four breaths,[58] and finally the classical list of five breaths. These five breaths were regarded as purely vital faculties responsible for respiration, digestion and the distribution of food through the

52. B.U. 3.1.3-6, but at Ka.U. 2.2 ear seems to take precedence over eye and speech.

53. C.U. 4.4-8.

54. C.U. 1.2.7-9.

55. C.U. 8.12.4-5.

56. B.U. 3.2.2; A.U. 1.1.4. Cp. B.U. 4.2.4.

57. B.U. 3.1.10; T.U. 1.5; Mt.U. 6.5. Cp. B.U. 2.2.1.

58. B.U. 3.4.1; 3.9.26.

body.[59] The respective functions of the five vital breaths are described in detail in the following passage.

> That breath which rises upwards that, assuredly is the *prāṇa* (breath). Now that which moves downwards, that, assuredly, is the *apāna* (breath). Now that, verily, by which these two are supported, that, assuredly, is the *vyāna* (breath). Now that which carries unto the *apāna* breath gross elements of food and distributes the subtle (elements) in each limb, that, assuredly, is called *samāna* (breath). It is a higher form of the *vyāna* (breath) and between them is the production of the *udāna* (breath). That which brings up or carries down what has been drunk and eaten is the *udāna* (breath).
>
> Mt.U. 2.6 (R)

In a few passages, the vital breaths are made to correspond with various faculties of perception and action *(karma-* and *jñāna-indriya),* as if the vital breaths were thought somehow to energize the faculties. Surprisingly little attention is paid to such speculation considering that the three sets of five could have been a bonanza for the Upaniṣadic preoccupation with correspondences.[60]

The Fifteen Vital, Perceptual and Volitional Faculties:

Five was apparently an attractive number to the Upaniṣadic sages. Eventually, by the addition of taste and touch — comparatively rare faculties in the *Upaniṣads* — to the more popular eye, ear and nose, the list of five empirical "faculties of perception or consciousness" *(jñāna-indriya* or *buddhi-indriya)* took the shape that it retained in virtually all post-Upaniṣadic Indian psychology.[61] Speech, like breath, eventually began to disappear from lists of perceptual faculties. On the basis of its function as an active as well as a perceptive faculty,

---

59. C.U. 3.13; 5.19-23; B.U. 1.5.3; T.U. 1.7; Mt.U. 2.6; 6.9. Cp. P.U. 3.

60. P.U. 3.5; C.U. 5.19-23.

61. See B.U. 4.3.23-29; 4.5.12; 2.4.11; P.U. 4.8; 4.2. Generic terms without enumerations at: K.U. 2.3.7; 2.3.10; 1.3.10; Mu.U. 2.6; 6.10; 6.11; 6.28; 6.30. Speech included at: B.U. 3.2.1-9; Mt.U. 6.11.

speech reappeared in another list of five, the five "faculties of action" *(karma-indriya).*[62] Some of the members of this list occurred from time to time in more archaic listings of correspondences between the individual and the universe.[63]

The "action faculties" *(karma-indriya)* are perhaps an odd concept to the modern mind. Nonetheless, they represent a rather admirable attempt to classify all human activity into five comprehensive and irreducible categories in the same way that perception may be reduced to five fundamental categories. These categories are: manipulation with the "faculty" of the hands, movement with the feet, speaking with speech, procreation with the penis and evacuation with the anus. The "faculties" of action, of course, must be thought of as representative of types of activity as usually performed. One could theoretically walk on one's hands or mix the functions of the faculties in other ways. It is an odd list, revealing more than anything else the types of activity which the ancient Indians considered important. The inclusion of procreation is notable in this respect. The omission of eating, however, is surprising. Perhaps this was considered essentially the prerogative of the digestive vital breaths.

Though these three groups of five faculties — 1) five perceptive, 2) five volitional, and 3) five vital faculties — appear to be the products of observation and deduction, the actual process by which these groups of faculties seems to have taken shape is surprisingly haphazard. One might have thought that the popularity of five as the number of members in the three sets of vital, perceptual and volitional faculties was based on the empirical necessity for there being five perceptual senses. This does not seem to have been the case. The five vital breaths apparently were consolidated into a group independently of a clear concept of the five empirical senses. For example, the complete set of vital breaths are made to correspond in several passages to incomplete and confused sets of the sense faculties.[64] This prompts the speculation that initially, the ritual and mythological

62. B.U. 4.5.12; 2.4.11; P.U. 4.8. Generic terms only at: Mt. U. 6.10; 6.28; 6.30.

63. C.U. 5.11.-23; A.U. 1.1.4.

64. C.U. 3.13; 5.19-23; T.U. 1.7.

significance of the number five,[65] rather than empirical necessity, accounted for the adoption of the number five as the membership of the various sets of faculties of the soul.

At any rate, the standard enumeration of the three groups of five perceptual, volitional and vital faculties were all gradually built up and gradually assembled into separate groups. The present study is most concerned with the development of the perceptual and volitional faculties and their subordination to *manas*, which in many listings is merely one of the perceptual faculties, on an equal footing with the rest. These lists of faculties often do not distinguish between volitional faculties and perceptual faculties either, though the distinction between the perceptual and volitional faculties on the one hand and the vital faculties on the other hand is observed more often. This situation emphasizes the fact that even in relatively advanced stages of Upaniṣadic psychology, there was no clear idea of exactly what constituted perception. Various odd combinations of perceptual, volitional and vital faculties are labeled occasionally with the later standard term *indriya*, occasionally with the terms breath *(prāṇa)* and divinity *(devatā)*, and occasionally with other sundry terms such as grasper *(graha)*, procurer *(avarodhanin)*, power *(bala)*, activities *(karmāṇi)*, knowledges *(jñānāni)*, and "numinous people" *(brahma-puruṣāḥ)*.[66]

The development of the two sets of five faculties of perception and action cannot be specifically traced, but various stages which point to a gradual development may be noted. In the most archaic stage, several of the sensual and/or volitional faculties are found interspersed with extraneous elements and along with extensive enumerations of universal correspondences. It is often not clear which faculties, if any, are meant by some of these terms. For example, in one passage the universal self is said to have five bodily constituents

65. See Knipe, David M., *In the Image of Fire*, Motilal Banarsidass, Delhi, 1975, pp. 1-7.

66. *Graha:* B.U. 3.2.1-9. *Avarodhanin:* Ks.U. 2.3. *Bala:* T.U. 3.10.2. *Karmāṇi:* B.U. 1.5.21. *Jñānāni:* K.U. 2.3.10; Mt.U. 6.30. *Brahma puruṣāḥ:* C.U. 3.13.6.

which correspond to various natural phenomena by being their sources. These correspondences are tabulated below for the sake of clarity.[67]

***Aitareya Upaniṣad* 1.1.4**

BODILY PART	FIRST EVOLUTE	SECOND EVOLUTE
mouth	speech	fire
nose	in-breath *(prāṇa)*	wind
eye *(akṣi)*	sight *(cakṣu)*	sun *(aditi)*
ear *(karṇa)*	hearing *(śrotra)*	quarters *(diś)*
skin	hair	plants
heart *(hṛd)*	mind *(manas)*	moon
navel	out-breath *(apāna)*	death
penis	semen	water

That eye and ear in the above table represent sense faculties is fairly clear from their correspondence to sight and hearing. Note also the technical differentiation between physical organ and faculty, though *cakṣu* and *śrotra* may mean simply eye and ear. One might suspect that mouth, nose and skin would represent taste, smell and touch, but their correspondents suggest otherwise. Speech and penis are two of the classical volitional faculties, but their placement makes

67. A.U. 1.1.4.

it doubtful that they are intended as such, and two of the vital breaths appear without apparent significance.

Another odd list of faculties occurs in the *Chāndogya Upaniṣad* in a passage in which several learned householders approach king Aśvapati Kaikeya to learn about *brahman*. Each householder gives his own theory of the nature of *brahman*, which in each case is said by the king to be only a part of the universal principle. The table of correspondences thus generated is as follows:[68]

sky	—	head
sun	—	eye
wind	—	breath
space	—	body
water	—	bladder
earth	—	feet

Of these, the head is totally extraneous as a faculty. Bladder might represent evacuation, but normally the anus is representative of that activity, nor is there anything to suggest that feet represent the faculty of motion. Body *(saṁdeha)*, usually under the name *śarīra*, sometimes seems to replace skin as the organ responsible for touch, but there is no indication that this is the case here. On the whole the table produced by Aśvapati's correspondences seems to be devoid of psychological content. However, Aśvapati is certainly not supposed to be ignorant of Upaniṣadic psychology. In the following verses of the same passage, he proposes a series of correspondences between the five vital breaths and five faculties which are probably to be taken as perceptive. With breath removed to the realm of pure vitality, it will be noted that skin, obviously representing the faculty of touch, appears in what would otherwise be an enumeration of the five "breath faculties". The correspondences he proposes are as follows:[69]

68. C.U. 5.11-18.

69. C.U. 5.19-23.

prāṇa	—	eye
vyāna	—	ear
apāna	—	speech
samāna	—	mind
udāna	—	skin

The same five vital breaths are said to correspond to the same faculties in the *Taittirīya Upaniṣad,* but the pairs are somewhat different.[70] Elsewhere in the Chāndogya *Upaniṣad* the correspondences above are exactly reproduced, except that the universal element wind *(vāyu)* replaces skin in corresponding to *udāna.*[71]

The foregoing might seem to suggest that the idea of the five vital breaths preceded the development of the faculties of sense and activity, but in the *Taittirīya Upaniṣad,* a listing of faculties and their functions generates the following table:[72]

speech	—	preservation *(kṣema)*
prāṇa	—	acquisition *(yoga)*
apāna	—	preservation
hands	—	*karma*
feet	—	movement
anus	—	evacuation
penis	—	procreation,immortality, bliss

The same passage also contains the following extraneous correspondences: cattle – fame, stars – light, space – all. Here, all five of the action faculties are mentioned, along with their standard functions (except for speech), while only two of the vital breaths are mentioned.

The only conclusion to be drawn from the foregoing is no conclusion with regard to the chronology of the genesis of the

70. T.U. 1.7.

71. C.U. 3.12-13. Each of these tables is extended considerably by adding numerous universal correspondences.

72. T.U. 3.10.3.

standard fifteen vital, perceptual and volitional faculties. The variations among the several lists cited suggest that the standard enumeration of fifteen faculties is the result of a process of gradual development by means of a trial and error process rather than by means of logical deduction from observation. In many incomplete, probably archaic lists, it is not at all clear that all of the faculties and organs mentioned are even intended to represent the classical *indriya*. For example, when additional faculties are mentioned in conjunction with the triad mind, speech and breath, it is often unclear whether speech is to be understood as on a par with the other volitional faculties mentioned, or whether it is to be understood as a perceptive member of the ancient triad.

For example, it is said in the *Kauṣītakī Upaniṣad* that the masculine, neuter and feminine names *(nāma)* of *Brahma* are to be acquired by breath, mind and speech respectively.[73] This suggests that speech is to be understood in its most common role as a perceptive faculty, but the entire process of the acquisition of the attributes of Brahma by the several faculties mentioned confuses the issue considerably. The correspondences at Ks.U. 1.7 are as follows.

FACULTY	—	ATTRIBUTE OF BRAHMĀ
prāṇa	—	masculine names
manas	—	neuter names
speech	—	feminine names
prāṇa	—	smells
eye	—	forms *(rūpa)*
ear	—	sounds *(śabda)*
tongue	—	tastes
hands	—	actions *(karma)*
body	—	pleasure and pain *(sukha-duḥkha)*
penis	—	procreation
feet	—	movement

73. Ks.U. 1.7. Cp. Ks. U. 2.15.

It will be noted that breath *(prāṇa)* appears twice, the second time as the sense faculty perceptive of odors. Body as perceptive of pleasure and pain apparently is meant to represent the sense of touch, but this is normally the function of skin *(tvak)*, and *sukha-duḥkha* seems rather an abstract way of expressing the tactile sensation more explicitly denoted by *sparśa*. Three of the five faculties of action are definitely intended, but the status of speech is unclear. In the classical scheme, speech is paired with the activity of speaking. Here it has its archaic function of perceiving names, but it shares this task with breath and mind. The issue is further confused in a later passage of the same *Upaniṣad*, where the same set of faculties, it is allowed, may be called breaths *(prāṇa)*.[74]

A similar question arises when the five standard "breath faculties" (mind, speech, breath, eye, ear) are supplemented with the addition of procreation and semen.[75] The latter two might well be intended as a substitute for the classical action faculty, penis, in which case speech might also be a faculty of action. On the other hand, this may be merely an addition made to the archaic list of vitalistic breath faculties in the context of a fertility rite, for the same passage gives the recipe for a concoction of which it is said, "If one should sprinkle this even on a dry stump, branches would grow and leaves spring forth".[76]

A similar problem occurs with reference to a passage in which the five breath faculties occur with the addition of the sense faculty skin, and semen, which again, may or may not represent the activity of procreation.[77] In this case, though, the faculties are mentioned in the following order: breath, speech, eye, ear, mind, skin, wisdom *(prajñā)*, and semen, which has the effect of dissociating the archaic triad of mind, speech and breath. This suggests that breath may be intended here as the sense faculty of smell. This otherwise rather unlikely possibility is strengthened slightly by the fact that the "inner controller" *(antaryāmin)* is said to dwell within and control each of

---

74. Ks.U. 2.15.

75. B.U. 6.3.2. Cp. B.U. 3.7.16-23.

76. B.U. 6.3.8-12.

77. B.U. 3.7.16-23.

these faculties. There is no clue, however, as to whether speech is to be taken in its ancient or its classical sense.

Be that as it may, speech and breath are certainly to be understood as faculties in Yajñāvalkya's exposition of the eight "graspers" (objects). Here only two action faculties — speech and hands — are mentioned but they are specifically described as such in the following manner:

> 3. Speech, verily, is a grasper. It is grasped by the over-grasper name *(nāma)*, for by speech one utters *(abhivādati)* names. ...
> 8. The hands, verily, are a grasper. They are grasped by the over-grasper action *(karma)*, for with the hands, one performs action.
> B.U. 3.2.2-8

Note that speech as the classical action faculty speaks names rather than perceiving them. In the same passage, breath is said to be responsible for smelling, but the verse on breath departs from the otherwise uniform format of the series of verses so as to include also the *apāna* (out-breath). Remember, out-breath is located in the nose, thus its association with smell.

> In-breath *(prāṇa)*, verily, is a grasper. It is grasped by the over-grasper out-breath *(apāna)*, for by the out-breath one smells odors.
> B.U. 3.2.2

It is also noteworthy that *manas* is treated in this passage by Yajñāvalkya as a separate faculty rather than as *sensus communis*, its over-grasper being desires *(kama)*, a motif which harks back to the *Ṛg Veda* itself. The terminology in the present passage is particularly interesting. The terms "grasper" *(graha)* and "over-grasper" *(atigrāha)*, of which a grammatically more strictly correct rendering would be "grasping" and "over-grasping", indicate a reciprocal relationship between faculty and object. If the variation noted in the verse dealing with breath is taken as a clue to the interpretation of this passage as a whole, the implication is that just as there can be no in-breath without an out-breath, there can be no perception without an object of perception, no doing without that which is done. Buddhism makes much of this notion, as the next chapter shows.

Not only the reciprocity implied in Yajñāvalkya's terminology is noteworthy. The choice of the term "grasping" implies a normative, moral or even psychopathological dimension in the process of perception. Seeing etc. is "a grasping". The objects of perception also grasp, and the term *atigrāha*, particularly with the long "ā" in *graha*, suggests "excessively grasping", even "predatory", like a fierce, dangerous animal. This, of course, is a particularly appropriate image in this passage with regard to mind and its object, desire.[78] This mistrust of perception, particularly passionate, grasping, desiring perception, is also a point of fundamental similarity between the *Upaniṣads* and Buddhism, where this attitude becomes considerably more pronounced.[79]

All in all, though technically incomplete with regard to the faculties of action, the account of the nature of perception at B.U. 3.2 is without a doubt one of the most insightful psychological teachings in the *Upaniṣads*. It must have been truly *avant-garde* in its time. It is interesting that after this progressive psychological lecture by Yajñāvalkya, this pupil *Ārthabhāga* still refers to death as the dispersion of the five archaic "breath faculties" into their corresponding universal counterparts. This suggests — as does the foregoing examination of the various enumerations of faculties found side by side in the *Upaniṣads* — that more progressive psychological ideas coexisted and interacted for many years with more conservative, Vedic beliefs about the nature of the human being. It appears to have taken quite some time for empirical observation to prevail over traditional beliefs and establish a systematic and defensible enumeration of a comprehensive set of categories of human perception and activity.

In the *Upaniṣads* overall, the five empirical sense faculties are listed in complete form more often than are the faculties of action. The tendency is to arrive at this complete enumeration by supplementing the archaic list of breath faculties — mind, speech,

78. See Monier-Williams, pp. 13 and 372.

79. See M1: 460 for similar imagery in the Buddhist context.

breath, eye and ear — with the sense faculties smell, taste and touch. As indicated above, smell is often tacked on to breath rather than linked to its more specific organ, the nose, and the faculty of touch is inconsistently represented — sometimes in classical terms as the interaction of skin *(tvak)* and tactile sensation *(sparśa)*[80] and sometimes as the interaction of the body and pleasure-pain *(sukha-duḥkha)*.[81] Moreover, the retention of the core of archaic breath faculties, in which context speech is a perceptive faculty, often has the effect of making it difficult to determine whether speech is to be understood as a faculty of perception or of action, even when the five empirical senses are listed in full.[82] However, the fact that speech does often occur as a sixth sense, along with the full array of five empirical senses, strongly suggests that in some circles it retained its status as a perceptual faculty even at a relatively advanced stage of psychological sophistication.

Even in passages which do away altogether with the archaic concept of the breath faculties and deal only with classical faculties, the role of speech is often questionable.[83] In the following, for example, speech usurps the position belonging naturally to touch. Its function is *vyākaraṇa*, an ambiguous term in this context which could mean "articulates (words)", but could also mean "reveals or makes manifest (names)". The latter possibility would duplicate the sense of hearing.

> Which is the soul *(ātman)?* That by which one sees, by which one hears, by which one smells odors, by which one reveals/articulates *(vyākaroti)* speech, by which one knows *(vijānāti)* sweet and non-sweet (tastes).
>
> A.U. 3.1.1

In all, it is probably most accurate to say that throughout the *Upaniṣads*, speech was considered just as much a faculty of perception

---

80. B.U. 3.7.16-23; 2.4.11; 4.5.12; C.U. 5.19-23; T.U. 1.7.
81. Ks.U. 1.7; 2.15; 3.5-6.
82. See Ks.U. 3.5 & 6; 1.7; 2.15; B.U. 4.3.23-30; 3.2.1-9; Mt.U. 6.11.
83. See A.U. 3.1.1; B.U. 2.4.11; 4.3.26; 4.5.12; Ks.U. 3.5; C.U. 3.13.3.

as the faculty of touch. Like speech, touch is often omitted from lists of sense faculties, and is often included only by way of the vague term pleasure-pain as experienced by the body in general.

The following passage suggests that the overall distinction between perception and action in general was not as clear-cut in Upaniṣadic times as the modern reader might tend to assume.

> For verily, without intelligence *(prajñā)* speech does not make known *(prajñāpayet)* any name whatsoever. 'My mind was elsewhere', he says, 'I did not cognise *(prājñāsiṣam)* that name.' for verily, without intelligence breath does not make known any odour ... the eye does not make known any form ... the ear does not make known any sound ... the tongue does not make known any taste ... the two hands do not make known any action ... the body does not make known pleasure or pain ... the generative organ does not make known any bliss, delight and procreation ... the two feet do not make known any movement whatsoever. 'Our mind was elsewhere', they say, 'we did not cognise that movement'. Without intelligence no thought *(dhī,* lit. vision) whatsoever would be effective. Nothing that can be cognised would be cognised.
>
> Ks.U. 3.7 (R)

Several of the archaic features noted in the Upaniṣadic treatment of the faculties appear in the above passage. The breath faculties are kept together as a group, which has the effect of mixing the classical action faculties with the sense faculties. Speech is represented as perceptive of name rather than performing the action of speaking. Breath rather than nose or smell *(ghrāṇa)* represents olfactory perception. The body as the organ of touch is said to experience pleasure and pain rather than tactile sensations *(sparśa)*. Anus, the fifth of the classical action faculties, is omitted, although one can certainly sympathize with the author in that the phrase "without intelligence, the anus does not make known any evacuation" would have been rather comical.

The passage does, however, represent *manas* as the *sensus communis*, which is relatively uncommon in the *Upaniṣads*, though it is a standard feature in later Indian psychology. Without the mind — which apparently conveys intelligence or consciousness to the faculties of sense and action — none of the faculties work. The fascinating point, however, is that given the presence of mind, they are all said to work in the same way, by cognising, or making known their respective objects, whether these be sensual perceptions or actions.

In modern physiological terms, no distinction seems to be made between the afferent (to the mind) and the efferent (from the mind) mechanisms of consciousness. The translations "make known" and "cognise", given our modern preconceptions, seem to imply that the mechanism suggested is exclusively afferent (to mind). In other words, rather than being produced by volitional mental activity, actions were thought to be perceived by the mind. In fact, however, if the uniformity of terminology in the preceding is significant, then exactly the opposite is implied. The mechanism of consciousness described in the *Upaniṣads* is, if exclusively anything, exclusively efferent (from mind). The universe we perceive is thought to be produced by mental activity, just as the actions we perform. Perhaps a conceptually more accurate rendering of *prajñāpayet* would be "make real" or "realize", in the sense of "accomplish or produce" with regard either to objects of perception or actions.

The conclusion that seems to emerge from the above observations is that what the modern reader tends to take as metaphorical in the *Upaniṣads,* was in many cases literal truth to the Upaniṣadic sages, if perhaps not to the average citizen of that age. In the present case, the difficulty in conceiving of perception and action as similar phenomena is overcome to a large extent if one assumes that the waking state of consciousness was viewed by some Upaniṣadic sages as fundamentally non-different from the state of dreaming.[84] Actions in a dream are readily seen to be similar to dream perceptions. Both are purely products of the mind. Thus, in the Upaniṣadic context the nature of the centrality and superiority of mind over the faculties of perception and action is perhaps misrepresented by the term *sensus communis.* Mind as a center was not thought of exclusively as a faculty which sorts and arranges the data of the sense faculties and commands the action faculties. Instead, it was thought of more as the point of origination of all of the modes, whether volitional or perceptual, through which the individual projects the universe. The mind is a

84. See B.U. 2.1.18; 4.3.9-18; C.U. 8.10.2; Ks.U. 4.19.

projection room rather than a control room. The various faculties — rather than being sources of information about the universe and channels of interaction with the universe — are thought of as a comprehensive enumeration of the means by which the soul creates the universe and its own apparent relationship thereto, as one does in a dream.

On the other hand, some Upaniṣadic passages do seem to represent *manas* or some other mental faculty as the coordinator of perception and action. This point of view is probably most clearly represented in various versions of the chariot simile which will be examined below.[85] At any rate, when approaching Upaniṣadic psychology, one must be constantly aware that the conceptual world-view that generates many of these ancient theories is often radically different from that of the modern West.

The Five Classical Sense Faculties:

Only a few Upaniṣadic passages clearly indicate an awareness of the classical groups of action and sense faculties.[86] Complete listings of the ten classical faculties of perception and action separated into these two specific categories are rarer still. There are only four such treatments, and these are confined to two of the thirteen principal *Upaniṣads*. Of these, one version in the *Praśna Upaniṣad* reveals its relative lateness by the extensive employment of Sāṁkhya technical terms.[87] The other simply names the ten faculties with mind as the central faculty.[88] The two other complete listings — in the *Bṛhadāraṇyaka Upaniṣad* — are actually parallel versions of Yajñāvalkya's famous teaching to his wife Maitrī. In these he corrects the omission of three of the action faculties noted earlier in his treatment of "grasper and overgrasper".[89]

85. K.U. 1.3.3; Mt.U. 2.6; 4.4.

86. P.U. 4.2; 8.4; B.U. 2.4.11; 4.5.12; K.U. 1.3.10; 2.3.7; 2.3.10; Mt.U. 2.6; 6.10; 6.11; 6.30; 6.31;

87. P.U. 4.8.

88. P.U. 4.2.

89. B.U. 2.4.11; 4.5.12. Cp. B.U. 3.2.2-9.

The two *Bṛhadāraṇyaka* treatments appear to be more archaic than the two in the *Praśna Upaniṣad* because of the confusion in the *Bṛhadāraṇyaka* with regard to the actions performed by the volitional faculties. The hands are said to perform to actions *(karma)*, while in the classical Sāṁkhya scheme the hands are restricted to manipulation *(vyāpāra)*.[90] The proto-Sāṁkhya enumeration of the faculties in the *Praśna Upaniṣad* gives "what is to be grasped" *(ādātavya)* as the object of the hands.[91] An even more archaic feature of Yajñāvalkya's account is the correspondence of speech to the *Vedas*, even though speech is grouped with the action faculties rather than the faculties of perception. The classical Sāṁkhya and the *Praśna* versions agree upon representing the function of speech as the production of speech in general.[92]

All four versions represent touch as the interaction of skin and tactile sensations *(sparśa)* rather than the vague interaction noted above between body and pleasure-pain. Breath is also removed entirely from all four enumerations. Nose represents the faculty of smell in Yajñāvalkya's version, and the more abstract term *ghrāṇa* represents smell in the *Praśna* account. The tabular comparison, on the facing page, of the *Bṛhadāraṇyaka*, *Praśna* and classical Sāṁkhya versions of the ten faculties and their functions may prove of interest, as they differ in several other minor details.

All of the above seems to indicate a gradual working out and a gradual acceptance of the doctrine of five empirical senses governed by mind. The starting point for this process appears to have been the five "breath faculties" — mind, speech, breath, eye and ear — all of which seem to derive from Vedic concerns with microcosmic-macrocosmic correspondences. By a haphazard process, speech was separated out and supplemented to form the standard list of five action faculties. Similarly, breath was supplemented to form the standard list of five vital breaths. Eye and ear were similarly augmented to make up the five empirical senses.

---

90. S.K. 26, *Gauḍapāda Bhāṣya*.

91. P.U. 4.8.

92. *Vāk vadati* at S.K. 26, and *Vāk ca vaktavyam* at P.U. 4.8. Mt.U. 2.6; 6.11. Cp Mt.U. 6.28; 6.30; K.U. 1.3.10; 2.3.7; 2.3.10; B.U. 4.4.17; C.U. 6.7; P.U. 6.14. Cp. B.U. 1.5.14-15; Ma.U. 3.

FACULTY	B.U. 2.4.11 4.5.12	P.U. 4.8	*SĀṀKHYA KĀRIKĀ* 26 (WITH COMMENTARY)
sight	*cakṣu — rūpa*	*cakṣu — draṣṭavya*	*cakṣu — rūpa*
hearing	*śrotra — śabda*	*śrotra — śrotavya*	*śrotra — śabda*
smell	*nāsikā — gandha*	*ghrāṇa — ghrātavya*	*ghrāṇa — gandha*
taste	*jihva — rasa*	*rasa — rasayitavya*	*rasana — rasa*
touch	*tvak — sparśa*	*tvak — sparśayitavya*	*sparśana — sparśa*
speech	*vak — veda*	*vak — vaktavya*	*vak — vadati*
manipulation	*hasta — karma*	*hasta — ādātavya* (taking)	*pāṇi — nānāvyāpāra* (manipulation)
motion	*pāda — adhvana*	*pāda — gantavya*	*pāda — gamana-āgamana*
evacuation	*pāyu — visarga*	*pāyu — visarjayitavya*	*pāyu — utsarga*
procreation	*upastha — ānanda* (bliss)	*upastha — ānandayitavya* (the blissful)	*upastha — ānandaṁ prajotpatyā* (bliss by procreation)

It is surprising indeed to discover that the fact that we have five empirical senses with which to experience the universe was not at all obvious to our forebears. The *Upaniṣads* are the earliest extant documents of the human rase which confirm this discovery. Moreover, so tentative were their conclusions that only one Upaniṣadic passage offers a theory regarding the actual mechanism of sensual perception.

> (One asks): Of what nature, verily, are these senses *(indriya)* that go forth (towards their objects)? ... There are enticing objects of sense and there are what are called luminous rays. Now the self *(ātman)* feeds on objects by the five rays.
>
> Mt.U. 6.31 (R)

Vitalistic passages, which are probably for the most part relatively early, represent what senses they do enumerate as more or less self-sufficient sources of information. For example, in some versions of the "dispute of the breath faculties" even the mind is expendable. The other faculties simply carry on performing their respective functions in its absence. More psychologically oriented passages depict the senses as types of consciousness rather than independent and apparently self-consciousness entities.[93] Thus the various faculties, which initially seem to have been understood as immediate faculties of the soul and on a par with *manas,* were gradually divided into perceptual and volitional faculties and cordoned off from consciousness itself. Consciousness increasingly came to be considered a more essential characteristic of the soul than the faculties of perception and action — more essential even than vitality itself as represented by the five vital breaths.

Initially in this process, *manas,* representing consciousness in general, was promoted from the ranks of the archaic breath faculties and advanced, as it were, a degree closer to the inner sanctum of the soul. This promotion of *manas* represents a decisive step away from vitalism and toward a psychological concept of the soul. *Manas,* however, was never able to overcome entirely its humble origins as a faculty of perception. As a result, a hierarchy of new levels of

93. E.g., Ks.U. 3.7; B.U. 1.5.3; 2.1.17.

consciousness was eventually introduced between the soul and *manas* as *sensus communis*. It is to this hierarchy of consciousness that this examination now turns.

Consciousness and Cosmogony:

The phrase "new levels of consciousness" is advisedly used. In many cases the Upaniṣadic faculties ranked above *manas*, as well as several supposed properties of *manas*, were apparently unknown to the authors of the *Ṛg Veda*. In Vedic times the terms used in the *Upaniṣads* to describe these faculties, functions and qualities of consciousness are either absent entirely, as *buddhi* and *ahaṁ-kāra*, or like *saṁjñā* and *vijñāna*, they denote far more prosaic concepts than they do in the *Upaniṣads*. Of the Vedic mental organs and faculties, *manas* and *hṛd* (heart) maintain basically equivalent positions in the Upaniṣadic scheme. *Manas* is still a dynamic faculty with perceptual, intellectual and volitional qualities. *Hṛd* remains primarily a locus of consciousness. The subordination to *manas* of *dhī* (visions) and *kratu* (mental power), implied in the *Ṛg Veda*, is made more specific in the *Upaniṣads*. *Kratu* comes to mean clearly "volition" or "will" in the *Upaniṣads*, and is thus divested of much of the magical potency it enjoyed in the Vedic scheme. *Dhī*, too, is a less supernormal faculty in the *Upaniṣads*. Its continued association with mental "vision" is beyond doubt, as is admirably demonstrated in Jan Gonda's *The Vision of the Vedic Poets*.[94] In the *Upaniṣads*, however, *dhī* no longer necessarily denotes a literal vision. Instead, in the *Upaniṣads*, the term more commonly denotes an idea, an intellectual "seeing", as in the phrase "I see, said the blind man". Both *dhī* and *kratu* are, however, of little direct importance in the Upaniṣadic scheme of consciousness.

Thee retention of Vedic content in the concept of *manas* is largely confined to retention of status. Even in the most archaic Upaniṣadic passages, the function of *manas* is conceived of psychologically rather than ritually. To be sure, the psychological function of *manas* is linked to the Vedic concern with cosmogony, a linkage which may be traced back to the characterization of *manas* as a cosmogonic principle

94. Gonda, *Vision*, pp. 245-58.

in the "Nāsadīya Sūkta". Upaniṣadic psychological cosmogonies, however, always emphasize the essential identity of the divine mind and the human mind. Creation is thus portrayed as essentially a process of perception, a tendency which eventually culminated in the sub-school of Advaita Vedānta known as *dṛṣṭi-sṛṣṭi-vāda*, "the theory that perception is creation".

It will be useful to clarify this concept before moving on to consider the hierarchy of supra-sensuous consciousness, because the exigencies of monistic cosmogony play an important role in the structure of this hierarchy. The idea that the universe is a projection or emanation of the universal principle through the hierarchy of individual consciousness and finally through the sense faculties is implicit in almost every Upaniṣadic cosmogony, other than a few theistic passages. This idea is not demonstrably present in any Vedic cosmogony, not even the "Nāsadīya Sūkta", which still represents creation as having taken place at a distant point in the past rather than in contemporary human consciousness. In general, Upaniṣadic cosmogonies are not so much explanations of human consciousness. In particular they are concerned with the rationale by which the human soul, in the state of release, may be identified with the universal principle. In the *Upaniṣads,* yogic release is conceived of as a rediscovery, within oneself, of *tad ekam,* "that unity", which, according to the Vedic theory, existed before creation. Release in the Upaniṣadic context is essentially a reversal of the creative process. This reversal is accomplished in contemporary human consciousness by the practice of yogic meditation.

Though the *Upaniṣads* as a whole point to some such contemplative practice, the yogic experience itself is not described specifically as such except in relatively late passages. The following lengthy citation from the *Maitrī Upaniṣad,* which is almost certainly post-Buddhist, nevertheless has the virtue of stating explicitly what is implicit in many earlier passages. It touches upon many of the issues that will be considered in the balance of this chapter.

> 17. Verily in the beginning this world was *Brahman.* ... At the dissolution of all he alone remains awake. Thus from that space, he awakes this (world) which consists of thought only *(cetāmātra).* By him alone is all this meditated on *(dhyāyate),* and in him it is

dissolved. ... He who is in the fire, and he who is here in the heart and he who is in the sun — he is one. ...

18. This is the rule for achieving this (oneness), control of the breath *(prāṇāyāma)*, withdrawal of the sense *(pratyāhāra)*, meditation *(dhyāna)*, concentration *(dhāraṇa)*, contemplative inquiry *(tarka)* and absorption *(samādhi)*, (this is) said to be the sixfold *yoga*. ...

19. Verily, when a knower has restrained his mind *(manas)* from the external, when his breath has put to rest the objects of sense, let him remain devoid of conceptions *(saṁkalpa)*. ...

20. When, by suppression of the mind, he sees through self, he sees the shining self ... then having the self through the self he becomes selfless *(nirātman)*. ...

25. He who has his senses indrawn as in sleep ... while in the cavern of the senses is not under their control, perceives him who is called Praṇava, the leader. ...

26. That having divided itself in limitless ways fills these worlds ... and as indeed the sparks issue from the fire, as rays from the sun, so do the breaths and the rest come forth again and again into the world in proper order. ...

27. The store house *(kośa)* which consists of the space in the heart, the blissful, the supreme abode, is our self, our *yoga* (goal) too and this the heat of fire and sun. ...

30. When the five forms of (sense) knowledge along with the mind stand still and the intellect *(buddhi)* stirs not, that, they say, is the highest state. ...

34. Even as a fire without fuel becomes extinct in its own place, even so thought *(citta)*, by the cessation of activity *(vṛtti)* becomes extinct in its own source. ... One's own thought, indeed, is *saṁsāra;* let a man cleanse it by effort. What a man thinks, that he becomes, this is the eternal mystery. ... So long should the mind be restrained *(nirodhavya)* in the heart till it reaches its end, that is knowledge, that is liberation. All else is but extensions of the knots (that bind us to this life). ... Mind, in truth, is the cause of bondage and liberation for mankind; for bondage if it is bound to objects; freedom from objects, that is called liberation. ...

35. He who knows this, is the knower. ... Having grasped oneness, he becomes identified with it. They who rise forth perpetually like spray drops (from the sea) like lightnings from the light within the clouds in the highest sky, they, by virtue of their entrance into the light of glory appear like crests of flame in the track of fire.

Mt.U. 6.17-35 (R)

As suggested in the above, the reversal of the creative process, the reabsorption of the universe into its source, was thought to occur in sleep and death as well as in yogic trance. The foregoing is obviously rather late Upaniṣadic material. It seems, in fact, to incorporate elements of Yogācāra Buddhism, but the same idea of the projection and re-absorption of the universe along with the senses in sleep, death, and trance, is expressed in earlier material as well.[95] For the purposes of this examination, however, the following passage from the *Kauṣītakī Upaniṣad,* though also possibly a late passage, is more typically Upaniṣadic in the style and content of its expression of the same idea.

> When a person is so asleep that he sees no dream whatever, he becomes one with that breathing spirit *(prāṇa)* alone. Then speech together with all the names goes to him; the eye together with all forms goes to it; the ear together with all sounds goes to it, the mind *(manas)* together with all thoughts *(dhyāna)* go to it. When he awakes, even as sparks proceed in all directions from a blazing fire, even so from this self the vital breaths *(prāṇa)* proceed to their respective stations, from the vital powers *(prāṇa)* the gods (i.e. the sense faculties) and from the gods the worlds.
>
> Ks.U. 3.3 (R)

The vitalistic terminology of the preceding, which is a notable feature of the *Kauṣītakī Upaniṣad* in general, will be dealt with further below. For the present, though, note that the *Kauṣītakī* consistently identifies *prāṇa* with the *prajñā-ātman,* the "intelligent self", so that the psychological orientation of the present passage is beyond doubt.[96] Radhakrishnan is probably right in identifying the gods *(deva)* with the senses, as this identification is explicitly made elsewhere in the *Kauṣītakī Upaniṣad.*[97] Though the *Kauṣītakī* is often content with the archaic "breath faculties", it exhibits also an awareness of the five empirical senses and most of the classical action

95. B.U. 4.3.7-38; C.U. 6.8; 6.15; etc.
96. See Ks.U. 3.2; 3.3; etc.
97. Ks.U. 2.3; 2.14.

faculties.[98] The present passage is obviously an account of the psychological projection of the universe.

At another point in the *Kauṣītakī Upaniṣad*, there is an enumeration of the ten "intelligence principles" *(prajñā-mātra)* and the ten "existence principles" *(bhūta-mātra)*, which correspond to the former by being their respective objects. Thus, in a system much like the classical Sāṁkhya system of *tanmātras*, a comprehensive analysis of the supposedly physical universe is thought to be accomplished by classifying objective phenomena according to the subjective faculty with which they correspond. Furthermore, it is clear that this analysis is intended to reflect the actual nature of reality in that the external universe is said to depend on the individual faculties like the rim of a wheel depends on the spokes.

> For as in a chariot the felly is fixed on the spokes and the spokes are fixed on the hub, even so these elements of existence are fixed on the elements of intelligence and the elements of intelligence are fixed in the breathing spirit *(prāṇa)*. This same breathing spirit is, truly, the intelligent self, bliss, ageless, immortal.
>
> Ks.U. 3.8 (R)

The reciprocity between faculty and object noted above in one of Yajñāvalkya's lectures in the *Bṛhadāraṇyaka Upaniṣad* is explicitly stated immediately before the preceding passage. This emphasizes the fact that the Upaniṣadic notion of the mutual dependence of faculty and object is somewhat different in conception than the similar Buddhist idea to be examined below. The Upaniṣadic notion of this reciprocity amounts to invariable concomitance: where there are faculties, there will be objects, but the faculties are more essential. This is like saying: where there is fire, there will be light, but the fire is more essential. This reciprocity is expressed in the following monistic terms:

> For, truly, if there were no elements of existence, there would be no elements of intelligence. Verily, if there were no elements of

98. Ks.U. 3.7-8.

> intelligence, there would be no elements of existence. For from either alone, no form whatsoever would be possible. And this (self) is not many.
>
> Ks.U. 3.8 (R)

The characterization of the conscious principle as breath, in the *Kauṣītakī Upaniṣad* and elsewhere, is particularly convenient for monistic cosmology. The supposed absorptive nature of breath and its universal counterpart wind is called upon to illustrate the absorption and projection of the faculties and, in turn, the universe. It is said, then, that when the divinities fire, sun, moon and lightning are extinguished, their breath *(prāṇa)* enters the wind *(vāyu)*.[99]

> 12. All these divinities, verily, having entered into wind, though they die in the wind do not perish (altogether). Therefrom, indeed, they come forth again. This with reference to the divinities: now with reference to the self.
>
> 13. This *Brahman* shines forth when one speaks with speech; likewise it dies when one speaks not, its light goes to the eye, its vital breath to the vital breath *(prāṇa)*. [A similar treatment of eye, ear and *manas* occurs.] All these deities, verily, having entered into the vital breath, though they die in the vital breath, do not perish (altogether). Therefrom, indeed, they come forth again.
>
> Ks.U. 2.12-13 (R)

This re-emergence represents a waking from sleep or a rebirth, both of which entail essentially a re-creation of the universe in the Upaniṣadic context. This concept, particularly as expressed in the *Maitrī* and *Kauṣītakī Upaniṣads*, has remarkable affinities with some of the ideas of Yogācāra Buddhism. Yogācāra, however, at least in its more precise formulations, does away with the concept of a common soul at the base of individual "creations" of the universe. A somewhat crude conceptual model of the Upaniṣadic theory may be imagined by picturing a sphere made up of many cones, all of which have their apex in the center. The cones would represent individual conscious

99. Cp. C.U. 4.3.1-3.

beings and the universe as projected through them, each having a common essence, the center of the sphere, which would represent the "self of intelligence" in the foregoing passages. Sleep or death would entail the retraction of a cone into the common apex, and waking or rebirth would be the re-projection of the cone from the center. Yogic release, however, the "fourth" state beyond waking, dream and deep sleep, would entail the re-absorption of a given cone forever.

Aside from the *Kauṣītakī* and *Maitrī Upaniṣads,* the other, generally earlier *Upaniṣads* are not so conceptually explicit regarding the projection of the universe through the faculties of the individual. For example, the re-absorption of the universe at death is described in the *Chāndogya Upaniṣad* as the reversal of the cosmogonic emanation of speech from mind from breath from heat from being.[100] Yajñāvalkya's explanation of dreaming also amounts to a projection theory of the universe.[101] In the most typical Upaniṣadic approach to this idea, however, the common apex of the aforementioned cones is represented by "the space within the heart *(hṛd* or *hṛdaya)*".

> 1. This is the truth. As from a blazing fire, sparks of like form issue forth by the thousands, even so, O beloved, many kinds of beings issue forth from the immutable and they return thither too.
>
> 3. From him are born life, mind, all the sense organs (also) ether, air, light, water and earth, the supporter of all. ...
>
> 10. The person himself is all this, work, austerity and Brahmā beyond death. He who knows that which is set in the secret place (within the heart), he, here on earth, O beloved, cuts asunder the knot of ignorance.
>
> Mu.U. 2.1.1-10 (R)

Radhakrishnan, following Śaṅkara, is no doubt correct in interpreting "secret place" *(guhyam)* as being in the heart, as many

---

100. C.U. 6.8; 6.15.

101. B.U. 4.3.7-38.

other passages are explicit in locating the universal principle, and in fact the universe itself, within the "space in the heart".[102]

> He should say, as far, verily, as this (world) space extends, so far extends the space within the heart. Within it, indeed, are contained both heaven and earth, both fire and air, both sun and moon, lightning and the stars.
>
> C.U. 8.1.3 (R)

This "space within the heart" is, of course, a psychological space, the subjective space *(antar-ākasa)*[103] behind the eyeballs, as it were. In this "space", to prevalent modern notions the external world is recreated in consciousness on the basis of sensual information. The Upaniṣadic theory is, in effect, a reversal of this notion, holding that the real universe is located entirely within this subjective space; external space and the things which fill it being illusory projections only imagined to exist.

Hṛd:

The location of the universe in the subjective "space within the heart" is essentially a cosmological extension of the notion that the heart is the seat of consciousness. Thus, it is said that, in sleep and at death, when the faculties of the individual are re-absorbed into consciousness, the "person made of consciousness" *(vijñāna-maya-puruṣa)*,[104] or in some cases the soul *(ātman)*,[105] descends into the heart. The notion of the heart as locus or seat of consciousness may be traced back even to the *Ṛg Veda*. Chapter 3 examined the close association of *hṛd* and *manas* as the primary loci of consciousness.

102. T.U. 2.1; 1.6.1; B.U. 2.3.1; 2.3.6; 4.4.22; C.U. 3.12.7-9; 8.3.3; K.U. 2.1.6; Mt.U. 6.27; 7.7. Cp. B.U. 2.3.5; 3.9.14-17; 4.3.7; 5.6; C.U. 3.14.3; P.U. 3.6; Mu.U. 2.1.4; Mt.U. 6.28.

103. Mt.U. 6.28. Cp. B.U. 3.9.25.

104. B.U. 2.1.17.

105. B.U. 4.4.1.

In the *Upaniṣads, manas*[106] and the "mind made person" *(mano-maya-puruṣa)*[107] are sometimes located in the heart, as is consciousness in general.[108] Though *hṛd* is generally regarded as the location of the innermost center of the human being,[109] it is also an occasion conceived of as a faculty rather than a location.[110] In this case it may be regarded as identical with manas.[111] More commonly, it is a faculty distinct from, though similar to *manas.* Thus, it is said in parallel phrases in three passages that ultimate reality is apprehended by the cooperation of heart, thought and mind *(hṛdā manīṣā manasābhiklpta).*[112]

In a similar passage, the heart is apparently represented as simultaneously a faculty and the location of the absolute, in this case conceived of theistically.

> His form is not seen; no one sees Him with the eye. Those who through heart and mind know Him as abiding in the heart become immortal.
>
> S.U. 4.20 (R)

The sublime nature of the heart as a faculty capable, in conjunction with *manas,* of perceiving ultimate reality is tainted by its supposed possession, again like *manas,* of several desirable and undesirable emotions. These range from grief *(śoka)* and desire *(kāma)* to tranquillity and satisfaction.[113] A passage in the *Aitareya Upaniṣad*

---

106. A.U. 1.1.4; 1.2.4.

107. B.U. 5.6; T.U. 1.6.1.

108. B.U. 4.4.22; T.U. 6.1.

109. S.U. 4.17; K.U. 1.2.20; 2.3.17; Ks.U. 4.19.

110. Cp. B.U. 5.3., where Prajāpati and *brahman* are said to be equivalent to the heart rather than located in it.

111. A.U. 3.2.

112. K.U. 2.3.9; S.U. 3.13; 4.17, adopting the reading of Śaṁkārānanda, Nārāyana and Vijñāna-bhikṣu for S.U. 3.13. Śaṅkara reads, instead of *manīṣa, manvīsa,* which he explains as *jñānesa,* "lord of knowledge". See Radhakrishnan's note.

113. See B.U. 4.3.22 *(śoka);* K.U. 2.3.14 and B.U. 4.4.7 *(kāma);* C.U. 8.3 (tranquil); C.U. 8.9.2 (satisfied); K.U. 2.3.15 and Mu.U. 2.2.9 (knots).

gives a list of the various qualities of heart and mind reminiscent of the extensive lists of "mental things" *(cetasikā dhammā)* in the Buddhist Abhidhamma literature.

> That which is the heart *(hṛdaya)*, this mind *(manas)*, that is perception *(saṁjñāna)*, determination *(ājñāna)*, consciousness *(vijñāna)*, intelligence *(prajñāna)*, wisdom *(medhā)*, insight *(dṛṣṭi)*, steadfastness *(dhṛti)*, thought *(mati)*, imagination *(manīsā)*, impulse *(jūti)*, memory *(smṛti)*, conceptualization *(saṁkalpa)*, will *(kratu)*, life *(asu)*, desire *(kāma)*, control *(vaśa)*, all these, indeed, are names of intelligence *(prajñāna)*.
>
> A.U. 3.1.2

At one point the functions of heart and mind as mental faculties are specifically differentiated. Here, the heart, whose function is wisdom *(vidyā)*, apparently is ranked above mind, the function of which is said to be conceptualization *(saṁkalpa)*.[114] But at another point the "mind-made, breath-bodied leader" *(mano-mayaḥ prāṇṁa-śarīra-netṛ)*, doubtlessly equivalent to the *mano-maya-puruṣa*,[115] is said to control the heart.[116] In one verse, the heart is said to assume the role normally assigned to *manas* as the support of forms *(rūpa)* and the eye, is being said that one knows *(jānati)* forms with the heart.[117] In this same passage, the heart is also said to function as the support of faith and truth, it being by heart that these are known.[118] It is even said that semen is supported on the heart, that a child who looks like its parents is "slipped from the heart" *(hṛdayād iva sṛpta)* or "made from the heart" *(hṛdayād iva nirmitta)*.[119] Interestingly,

---

114. B.U. 2.4.11.

115. Radhakrishnan's translation of this phrase, "consists of mind and is the leader of life and body" is probably wrong, since the phrase *mano-mayaḥ prāṇa-śarīra* is a common adjective for *puruṣa*.

116. Mu.U. 2.2.8.

117. B.U. 3.9.20. Cp. B.U. 1.5.3.

118. B.U. 3.9.21 & 23.

119. B.U. 3.9.22.

Yajñāvalkya, the speaker of these verses, says elsewhere that it is because of *manas* that a son resembles his father.[120]

As some of the preceding might suggest, the heart is also said to serve a vital function in a few passages. For example, *prāṇa* is said to reside in the heart.[121] In an interesting variation on the audible universal fire within oneself, one is said to hear the space within the heart when one covers one's ears.[122] The vitalistic function of the heart is recalled too in the theory of the extremely subtle channels *(hīta* or *nādi)*, as fine as "a hair divided a thousandfold",[123] which are said to radiate from the heart like spokes from the hub of a wheel.[124] In one verse, these are said to be the thoroughfares of the "diffused breath" *(vyāna)*,[125] but elsewhere it is the "intelligent soul" *(prajñā-ātman)* which is said to resort to these channels during dreamless sleep.[126]

The unconsciousness of sleep is thought to be paralleled by the unconsciousness after death, which is also represented as entrance into these channels.[127] Rebirth is said to result from passage of the soul through any of the numerous secondary channels, while liberation is the result of its passing the head.[128] All of these channels are supposed to be connected with the rays of the sun.[129] This appears to be a metaphorical expression of the identity of the individual with the universal principle, though apparently only passage though the central channel is sufficient to gain absolute unity with this principle.[130]

---

120. B.U. 4.1.6.

121. B.U. 2.3.5. Cp. C.U. 3.12, where the breath faculties are said to be established on the heart.

122. Mt.U. 6.22.

123. B.U. 4.2.

124. Mu.U. 2.2.6. Normally there are said to be 101 channels (C.U. 8.6; K.U. 2.3.16). At P.U. 3.6, there are said to be 101 main channels, each of which has 100 finer channels, each of which has 72,000 super fine branches, a total of 101 + 10,100 + 727,200,000 = 727,210,101 channels.

125. P.U. 3.6.

126. C.U. 8.6; B.U. 2.1.17-19. Cp. B.U. 4.3.20; Ks.U. 4.19.

127. B.U. 4.2.3; C.U. 8.6; K.U. 2.3.16.

128. C.U. 8.6.6; K.U. 2.3.6; CP. A.U. 1.3.2.

129. C.U. 8.6.1; Mt.U. 6.30. Cp. P.U. 4.2; K.U. 2.3.6.

130. C.U. 8.6.6; K.U. 2.3.6; Mt.U. 6.30. Cp. A.U. 1.3.12.

This theory of subtle channels in the body, through which a person's vitality and consciousness is supposed to flow, was made much of in tantric systems, particularly Kuṇḍalinī Yoga. In this system, the heart and the crown of the head — mentioned in these Upaniṣadic texts — are two of the *cakras*, or "psychic centers" in the body. It is possible that an ancient form of some such system underlies many of the rather confusing aspects of the heart in the *Upaniṣads*, in particular its sexual aspect as the support of semen. The heart is also said to be the bed chamber of Puruṣa and Virāj, the universal couple, whose "place of movement *(saṁcaraṇi)*", a fairly obvious sexual euphemism, is said to be the central channel.[131] Many of these same ideas are prominent in Buddhist *tantra* as well, in particular the sexual aspects of the channels and the importance of the semen *(śukra* or *bindu*, Tib. *thig-le)*, representing *bodhi-citta* and/or *śunyatā*, and said to be active within the channels and *cakras*.[132]

In general, though, the *Upaniṣads*, depict the heart as the location of consciousness. The location of the universe and the universal principle in the heart is indicative of the ascendancy of psychological over vitalistic concepts of the nature of the soul and the universe. It is perhaps worth noting that, as in the *Ṛg Veda*, *hṛd* is not identified with the biological organ in the *Upaniṣads*.[133] Again, the term might be better understood as simply "center". It is interesting too that with all the Upaniṣadic concern with the empirical signs of life — breath, warmth, the sound of the digestive fire — the beating of the heart is never mentioned. It is perhaps also noteworthy that though the early Buddhists borrowed many Upaniṣadic psychological terms, the use of *hṛd* as a technical term was not adopted until the appearance of the *hadaya-vatthu* in the Abhidhamma and commentarial literature of Theravāda Buddhism. This may be because of the term's strong

131. B.U. 4.2.3; Mt.U. 7.11; S.B. 10.5.2.11-12.

132. See David Snellgrove, *The Hevajra Tantra*, vol. 1, Oxford University Press, London, 1959, index and glossary under *"bindu"* and *"thig-le"*. See also Lama A. Govinda, *Foundations of Tibetan Mysticism*, Rider, London, 1969, index under *"śukra, bindu, thig-le"*. See also Garma C. Chang, *Teachings of Tibetan Yoga*, University Books, Secaucus, N.J., 1963, pp. 55-81.

133. The only possible exception is the reference at B.U. 4.2.3 to the "net like structure" in the heart, which probably, however, refers to the subtle channels and not to an anatomical feature.

connotation of psychological centrality, which of course, Buddhism shunned.[134]

Manas:

Within the "space within the heart", the seat of consciousness, there developed a fairly extensive hierarchy of consciousness in the *Upaniṣads*. Generally, the lowest level of supra-sensuous consciousness is assigned to *manas*, presumably because of its association with mundane consciousness as *sensus communis*. *Manas*, however, is also sometimes depicted as the supreme faculty of the soul, capable of apprehending ultimate truth.[135] Elsewhere, however, it is specifically denied that *manas* is capable of apprehending ultimate truth,[136] and *manas* is often represented as an intermediate level of consciousness with several levels above it. These levels will be examined below, but first it is useful to examine some of the characteristics of *manas* which eventually necessitated the introduction of purer levels of consciousness above it.

The most common characteristic or function of *manas* in the *Upaniṣads* is *saṁkalpa*, probably best rendered as "conceptualization", which is sometimes represented as the simple object of *manas* in the same way objects of the sense faculties are treated.[137] It is clear, however, that *saṁkalpa* is not to be regarded as a mere sensual object, and that its association with *manas* belongs primarily to the stage of Upaniṣadic psychology in which *manas* is considered a super-sense presiding over the others. From one point of view, *manas* creates ordered conceptualizations from sensual information. In the Upaniṣadic scheme, however, the reverse is more commonly the case, and *manas*, by conceptualization, is thought to provide the template for an orderly universe.[138] Thus, it is said of the person who knows the soul:

134. See E.R. Sarathchandra, *Buddhist Psychology of Perception*, p. 38.

135. K.U. 2.3.9; 2.1.11; S.U. 3.13; 4.17.

136. K.U. 2.3.12.

137. B.U. 2.4.11; 4.5.12; Ks.U. 3.2.

138. Cp. C.U. 7.4.3.

> 1. If he becomes desirous of the world of the fathers *(pitṛ-loka)*, by the mere thought *(saṁkalpa)*, fathers arise. Possessed of the world of the fathers he is happy.
>
> 2-9. [Similar treatments of various other worlds occur.]
>
> 10. Of whatever object he becomes desirous, whatever desire he desires, out of his mere thought it arises. Possessed of it he is happy.
>
> C.U. 8.2.1-10 (R)

Manas, however, is the repository of several functions and characteristics of which *saṁkalpa* is only the most frequently mentioned. Some of the various enumerations of the attributes of *manas*, which may include both good and bad qualities, are reminiscent of the extensive analytical lists of *dhammas*, the "objects" of *manas*, which were developed in the Buddhist Abhidhamma literature. Of these desire *(kāma)*, and volition *(kratu)* have already been noted. These two attributes of *manas* relate to *saṁkalpa* as creative conceptualization in what is perhaps a surprising way, i.e. through the mechanism of *karma* and rebirth.

The creative aspect of *kratu* in the *Ṛg Veda*, where "mental power" is a more satisfactory translation of the term, is in effect transferred to *saṁkalpa* in the Upaniṣadic scheme. This leaves *kratu* as a purely volitional force in the *Upaniṣads*. Cited above was a causal sequence reminiscent to some extent of the Buddhist doctrine of *pratītyasamutpāda*, according to which: as the desire *(kāma)*, so the will *(kratu)*; as the will, so the act *(karma)*; as the act, so the attainment in rebirth.[139] In the initial stages of Upaniṣadic psychology, transmigration was viewed as the simple passage of the individual soul to another body, like an caterpillar crawling from leaf to leaf at B.U. 4.4.3. There is also evidence, however, of a long tradition assigning a creative function to the soul. In fact, in the verse immediately following the caterpillar simile the soul is said to fashion a new body like a smith casting gold.[140] These two ideas, which appear to be the result of a synthesis of Vedic and non-Vedic material, were gradually dovetailed in the concept that death and rebirth actually represent the

---

139. B.U. 4.4.5.

140. B.U. 4.4.3-4.

absorption by and re-projection from the soul of the faculties and their objects. According to this concept, the nature of the universe is determined by the various qualities of the mind through which it is projected, as light is colored by a tinted lens.

The tint of the lens would be analogous to the numerous good and bad qualities said to exist in *manas*, the lowest purely conscious level of the soul. The early stages of attempts to categorize the qualities of the human mind are probably reflected in passages such as the following. This passage does not specifically locate these qualities in *manas* or in any other particular faculty, but enumerates them alongside the faculties as being encompassed in the individual *cum* universal principle.

> That soul *(ātman)* is, indeed, *brahman*, characterized *(-maya)* by consciousness *(vijñāna)*, mind *(manas)*, breath *(prāṇa)*, sight, hearing, earth, water, wind, space, heat *(tejas)*, non-heat, desire *(kāma)*, non-desire, anger, non-anger, *dharma*, *adharma*, everything. Thus it is said, "made *(-maya)* of this, made of that". As one acts, as he behaves, so he becomes. The doer of good becomes good. The doer of evil becomes evil. Good comes of good action, bad of bad. Thus it is said, "This person *(puruṣa)* is characterized by desire *(kāmamaya)*". As is the desire, so is the will *(kratu)*. As is the will, so the deed performed. As is the deed performed, so the attainment.
>
> B.U. 4.4.5

Elsewhere a similar enumeration of human qualities is specifically located in the *manas*, which is also represented as the *sensus communis*.[141]

> Three he made for himself. Mind speech and breath he made for himself. (It is said) "My mind was elsewhere, I did not hear". Indeed, one sees with the mind; one hears with the mind. Desire *(kāma)*, conceptualization *(saṁkalpa)*, doubt *(vicikitsā)*, faith *(śraddhā)*, non-

141. Cp. Mt.U. 6.30.

> faith, steadfastness *(dhṛti)*, non-steadfastness, shame *(hrī)*, vision *(dhī)*, fear *(bhī)*, all this is mind *(manas)*.
>
> B.U. 1.5.2

An even more extensive list of such qualities of *manas* was quoted above in a citation from the *Aitareya Upaniṣad*.[142]

In general, the principal *Upaniṣads* are content with such more or less random listings of the qualities of *manas*. A more purposeful enumeration of qualities, including conceptualization *(saṁkalpa)*, determination *(adhyavasāya)* and conceit *(abhimāna)*, occurs several times in the *Maitrī Upaniṣad* as a definition of the characteristics *(liṅga)* of the *puruṣa* or *kṣetra-jña* ("knower of the field"). In this context, both of these terms, as in Sāṁkhya technical terminology, appear to be epithets of the soul in general.[143] A similar passage, however, by referring to a specific definition of *manas*,[144] suggests that this enumeration applies specifically to *manas* as a faculty of the soul.

> Indeed, one sees with the mind, one hears with the mind. Desire, conceptualization, doubt ... all this is mind. Borne along and defiled by the stream of qualities *(guṇa)*, unsteady, fickle, bewildered, full of desire, distracted, one comes to conceit. Thinking, "I am he; this is mine", he entangles himself with himself as a bird in a snare. Thus, the person *(puruṣa)*, characterized by determination *(adhyavasāya)*, conceptualization *(saṁkalpa)* and conceit *(abhimāna)*, is bound. The opposite of that is liberated. Therefore stand free of determination, conceptualization and conceit. This is the path to *brahman*.
>
> Mt.U. 6.30

The definition offered here is purposeful and systematic. It seeks to categorize exhaustively the characteristics of the deluded mind under three headings, conceptualization, determination and conceit. It implies that the mind falls prey to its own conceptualizations by objectively

142. A.U. 3.2.

143. Mt.U. 2.5; 5.2; 6.10; 6.30.

144. B.U. 1.5.3. Cp. B.U. 4.4.6.

concretizing them through determination and subjectively setting up the egoistic self as existing over against these objects through conceit.

If such are the characteristics of the deluded mind, the mind relieved of these faults is sublime, but ambiguously so.

> The mind *(manas)* it is said, is of two kinds, pure and impure, impure from contact with desire and pure when freed from desire. By freeing mind from sloth and distraction and making it motionless, he becomes delivered from his mind, then that is the supreme state. ... Mind, in truth, is the cause of bondage and liberation for mankind; for bondage if it is bound to objects; freedom from objects, that is called liberation.
>
> Mt.U. 6.34 (R)

In general, as the foregoing discussion suggests, *manas* is more associated with mundane, sensual consciousness and activity than with pure consciousness, which is here characterized simultaneously as freedom of *manas* and freedom from *manas*. The pure, essential consciousness of the soul gradually came to be associated with a hierarchy of levels of consciousness purer and less active than *manas*, and the role of *manas* in the attainment of liberation became largely negative.[145]

> When the five senses and mind stand down (i.e. cease functioning), and the intellect *(buddhi)* does not stir, that is said to be the supreme attainment.
>
> K.U. 2.3.11

Faculties Derived from √*jñā:*

One source of terms for these purer levels of consciousness is the verbal root √*jñā*, "to know". In the *Ṛg Veda*, derivatives of this root occur in the forms *sam* + √*jñā*, meaning "to be in agreement", and *vi* + √*jñā*, meaning "to know" or occasionally "to know separately, discriminate". Such terms have no particular psychological significance in the *Ṛg Veda*. In the *Upaniṣads*, however, three derivatives of √*jñā*

145. Cp. K.U. 1.2.24; Mt.U. 6.19.

in particular denote more or less precise psychological concepts. These terms — *saṁjñā, vijñāna* and *prajñā* — have been noted above in several contexts. Unprefixed derivatives of √*jñā*, normally *jñāna*, usually mean simply "knowledge",[146] though derivatives of √*vid*, such as *veda*, are more common in this sense. *Jñāna* also occurs occasionally in the plural, in which case it designates the senses, as is common in the in the technical term *jñāna-indriya* (sense faculty).[147] In a few cases, *jñāna* is used synonymously with *vijñāna*,[148] but in general it is psychologically an insignificant term in the *Upaniṣads*.

Of the three psychologically significant derivatives of √*jñā* — *saṁjñā, vijñāna* and *prajñā* — *saṁjñā* (perception) is the least frequent and the least exalted. Sometimes it seems to mean simply "known as",[149] but it also occurs in contexts where it obviously refers to a faculty, though not a particularly essential faculty.[150]

> This great being *(bhūta)*, infinite, limitless, is a mass of consciousness *(vijñāna-ghana)*. Arising from these elements *(bhūta)*, back to them one perishes, and there is no more perception *(saṁjñā)*.
>
> B.U. 2.4.12

Obviously this passage represents *saṁjñā* as a lower order of consciousness than *vijñāna*. Here, *saṁjñā* probably refers to sensual consciousness, and is thus probably similar in meaning to the term *saññā* in Pāli Buddhist literature, though there are too few Upaniṣadic occurrences of the term to justify definite conclusions.

Two other psychologically significant derivatives of √*jñā* — *prajñā* and *vijñāna* — are more common in the *Upaniṣads* than the term *saṁjñā*. Both of these terms occur with basically three different

---

146. Mt.U. 6.34; 7.8; Mu.U. 3.1.8; 3.2.5; 1.1.8; Ma.U. 10.

147. K.U. 2.3.10;Mt.U. 6.30.

148. K.U. 1.3.13; T.U. 2.1.1. Cp. C.U. 7.7.2, where *vijñāna* and *jñāna* occur as synonyms meaning "knowledge".

149. Mt.U. 2.5; 6.10. The phrase *puruṣa-saṁjñā* at Mt.U. 2.5 almost has to be taken thus, but the statement that the world is *sukha-duḥkha-moha-saṁjñā* could be construed as a *dvandva* compound: "pleasure, pain, delusion and perception".

150. See also B.U. 4.5.13; A.U. 3.2.

meanings. They may, like *saṁjñā*, refer to sensual consciousness. They often mean simply "wisdom" *(prajñā)*,[151] or "understanding" *(vijñāna)*.[152] Most often though, they denote the pure "stuff" or essence of abstract consciousness, from which *manas* and the mundane senses emanate.

The equation of breath *(prāṇa)* with the *prajñā-ātman* is a common feature in the *Kauṣītakī Upaniṣad*,[153] and is an instance of the Upaniṣadic tendency to retain archaic vitalistic terminology for the expression of psychological theories of the soul. The phrase *prajñā-ātman*, though not identified with breath, also occurs in the *Aitareya Upaniṣad*,[154] as does the specific identification of *prajñā* with *brahman*.[155] The *Maitrī Upaniṣad*, on the other hand, states that *prajñā* is only one of the many characteristics *(liṅga)* of the soul *(ātman)*.[156]

The overall intent of *prajñā* as a psychological term is perhaps best stated in the *Māṇḍūkya Upaniṣad*, where *prajñā* is associated with the state of deep sleep, the penultimate level of the soul.

> 5. Where one, being fast asleep, does not desire any desire whatsoever and does not see any dream whatsoever, that is deep sleep. The third quarter is *prajñā*, whose sphere (of activity) is the state of deep sleep, who has become one, who is, verily, a mass of cognition *(prajñāna-ghana)*, who is full of bliss, whose face is thought *(ceto-mukha)*.
>
> 6. This is the lord of all, this is the knower of all, this is the inner controller; this is the source of all; this is the beginning and end of beings.
>
> Ma.U. 5-6 (R)

The essence of consciousness as denoted by the term *prajñā*, then, is thought to be experienced when consciousness *per se* ceases.

---

151. K.U. 1.1.14; 1.1.28; 1.2.24; Ks.U. 1.5; B.U. 4.4.21; S.U. 4.18; P.U. 2.13.

152. Ks.U. 3.3; C.U. 7.7.1; 7.8.1; 7.26.1; B.U. 2.4.5; 2.4.13; Mu.U. 1.2.12; 2.2.1; 2.2.7; 3.2.6.

153. Occurring specifically in five verses: Ks.U. 2.14; 3.2; 3.3; 3.8; 4.20.

154. A.U. 3.1.4.

155. A.U. 3.1.3.

156. Mt.U. 6.31.

As a psychological term, *prajñā* is in many ways similar to *vijñāna*, which may also be applied to the entire range of consciousness, from mundane to sublime.

> When this one fell asleep, then the consciousness-made person *(vijñāna-maya-puruṣa)*, by consciousness *(vijñāna)* having taken in the consciousness of these breath faculties *(prāṇa)*, rests within the space within the heart.
>
> B.U. 2.1.17

The reason for this broad significance of *vijñāna* is probably the same reason that seems to underlie the occasional use of the term *prajñā* to denote mundane consciousness, i.e. *vijñāna* also represents the essential stuff of consciousness which is tainted by sensual discrimination.

> Visualization *(dhyāna)* is directed to the highest reality within and to the perceptible *(lakṣya)*. Therefore undiscriminated consciousness *(vijñāna)* comes to be discriminated, but when the mind *(manas)* is dissolved, the bliss *(sukha)* witnessed by the soul is *brahman*, the immortal, the radiant. That is the destination. That is the world.
>
> Mt.U. 6.24

In most cases, the phrase *vijñāna-maya*, whether it refers to *puruṣa* or to *ātman*, obviously denotes the essential consciousness of the soul. The phrase *vijñāna-ātman*, analogous to *prajñā-ātman*, occurs,[157] as does the specific identification of *vijñāna* with *brahman*.[158] Of the two parallel versions of Yajñāvalkya's discourse to Maitrī, one describes the soul *(ātman)* as a *prajñā-ghana*, the other as a *vijñāna-ghana*, meaning "mass of consciousness" in either case.[159] Like *prajñā*, *vijñāna* is also conceived of as the subtle consciousness of deep

---

157. P.U. 4.9; 4.11.

158. B.U. 3.9.28; T.U. 3.5.1.

159. Cp. B.U. 4.5.13 *(prajñā-ghana)* and B.U. 2.4.12 *(vijñāna-ghana)*. See also Ma.U. 5 *(prajñāna-ghana)*.

sleep,[160] which is thought to be similar to the state immediately after death.

Neither the state of deep sleep nor the post-mortem state, however, ultimately was judged to be equivalent to the essential nature of the soul. Some passages suggest as much, but others explicitly refer to aspects of the soul even more essential than pure, passive consciousness. It is in this context that the meaning of *vijñāna* and *prajñā* begin to diverge. *Vijñāna* became a standard technical term for the penultimate level of the soul. *Prajñā* was increasingly associated specifically with wisdom rather than a theoretical level of consciousness. "Wisdom", in fact, is the exclusive meaning of *prajñā* or *paññā* by the time of early Buddhist literature. *Vijñāna*, on the other hand, tended to lose its connotation of "knowledge" and became a general psychological term probably best translated as simply "consciousness". The generality of the term, notable in early Buddhist literature, probably stems originally from the fact that in the *Upaniṣads*, as the ultimate or penultimate level of the soul, *vijñāna* was thought to emanate into all lower levels of consciousness, including the several faculties of perception and action. Thus, as the essential stuff of consciousness, it could be said to be present wherever there is any manifestation of consciousness of any type.

Citta:

Before turning to the various specific doctrines of the several layers of the soul, which do much to clarify Upaniṣadic psychological terminology, one more general term requires attention. As in the *Ṛg Veda*, various nominal derivatives of the verbal root √*cit* occur in the *Upaniṣads* with the basic meaning "thought". The most common forms are *citta* and *cetas*. These synonymous terms differ from *vijñāna* and *prajñā* as psychological terms only subtly in that they imply the process of consciousness rather than the stuff of consciousness. They differ subtly from *manas* in a similar way, implying process rather than faculty, but the derivatives of √*cit* are general enough in meaning that they can substitute for any of these terms. Perhaps the clearest

160. B.U. 2.1.17.

characterization of *citta* is the following passage, in which lack of *citta* does not mean a lack of the stuff of consciousness or any faculty of consciousness, but merely a deficient functioning of consciousness.[161]

> Even if a man be possessed of much learning, but is unthinking *(acitta)*, people say of him that he is nobody, whatever he may know. Verily, if he did know he would not be so unthinking. On the other hand, if he is thoughtful, even though he knows little, to him people are desirous of listening.
>
> C.U. 7.5.2 (R)

Citta may be associated with sensual consciousness, as in the following verse, where the departure of *citta* marks the end of such consciousness.

> When a sick person about to die gets to such weakness as to fall into a stupor *(sammoha)* they say of him, his thought *(citta)* has departed, he does not hear, he does not see, he does not speak with speech, he does not think *(dhyāyati)*.
>
> Ks.U. 3.3 (R)

As a purified *manas* is said to be capable of grasping the ultimate truth, so is a purified, serene *citta* said to be capable of the same.[162]

> This subtle soul *(ātman)* in which the fivefold breath faculties *(prāṇa)* are merged is knowable by thought *(citta)*. The thought of all beings is entangled with the breath faculties, when purified, the soul shines forth.
>
> Mu.U. 3.1.9

However, as in the case of *manas*, the purification of *citta* also seems to involve its cessation.

---

161. Cp. Mt.U. 6.7.

162. See also Mt.U. 6.20; 6.34. Cp. Mt.U. 4.4; Mu.U. 2.2.3.

> The one goes quickly to that condition (of liberation); as a lump of iron buried in the earth quickly becomes earth ... so does thought *(citta)* perish along with its basis *(āśraya)*.
>
> Mt.U. 6.27

In other cases derivatives of √*cit* seem to be construed as the essence of the soul and universe, as in the following passages, where thought is said to be the fundamental characteristic of both the individual and the universal soul.

> This body is like a cart, without thought. By the power of what supersensuous being is it made to arise with thought *(cetanavat)*; or who is its mover?
>
> Mt.U. 2.3

> The enjoyer *(bhoktṛ)* of this (universe) is without qualities *(nirguṇa)*, but because of its being an enjoyer, it must have thought *(caitanya)*.
>
> Mt.U. 6.10

Elsewhere, *buddhi, manas* and *aham-kāra*, three of the suprasensuous levels of the soul, are all said to be the "thought aspect" *(cetanavatī)* of the universal principle.[163] Thus, the derivatives of √*cit*, which were never specifically ranked in any of the Upaniṣadic hierarchies of consciousness, comprise the most general set of terms for consciousness in the *Upaniṣads*.

It is interesting that the idealistic tendency of the *Upaniṣads* to regard the world as a creation of consciousness is most explicitly stated with recourse to terms derived from √*cit*, in a few late passages remarkably reminiscent of Yogācāra Buddhism.[164]

---

163. Mt.U. 6.5.

164. See also Mt.U. 2.5; 5.2.

> At the dissolution of all, he alone remains awake. Thus from that space, he awakes this (world) which consists of thought only *(cetāmātra)*.
> Mt.U. 6.17 (R)

It is doubtlessly with reference to the theory of rebirth as the re-creation of the universe that the volitional aspects of *citta* as the criterion of rebirth are to be understood.[165]

> One's own thought, indeed, is *saṁsāra;* let a man cleanse it by effort. What a man thinks, what he becomes, this is the eternal mystery.
> Mt.U. 6.34 (R)

The careful reader will have noted that most of the psychologically significant derivatives of √*cit* occur in relatively late passages, the majority being in the *Maitrī Upaniṣad*. The explanation behind the late rise to popularity of these terms is probably an increasing Upaniṣadic interest in idealistic metaphysics rather than psychological analysis. *Citta* is a handy term in this context by virtue of being a general term for consciousness without any specific psychological connotations. At any rate, *citta* is the last of the general terms for consciousness to be examined here. The rest of the terms to be considered are more specific in that their occurrence is almost entirely confined to the context of various hierarchical schemes of consciousness. *Manas* and *vijñāna* also occur in several of these integrated schemes, with the result that the precise meanings of these terms become much clearer than they would be otherwise.

Hierarchies of Consciousness:

The terms *buddhi* and *ahaṁkara* will immediately be recognized as the two primary *sattvika* evolutes of *prakṛti* in the classical Sāṁkhya system. It iṣ in the context of what are obviously proto-Sāṁkhya passages that these terms most often occur in the *Upaniṣads.* The term *kśetra-jñā*, which also makes its debut in the *Upaniṣads,* is

---

165. See the rest of Mt.U. 6.34 and Mt.U. 6.20.

typical Sāṁkhya euphemism for *puruṣa*. The meanings of these Upaniṣadic technical terms are roughly similar to their classical counterparts. However, the cardinal doctrines of Sāṁkhya, namely the plurality of individual souls *(puruṣa)* and their strict separation from matter *(prakṛti)* are lacking in most if not all Upaniṣadic passages. Instead, the most obvious Upaniṣadic prefigurations of Sāṁkhya are either monistic, as in the *Kaṭha* and *Maitrī Upaniṣads*, or theistic, as in the *Śvetāśvatara Upaniṣad*. These two Upaniṣadic points of view are clearly illustrated in the following passages.

This (world) was darkness *(tamas)* in the beginning, a unity. That was in the supreme. When impelled by the supreme it goes to differentiation. That form is *rajas*. That *rajas*, when impelled, goes to differentiation. That is the form of *sattva*. That *sattva* impelled, the essence flowed forth. That part is this field-knower, which is thought-only and (is found) in (all) souls *(cetā-mātraḥ pratipuruṣaḥ kṣetrajña)*.
Mt.U. 5.2

13. The permanent of the permanent, the thought *(cetana)* of thoughts, the one among the many, he grants desires. Having known god, the cause, by practising Sāṁkhya and Yoga, one is freed from all snares.

16. He is the all-maker, all-knower, self-originated, the conscious *(jñaḥ)*, maker of time, possessor of (all) qualities, all-wise, the ruler of nature and the field-knower *(pradhāna-kṣetrajña-pati)*, the lord of qualities *(guṇa)*, the cause of *saṁsāra*, liberation, stability and bondage.
S.U. 6.13-16

The *Śvetāśvatara* passage is apparently theistic, and though the version of Sāṁkhya metaphysics adopted by the orthodox Yoga school allows for a theistic god, this god could not be styled the ruler of the *kṣetrajña*, i.e. the soul *(puruṣa)*. Nor could this god be considered the ruler of material nature, *pradhāna* or *prakṛti*, since god, in the classical Yoga system is only an instance of a soul which has never been associated with *prakṛti*. The *Maitrī* passage on the other hand employs Sāṁkhya technical terms in a monistic context. Here, the *kṣetrajña* represents a universal soul standing behind all individual souls, which are apparently labeled *puruṣa* in this passage.[166] Moreover, this universal *kṣetrajña* is said to be the source of the three classical *guṇas* of *prakṛti*, all of which is a far cry from the theories of classical Sāṁkhya.

Ahaṁkāra, another technical term typical of Sāṁkhya, is the second *sattvika* evolute of *prakṛti*, and means literally "I-maker", i.e. "self-sense" or "ego". It occurs in three proto-Sāṁkhya passages in the *Upaniṣads*, but always as an evolute of the soul rather than, as in the classical system, an evolute of matter *(prakṛti)*.[167] The term occurs once more in an earlier passage in the *Chāndogya Upaniṣad*, but without apparent connection to Sāṁkhya terminology, the *ahaṁkāra-ādeśa* ("teaching with regard to I-making") being in that passage the monistic meditation "I am all this (world)".[168]

Sāṁkhya, of course, means literally "enumeration", so it is perhaps not surprising that the majority of hierarchical enumerations of the several levels of consciousness in the *Upaniṣads* involve some Sāṁkhya terminology. In the classical Sāṁkhya system, however, the enumeration is essentially of the various evolutes of matter *(prakṛti)*, some of which only appear to have consciousness. In the *Upaniṣads*, these enumerations represent an attempt to shade individual consciousness off into the universal soul without admitting any sharp demarcation between the two. It is almost exclusively in the context of such attempts that the term *buddhi* appears.[169] It is not altogether clear why "intellect" is the most common translation offered for the term *buddhi*, since in both the classical Sāṁkhya system as well as in the majority of Upaniṣadic contexts, the term represents passive, non-conceptual consciousness. Generally speaking, it may be regarded as representing the upper level of *vijñāna* while *manas* represents the lower, sensual level. The derivation of the term from the root √*budh*, "to wake up", suggests "awareness" as a more satisfactory translation.

166. See also Mt.U. 2.5.

167. S.U. 5.8; Mt.U. 6.5; P.U. 4.8.

168. C.U. 7.25.

169. Exceptions being S.U. 3.4, where Rudra is asked to "endow us with a clear *buddhi*", and Mt.U. 6.31, where mention is made of those who hold that the *ātman* is comprised of *buddhi, dhṛti, smṛti* and *prajñā*. Cp. Mt.U. 6.7.

In the classical Sāṁkhya system, *buddhi* is the first, most sublime *sattvika* evolute of *prakṛti*, followed by *ahaṁkāra* and then *manas*. In the only Upaniṣadic passage which actually ranks these three aspects of consciousness, however, *ahaṁkāra* comes out on top of *buddhi* and *manas*.[170] This passage also differs from the classical scheme by ranking *citta* (thought), *tejas* (heat), and *prāṇa* (breath) above *ahaṁkāra*, as well as by resolving the whole scheme into the "supreme soul".[171] Elsewhere, though, the phrase *buddhi-ādi* "awareness etc." implies the preeminence of *buddhi* in the hierarchy of consciousness. The passage in question is highly obscure, but worth quoting inasmuch as it is an obvious prefiguration of the Sāṁkhya scheme of the evolution of the *tattvas* or "basic reals".

> The nature of (perceptual) food (arises) from inherent transformation *(pariṇamatvāt)*. Thus there is perception *(upalabdhi)* of nature's *(pradhānasya)* becoming distinguished. For tasting (it) arise awareness etc. *(buddhi-ādi)*, determination, conceptualization and conceit *(adhyavasāya-saṁkalpa-abhimānā)*. Then arise the five sense objects *(indriya-artha)* for tasting, and thus all of the sense activities *(indriya-karmāṇi)* and vital activities *(prāṇa-karmāṇi)*.
>
> Mt.U. 6.10

The categories and terminology of the foregoing obviously resemble those of the classical Sāṁkhya system, and something similar to the evolution of the *tattvas* is obviously implied. It would be inadvisable, however, to interpret the preceding passage along classical Sāṁkhya lines because of the overt monism of the *Maitrī Upaniṣad* in general. It is, at any rate, probably a very late passage as Upaniṣadic passages go.

A much less esoteric, and probably much earlier proto-Sāṁkhya hierarchy of consciousness occurs in the form of the Upaniṣadic chariot simile, which, in its most archaic form is found in the *Kaṭha Upaniṣad*. Actually, an extremely early reference to a chariot in the *Ṛg Veda* appears in retrospect to have psychological significance, but

170. Cp. P.U. 4.8; Mt.U. 6.5 and S.U. 5.8, where no ranking seems to be implied.

171. P.U. 4.7.

nothing is ever made of it in the Vedic theory of consciousness. It occurs, moreover, in a hymn dedicated to the weapons of war.

> 6. Upstanding in the car the skilful charioteer guides his strong horses on withersoe'er he will. See and admire the strength of those controlling reins which from behind declare the will *(manas)* of him who drives.
>
> 7. Horses whose hoofs rain dust are neighing loudly, yoked to the chariots *(rathebhiḥ saha),* showing forth their vigour. With their forefeet descending on the foemen, they, never flinching, trample and destroy them.
>
> *Ṛg* 6.75.6-7 (G)

The chariot described in the *Kaṭha Upaniṣad,* by contrast, is of obvious psychological significance.

> 3. Know the soul *(ātman)* as the rider of the chariot, and the body as the chariot itself. Know awareness *(buddhi)* as the charioteer, mind *(manas)* as the reins.
>
> 4. The faculties *(indriya)* are said to be the horses; objects are their ranges. That which is yoked *(yukta)* to the soul, faculties and mind, the wise declare is (called) "the enjoyer" *(bhoktṛ).*
>
> 5. He who is not conscious *(avijñānavān),* with an always unyoked *(ayukta)* mind, his faculties are uncontrolled, like bad horses for a charioteer.
>
> 6. But he who is conscious, whose mind is always yoked, his faculties are controlled, like good horses for a charioteer.
>
> 7. He who is not conscious, who is mentally unstable *(amanaska)* and always impure, does not reach the goal, and he returns to *saṁsāra.*
>
> 8. But he who is conscious, who is mentally stable and always pure, he reaches the goal from which he is not born again.
>
> 9. The man with consciousness as the charioteer, who holds the mental reins, he reaches the end of the journey, the supreme place of Viṣṇu.
>
> 10. Beyond the faculties are the objects, and beyond the objects is the mind. Beyond the mind is the awareness *(buddhi),* and beyond awareness is the great soul *(ātmā mahan).*
>
> 11. Beyond the great *(mahat)* is the unmanifest *(avyakta),* beyond the unmanifest is the person *(puruṣa).* Beyond the person there is nothing whatsoever. That is the end. That is the supreme state.
>
> 12. This soul hidden in all beings does not shine forth, but is seen by subtle seers with keen and subtle awareness.

13. Let the wise man restrain speech in mind, restrain that (mind) in the conscious soul *(jñāna-ātman);* restrain the consciousness *(jñāna)* in the great; restrain that in the tranquil soul *(śānta-ātman).*

K.U. 1.3.3-13

The chariot model of consciousness is perhaps the clearest Upaniṣadic treatment of *manas* as *sensus communis*. A version of the chariot simile which occurs in the *Maitrī Upaniṣad* is explicit in putting both the faculties of perception and the faculties of action under the control of *manas*. It is somewhat confusing, however, in that it identifies *manas* with the charioteer, the reins with the perceptual faculties and the horses with the action faculties, even though perception would not seem to control action.[172] In the above citation, the translation "conscious" for *vijñānavān* is, of course, open to question, as "having understanding", Radhakrishnan's rendition, is also a plausible choice. Certainly "conscious" must be taken as meaning alert, introspective consciousness rather than mere sentience.

At any rate, the equation of *vijñāna* with the charioteer and thereby with *buddhi* in verse nine is fairly clear. This position, a rank above *manas*, is the position *vijñāna* enjoys in the five-*kośa* hierarchy of the soul. The fate of the individual is represented as being in the hands of *buddhi*, in what is obviously an attempt to isolate the *ātman*, the rider of the chariot, from the realm of sensual and volitional activity. To insure that this is understood, the terms of the original analogy are transgressed in verses ten and eleven with two more Sāṁkhya technical terms. These, however, obviously do not carry their classical meanings here. *Mahan* or *mahat*, in the first place, is a synonym for *buddhi* in classical Sāṁkhya, whereas here the *ātmā mahan*, abbreviated as *mahat* in verse eleven, is said to be the rider of the chariot, the soul itself. *Avyakta* (unmanifest) is a euphemism for *prakṛti* in the classical system, but could not mean that here. Instead if must refer to pure being, which, under various names, is often called *avyakta* in other Upaniṣadic passages.[173] Puruṣa is obviously

---

172. Mt.U. 2.6.

173. K.U. 1.3.11; 2.3.7-8; Mt.U. 6.10; 6.22; 2.7.

intended as a yet higher level of being, even further removed from sensual and volitional activity.[174]

Does active consciousness, then, play an entirely negative role in the attainment of release? The classical Sāṁkhya answer is "yes". In that system, *buddhi*, etc. are merely evolutes of matter. The *Upaniṣads* vacillate on this point and contradict themselves repeatedly. For example, it is said in verse twelve of the preceding citation that the ultimate soul may be seen with a "keen and subtle awareness *(buddhi)*". This view seems to be reiterated in the less ancient second section of the *Kaṭha Upaniṣad*, where it is said that one should awake *(boddhum)* before the body perishes or else one will be reborn.[175] Presumably *boddhum* means in this context "to perceive by *buddhi*", but the verse is followed by a series of verses stating that as a condition for liberation the five senses and mind *(manas)* must cease to function and *buddhi* must not stir. Further, they state contradictorily that the ultimate soul is to be apprehended *(abhiklpta)* by heart *(hṛd)* and *manas*, and that it is not to be apprehended *(prāptum)* by *manas*.[176] In the end, the latter is the predominant view. Particularly in later verses, active consciousness is usually said to be opposed to the ultimate attainment, which is increasingly characterized as non-consciousness.

> That which is non-thought *(acitta)*, which stands in the midst of thought, the unthinkable *(acintya)*, the hidden, the highest, let a man merge his thought there. Then will this living being *(liṅga)* be without support *(nirāśraya)*.
>
> Mt.U. 6.19 (R)

Is release, then, merely like going to sleep? Again, there is contradictory material in the *Upaniṣads*, but the predominant answer is that yes, it is,[177] as well as something more. We have seen Maitrī's consternation when Yajñāvalkya told her that there is no more *saṁjñā*

174. See K.U. 2.3.6-8.

175. K.U. 2.3.4.

176. K.U. 2.3.9-12.

177. B.U. 2.1.18; C.U. 8.11.3.

after death, which in that context apparently means after the death of one who has attained release.[178] In one version of this teaching, though, Yajñāvalkya assures her that the soul is imperishable and indestructible,[179] so presumably there is more to the soul than *saṁjñā*. This could be *vijñāna*, since Yajñāvalkya has defined the soul as a "mass of consciousness" *(vijñāna-ghana)*, but in the following verses, the survival of *vijñāna* seems to be refuted along with that of the senses and *manas*. Apparently union with the absolute entails putting an end to consciousness, though it also entails reaching the source of consciousness, as well as eternal life.[180]

> Where there is duality, as it were, there one sees another, smells ... tastes ... speaks ... hears ... thinks *(manute)* ... touches ... is conscious of *(vijānāti)* another. But where everything has become one's own soul, what and by what should one see ... of what and by what should one be conscious? How should one be conscious of that by means of which he is conscious of all this? That soul is not this, not that *(neti neti)*. ... How should one be conscious of the cognizer *(vijñātṛ)* itself?
>
> B.U. 4.5.15

In other words, though the soul is the source of consciousness, that consciousness cannot be conscious of its source.[181] Consciousness, in other words, can only be conscious of that which is other than itself, but it is precisely that content which constitutes the impurity of consciousness. Pure consciousness is, then, of necessity, non-consciousness, and consciousness, of necessity, is impure. It will be remembered that the creation of the universe is said to have started with an attempt by the soul to know itself, thereby initiating the creative condition of illusory duality.

> 1. In the beginning this (world) was only the self *(ātman)*, in the form of a person *(puruṣa)*. Looking around he saw nothing else than the self. He first said, 'I am'. ...

178. B.U. 2.4.12-13; 4.5.13.

179. B.U. 4.5.14.

180. Similar ideas at B.U. 3.4.2; C.U. 7.24; 8.11.

181. B.U. 3.7.23; 3.8.11; 4.23-31.

> 2. He was afraid. Therefore, one who is alone is afraid. This one then thought to himself, 'Since there is nothing else than myself, of what am I afraid?' Thereupon his fear, verily, passed away, for, of what should he have been afraid? Assuredly it is from a second that fear arises.
>
> B.U. 1.4.1-2 (R)

This fear is apparently the same as the "fear of the knower" mentioned in the *Taittirīya Upaniṣad.*

> When, however, this (soul) makes in this one the smallest interval, then, for him, there is fear. That, verily, is the fear of the knower, who does not reflect.
>
> T.U. 2.7.1 (R)

The "fear of the knower", however, is not as fearful to the average person as the fear of being a non-knower. Even Indra, the king of the gods, does not find such a prospect appealing. Thus, in reaction to the teaching that the essence of the soul is reached in deep sleep, he says:

> Venerable Sir, in truth this one does not know himself that I am he, nor indeed the things here. He has become one who has gone to annihilation. I see no good in this.
>
> C.U. 8.11.2 (R)

This hesitation to strive for permanent unconsciousness is apparently, as one would expect, a common reaction among Upaniṣadic students, but it is held to be the result of a deficient understanding of things spiritual.

> If one clearly beholds the divine soul, as the lord of what has been and what will be, he does not shrink away from it.
>
> B.U. 4.4.15

The negative aspects of the Upaniṣadic conclusions about the nature of the soul and spiritual liberation are offset to some extent by the adoption of the term "bliss" *(ānanda)* to denote the mystical abandonment of individual consciousness. The term bliss as applied to the yogic mystical experience is evocative of the ancient Vedic concept of hedonistic bliss in a corporeal form in heaven.

> Make me immortal in that realm where happiness *(ānanda)* and transports, where joys and felicities combine, and longing wishes are fulfilled.
>
> *Ṛg* 9.113.11 (G)

In the *Upaniṣads,* however, the term bliss is employed as a euphemism for the indescribable experience of mystical non-duality. It is not to be understood as the positive experience of a pleasant state of consciousness, for it is said that "pleasure and pain do not touch the bodiless" soul.[182]

> He becomes (transparent) like water, one, the seer without duality. This is the world of Brahmā. ... This is the highest goal; this is the highest treasure; this is the highest world; this is his greatest bliss. On a particle of this very bliss other creatures live.
>
> B.U. 4.3.32 (R)

A conceptual attempt to describe this bliss is made by multiplying human bliss repeatedly by 100 to compute the blissfulness of bliss in various levels of existence, such as *gandharvas,* the ancestors in heaven and the gods. The computation reaches the conclusion that the bliss of Brahmā is one hundred quintillion times more blissful than the bliss of a young man, healthy, wealthy and wise.[183] This exponential *tour de force* is, of course, actually meant to convey the inconceivability of the blissfulness of the mystical experience, which apparently is equal to that of Brahmā. The term bliss, then, is actually a technical term indicating the positive, but inexpressible nature of the

---

182. C.U. 8.12.1.

183. T.U. 2.8.1.

mystical experience, which is said to be unity with the universal principle.

> The knower of the bliss of *brahman*, from which speech and mind (*manas*) turn back without success, does not fear anything whatsoever.
> T.U. 2.9

The term bliss takes on specifically psychological significance in the Upaniṣadic doctrine of the five levels of the soul, which are later called the five sheaths *(kośa)*. In this doctrine, the yogic experience is incorporated into the hierarchy of the soul and said to be the innermost essence of the individual and the universe. The classical Advaitin definition of the individual *cum* universal principle as *sat-cit-ānanda* (being-consciousness-bliss) does not appear in the principal *Upaniṣads* themselves, but the identification of the bliss of the mystical experience with the absolute principle is not uncommon.[184] The state of deep sleep is sometimes described as bliss,[185] but some passages postulate a fourth state of the soul, beyond waking, dream and deep sleep, which is also identified with the mystical experience. Both the doctrine of the fourth state of the soul and the doctrine of the *ānanda-maya* level of the soul, then, appear to be similar and relatively late maneuvers to overcome some of the off-putting aspects of the idea that the ultimate attainment is a state of non-consciousness.

This fourth *(turīya* or *caturtha)* state is something of a mystery. It is characterized at one point in the *Maitrī Upaniṣad* as non-consciousness *(acitta)*,[186] while elsewhere in the same *Upaniṣad* the ultimate soul is specifically said to be conscious *(caitanya)*.[187] The *Māṇḍūkya Upaniṣad*, however, which contains the most detailed exposition of the four states of the soul, denies that the fourth state is either a state of consciousness or a state of non-consciousness. The *Māṇḍūkya Upaniṣad* extols the state of deep sleep as a state in which

---

184. See B.U. 3.9.28.7, where *brahman* is defined as *vijñānam ānanda*, "consciousness and bliss".

185. B.U. 2.2.19; Ma.U. 5.

186. Mt.U. 6.19.

187. Mt.U. 6.10.

one becomes a unified mass of consciousness *(prajñāna-ghana)*. This state is characterized as bliss *(ānanda-maya)* and is said to be the lord (Īśvara) and source of all, but the *Upaniṣad* postulates a fourth and even more essential level of being.

> (*Turīya* is) not that which cognises the internal (objects), not that which cognises the external (objects), not what cognises both of them, not a mass of cognition *(prajñāna-ghana)*, not cognitive *(prajñā)*, not non-cognitive. (It is) unseen, incapable of being spoken of, ungraspable, without any distinctive marks, unthinkable *(acintya)*, unnamable *(avyapadeśya)*, the essence of the knowledge of the one self, that into which the world is resolved, the peaceful, the benign, the non-dual, such, they think, is the fourth quarter. He is the self; He is to be known.
>
> Ma.U. 7. (R)

The fourth state in many ways appears to be a metaphysical abstraction arrived at on the basis of logical necessity rather than psychological introspection. It is mentioned elsewhere in the *Upaniṣads* and equated with the three-fourths of the Vedic Puruṣa which is said to have "gone up" at the beginning of creation. The mundane fourth is equated with the states of waking, dream and deep sleep.[188]

While the *Māṇḍūkya Upaniṣad* sometimes characterizes the third state of the soul as *ānanda-maya*, it is clear that when bliss *(ānanda)* describes the supreme, innermost soul, it represents a concept similar to the fourth state. The *Māṇḍūkya Upaniṣad* presents the fourth state of the soul as being beyond deep sleep characterized by *prajñā*. Elsewhere the "soul made of bliss" *(ātmā-ānanda-maya)* is characterized as superior to the *vijñāna-maya-ātman*.

> Different from and within the consciousness-made is the soul made of bliss. By that, this is filled.
>
> T.U. 2.5

188. Mt.U. 7.11. See *Ṛg* 10.90.

Like the fourth state of the soul, the *ānanda-maya-ātman* is identified with *brahman*, which is characterized as transcending the duality of conscious and non-conscious.

> Having emanated it (the universe), he entered it. Having entered it, he became both the existent *(sat)* and the beyond *(tyat)*, the defined and the undefined, the founded and the non-founded, the conscious *(vijñāna)* and the non-conscious, the true and the false.
>
> T.U. 2.6

It is perhaps worth noting that, at different points in the *Upaniṣads*, all four of the terms in the Buddha's "four-cornered" *(catuṣ-koṭi)* negation appear as statements about the nature of the soul, which is said in different contexts to be conscious, non-conscious, both conscious and non-conscious and neither conscious nor non-conscious.

At any rate, again like the fourth state of the soul, the *ānanda-maya* level is represented as an abstract metaphysical, cosmological principle, apparently equivalent to being itself.

> Nonexistent was this (world) in the beginning. From that, being was born. It made itself a soul; therefore it is called well-made. That well-made is indeed the essence. Thus, having attained the essence, one becomes blissful. Who could exhale, who inhale if there were not this bliss in space?
>
> T.U. 2.7

> The store house which consists of the space in the heart, the blissful, the supreme abode, is our self, our *yoga* (goal) too and this the heat of fire and sun.
>
> Mt.U. 6.27 (R)

With the doctrine of bliss as the ultimate essence of the individual and the universe, the upward spiral of the increasingly abstract Upaniṣadic notion of the soul comes to an end, with the conclusion that neither vitality nor consciousness are sufficient as characterizations of the ultimate nature of the human being and the universe as revealed in the yogic experience of non-duality. The exposition of the five levels of the soul, later known as the five "sheaths" *(kośa)*,[189] as found in the *Taittirīya Upaniṣad*,[190] provides an occasion to review the entire course of the development of the Upaniṣadic concept of the soul. The archaic vitalistic concepts reappear as the first two sheaths, the food-made *(anna-rasa-maya)* and the breath-made *(prāṇa-maya)*. The *Taittirīya Upaniṣad* has a predilection for the number five, and each of the levels of the soul is said to be fivefold. The five parts of each sheath are made correspond to five parts of a person — head, right side, lift side, body, and lower part.[191] The food-made soul, which probably represents not only the body, but also the material universe in general is the outer shell, as it were, of the essential soul. Its fivefold nature probably indicates the five elements — space, wind, fire, water and earth. This is not specified in the text, but the following passage seems to suggest this conclusion.

> He who knows *Brahman* as the real, as knowledge and as the infinite, place in the secret place in the heart and in the highest heaven realizes all desires along with *Brahman*, the intelligent. From this Self *(ātman)*, verily, ether arose; from ether air, from air fire; from fire water; from water the earth; from the earth herbs; from herbs food; from food the person *(puruṣa)*. This, verily, is the person that consists of the essence of food *(anna-rasa-maya)*. This, indeed, is his head; this the right side; this the left side; this the body; this the lower part, the foundation.
>
> T.U. 2.1 (R)

Here, "food" (anna) probably represents matter in general, which is composed of the five elements, while the body is said to be composed of the essence of food *(anna-rasa)*. Food often represents matter in the *Upaniṣads*, but this interpretation is somewhat doubtful in the present passage, where its origin from herbs implies that only edible matter is intended. The next verse, however, calls food the "universal herb"

---

189. These levels of the soul are not specifically called *kośa* in the principal *Upaniṣads*, although this came to be the standard term in later literature. This terminology is suggested at Mt.U. 6.27.

190. T.U. 2.2-5; 3.2-6. The only other complete enumeration is at Mt.U. 6.13.

191. T.U. 2.1. See also T.U. 1.7.

(sarvauṣada) and recalls a pun cited above which allows that the universal principle is called Aditi because it eats *(atti)*.[192] All things considered, it is difficult to imagine that "food" is not a double-entendre in this highly sophisticated, synthetic doctrine, which attempts to combine several Upaniṣadic concepts into an integrated scheme.

> Verily, those who worship *Brahman* as food obtain all food. For food, verily, is the eldest born of beings. Therefore is it called the healing herb for all *(sarvauṣada)*. From food are beings born. When born they grow up by food. It is eaten and eats things. Therefore is it called food.
>
> T.U. 2.2 (R)

The five parts of the breath-made soul *(ātmā prāṇa-maya)* include only three of the five vital breaths, *prāṇa, vyāna* and *apāna*, the other two parts being space and earth. The reason for this substitution is unclear, as the standard enumeration of five vital breaths, including *udāna* and *samāna* occurs earlier in the same *Upaniṣad*.[193] The breath-made soul is extolled as in genuinely vitalistic passages, but the reward for those who worship *brahman* as the breath — i.e. for those who conceive of vitality as the essence of the individual and the universe — is not as great as the reward of those who hold more sophisticated views about the nature of the soul.

> The gods breathe along with breath *(prāṇa)*, as also men and beasts. Breath is the life *(āyu)* of all beings. Therefore, it is called the life of all *(sarva-āyusa)*. Those who meditate upon *brahman* as breath attain a full life *(āyu)*, for breath is the life of beings.
>
> T.U. 2.3

192. B.U. 1.2.5. Cp. *Ṛg* 1.59.10: "Aditi is the sky; Aditi is the atmosphere; Aditi is the mother; Aditi is the father". (From Radhakrishnan's note on B.U. 1.2.5).

193. T.U. 1.8. Śaṅkara interprets space and earth as representing the other two vital breaths.

The third, "mind-made soul" *(ātmā mano-maya)*, "different from and within" the vital, breath-made soul, is said to have five parts corresponding to various Vedic scriptures. The five empirical senses would have made for a neat model, but may not have been recognized by the author of even the present relatively late passage. Earlier, the *Taittirīya Upaniṣad* lists eye, ear, mind, speech, and skin as the five sensual faculties.[194] At any rate, it is clear by virtue of its placement in the present hierarchy that *manas* represents active, sensual consciousness, the midpoint of the human spectrum, where the mundane and the divine meet and interact. It interesting that part of the definition of bliss is inserted in the definition of the *mano-maya* level of the soul, apparently as an indication of the limitations of *manas*, which is said not to be able to apprehend bliss, the essence of the soul.

> The knower of the bliss of *brahman*, from which speech and mind *(manas)* turn back without attaining it, does not fear at any time. This (the *mano-maya-ātman*) is the embodied soul *(śarīra-ātman)* of the former (the breath-made soul).
>
> T.U. 2.4

Pure consciousness, as represented by the "consciousness-made soul" *(ātmā vijñāna-maya)*, is said to be "different from and within" the mind-made soul. It is the penultimate level of the soul, isolated by the mediating *manas* from the physical universe and body, as well as from fleeting vitality. The *manas* is held responsible for the defilement associated with perception and volition, leaving the more essential consciousness free from taint. Analogous to *buddhi*, the driver of the chariot, *vijñāna* is said to direct the deeds, but apparently not actually to perform deeds and thereby become karmicly involved.

> Consciousness directs (*tanute*, lit. "spins out") the sacrifice, and it directs the deeds *(karmāṇi)* also. All the gods worship consciousness as the (form of) *brahman* which is eldest. If one knows *brahman* as

---

194. T.U. 1.8.

consciousness and does not neglect it, having left all the evil in the body, he attains all desires.

T.U. 2.5

The five parts of the consciousness-made soul are said to be faith *(śraddhā)*, order *(ṛta,)* truth *(satya)*, *yoga*, and "the great" *(mahaḥ)*, which may or may not be a specific reference to *buddhi*, which is sometimes called *mahat* in the Sāṁkhya system.

"Different from and within" the consciousness-made soul, is the "soul made of bliss" *(ātmā ānanda-maya)*. Apparently this ultimate and innermost level of the soul is meant to be equivalent to the absolute principle, although according to the enumeration of its five "parts", *brahman* is said to be its foundation, the other four parts being *priya*, *moda*, *pramoda* and *ānanda*, all of which mean essentially "bliss". Śaṅkara devotes a lengthy argument to establishing that the *ānanda-maya* level of the soul is to be regarded as conditioned, and therefore not identical with *brahman*. This in itself is an indication that the *ānanda-maya* level of the soul was commonly identified with the absolute. The *Brahma Sūtra* specifically states the identity of the *ānanda-maya* and *brahman*, and Śaṅkara follows suit in his commentary, contradicting his exegesis of the *Taittirīya* passage.[195]

At any rate, the recapitulation of the five levels of the soul in the third chapter, the "Bhṛgu Valli" of the *Taittirīya Upaniṣad*, amounts to a progressive definition of *brahman*. Bhṛgu, the son of Varuṇa, desirous of knowing ultimate reality, is given by his father the hint that:

That, verily, from which these beings are born; that by which, when born, they live; that into which, when departing, they enter; that, seek to know. That is *Brahman*.

T.U. 3.1 (R)

195. Cp. Śaṅkara's commentary on T.U. 2.5-7 and B.S. 1.1.12-19. See also his comment on T.U. 3.6.

By performing repeated austerities *(tapas)*, Bhṛgu comes successively to the conclusions that *brahman* is food, breath, mind, consciousness, and finally bliss, which apparently is the correct answer.

> He knew that *Brahman* is bliss. For truly beings here are born from bliss, when born, they live by bliss, and into bliss, when departing, they enter.
>
> T.U. 3.6 (R)

Here, Śaṅkara seems to accept the identity of the *ānanda-maya* soul and *brahman*, offering the following exegesis.

> Thus becoming pure through concentration and failing to find the characteristics of *brahman*, in their fullness, in the selves composed of the vital force, etc., Bhṛgu penetrated inside by degrees, and with the help of concentration realized the innermost bliss that is *brahman*.[196]

Early Buddhism and the "Two Soul" Doctrine:

With the doctrine of the absolute as *ānanda*, the *Upaniṣads* approach early Buddhist soteriology so closely that the only difference between *ātman* and *nirvāṇa* is that *ātman* is thought to generate and maintain the universe, while the Buddha denied an ontological relationship between *saṁsāra* and *nirvāṇa*. The Buddha's approach to ultimate reality is, however, a self-conscious dialectic which rejects tradition and dogma as sources of knowledge, and claims to deal only with that which can be perceived and inferred from human experience. Since this experience does not provide adequate terms for the expression of the absolute, the Buddha refused to speculate upon its nature, i.e. its relationship to the world. In other words, he would not say what it is like simply because it is not like anything else. For the Upaniṣadic sages, however, the Vedic revelation *(śruti)* provided an extra source of knowledge which made a doctrine of the relationship between the absolute and the world possible, and, for the sake of orthodoxy, imperative.

---

196. Śaṅkara's commentary on T.U. 3.6, from Swami Gambhirananda, *Eight* Upanisads, Advaita Ashrama, Calcutta, vol. 1, p. 379.

The only real difference between the Buddhist and Upaniṣadic absolutes is that while both are held to be ultimately inexpressible, *ātman* is an inexpressible "something". The "somethingness" of *ātman* derives from the Vedic doctrine that there exists "that one", the monistic cosmogonic principle, which is the source and ground of the mundane universe. By seeing the diverse universe, however, one does not see *ātman*. In fact, one only sees *ātman* when one ceases to see diversity, so that even though the *Upaniṣads* consistently assume an ontological continuity between *ātman* and *saṁsāra,* they say, like Buddhism that existence as we know it is antithetical to ultimate reality. Consciousness and ultimate reality are also held to be mutually exclusive in both the *Upaniṣads* and early Buddhism. There is also a notable idealistic tendency in early Buddhism not to draw a distinction between the "physical" universe and the universe as experienced by consciousness.

There is, in other words, a Vedic cosmological content in the Buddhist doctrine of *nirvāṇa.* In other heterodox systems such as Jainism or Ājīvikism one's individual soul is thought to reach some sort of salvation within the context of the given universe. Buddhist *nirvāṇa* by contrast represents a radical transcendence of the universe based on an understanding of its ultimate nature, which, it is held, is fathomed by means of an introspective examination of human consciousness.

Most commonly in early Buddhism, *nirvāṇa* is spoken of as the cessation of various psychopathological states which are held to be both the cause and the result of the individual's involvement in *saṁsāra. Nirvāṇa,* for example, is said to be the cessation of desire *(taṇhā)*[197] or the cessation of greed, hatred and delusion.[198] It is also spoken of in metaphysical terms, however, as the cessation of existence *(bhava)* or as the uncompounded *(asaṅkhata).*[199]

197. S5: 421; S3: 190; S1: 136; A2: 34; M1 191.

198. S4: 251; 359; 371.

199. Cessation of *bhava:* S2: 117. *Asaṅkhata:* S4: 251; 359. For this and other terms see the "Asaṅkhata-saṁyutta", S4: 359-372. See also Walpola Rahula, *What the Buddha Taught,* revised ed., 1967, p. 35-44.

> Monks, there exists that condition wherein is neither earth nor water nor fire nor air. ... Thence, monks, I declare is no coming to birth; there is no going (from life); therein is no duration; thence is no falling; there is no arising. It is not something fixed, it moves not on, it is not based on anything. That indeed is the end of ill *(dukkha)*. ... Monks, there is not-born, a not become *(abhūta)*, a not made, a not-compounded *(asaṅkhata)*. Monks, if that unborn, not-become, not-made, not-compounded were not, there would be apparent no escape from this here that is born, become, made, compounded.
>
> *Udāna*, p. 80 (SBB)

Thus, even though *nirvāṇa* is said to be the cessation of existence *(bhava,* lit. "becoming"), and even though it lacks any of the characteristics of that which is normally said to exist, the Buddha makes the uncharacteristic declaration, "There exists that condition". His refusal elsewhere to state whether after death a person who has realized that condition "exists, does not exist, both exists and does not exist or neither exists nor does not exist" is well known.[200]

The Buddha's dilemma in this context is in many ways very similar to that of the Upaniṣadic sages with reference to the nature of the absolute. This dilemma arises from two basic "properties" of the absolute which both the *Upaniṣads* and Buddhism accept: 1) It has nothing in common with existence as we know it, but 2) nevertheless, it is such a potent reality that in the face of the absolute, existence as we know it must be re-evaluated as inconsequential. The first "property" makes anything one says about it wrong, and the second demands that one say something about it anyway.

In their re-evaluations of empirical reality, both the *Upaniṣads* and Buddhism agree on two fundamental points: 1) The perception of the objects of the world as existing in and of themselves is illusion, and 2) the notion of an individual subjective essence is illusion. In both systems, it is only with reference to the potent super-reality of the mystical experience of transcendence of the individual, ego-centric viewpoint that object and subject may be said to be illusory or unreal. In neither system is the inconsequentiality or illusoriness of the

200. M1: 426.

mundane world construed as non-existence *per se*. Instead it is thought to be the result of a wrong seeing of reality.

At this point the *Upaniṣads* and Buddhism part company. Committed to the cosmogonic monism of the orthodox Vedic tradition, the *Upaniṣads* declare on the basis of revelation that the reality which is seen wrongly is the monistic universal principle, *ātman-brahman*, the ground of existence *(sat)*. The thoroughgoing monism of the *Upaniṣads* also holds that it is ultimately this same universal principle which sees wrongly; *ātman-brahman* is the essence of consciousness *(cit)*. This is an aspect of monism not anticipated in the ancient *Vedas*. It appears to be an outgrowth of the Upaniṣadic conviction that the pinnacle of yogic meditational experience is a rediscovery of the monistic principle within one's own consciousness; *ātman-brahman* is mystical bliss *(ānanda)*.

The Buddha was in essential agreement with the Upaniṣadic sages on the assertion that the eternal is to be discovered internally through meditation, but he refused to characterize *nirvāṇa* as either the source of the world or the source of consciousness. Wrong seeing is not, then, in the Buddhist context, a wrong seeing of *nirvāṇa* or a wrong seeing by *nirvāṇa*. Wrong seeing is ignorance *(avidya)* of the true nature of the world, regardless of the world's source or lack thereof. Though the Buddha did not accept an ontological essence of existence, he did not dogmatically reject one either.

> The world rests on two doctrines, being and non-being, but he who rightly sees the arising of the world as it really is, does not hold that there is non-being in the world, and he who rightly sees the cessation of things as it really is, does not hold that there is being in the world. ... That "everything exists" is one extreme and that "nothing exists" is the other extreme.
>
> S2:17 (PTS)

In the Buddhist context, the inconsequentiality or illusoriness of the world is because of the impermanence of everything in it. This impermanence, it is held, is demonstrable in that it can be observed that nothing exists independently of causes and conditions external to itself. In other words, impermanence, analytically viewed, is interdependence. The most fundamental interdependence in Buddhism is the interdependence of consciousness and object of consciousness. Thus, the cardinal doctrine of *paṭiccasamuppāda*, "conditioned or interdependent arising", is couched in primarily psychological terms. It is essentially an explanation of the mutually conditioned arising of consciousness and its objects. This indicates that in a way the Buddhist doctrine of *nirvāṇa* does have a metaphysical, cosmological significance in that the world is dealt with in Buddhism, as in the *Upaniṣads*, as the sum total of the objects of consciousness. When, by the realization of *nirvāṇa*, consciousness ceases, the known world must also cease. Whether there is an independently existing objective world standing behind that which is known to consciousness is a moot point for Buddhism. Thus, the viewpoint of the historical Buddha was actually very similar to that of the Upaniṣadic sages who held that consciousness and its objects are interdependent by virtue of the fact that the world is a projection of the universal principle through consciousness. In the Buddhist context, however, it must be emphasized that the interdependence of consciousness and its objects is viewed as an analytical fact rather than mythologically as a cosmogonic fact.

In the *Upaniṣads* with the exception of the theistic *Śvetāśvatara Upaniṣad*,[201] it is assumed that which is experienced at the pinnacle of yogic meditation is the monistic, ontological source of the universe. This, of course, derives from the Vedic preoccupation with cosmogony and "that one" which existed "in the beginning", although the *Upaniṣads* are not unanimous in predicating existence of the individual *cum* universal soul.[202] It is, at any rate, consistently portrayed as the unitary material and efficient cause of the universe. It works through a process which, though sometimes described mythologically, amounts to emanation of the universe through the conscious faculties of the individual.

This doctrine later attracted Buddhist criticism based on the argument that the eternal cannot be the cause of the impermanent. There is little evidence of the recognition of such problems in the *Upaniṣads* themselves, but there is ample evidence of concern over

---

201. See S.U. 1.1-3; 6.9; 6.13; 6.19.

202. T.U. 2.6.1; 2.7.1; Mt.U. 2.4; 6.20; 6.23; 6.31.

the implications of *karma* and rebirth with regard to psychological monism.

At different points the absolute principle, under various names, and obviously identified with the individual essence, is specifically said to be the cause of the universe.[203]

> Whoever has found and awakened to the self that has entered into this perilous and inaccessible place (the body), he is the maker of the universe, for he is the maker of all. His is the world; indeed he is the world itself.
>
> B.U. 4.4.13 (R)

Moreover, the absolute is repeatedly characterized as the foundation of subjective consciousness as well: the seer of seeing, knower of knowing, doer of doing, etc.[204] Volitional causation, however, constitutes *karma*. According to the theory accepted in the *Upaniṣads* and Indian religion in general, *karma* necessarily entails the eventual transformation of the doer thereof in accordance with the nature of the act, even if the act be only thought. Such a fate is, not appropriate for the eternal, universal principle. Nonetheless, its simultaneous role as the individual essence suggests that the creator must be affected by its own creation through the karmic results accruing to reincarnating individuals.

Therefore, the hierarchies of the soul which developed in the *Upaniṣads* appear to be more than systematizations of psychological theory. These hierarchies are also an attempt to overcome the problem which arises when the absolute is identified with the essence of the transmigrating individual. In terms of the chariot simile, of the chariot is to be excused from direct volitional and sensual activity even tough the chariot and the journey are for his purposes. He might be held accountable by an ignorant gardener if the chariot ran through his flower bed, but according to Upaniṣadic thinking, actually:

---

203. *Puruṣa* and *Īśa:* Mt.U. 6.18. *Brahman:* Mu.U. 1.1.1; 3.1.3; Ks.U. 4.19. *Ātman:* B.U. 4.3.10; 4.4.13.

204. C.U. 7.8.1; 7.9.1; Ks.U. 3.8; B.U. 1.4.7.

> Verily, this self, the seers declare, wanders here on earth in every body (from body to body) unaffected, as it seems, by the light or the dark fruits of action.
>
> Mt.U. 2.7 (R)

This type of attempt to isolate the soul in its universal aspect from the individual aspect of the soul eventually lead to the doctrine of two souls. More properly, there were held to be two aspects of the soul, the conditioned and the eternal, or in classical terms, the individual "living soul" *(jīva-ātman)* and the "ultimate soul" *(param-ātman)*. This doctrine is often invoked in Upaniṣadic exegesis, but it is only obliquely mentioned in the texts of the principal *Upaniṣads* themselves. The *Bṛhadāraṇyaka Upaniṣad* at 4.4.6 refers to the transmigrating *liṅga,* which term, in the form *liṅga-śarīra,* or alternatively *sūkṣma-śarīra* ("subtle body"), came to be a standard term for the reincarnating aspect of the soul in post-Upaniṣadic psychology. A simple two-soul doctrine, in which the two are soul and body, or literally "intelligent soul" *(prajñā-ātman)* and "body-soul" *(śarīra-ātman),* occurs in the *Upaniṣads.*[205] This may be a prototype for the more developed theory, also occurring in a few passages, which distinguishes the individual and the ultimate aspects of the soul.[206]

> He, verily, is the seer, the toucher, the hearer, the smeller, the taster, the perceiver, the knower, the doer, the thinking self, the person. He becomes established in the supreme undecaying self.
>
> P.U. 4.9 (R)

The two soul doctrine is implied again in the *Maitrī Upaniṣad,* where it is said, with reference to the chariot simile, that the rider of the chariot (the *ātman* in the *Kaṭha Upaniṣad's* version) attains union with the *ātman,* obviously something more than the soul as rider of the

205. B.U. 4.3.35; Ks.U. 4.20.

206. See also Mt.U. 3; S.U. 3.18-21; K.U. 1.3.1; 2.2.9-15; Mu.U. 3.1.

chariot.[207] The *Maitrī Upaniṣad* also contains an explicit statement of the doctrine of two souls as well as the rationale behind the doctrine.

> Reverend One, if you thus indicate the greatness of this self then there is that other, different one also called self, who, affected by the bright or dark fruits of action, enters a good or an evil womb, so that his course is downward or upward and he wanders about, affected by the pairs (of opposites like pleasure and pain).
>
> Mt.U. 3.1 (R)

The unity of the individual and the ultimate soul, however, is said to be pre-existent, eternal, in fact. The condition for the realization of this unity is only metaphorically described as the individual soul attaining a goal or reaching a destination. Actually, this unity is said to be realized upon the cessation of the hierarchy of consciousness.[208]

> When the five (sense) knowledges *(jñānāni)* together with mind *(manas)* cease, and the intellect *(buddhi)* does not stir, that, they say, is the final destination.
>
> K.U. 2.3.10

On the one hand, that this state is said to be attained when active consciousness ceases is due to the nature of meditational experience. On the other hand, such a doctrine is an expedient for monism in that karmic entanglement can be associated with the non-essential faculties of consciousness. The essential soul may then stand aloof behind the whole process as the ultimate source of the universe wherein the modification and rebirth of the non-essential consciousness occurs. The essential soul, as that which stands behind the non-essential, active soul, is characterized in the no doubt late *Maitrī Upaniṣad* as "that which causes to cause" *(kārayitṛ)*, rather than "that which causes" *(kartṛ)*.[209] The *kartṛ*, which is elsewhere a euphemism for the ultimate

---

207. Mt.U. 4.4.

208. The following citation is quoted at Mt.U. 6.30.

209. Mt.U. 3.2-3.

soul,[210] is identified instead with the "elemental soul" *(bhūta-ātman)*. In another chapter of the *Maitrī Upaniṣad*, matter *(pradhāna)* is said to be the cause *(kartṛ)* of the elemental soul.[211] This sounds like classical Sāṁkhya dualism, but the *bhūta-ātman* is defined in context as "the body", not as "in the body", as Radhakrishnan translates.[212] The concept presented here has only superficial resemblance to the *liṅga-śarīra* of Sāṁkhya.[213]

When the Upaniṣadic synthesis of *Veda* and *yoga* was eventually worked out in more systematic ways, different combinations of the various mental, sensual, and volitional faculties were equated with the active, individual, transmigrating soul. Some of the passages noted above, which prefigure the classical two-soul theories of Advaita Vedānta and Sāṁkhya, contain similar ideas without explicitly stating precisely which faculties comprise the individual aspect of the soul.[214]

Perhaps surprisingly, this doctrine of the two aspects of the soul is relevant to the Buddhist denial of the soul. The Upaniṣadic concept of two souls provides a precedent for the idea that rebirth does not necessarily involve a reincarnating soul, as required by the rebirth doctrines of the Jains or Ājīvikas. In the Buddhist system, however, release is also held to be independent of the existence of an eternal entity, whether individual or universal. It is here, again, that Buddhism parts company with the *Upaniṣads* and their doctrines as developed in Advaita Vedānta and Sāṁkhya.

Of the orthodox schools, Sāṁkhya took the boldest approach to the problem by declaring that the existential, transmigrating consciousness is absolutely separate from the soul, and is, in fact, merely an epiphenomenon of matter *(prakṛti)*.

---

210. B.U. 4.4.3.

211. Mt.U. 6.10.

212. Mt.U. 3.2.

213. *Śarīra*, however, is defined in the same passage as the five elements *(mahābhūta)* and the five sense potentials *(tanmātra)*, which suggests at least the possibility of sentience, although the precise meaning of these verses is unclear.

214. Mt.U. 6.30; K.U. 2.3.10; P.U. 4.9. See K.U. 1.3.1.

> Nothing, therefore is bound; nothing released, likewise not anything transmigrates. (Only) *prakṛti* in its various forms transmigrates, is bound and is released.[215]

In the Sāṁkhya system, the active, transmigrating soul is held to be actually only a conglomerate of apparently conscious evolutes of matter *(prakṛti)*. It is called the *liṅga-śarīra* or *sukṣma-śarīra* (subtle body) and is said to consist of awareness *(buddhi)*, ego *(ahaṁkāra)*, mind *(manas)*, the five sense faculties, their five potential objects *(tanmātra)* and the five action faculties. The individual, but eternal and essentially cosmological plurality of souls *(purusa)* are said only to witness the activity of the evolutes of *prakṛti*. These souls remain unconcerned, unchanged and absolutely independent.

The Advaita Vedānta system, however, being bound to the tradition of Vedic and Upaniṣadic monism, is not free to make such a radical distinction in order to explain the transmigration of the soul. It must maintain that at some level, the individual soul is identical to the supreme soul without there being a sharp demarcation. Various approaches to defining the transmigrating entity are employed according to the nature of the text being commented upon, but in each case it is necessary that when the various adjuncts *(upādhi)* are removed, or the various sheaths *(kośa)* peeled off, the supreme soul, the universal principle, must be there at the core of each individual. According to some Advaitins — such as Suresvara, Śaṅkara's sub-commentator — the "subtle body" or transmigrating entity is composed of the *prāṇa-*, *mano-* and *vijñāna-maya* sheaths.[216] Śaṅkara himself inconsistently defines the subtle body more along Sāṁkhya lines as a combination of twelve,[217] seventeen,[218] or nineteen[219] of the vital, sensual, volitional and mental faculties of the soul.

In the end, however, the doctrine of two souls, particularly in the context of Advaita Vedānta, does little to solve the Upaniṣadic

---

215. S.K. 62; from Gerald James Larson, *Classical Sāṁkhya*, p. 279.

216. See Radhakrishnan's note on T.U. 2.1. and Rene Guenon, *Man and His Becoming According to the Vedānta*, p. 77.

217. B.U. 4.4.2.

218. B.U. 3.7.2.

219. Ma.U. 3.

dilemma, since the two must ultimately be identical. Ultimately, it is clear that the Vedicly inspired Upaniṣadic monism and the yogic doctrine of rebirth conditioned by *karma* are not compatible in any meaningful way, for the true soul must not be held responsible for actions, even though it is the ultimate cause of activity.[220] Volition, actions and their results must be considered illusory in such a system of thought. Indeed, the amorality of the Advaita system, which evolved from just such considerations, was one of the main objects of attack by later commentators such as Rāmānuja and Madhva, who returned to the original non-Vedic position of genuinely individual souls. This position, it should be noted, seems to be the overall intent of the *Śvetāśvatara Upaniṣad* with regard to the nature of the individual.

Ironically, the ingenious, though problematic speculations of mainstream Upaniṣadic psychology were most successfully resolved by the heterodox Buddha. The Buddha may not have been directly aware of mainstream Upaniṣadic teachings, but he made stunning use of the fundamental Upaniṣadic insight, namely that it is wholly within human consciousness that both the curse and the salvation of mankind reside.

> Mind, in truth, is the cause of bondage and liberation for mankind; for bondage if it is bound to objects; freedom from objects, that is called liberation.
>
> Mt.U. 6.34 (R)

> Friends, I declare that the world, the cause of the world, the cessation of the world and the path leading to the cessation of the world lie within this fathom-long carcass with its perceptions and mind.
>
> S1:62

At the same time, by rejecting the existence of a universal and/or individual soul, the Buddha was able to avoid the *Upaniṣads'* problems with attempting to dovetail cosmology, *karma*, rebirth, and release.

---

220. See C.U. 8.1.5; K.U. 1.2.14; 1.2.18-19; B.U. 4.4.22-23; Mt.U. 2.7.

Chapter 6

The Fundamentals of Buddhist Psychology

The reader with an appreciation for the gradual accumulation of human knowledge over the ages doubtless will have been impressed by the ingenious psychological and cosmological speculations of the Upaniṣadic sages. Early Buddhist psychology, on the other hand, is impressive precisely because of the absence of such speculation. The genius of the Buddha consisted primarily in his uncanny intuition for avoiding what is not arguably true and his ability to state the sublime, without speculation, mythology or metaphysics, purely on the basis of an incisive and persuasive analysis of human consciousness as experienced. The historical Buddha was fortunate, however, in being in a position to benefit from a wealth of cumulative human knowledge. The nature and development of the psychological knowledge at his disposal has been the subject of the bulk of the present work, which will now examine the way in which the Buddha employed and in some cases transformed the psychological terms and concepts available to him into his own fresh and ingenious psychological doctrine.

Many Buddhists will be quick to argue that the Buddha's insight was unique and spontaneous, not merely a critical and creative re-working of existing philosophical traditions.[1] Many non-Buddhists, particularly Hindus, prefer to argue just the opposite, perhaps denying even creative insight to the Buddha.

Without evaluating the origins or originality of the Buddha's insights themselves, the present chapter assumes simply that the most reasonable point to start in seeking to understand the basic psychological terms and concepts of early Buddhism is with the terms and concepts of antecedent psychological thought in India. In the

1. See A3: 8.

absence of compelling evidence to the contrary, where the Buddha used similar terms, one must assume that he had in mind similar concepts. The early *Upaniṣads* and some *Brāhmaṇa* material are all we have, other than the early Buddhist *suttas* themselves, in the way of literature representing roughly the age of the Buddha. The Jains, Ājīvikas and other contemporary heterodox sects left no textual material verifiably representative of this age. It is not clear precisely how much access the Buddha had to the Upaniṣadic tradition, which though orthodox, must not be imagined to represent the Brahmanism which the Buddha often criticized on the basis of caste discrimination, ritualism and dogmatism.[2] It is unlikely that the Buddha had direct access to the principal *Upaniṣads* examined in the foregoing chapters. Nevertheless, some of the fundamental concepts of the early Buddhist theory of the nature of human consciousness and some of the central concerns of Upaniṣadic psychology are similar to an extent that would make it difficult to believe that the Buddha did not have some access to an orthodox tradition of knowledge that is represented in these *Upaniṣads*.

Doubtlessly, yogic traditions of the time had a much greater influence upon the Buddha than did the orthodox tradition standing behind the *Upaniṣads*, but unfortunately, there are no extant texts which record the state of yogic speculations before the rise of Buddhism. This so-called "yogic" tradition is necessarily only a postulate, but without such a postulate, it is impossible to understand the development of orthodox thought in the *Upaniṣads*. The *Ṛg Veda*, which is traditionally held to be the sole basis of Upaniṣadic thought, is primarily vitalistic in its approach to the nature of the human being. The *Upaniṣads* are primarily psychological. The *Ṛg Veda* lacks the important concepts of the soul, rebirth and release. These are fundamental psychological concepts in the *Upaniṣads*. In elucidating them, the Upaniṣadic sages did not hesitate to devalue severely the Vedic doctrines of the efficacy of ritual, the supremacy of the priesthood, and a heavenly afterlife.

---

2. See D3: #13; M3: 169.

The *Upaniṣads* are indifferent and even hostile toward several fundamental Vedic doctrines, and are concerned primarily with several apparently non-Vedic notions which have been labeled here "yogic" for the sake of convenience. Beyond the doctrines of the soul, rebirth and release, it is impossible to say, given the absence of textual evidence, what else the Upaniṣadic sages may have borrowed in the way of psychology from this postulated yogic tradition. Perhaps the notion of a layered consciousness is also a yogic borrowing, but as noted in the previous chapter, there is every indication that the notion of a layered consciousness informed by the five empirical senses and *manas* was laboriously worked out in the *Upaniṣads* themselves.

The *Upaniṣads* also show a notable movement from a vitalistic to a psychological notion of the essential nature of the soul. This also may be an Upaniṣadic contribution to Indian psychology. On the other hand, the original yogic notion of the soul may have been a notion of a conscious soul, and Upaniṣadic vitalism may be only a superimposed retention of Vedic vitalistic concerns. Then again, perhaps both the vitalistic and psychological notions of the soul found in the *Upaniṣads* are parallel developments of a primitive yogic soul theory. Chronological stratification of the *Upaniṣads* is at present in too crude a state to lend persuasive support to any of these possibilities. It is at least clear that for Upaniṣadic thinkers a psychological notion of the soul proved more amenable to the exigencies of monism than did a vitalistic concept of the soul. Ever since the *Upaniṣads,* the vast preponderance of Indian speculation on the nature of the human being has been psychological rather than vitalistic in orientation.

Early Buddhist psychology exhibits a deep, though perhaps not immediately apparent similarity with fundamental concepts of Upaniṣadic psychology, and an analysis of the existing textual evidence dictates the conclusion that early Buddhism is not purely yogic in its backgrounds. In the absence of evidence to the contrary, one has no alternative but to conclude that Buddhism owes something of its origins to essentially orthodox psychological speculations of the sort contained in the ancient *Upaniṣads.*

Previous chapters have already noted several broad similarities between early Buddhist psychology and even earlier Indian thought, both orthodox and heterodox. Like the majority of its heterodox siblings, Buddhism accepts rebirth and yogic release. Buddhism denies the soul, however, and the soul which is denied is not only the individual, changing soul of the heterodox traditions, but also the eternal, universal soul of Upaniṣadic ilk, which appears to be a concept resulting from a synthesis of Vedic monism and yogic psychology. Moreover, the Buddhist doctrine of *nirvāṇa* bears as much in common with the more sophisticated of the Upaniṣadic soteriological theories as with the theories of Jainism or Ājīvikism. Beyond these broad indications of orthodox influence in Buddhism, however, there is surprisingly little direct reference to Upaniṣadic ideas in the early Buddhist *suttas*.

The "Brahmajāla" and "Sāmaññaphala Suttas" of the *Dīgha Nikāya* contain the most extensive treatment of specific doctrines rejected by the Buddha. There is some indication of Upaniṣadic philosophy in some of these rejected doctrines, particularly in reference to the "eternalists" *(sassatavāda)* and "semi-eternalists" *(ekacca-sassatika)*. The grounds upon which they are said to base their doctrines, however, are in most cases recollection of past births, which is not a feature of Upaniṣadic metaphysical speculations. One of the mythological treatments of semi-eternalism offered in the "Brahmajāla Sutta", however, is vaguely reminiscent of the archaic Upaniṣadic creation theories based on desire *(kāma)* occurring within the original, cosmogonic principle. It is said in the "Brahmajāla" that the first being to descend from the "World of Radiance" at the beginning of a world cycle, forgetting his previous state, desired companionship. When other beings descended later because of exhausted merit, he and they thought that he was their creator.[3]

In the "Brahmajāla Sutta", the "annihilationist" *(uccheda-vāda)* denial of several progressively more subtle souls is vaguely reminiscent of the *Taittirīya Upaniṣad's* five *kośa* or multiple soul doctrine. According to the annihilationists, the first soul is the body, made of four elements. The second is divine *(dibba)* and sensuous *(kāmāvacara)*, and the third is mind-made *(mano-maya)*. The topmost souls, however, are defined in specifically Buddhist terms and are

3. D1: 17.

identified with the four "formless meditative absorptions" *(arūpa-jhāna)*. All seven souls, of course, are said by the annihilationists to perish utterly upon death.[4] This materialist doctrine is paralleled by the Buddhist reference to the three "soul-apprehensions" *(atta-paṭilābbha)*, which are the physical *(olārika)*, the mind-made *(mano-maya)*, and the formless *(arūpa)*, each of which is denied in Buddhism and said to be only a worldly convention of language.[5]

Thus, though the classical five *kośa* doctrine of the soul is not reproduced exactly in early Buddhist literature, there is evidence of an awareness of the broad outlines of Upaniṣadic speculations regarding the layered soul. The Buddhist "formless soul-apprehension" may be roughly equivalent to the Upaniṣadic *ānanda-maya-ātman*. *Arūpa* obviously represents the supra-conscious experience of meditational absorption, which according to the Buddha may be mistaken for a soul. Again in the "Brahmajāla Sutta", possible reference is made to the Upaniṣadic confusion over whether the soul is conscious (has *saññā*), or non-conscious or both conscious and non-conscious.[6] This analysis is typically Buddhist, however, and need not necessarily indicate familiarity with Upaniṣadic doctrine as such.

Elsewhere in the *Nikāyas* reference is made to the dispersion upon death of the body parts and senses of the individual into universal sources, the five elements, but the statement is made by a materialist denying afterlife rather than in the context of the Vedic theory of dispersion described above.[7] The Pāli *suttas* make definite reference to the Vedic practice of maintaining dead ancestors with food offerings,[8] but neither post-mortem dispersion nor ancestral maintenance are specifically Upaniṣadic doctrines, and both ideas are too universally common to be definitely linked even with Vedic sources.

---

4. D1: 34. Cp. D1: 195.
5. D1: 202. See also D1: 186-87.
6. D1: 31-33; 40. See M1: 231.
7. M1: 515.
8. A1: 155; A5: 269; S2: 170.

The Buddha agrees with the Upaniṣadic sages in holding that knowledge of the three *Vedas* is not sufficient to gain union with Brahmā.[9] He also agrees with them concerning the bliss of heaven which, he says, compares with the greatest human bliss as the Himalayas to a pebble.[10] In the Buddhist scheme, of course, neither the attainment of heaven nor union with Brahmā is ultimate or permanent. As in some Upaniṣadic passages, however, questions about the ultimate, *nibbāṇa* or *nirvāṇa* in the Buddhist context, are said to "go too far".[11] Unlike in the Upaniṣadic context, one's head is not likely to fall off for asking such questions, although such a punishment threatens one who knowingly lies to the Tathāgata (the Buddha).[12]

The Buddha seems to be poking fun at monism when he recounts the story of an encounter with Brahmā in which the Buddha cautions the god lest his knowledge of "the allness of all" turn out to be vain and empty.[13] On the other hand, in the Buddhist context, perception of diversity *(nānattasaññā)* is said to be a defilement of the mind *(cittassa upakkilesa)* in much the same terms and context that "seeing diversity" *(nāneva paśyati)* in the *Upaniṣads* is said to prevent release and lead to rebirth.[14]

Yoga practice in general is an integral part of the Buddhist path to enlightenment, and the monks are exhorted to practice *yoga* by that name.[15] Even the experience of colors on the Upaniṣadic "narrow, ancient path" is roughly approximated in Buddhist texts with reference to jhānic experiences.[16] In all, it is quite likely that T.W. Rhys-Davids is correct in his suspicion that much of Buddhist meditational

---

9. D1: #13
10. M3: 172-77.
11. M1: 304. Cp. B.U. 3.6.1.
12. D1: 95.
13. M1: 329. Cp. M1: #1.
14. M3: 162. Cp. B.U. 4.4.19.
15. M1: 472.
16. M2: 13-14. Cp. B.U. 4.4.9.

technique was borrowed from antecedent practice.[17] Such practices probably also antedate the *Upaniṣads* and probably belonged originally to a non-Vedic *yoga* tradition of which Buddhism was ultimately the most successful heir.

Otherwise, though the soul is denied in Buddhism, several of the similes with which the soul is described in the *Upaniṣads* do appear in early Buddhist literature. This is most notable with reference to the miraculous *mano-maya-kāya* (mind-made-body) which is said to be drawn out of the physical body like a reed from its sheath, a snake from its slough or a sword from its scabbard. In the *Upaniṣads*, similar similes describe the intimate relationship between the soul and the body.[18] In the *Suttanipāta*, the simile of a drop of water on a lotus leaf describes the sage *(muni)*, who does not cling to perceptions. The same simile describes the supreme self as opposed to the active self in the *Maitrī Upaniṣad*.[19] Such similes, however, are likely to have been common idiomatic currency at the time of Buddha and do not necessarily indicate familiarity with the *Upaniṣads* themselves.

Denial of the Soul

On the basis of the foregoing, it is clear that though the Buddha probably did not have direct access to precisely the material which is contained in the principal *Upaniṣads*, he was aware of philosophical and psychological speculations of the type recorded in these *Upaniṣads*. Such familiarity is suggested also in the similarity between the layered models of consciousness found in both the *Upaniṣads* and Buddhism. On a deeper, conceptual level, the debt of Buddhism to a synthesis of *yoga* and *Veda* similar to that recorded in the *Upaniṣads* is even more evident.

In the first place, the Buddhist denial of the soul may be viewed as a solution to the Upaniṣadic problem of resolving the contradictions involved in associating cosmogony, individuality, *karma* and rebirth

17. See T.W. Rhys Davids, *Early Buddhism*, pp. 86ff.

18. M1: 17-18; D1: 88.

19. Sn. #813. Cp. Mt.U. 3.2.

with an eternal, changeless soul. These contradictions eventually gave rise to various two-soul theories in the orthodox context. The Buddha, not being under the constraints of orthodoxy, simply denied the existence of any type of permanent soul *(ātman, paramātman, puruṣa,* etc.) standing behind the active, transmigrating soul *(jīvātman, liṅga-śarīra,* etc.). This denial is a logical consequence of the same Upaniṣadic thought which affirmed the existence of an eternal soul in the first place. The *Upaniṣads* themselves conclude that the monistic world soul, though somehow mysteriously connected to the individual, paradoxically is not affected by the actions of the individual. The Buddha identified this concept as a speculation which could be neither verified nor falsified, and which, when incorporated into a theory of the nature of individual human consciousness, necessarily produces contradictions.

Removing the eternal soul from Upaniṣadic psychological speculations leaves only the transmigrating, individual soul, which is, apart from the fact that it is called a soul, very similar to the Buddhist model of consciousness. In both theories there is a hierarchy of consciousness with *vijñāna* or some form of basal consciousness at the upper end. In both theories, five senses, in conjunction with *manas* as *sensus communis*, are the channels through which consciousness is informed. In both systems, this sensory information is processed and interpreted by several cooperative levels of consciousness. In both systems, this sensory interaction with the apparently external world is regarded as an undesirable disturbance of consciousness, and in both systems, the termination of this interaction, through wisdom and meditation, is considered tantamount to the realization of the *summum bonum* of human existence. It could be argued that these were all characteristics of ancient yogic psychology and that the world soul of the *Upaniṣads* was merely tacked on to such a theory, while the Buddha accepted the ancient yogic theory with only slight modifications. This would account for the similarity of the Upaniṣadic and Buddhist models of consciousness, but not for the Buddha's vigorous denial of any type of permanent entity standing behind the process of consciousness, for such an entity is not postulated in either Jainism or Ājīvikism. It is interesting in this connection that the Buddha is not recorded as criticising the Jains for their belief in a soul. This is probably the case because the early Jain and Ājīvika theory of an evolving soul is not much different from the Buddhist theory of evolving consciousness, except, that is, at the point of release, where the Buddhists held that consciousness ceases. It is interesting too that most of the Buddhist critique of the concept of a soul is directed at an individual soul similar to the *puruṣa* of the Sāṁkhya system. The two-soul theory of Sāṁkhya, however, also appears to be a result of a synthesis of yogic and Vedic concerns, rather than a purely yogic doctrine.

It is clear that the Buddha denied the universal soul as well as the individual soul, though some scholars doubt that the Upaniṣadic *ātman* is denied in Buddhism. In the "Alagaddūppama Sutta", for example, the Buddha rejects the following view as "utter and complete folly", noting that it is held even though the soul *(atta,* Skt. *ātman)* is said to be incomprehensible *(anupalabbhamāna)*.

> The soul (is) the world. After (death) I will become that permanent, stable, eternal, unchanging thing. Like the eternal will I stand.
>
> M1: 138

The Buddha also notes the contradictions in monism which appear originally to have given rise to the theory of two souls. Thus, in the "Brahmajāla Sutta" he notes that some sages are prepared to assert the eternality of soul and world even while accepting rebirth conditioned by *karma*.[20]

> The soul and the world are eternal, barren, a steadfast peak, like a pillar firmly fixed, and these beings, though they move on, transmigrate *(saṁsaranti)*, pass away and arise, are eternally the same.
>
> D1: 16

He also notes, in terms reminiscent of Upaniṣadic paradoxes, the verbal and conceptual confusion in monism that results from

---

20. Cp. M2: 233.

identifying the individual essence with the eternal, universal super-soul.[21]

> 'There is for me a self *(atta)*' — the view arises to him as though it were true, as tough it were real. Or, 'there is not for me a self'. ... Or, 'Simply by self am I aware of self'. ... Or, 'Simply by self am I aware of not-self'. ... Or, 'Simply by not-self am I aware of self' — the view arises to him as though it were true, as though it were real.
> M1: 8 (PTS)

Even the post-Upaniṣadic two-soul theory of Sāṁkhya and Advaita, which identifies the transmigrating soul with various groups of individual sensual and mental faculties, is approached with a degree of detail, though strictly speaking inaccurately, in a treatment of semi-eternalism in the "Brahmajāla Sutta".

> He gives utterance to the following conclusion of his own, beaten out by his argumentations and based on his sophistry: "This which is called eye and ear and nose and tongue and body *(kāya)*,[22] is a soul *(atta)* which is impermanent, unstable not eternal, a changing thing. But this which is called thought *(citta)*, or mind (manas), or consciousness (viññāṇa) is a soul which is permanent, steadfast, eternal, an unchanging thing, which will remain eternally the same."
> D1: 21

It is interesting that a similarly specific characterization of the *liṅga-śarīra* (transmigrating soul) does not occur in the early *Upaniṣads* themselves. In the orthodox schools, of course, *citta, manas* and *vijñāna* would also be included in the changeable soul, but the basic two-soul idea is expressed clearly enough in the above passage.

It is thus clear that some of the sages with whom the Buddha was familiar asserted an eternal soul, but were willing to admit the necessity of a less essential soul or identity which undergoes

---

21. Cp. Mt.U. 6.20, etc.

22. Identifying the sense of touch with the body in general, as noted in the *Upaniṣads*.

transmigration in *saṁsāra*. This transmigrating soul, they thought, was made up of several of the sensual and/or mental faculties of the essential soul. There is no hint in the above passage whether the eternal soul mentioned was considered universal, as in Advaita, or individual as in Sāṁkhya. Be that as it may, the two-soul theories of both of these schools are a reaction to the problem of coordinating the theory of *karma* and rebirth with an eternal soul. The Buddhist denial of the classical two-soul theory seems to indicate that the Buddhist denial of the soul was in part a conscious attempt to simplify and render more coherent the doctrine of rebirth.

Many Westerners find difficulty in conceiving of rebirth and salvation without a soul, an individual essence which is reborn and saved. Actually, however, the non-soul doctrine of Buddhism offers a solution to the conceptual problems surrounding an eternal, universal soul of Upaniṣadic ilk. Even an eternal individual soul, such as that of Sāṁkhya, shares many of the same problems. A non-eternal, changing soul, such as the soul of the Jains, could not meaningfully be called a soul, according to Buddhist thinking, because identity *per se* cannot inhere in that which changes. In other words, if the soul changes, it is just like everything else, impermanent, conditioned, and thereby not self, not self-determined, not self-defined.

The Buddha's most common denial of the soul is based on his own supposedly comprehensive analysis of the human being into five aggregates. Each of these, he argues, may be seen to be impermanent and conditioned by circumstances external to itself.[23] The dependence of aggregates upon other conditions is demonstrated primarily by means of the formula of conditioned arising *(paṭiccasamuppāda)*.[24] The Buddha's own supposedly verifiable psychological analysis is thus the primary means by which he demonstrated the absence of a stable essence of individual identity. Perhaps the most comprehensive Buddhist treatment of erroneous theories affirming the soul is the twenty-fold denial of the soul as identical to one of the five aggregates (1-5), as in one of the aggregates (6-10) as independent of

23. See M1: 230; 421; M3: 115, 265.

24. See M3: 115.

them (11-15) or as their owner (16-20).[25] Denial of the soul in Buddhism, then, is based primarily on the proposition that no independent, permanent entity can be observed in human consciousness, with the further argument that where only impermanence is observed permanence cannot be inferred.

In addition to denying permanence to any of the conscious or physical attributes of the individual, the Buddha is careful to deny that any of the meditational absorptions *(jhāna)* are permanent.[26] This, in effect, is a denial of the Upaniṣadic definition of the soul as bliss *(ānanda)*, a state of being beyond empirical consciousness. Thus, Buddhism holds that the various faculties and aspects of individual consciousness are themselves impermanent, and that they cannot be developed or refined into anything permanent. Nibbāṇa, which is permanent involves the cessation of all that is impermanent and conditioned, and thus it too is not soul in that it cannot be compared to any aspect of the individual.[27] The important difference between Buddhist and Upaniṣadic soteriological concepts is that while the *Upaniṣads* attempt to represent the eternal as a refined aspect of the individual and the world, the Buddhist *suttas* make an absolute distinction between unborn, eternal *nibbāṇa* and the changing individual and universe.

> Monks, if that unborn, not-become, not-made, not-compounded were not, there would be apparent no escape from this here that is born, become, made, compounded.
>
> *Udāna*, p. 80 (SBB)

The Buddhist concept of *nibbāṇa* is nonetheless similar in many respects to the Upaniṣadic characterization of the essential soul as non-conscious. Eternality and individuality were recognized as mutually exclusive at an early stage in Indian philosophy. Witness the consternation that arose in some Upaniṣadic aspirants as a result

---

25. M1: 300.

26. M3: 27-28; M1: 41-42; M1: 351-54; M2: 265.

27. M3: 64 (PTS tsl., p. 108, n. 1) Dhp. #277-79.

of the teaching that there is no consciousness in the ultimate soul.[28] There are several instances in the *Nikāyas* as well of a similar reaction to the Buddha's teaching of non-soul.[29]

Aside from the Buddhist denial of an essential unity underlying the various aspects of individual consciousness, the picture of the individual in early Buddhist is strikingly similar in many respects to the sophisticated Upaniṣadic models. The similarity between the chariot simile of the *Kaṭha Upaniṣad* and the five aggregates, for example, is obvious. The Buddhist analysis of consciousness, however, is systematically organized around the five aggregates, whereas there is little consistency in the principal *Upaniṣads* with regard to psychological matters. The five empirical senses, which were laboriously determined in the *Upaniṣads*, are taken for granted and consistently recognized in early Buddhist literature.[30] The predominant Buddhist tendency is to list *manas* as a sixth sense,[31] on a par with the other five, but its separate status a *sensus communis* is also recognized,[32] as is common in the *Upaniṣads*. Again, as in the *Upaniṣads*, *manas* in Buddhism is more than merely *sensus communis*, for it is said to function independently of the five empirical senses in certain of the higher meditational absorptions.[33] As the most versatile perceptual faculty, *manas* is functional at all levels of perceptual consciousness, which in the Buddhist scheme, must invariably have an object. Whenever the object of consciousness is non-physical, as, for example, in these higher *(arūpa)* absorptions, the faculty by which it is perceived is *manas*.

As in the five-soul doctrine of the *Taittirīya Upaniṣad* or the chariot simile of the *Kaṭha Upaniṣad*, early Buddhism also recognizes levels, or more properly aspects of consciousness beyond *manas*. The

---

28. B.U. 2.4.13; C.U. 8.11.1.

29. M1: 136, 487.

30. M1: 245, 505; M1: 292-93. Sn. #759.

31. M1: 273, 346; M2: 257; M3: 32, 56, 62, 137, 239.

32. M1: 295, 310; M1: 292-93; M3: 9 (see PTS tsl., p. 355, n. 2); S5: 218; A1: 199.

33. M1: 293.

most notable similarity in this regard is between the Upaniṣadic *vijñāna* and the Buddhist Pāli equivalent *viññāṇa*, in both systems the broadest, most basic term for consciousness in general. The "layering" of consciousness in Buddhism must be approached with caution, however, because differentiation between various aspects of consciousness in the Buddhist scheme is for the purpose of analysis, not for the purpose of ranking aspects of consciousness into a hierarchy of levels that approach an essential soul. Thus, the occurrence of *viññāṇa* in the position farthest removed from *rūpa* (form) in the enumeration of the five aggregates, or as the first term for consciousness in the enumeration of *paṭiccasamuppāda*, should not be taken as implying that *viññāṇa* represents a higher aspect of consciousness than the other terms employed in these formulas.

Most of the psychological terms in early Buddhism represent aspects of *viññāṇa*. In this way the term is similar in meaning to the Upaniṣadic *vijñāna*. The generality of the Buddhist term has a somewhat different significance from the generality of the Upaniṣadic term. In the Buddhist context, a thing has no existence independent of its aspects and attributes. A book is not a book without pages. It is technically wrong in the Buddhist context to think of a book as *having* pages. Instead, a collection of pages, hopefully along with other more stringent conditions, *is* a book. There is no abstract book, apart from the pages, which could *have* pages. Similarly, consciousness in general as designated by *viññāṇa* does not *have* aspects such as feeling, perception, etc.; it *is* all of these aspects together. In the *Upaniṣads*, *vijñāna* is a general term for consciousness by virtue of the fact that it is thought of as an inner, essential consciousness which somehow emanates into other, less essential levels of consciousness such as manas and the senses.

> When this one fell asleep thus, then this person made of consciousness *(vijñāna-mayaḥ puruṣaḥ)*, having retrieved by consciousness the consciousness of these breath faculties *(prāṇa)*, rests in the space within the heart.
>
> B.U. 2.1.17

In early Buddhism, on the other hand, *viññāṇa* is a general term for consciousness, merely because all instances of consciousness may be called *viññāṇa*. The Upaniṣadic *vijñāna* and Buddhist *viññāṇa*, then, refer generally to the same phenomenon, but they mean different things because the concepts underlying them are different. In the *Upaniṣads*, *vijñāna* is the very stuff of consciousness, while in Buddhism *viññāṇa* is merely a designation for consciousness in general.

Citta, a more common term in early Buddhism than in the *Upaniṣads*, is also used in much the same way in both systems. In general, it is synonymous with *viññāṇa* or *vijñāna*, but connotes the activity of consciousness rather than the stuff of consciousness. Though particularly in the Buddhist context there is no real distinction between consciousness and its activity, perhaps again the translation "thought" for *citta* will serve to distinguish if from *viññāṇa*.

Citta would not be an appropriate term with reference to the functioning of the five empirical senses, which, when stimulated are a form of *viññāṇa*, but not a form of *citta*. Wherever *manas* functions, however, as a separate sense or *sensus communis*, *citta* would be an appropriate designation of consciousness and more or less interchangeable with *viññāṇa*. *Citta* also retains in Buddhist usage the volitional, moral, connotation it had even in the *Ṛg Veda*. In early Buddhism *citta* (as in *citta-saṁkhāra)*, and particularly its grammatical relative *cetana*, implies "will", thus supplanting the Upaniṣadic *kratu*.

The basic Buddhist model of consciousness also involves a number of terms and concepts which do not exhibit an obvious relationship to antecedent Upaniṣadic material. The fact remains that the framework of Buddhist psychology — several coexisting, cooperative levels of consciousness — may be arrived at simply by subtracting the essential soul from Upaniṣadic speculations. It bears repeating, though, that the Upaniṣadic hierarchy of aspects of individual consciousness was the result of an attempt to separate the existential individual from the changeless, eternal soul, and at the same time somehow to shade one off into the other without making a sharp distinction between the individual and the ultimate. The descriptive accuracy of the resulting analysis was a secondary consideration, enhancing the credibility of dogmatic belief in a soul standing at the base of empirical consciousness. Excessive concern with the workings of consciousness was even discouraged.

> Speech is not what one should desire to understand, one should know the speaker. Odour ... form ... sound ... taste of food ... the deed is not what one should desire to understand, one should know the doer. ... Mind is not what one should desire to understand, one should know the minder [the thinker].
>
> Ks.U. 3.8 (R)

The Buddha's advice would have been diametrically opposite, for the bulk of his prescription for overcoming suffering consists in seeking to know the functioning consciousness in detail, and thereby eventually to control it.

> Herein (in this teaching) a monk dwells practising body-contemplation on the body ... feeling-contemplation on the feelings ... mind-contemplation on the mind *(citta)* ... mind-object contemplation on the mind-objects *(dhamma),* ardent, clearly comprehending and mindful, having overcome covetousness and grief concerning the world.[34]
>
> M1: 56

It would be impossible to delineate precisely Buddha's debt to the Upaniṣadic synthesis of *yoga* and *Veda*, but it is clear that the soul which is denied in Buddhism is not a purely yogic concept. Instead, the soul denied in Buddhism appears to contain an admixture of orthodox speculation of the type found in the *Upaniṣads* and traceable back to Vedic concerns with cosmogonic monism. On the basis of the textual evidence available, it appears that the essentials of the hierarchy paradigm of consciousness employed in Buddhism were originally developed in the *Upaniṣads* in order to facilitate a synthesis of Vedic monism and yogic concepts of soul, rebirth and release. When the world-soul is removed from Upaniṣadic psychological

34. Translation from: Nyanaponika, *The Heart of Buddhist Meditation*, p. 117.

speculations, a model of consciousness remains which is remarkably similar to the Buddhist model.

Each of these points suggests orthodox influence in Buddhism. Even more persuasive is the deep conceptual similarity between the psychological cosmologies expressed in the *Upaniṣads* and the Pāli *suttas*. Buddhist psychology, though it discards the world-soul of the *Upaniṣads*, remains cosmological in a way that is alien to either Jainism or Ājīvikism. In both of these systems, release is attained within the context of the given universe, and in neither system does release have any particular cosmological implications. In the Pāli *suttas*, however, the universe is not merely a given. The Buddha seeks to include in his psychological theory an explanation of the nature of the universe and to coordinate this explanation with the Buddhist concept of release. Even though the Buddha denies the cosmological soul of the *Upaniṣads*, he retains the essentially Upaniṣadic cosmological insight that the world cannot be considered independently of the mind which perceives it.

> Friends, I declare that the world, the cause of the world, the cessation of the world and the path leading to the cessation of the world lie within this fathom-long carcass with its perceptions and mind.
>
> S1: 62

Having done away with the Upaniṣadic world-soul, the Buddhist concept of the interdependence of the world and consciousness concentrates on the interdependence of the perceiver and the perceived. The interdependence of the perceiver and the world perceived is an Upaniṣadic insight which, as elucidated in Buddhism, remains viable and informative even in the present scientific age.

Vitality

Perhaps the best place to begin an examination of the early Buddhist concept of the interdependence of consciousness and the world is with an examination of the Buddhist treatment of vitality. The so-called "life faculties" appear in the Pāli *suttas* more or less exactly as they do in the *Upaniṣads*, although there is little concern with the vital faculties in Buddhism. In this respect, early Buddhism does not present a significant advance over the quaint speculations of that age. As the *Vedas* and *Upaniṣads*, in early Buddhism breath is associated with meterological wind *(vāyu)*. The five "vital winds" *(vāta)* enumerated in the suttas correspond roughly to the five "vital breaths" *(prāṇa)* of the *Upaniṣads*.[35] Breath (Pāli: *pāṇa)* is considered the most general criterion for determining what is alive, and thus the first of the five "bases of training" *(sikkhapada)* or "precepts" *(sīla)* involves abstinence from "assaulting that which has breath" *(pāṇatipata)*. The cutting off of breath *(pāṇa-upaccheda)* is a symptom of death,[36] and one is said to live as long as breath endures.[37] Interestingly, however, breath is said to cease in the fourth *jhāna*.[38] There is even mention of a specific "breathless absorption" *(appāṇaka-jhāna)* in which, we are assured, the meditator does not cheat by breathing through his ears.[39] Such naïveté suggests that to some extent the claim that breath ceases in meditation may be the work of over-zealous Buddhists seeking to attribute the supposedly miraculous feats of *yogins* to their own master.

The Buddhists were probably reluctant to accord too high a vital status to breath because of its identity with the soul in the Upaniṣadic tradition. The more essential life faculties, according to early Buddhism, are *āyu* (life-span) and *usmā* (warmth). Under normal conditions, a living body *(kāya)* is said to possess a minimum of three

35. M1: 422; S4: 218.

36. M1: 327.

37. D1: 85.

38. D3: 266.

39. M1: 243; M2: 212.

things: *āyu, usmā,* and *viññāṇa.*[40] However, in the topmost meditational absorption, *saññā-vedayita-nirodha* (cessation of perception and feeling), *āyu* and *usmā* are said to be present, but *viññāṇa* is replaced by "purified sense faculties" *(indriyāni-vippasanāni),* for reasons that will be discussed below. Sāriputta, the author of the foregoing vitalistic speculations, is careful to avoid what might be construed as a vitalistic soul theory by specifying that *āyu* and *usmā* are interdependent. He also refers to them as *saṁkhāra,* apparently implying, in this context, that they are the result of past *karma.* He says too that these particular *saṁkhāra* are not "things which can be felt" *(vedaniyā dhammā).* Why? Because if they could be felt, or experienced, they could not be present during the cessation of feeling and perception.[41]

Otherwise, the term *āyu-saṁkhāra* occurs synonymously with *jīva-saṁkhāra* in the "Mahāparinibbāṇa Sutta" in a highly suspect group of passages seeking to explain why the Buddha died.[42] Immediately following this section — which blames the Buddha's death on Ānanda's failure to petition him to live on for an aeon — is a more sober and characteristic declaration by the Buddha that whatever is born must die.[43] This declaration, repeated to the grief-stricken Saṅgha by the venerable Anurudda after Buddha's death,[44] appears to be the original substance of the explanation of Buddha's death.

Be that as it may, it is clear that the term *āyu* retains the meaning "life span" as in the *Ṛg Veda.* In the "Mahāparinibbāṇa Sutta", the Buddha is said to renounce the rest of his natural life span, as if it were a continuously present though diminishing quantity.[45] Elsewhere, violent behavior is said to produce a short *āyu* in the next birth, whereas non-violence is karmicly conducive to a long *āyu.*[46] This

---

40. D2: 335, 338; M1: 296.

41. M1: 296.

42. D2: 99; 106-107.

43. D2: 118-19.

44. D2: 158.

45. See also D2: 118.

46. M3: 203.

again emphasizes the karmic associations of *āyu* as a *saṁkhāra*. *Usmā*, or warmth, being interdependent and co-terminal with *āyu*, must be the physical manifestation of the presence of karmicly-produced "life foundation" or "life construction" *(āyu-saṁkhāra)*. As in the *Upaniṣads*, this warmth is associated with fire or heat in general and recognized as being responsible for digestion.[47]

The Fundamental Concepts of Buddhist Psychology:

In themselves, these vitalistic speculations are of little importance in Buddhist psychology. The enumeration of the minimum conditions of human life which arises from them, however, is a convenient place to begin this study. The most detailed treatment of human life at its basal level occurs in the "Mahā Vedalla" and "Cula Vedalla" *Suttas* of the *Majjhima Nikāya*, where Sāriputta says:[48]

> In regard to this body *(kāya)*, your reverence, when three things are god rid of: vitality *(āyu)*, heat *(usmā)* and consciousness *(viññāṇa)*, then does this lie cast away, flung aside like unto a senseless log of wood.
>
> M1: 296 (PTS)

On the basis of the characteristics of *vijñāna* as described in the *Upaniṣads*, the location of *viññāṇa* here at the basal level of mere life is not surprising. In the *Upaniṣads*, *vijñāna* or its occasional synonym *prajñā* is associated with deep sleep. In the *Taittirīya Upaniṣad's* five-soul theory, it is identified with the next innermost essence of the person.

The parallel Buddhist association of *viññāṇa* with basal consciousness is borne out in its importance in the mechanism of rebirth, which in several passages is described as the descent *(avakkanti)* of *viññāṇa* into the womb.[49] In the *Upaniṣads*, the

47. M1: 422.

48. Cp. S2: 253; S3: 80, 169; S5: 311; A1: 132; A4: 53.

49. S2: 13 91, 101, 104; M1: 165; A1: 176; D2: 62. Cp. D3: 103.

departure at death of the soul *(ātman or puruṣa)*, along with breath *(prāṇa)* and *vijñāna*, is described in similar terms with various modifications of the verbal root √*kram*.[50] The Buddha, possibly because of a widespread association of basal consciousness with the soul, took particular pains to emphasize that *viññāṇa* must not be thought of as a soul. In addition to his frequent characterization of the five aggregates, including *viññāṇa*, as non-soul, there occurs the stern and specific rebuke to the monk Sati son for teaching that *viññāṇa* survives death as an entity.[51] At another point it is observed that it would make more sense to think of the body as soul since it may persist for some time.

> But this, brethren, that we call thought *(citta)*, that we call mind *(manas)*, that we call consciousness *(viññāṇa)*, that arises as one thing, ceases as another whether by night or by day.
>
> S2: 94 (PTS)

Several passages state further that *nibbāṇa* is not to be understood as a state of *viññāṇa*. After the final attainment of the *summum bonum*, after one's last death *(parinibbāṇa)*, *viññāṇa* ceases,[52] or is not reinstated.[53] This doctrine is somewhat similar to the Ājīvika doctrine that some aspect of the individual transmigrates for a set amount of time, like a ball of string unravelling. Ultimately, this process necessarily results in total annihilation, the end of the string, which is characterized as an end of suffering *(dukkha)*, and therefore is in some sense, a *summum bonum*.[54] In the Buddhist context, of course, *nibbāṇa* is in no sense inevitable or predetermined. More important in the present study is that according to Buddhism the *viññāṇa* which

---

50. See B.U. 4.3.8; 4.4.2.
51. M1: 256-59.
52. D1: 54.
53. S1: 122; S3: 106.
54. D1: 54.

establishes a link between rebirths, is not like a string, but like a stream.[55]

In considering the Buddhist metaphor, one must be careful not to think of a stream as a string. A string is self-determined as it unravels, while a stream, as it flows along, is in constant interaction with its environment and changing at every instant. One cannot cross the same proverbial river twice, for it will have become a different river. It is also unwise to lay too much stress on the occasional metaphorical treatment of consciousness as a stream. It is better to observe precisely how, in early Buddhism, the continual changing of *viññāṇa* is said to occur. Somewhat like a stream, it changes in relation to its environment, which in the case of *viññāṇa* is comprised of the objects of consciousness. Without and object *(ārammaṇa)*, *viññāṇa* does not arise or "become established" *(patiṭṭha)*.[56] Given an object, it arises conditioned by that object. The nature of *viññāṇa* at any given time is determined by the nature of its object. The most general designation for the necessary objective counterpart of *viññāṇa* is *nāma-rūpa* (name and form), which term is employed in early Buddhist literature in much the same way that it is used in the *Upaniṣads*, to denote the conceptual and apparitional aspects of any individual object.

There is a tendency among both ancient and modern interpreters of early Buddhism to construe *nāma-rūpa* as a general designation for the two basic aspects of an individual human being, namely consciousness and body.[57] Thereby, the intriguing term is oversimplified and glossed, often with the unfounded assertion that *nāma* represents the four non-material aggregates *(vedanā, saññā, saṁkhāra and viññāṇa)* and that *rūpa*, the fifth aggregate, represents the body. Even Buddhaghosa, who is normally careful to avoid this oversimplification of *nāma-rūpa*, does at one point in the

---

55. See D3: 105; M2: 262; and Walpola Rahula, *What the Buddha Taught*, 1967, p. 25.

56. S2: 65.

57. C.A.F. Rhys-Davids, *Buddhist Psychology*, 1914, pp. 6-9. Rune Johansson, *The Psychology of Nirvāṇa*, 1969, pp. 78-80. E.J. Thomas, *The History of Buddhist Thought*, 2nd ed., 1951, pp. 63-70.

Visuddhimagga suggest that *nāma-rūpa* is a twofold designation of the five aggregates.[58] His usual care in this regard is no doubt a result of the fact that at no point in the early *sutta* literature is *nāma* defined as the four non-material aggregates. Instead, it is defined as or said to involve, *vedanā, saññā, cetanā, phassa* and *manasikāra*. *Rūpa* is consistently defined as the four great elements.[59] *Rūpa*, moreover, means "form" in general, not specifically "body". *Kāya* is the standard term for body. Body, of course, is one type of form, and as such is also said to be composed of the four great elements.[60] When the physical and conscious aspects of the individual are specifically intended, however, *kāya* indicates body, and either *citta*[61] or *viññāṇa*[62] indicate consciousness in general.

If *nāma-rūpa* is taken to mean "consciousness and body", the *paṭiccasamuppāda* formula may be, and often is, interpreted more or less persuasively as an explanation of rebirth. The phrase *"viññāṇa* conditions *nāma-rūpa"* then seems to mean simply that consciousness somehow enters or arises in the womb and that a mind and body start to develop. There is, however, no indication in the early *sutta* literature that the first four links of the standard enumeration of *paṭiccasamuppāda*, culminating with the phrase *"viññāṇa* conditions *nāma-rūpa"*, are to be construed as confined to the explanation of rebirth. Instead, the conditioning of *nāma-rūpa* by *viññāṇa* refers to the arising of any instance of consciousness, which "arises as one thing, ceases as another whether by night or day". The conditioning of *nāma-rūpa* by *viññāṇa*, of course, may describe the arising of consciousness in rebirth,[63] but rebirth is also described as the descent

58. Vsm. 14.11. Normally he defines *nāma* as comprised of *vedanā, saññā* and *saṁkhāra,* as at Vsm. 17.187. This definition may be based on an inference from S3: 58, where it is stated that there can be no *viññāṇa* without *rūpa, vedanā, saññā* and *saṁkhāra,* while it is often said that there can be no *viññāṇa* without *nāma-rūpa*.

59. S2: 3; M1: 53.

60. M1: 144; 190; 500.

61. M1: 237, 276; M3: 18; D1: 20; D3: 32; A2: 137; S2: 94; S3: 2-5; S5: 66.

62. D2: 335, 338; M1: 296; M2: 17; M3: 18. Cp. M1: 144; D1: 176.

63. See D2: 63; S2: 91.

of *nāma-rūpa*.[64] One passage which describes rebirth as the result of *viññāṇa* omits *nāma-rūpa* altogether and starts with the six senses, i.e. the six types of *viññāṇa*, as the condition for sensual contact *(phassa)*.[65]

The general and specific inconsistencies which result from interpreting *nāma-rūpa* as consciousness and body, and *paṭiccasamuppāda* as merely an explanation of rebirth are too numerous to catalogue. If the *Upaniṣads* are taken as the source of our understanding of the term *nāma-rūpa*, the bulk of the psychological material in the early Buddhist *suttas* will be far more satisfactorily and consistently explained than if the term is taken to mean consciousness and body.

The following discussion assumes the obvious: that the Buddha used the term *nāma-rūpa* when, in the common parlance of his age, it meant approximately what he wanted to say. There is no doubt that the term literally means "name and form". At the time of the Buddha, and for several hundred years before and after his lifetime, the term implied "individuality", a connotation which was based on the archaic idea that names were inherent qualities of individual things. More abstractly, name was that which was thought to account for the relationship among different forms which were nonetheless similar enough to be given the same verbal designation. In this sense, the term *nāma* is similar to "a concept". Thus, when it is said in the *Upaniṣads* that creation consisted of the differentiation of the universe by means of *nāma-rūpa*, what is implied is that the myriad discrete entities thus produced were and still are related in an orderly fashion by virtue of the fact that they bear names. These names make possible the conceptual ordering of manyness.[66] Language was thought of as a discovery of the inherent conceptual relationships among things, so that from a very early period in Indian thought, conceptualization was regarded as primarily a verbal phenomenon.

---

64. S2: 89-90, 104.

65. S2: 13.

66. B.U. 1.4.7; C.U. 6.3.2-3; C.U. 8.14.1.

One should not suppose that all of these implications of the term *nāma-rūpa* are specifically intended in every instance of the term, particularly as it occurs in Buddhism, which rejected from the beginning many orthodox linguistic notions. In general, however, the term *nāma-rūpa* is a comprehensive designation of the individuality of a perceived thing. It refers to both the appearance and the conceptualization of a given object of consciousness. As such it is employed in early Buddhism in much the same way in which it is used in the *Upaniṣads*.

> Just as the flowing rivers disappear in the ocean casting off name and shape, even so, the knower, freed from name and shape, attains to the divine person, higher than the high.
>
> Mu.U. 3.2.8 (R)

> A seeing man will see name and form, and having seen he will understand those (things); let him at pleasure see much or little, for the experts do not say that purity exists by that.
>
> Sn. #909 (SBE)

> I will explain to thee by what name and shape are totally stopped; by the cessation of consciousness *(viññāṇa)* this is stopped here.
>
> Sn. #1037 (SBE)

> As a flame extinguished by the force of the wind ... so a sage, freed from name-and-form goes to rest and cannot be verbally characterized.
>
> Sn. #1073

With this understanding of *nāma-rūpa*, an examination of the early Buddhist treatment of the arising of consciousness in relation to objects of consciousness may proceed.

In response to the wayward monk Sati's characterization of *viññāṇa* as "that which runs on, fares on, not changed *(anañña)*", the Buddha offers the following.

> In many a figure has consciousness generated by conditions been spoken of by me to you, monks, saying: 'Apart from condition there is no origination of consciousness'.
>
> M1: 259 (PTS)

The "many figures" in which the generation of *viññāṇa* by conditions is explained elsewhere by the Buddha fall into essentially two main categories: 1) the analysis of *viññāṇa* into six types, comprising the five senses and mind, and 2) the conditioned arising of *viññāṇa* according to various forms of *paṭiccasamuppāda*.

By far the most common definition of *viññāṇa* is that it is of six kinds with reference to the five empirical senses and *manas*. It is said to be dependent upon them as fire is dependent upon its fuel, and to be defined by them as fire is characterized according to the nature of its fuel.[67]

> It is because, monks, an appropriate condition arises that consciousness is known by this or that name: if consciousness arises because of eye and material shapes *(rūpa)* it is known as visual consciousness; if consciousness arises because of ear and sounds ... nose and smells ... tongue and tastes ... body and touches ... mind and mental objects, it is known as auditory ... olfactory ... gustatory ... tactile ... mental consciousness. Monks, as a fire burns because of this or that appropriate condition, by that it is known: if a fire burns because of sticks ... chips, etc. it is known as a stick-fire ... a chip-fire, etc.
>
> M1: 259 (PTS)

The conditions governing the arising of consciousness are more precisely stated in the following formula in the "Madhupiṇḍika Sutta".

> Visual consciousness, your reverences, arises because of eye and material shapes; the meeting of the three is a sensory impingement *(phassa)*.
>
> M1: 111 (PTS)

---

67. Cp. Mt.U. 6.34.

This "sensory impingement", literally "touch" or "contact", is similarly treated with reference to the other senses and *manas*. Technically speaking, *phassa* does not automatically result from the mere physical juxtaposition of organ and object. The object must be present to consciousness. The contact, termed *samannāhāra* (lit. "bringing well along") in the following passage from the "Mahā Hatthipadopama Sutta", must be "appropriate" *(tajja,* lit. "born from that"). In other words, it must be effective in producing consciousness.

> If, your reverences, the eye that is internal is intact and external forms *(rūpa)* come within its range, but without appropriate contact *(samannāhāra),* then there is no appearance of the appropriate type of consciousness. But when, your reverences, the eye that is internal is intact and external forms come within its range and there is the appropriate contact, then there is thus an appearance of the appropriate type of consciousness.
>
> M1: 190

Comparing the two preceding passages, two equations emerge: 1) faculty + object + *viññāṇa* = *phassa/samannāhāra,* and 2) faculty + object + *phassa/samannāhāra* = *viññāṇa.* Thus, *viññāṇa* is as necessary for sensual contact as sensual contact is for *viññāṇa.* The "Mahā Hatthipadopama Sutta" continues its analysis by saying that given faculty, object, appropriate contact and the appearance of the corresponding type of consciousness:

> Whatever is *rūpa* in what has thus come to be is called the grasping-aggregate of form *(rūpa-upādāna-khandha).* Whatever is *vedanā* in what has thus come to be is called the grasping-aggregate of feeling. Whatever is perception *(saññā)* ... formations *(saṁkhāra),* ... consciousness *(viññāṇa)* in what has thus come to be is called the grasping-aggregate of perception ... formations ... consciousness. Thus, one comprehends the collecting, the assembling, the coming together of these five grasping-aggregates.
>
> M1: 190

Rūpa, which first appears specifically as the object of visual consciousness, is expanded in the above citation to include the objects of any type of consciousness, once they have actually become present to consciousness.

The fascinating point about the above is that *rūpa*, as a *khandha*, an aggregate, is said to come into existence on the basis of the functioning of consciousness, even though, as the specific object of vision, it is a condition for the arising of that very consciousness. In either case, it is manifestly impossible to construe *rūpa-upādāna-khanda* as the body. Instead, on the one hand it is an objective condition for the arising of consciousness. On the other hand, like all of the five aggregates, it results from the fulfilment of the conditions necessary for the arising of consciousness. Nonetheless, in the opening statement of the above passage, *rūpa* is emphatically defined as a body, "a space enclosed by bones and sinews and flesh and skin". This must be a commentarial corruption in the text. Such a definition of *rūpa* is absolutely inappropriate in either context in which the term is used in the "Mahā Hatthipadopama Sutta".[68] These two contexts, again, are: 1) as an aspect of that which arises when all of the conditions for any of the six types of consciousness are met, and 2) as the specific object of visual consciousness.

There is a tendency in Indian psychology in general to substitute vision for all of the senses, and this probably accounts for the two contexts in which *rūpa* is used here. When the arising of consciousness is being analyzed, an appropriate object, or *rūpa* is a condition, but from the opposite point of view, the arising of consciousness is a condition for the arising of *rūpa*. Therefore, as consciousness does not arise without an object, so an object does not arise without consciousness. This is borne out in many other passages, perhaps most specifically where it is said that the four great elements — which are the standard definition of *rūpa* — cease when *viññāṇa* ceases.[69]

---

68. This is, to my knowledge, the only context in the early *sutta* literature which so emphatically defines *rūpa* in the sense that *kāya* is normally understood.

69. D1: 222-23.

The above considerations suggest that the five aggregate analysis is entirely an analysis of consciousness as experienced. When sufficient conditions exist and consciousness actually arises, the five aggregates are brought into the picture as an analysis of that consciousness. *Rūpa-khandha* is the apparently external, objective content of that consciousness. This again is consistent with observations in earlier chapters that *rūpa* does not connote substance, but rather appearance. The four great elements, at least when they are enumerated as a definition of *rūpa-khandha,* are not necessarily a primitive periodic table, but rather an analysis of how "matter" is experienced. It is well known that the four elements are construed in the *Abhidhamma* and commentarial literature as being abstract representations of various qualities of matter as experienced (i.e. solidity, fluidity, heat and motion.[70] There is little evidence of an abstract interpretation of the elements in the *suttas* themselves,[71] but there is also little to suggest that an independently existing material world was postulated.

In relation to this point, *paṭiccasamappāda,* the second means by which the conditions for the arising of consciousness are set forth, is relevant. In this formula, the relationship between *viññāṇa* and *nāma-rūpa* is very similar to what appears to be the relationship of *viññāṇa* and *rūpa* in the "Mahā Hatthipadopama Sutta", where *rūpa* is a condition for the arising of *viññāṇa* and the arising of *viññāṇa* is, in turn, a condition for the arising of *rūpa*. It is not uncommon to find the formula of *paṭiccasamuppāda,* minus the first two links in the standard chain, beginning with the reciprocal conditioning of *viññāṇa* by *nāma-rūpa* and *nāma-rūpa* by *viññāṇa*.[72] In this connection, it is no doubt significant that the entire twelvefold enumeration of *paṭiccasamuppāda* is not listed anywhere in the *Dīgha Nikāya*.[73] Moreover, the tenfold enumeration of *paṭiccasamuppāda* in the

---

70. See: Y. Karunadasa, *Buddhist Analysis of Matter,* Ch. 2.

71. But see M1: 421-23.

72. D1: 223; D2: 32; S2: 104, 113. Cp. D2:62-3; S2: 6, 8, 12; S3: 102.

73. See T.W. Rhys-Davids' "Introduction to the Mahā-nidāna-suttanta", SBB, vol. 3, p. 42. Cp. S2: 104.

"Mahāpadana Sutta" treats the mutual conditioning of *nāma-rūpa* and *viññāṇa* in a way that would seem to preclude any further conditions beyond the ten commonly recognized in the *Dīgha* Nikāya.

> Consciousness is the condition of name-and-form. ... Name-and-form is the condition of consciousness. ... Consciousness turns back from name-and-form, it does not go beyond. Only as follows can one be born, or age, or die, or pass away or arise, that is to say: consciousness conditions name-and-form; name-and-form conditions consciousness; name-and-form conditions the six spheres; the six spheres condition contact *(phassa);* contact conditions feeling *(vedanā);* feeling conditions desire *(taṇhā);* etc.
>
> D2: 32

The "Mahanidāna Sutta" of the *Dīgha Nikāya* opens with an even shorter, no doubt archaic ninefold enumeration of *paṭiccasamuppāda* which omits the six sense spheres *(salāyatana)* from the tenfold *Dīgha Nikāya* formula. This makes *nāma-rūpa* the direct condition of sensual contact *(phassa),* as well as the reciprocal condition of *viññāṇa.*[74] Following this short list is an explanation of *nāma-rūpa* which is highly instructive and which proves that the omission of the sense spheres in this treatment was not merely an oversight.

> "That name-and-form conditions contact should be understood in the following way. If, Ānanda, those modes, characteristics, signs, indications by which the name-group *(nāma-kāya)* is manifested were absent, would there be the manifestation of verbal contact *(adhivacana-samphassa)* in the form-group *(rūpa-kāya)?"*
>
> "There would not, venerable sir."
>
> "If, Ānanda, those modes, characteristics, signs, indications by which the form-group is manifested were absent, would there be the manifestation of sensual contact *(paṭigha-samphassa)* in the name-group?"
>
> "There would not, venerable sir." ...
>
> "And if, Ānanda, those modes, etc. by which (both) name and form are manifested were absent, would there be any manifestation of (any kind of) contact *(phassa)?"*

---

74. D2: 56.

"There would not, venerable sir."

"Therefore, Ānanda, this is the cause, the basis, the origin, the condition of contact, namely name-and-form."

D2: 62

This passage is essentially a rational abstraction of the cosmogonic *nāma-rūpa* of the *Upaniṣads,* where the differentiation of the universe is said to be accomplished by means of name and form. Recalling the association of name and conceptualization in the general Indian context, it is clear that the interdependence of concept *(nāma)* and conceptualized *(rūpa),* or name and named, is also stated in this passage. It is also noteworthy that the analysis of *nāma-rūpa* in the "Mahānidāna Sutta" has the effect of generating two types of contact *(phassa):* verbal *(adhivacana)* and sensual *(paṭigha,* lit. "striking against"). It is this very contact which is necessary for the arising of *viññāṇa.* This expression of a twofold concept of contact may well relate to the fact that in the *arūpa-loka* or in the *arūpa-jhānas, rūpa* technically is not possible as a condition for the arising of consciousness. Nonetheless, consciousness is present in these states, except, that is, for the fourth *arūpa-jhāna,* which is said not to be a "foothold of *viññāṇa*".[75] In these subtle states, consciousness apparently is conditioned by a verbal concept *(nāma)* such as "space is infinite", "consciousness is infinite", or "there is nothing", but not by a form *(rūpa).*

The *adhivacana,* verbal-conceptual aspect of *phassa* is of more immediate importance with reference to the conditioning of feeling *(vedanā)* by *phassa,* and the consequent conditioning of perception *(saññā)* by *vedanā* in the normal course of human consciousness. Like *viññāṇa,* or consciousness in general, and like *phassa,* both of these aggregates *(vedanā* and *saññā)* may be classified as sixfold with reference to the five senses and *manas.*[76] Both *vedanā* and *saññā,*

---

75. See L. de la Vallée Poussin, *Théorie des douze causes,* p. 16. See also Poussin's "Cosmology" article, ERE, vol. 4, p. 137. See Vbh: 138, where *viññāṇa* is said to condition only *nāma.*

76. D3: 244; M1: 398; M3: 281.

however, have a conceptual content as well. Interestingly, *vedanā* is specifically said to have both a physical *(kāyikā)* and a mental *(cetasikā)* aspect,[77] and both *vedanā* and *saññā* are together said to comprise *citta-saṁkhāra.*[78] The conceptual nature of *vedanā* is evident even in the standard enumeration of the three types of *vedanā*, painful *(dukkha)*, pleasant *(sukha)* and neutral *(adukkham-asukha)*,[79] for these in themselves are minimal verbal-conceptual constructs. The "Satipaṭṭhana Sutta" notes too that these three minimal concepts may also occur with reference to non-material *(arūpa)* things, presumably on the basis of *adhivacana-samphassa.*[80] *Saññā* is characterized as a more developed verbal conceptualization than *vedanā* in the following definition, which obviously must be taken as exemplary rather than comprehensive.

> Your reverence, if it is said, 'He perceives, he perceives *(sanjānāti)'*, it is therefore called 'perception'. And what does he perceive? He perceives what is dark green and he perceives what is yellow and he perceives what is white.
>
> M1: 293 (PTS)

The three terms, *viññāṇa* as consciousness in general, *vedanā* as feeling, and *saññā* as perception of specific features, may be differentiated for the purpose of analyzing conscious experience. They do not, however, denote separate entities which arise, each dependent on the former, in a temporal or even a linear causal sequence, as might be imagined by noticing their respective positions in the enumeration of *paṭiccasamuppāda* or of the five aggregates. Instead, they all occur together and are actually aspects of the same thing.

> That which is feeling, sir, and that which is perception, and that which is consciousness, these things are associated, not dissociated. Having

77. S4: 231. Cp. M1: 302, 398.
78. M1: 301.
79. M1: 293, 302, 398.
80. M1: 59.

> analyzed and analyzed, it is not possible to declare a basis of differentiation. What one feels, sir, that one perceives. What one perceives, of that one is conscious.
>
> M1: 293

Even though *saññā* is not technically a member of the standard enumeration of *paṭiccasamuppāda,* the relationship among *vedanā, saññā* and *viññāṇa* is described in the above passage as a type of conditioned arising. This in itself is not surprising. The basic definition of *paṭiccasamuppāda* is the well-known phrase: "When this is, that is. From the arising of this, that arises. When this is not, that is not. From the cessation of this, that ceases."[81] Thus, the term may properly be applied to any set of results dependent upon necessary and sufficient conditions. It is likely that the standard twelvefold formula developed over some time, though possibly within the Buddha's lifetime, as a result of the consolidation of various cause and effect relationships governed by the general formula "When this is, that is, etc." The relationship among the three aspects of consciousness in question in the preceding passage is clarified by Mahākaccana in the "Madhupiṇḍika Sutta" as follows.

> Conditioned by eye (etc.) and form *(rūpa,* etc.), sir, visual consciousness (etc.) arises. The conjunction of the three is contact *(phassa).* Contact conditions feeling *(vedanā).* What one feels, that one perceives *(sañjānati);* what one reasons about *(vitakketi);* what one reasons about, that one proliferates *(pappañceti);* what one proliferates, that is the source of the various perceptual proliferations which assail a person in the past, the future and the present with regard to forms (etc.) of which the eye (etc.) may be conscious.
>
> M1: 111-12

Thus, the arising of *saññā* is implied in the standard formula of *paṭiccasamuppāda* by the arising of *vedanā* conditioned by *phassa.*

---

81. M1: 262; M2: 32; M3: 63; S2: 28, 65, 95; Ud. #1. See Poussin, *Théorie des douze causes,* p. 50. Walpola Rahula, *What the Buddha Taught,* p. 53.

Beyond *vedanā*, the *paṭiccasamuppāda* formula deals with psychopathology, rather than theoretical psychology, by enumerating desire, grasping etc. Let us then pause here to consider the implications of the relationships between the fundamental theoretical concepts of Buddhist psychology and to consider an integrated interpretation of the foregoing ancient Buddhist material that may render it more accessible to the modern reader.

This integrated interpretation, though somewhat speculative, need not stray from actual ancient Buddhist material. In fact, it may be supported at every point as a valid interpretation thereof. The basis of the present interpretation is generated by considering the two immediately preceding passages in conjunction with the archaic ninefold enumeration of *paṭiccasamuppāda* found in the "Mahānidana Sutta". On this basis, it will be noted that the initial stages of the interdependent arising of consciousness and object of consciousness turn back upon each other at every point and form a self-contained unit, as illustrated in the following diagram. (Arrows show direction of influence).

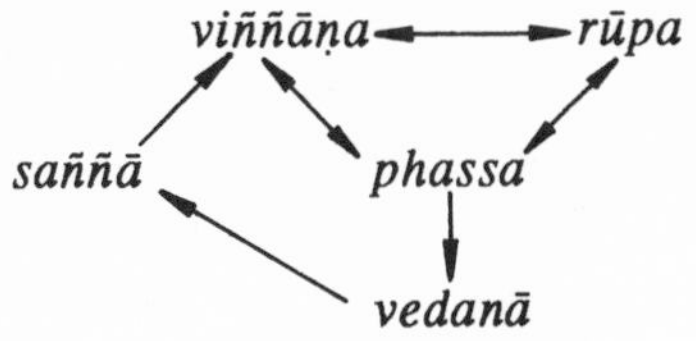

It is important that, when several versions of these relationships are considered, there is seen to be no starting point as such in the complex diagrammed above. Yet in a sense, *viññāṇa* is the focus of these relationships. Having arisen on the basis of contact with an object of consciousness *(rūpa)*, it recycles into itself, as it were, through the *vedanā* and *saññā* aspects of *viññāṇa*, so that consciousness is like a dog chasing its own tail. It takes aspects of itself as an object and may arise on the basis thereof.

When *viññāṇa* arises on the basis of *vedanā* and *saññā (yaṁ vedeti, taṁ sañjānāti);* the contact *(phassa)* said to be necessary for the arising of *viññāṇa* must be conceptual *(adhivacana)*, rather than sensual *(paṭigha)*. It must be supposed that this contact occurs on the basis of the sixth sense, *manas*. An interpretive diagram of the foregoing material would appear as follows:

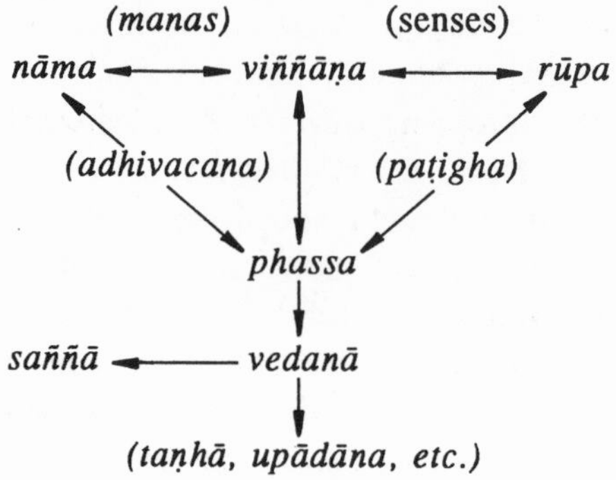

The distinction between *nāma* and *rūpa* in the above treatment is justified in the "Mahānidana Sutta". Its archaic ninefold treatment of *paṭiccasamuppāda*, omits the six-sense spheres as a separate causal link between *nāma-rūpa* and *phassa*, and simply states that name-and-form is the condition of contact. Contact, rather than being of six kinds with reference to five senses and *manas*, is characterized as being of two kinds, verbal *(adhvacana)* and sensual *(paṭigha)*. One might suspect that *adhivacana samphassa* is the specific privilege of *manas* while the senses "strike against" *(paṭigha)* their grosser objects. In other words, it appears that in this archaic formula *adhivacana* (verbal) and *paṭigha* (sensual), as categories of *phassa*, fulfill the role normally assigned to the more commonly enumerated six kinds of *phassa*. *Nāma-rūpa* thus appears to be a dual categorization of the six types of objects of consciousness. This is precisely how the commentary interprets the present passage. Therefore, if *nāma-rūpa* is to be identified with any other set of terms in the Buddhist system, it must be with the six "external" sense spheres and not with the five aggregates. The integrated interpretation of the preceding passages also suggests that the so-called "external" object *(dhamma)* of *manas*, the sixth type of *viññāṇa*, may be equated with the conceptual content of previous consciousness as indicated by the terms *vedanā* and *saññā*.

Recalling the components of *nāma* listed in the early *Nikāya* literature as *vedanā, saññā, cetanā, phassa,* and *manasikāra,*[82] it will be recogniszed that this interpretation is borne out to a considerable degree in the terminology of early Buddhist literature. This enumeration of the components of *nāma* in the early *Nikāya* literature seems to be actually an enumeration of the conditions surrounding consciousness of a name, i.e. a concept generated by previous consciousness. If this is so, then of these five conditions, *phassa* is to be interpreted specifically as *adhivacana-samphassa,* based on 1) the conceptual content of *vedanā* and *saññā* (for example: "pleasant and red"), and 2) the naming of this conceptual content by *manas,* (for example: "an apple"). The term *manasikāra,* often translated "attention", but meaning literally "making or doing in the mind", apparently refers to the specific functioning of *manas* in perceiving the conceptual *(nāma)* aspect of a given object *(rūpa).* It will be noted as well that since *vedanā* and *saññā* are invariably aspects of the arising of consciousness, there can be no actual instance of consciousness of a form without an accompanying verbal/conceptual content. In other words, there is no *rūpa* without a *nāma.* This situation is reflected no doubt in the status of *manas* as *sensus communis.* The five empirical senses "resort to" *manas,* not only in the sense that the mind as *sensus communis* sorts and arranges the information they convey. They also resort to *manas* in the sense that, as the faculty responsible for *adhivacana-samphassa,* (verbal/conceptual contact), *manas* supplies the *nāma,* partly on the basis of previous consciousness, for the *rūpa* conveyed by the five senses.

The implication of the foregoing is that according to early Buddhist psychology, there are no "external" objects as such, but only apparent objects based on the objectivization of certain aspects of consciousness. Consciousness, however, depends on the fulfillment of certain minimum conditions, one of which is an appropriate, i.e. accessible object. From an overarching point of view, what is

---

82. S2: 3; M1: 53.

described is the constant, reciprocal interaction between object and consciousness, each determining the nature of the other.

For the sake of analysis, a hypothetical starting point in the arising of consciousness may arbitrarily be selected. Thus, some analyses start with the six internal and external sense spheres as the origin of consciousness.

> Six internal (sense) spheres *(āyatana)* are to be known. ... Six external (sense) spheres are to be known. ... Six groups of consciousness *(viññāṇa-kāya)* are to be known. ... Six groups of contact *(phassa-kāya)* are to be known. Visual consciousness (etc.) is conditioned by eye (etc.) and form (etc.). The conjunction of the three is contact. Contact conditions feeling *(vedanā)*. When it is said that six groups of feeling *(vedanā-kāya)* are to be known, it is with reference to this conditionality.
>
> M3: 281

But "three things come together" are *phassa,* not two. Contact between the internal and external sense spheres presupposes the existence of consciousness. On the other hand, consciousness presupposes the existence of contact between the internal and external sense spheres. This situation appears to be responsible for the tendency in early enumerations of *paṭiccasamuppāda* to qualify immediately the assertion that *viññāṇa* is the condition of *nāma-rūpa* with the counter assertion that *nāma-rūpa* is the condition of *viññāṇa, nāma-rūpa* representing the conceptual and apparitional aspects of the object of consciousness. The original inclusion of the six sense spheres *(salāyatana)* — conditioned by *nāma-rūpa* and the condition of *phassa* — in the standard *paṭiccasamuppāda* formula amounts to a more detailed definition of *nāma-rūpa* as the apparently objective content of consciousness. *Nāma-rūpa* determines and is determined by consciousness according to the six avenues through which this interaction may be observed to take place.

By way of illustration of the foregoing, let us start arbitrarily and hypothetically with an unspecified yet discrete object, a *nāma-rūpa.* For simplicity's sake let us suppose that the contact *(phassa)* it generates in conjunction with appropriate *viññāṇa* is purely sensual, say visual. ["Three things come together are contact"] Suppose the *vedanā* aspect of *viññāṇa* which arises therefrom ["Contact conditions feeling"] is "pleasant", and that *saññā* arises as "red, round". ["Whatever one feels, one perceives"] This conceptual content cycles into *viññāṇa* by means of *adhvacana-samphassa* (verbal, conceptual contact) through the faculty of *manas*. ["Whatever one perceives, of that one is conscious"] This conceptual content determines to some extent the nature of the object, and to a similar extent the object determines the nature of consciousness. ["Consciousness conditions name-and-form; name-and-form conditions consciousness"] Within this self-contained cycle a fairly precise notion of the object of consciousness may be built up, perhaps: "pleasant, red, round, hard, smooth: an apple!" At this point, if not before, or rather if not at a more basic level, consciousness may become more than mere awareness of an object. There may come to be, in the broad Buddhist sense of the term, a moral or karmic interaction as well. Suppose, for example, one is hungry, or even merely that one is at a fruit stall. One may, then, come to interact volitionally with that pleasant red, round, smooth, hard object. One may then be disappointed to find, on the basis of further functioning of the interdependent network of perceptual consciousness, that it is in fact a child's ball. It may then become an unpleasant object, particularly if one is very hungry, or merely an annoyance to the shopper at a fruit stall. On the other hand, a child dragged along on shopping day might be elated to find a lovely ball among all those boring fruits.

Thus, some of the qualities of a given object are not inherent in the object itself. The interdependence of consciousness and object is literal and observable, not merely theoretical. Consciousness is not merely the recognition of an independently existing environment. This observation suggests that the self-contained perceptual network diagrammed above, is not truly self-contained. On the one hand, it tends to move beyond mere perceptual interaction with the object at hand into the moral realm of willful interaction therewith. This tendency is expressed in the standard *paṭiccasamuppāda* formula with the observation that desire *(taṇhā)* is conditioned by *vedanā*. Beginning with this link, the moral, psychopathological portion of conditioned arising is set forth. On the other hand, however, on the basis of the theory of *karma*, it is thought that volitional activity of any kind, by mind *(citta)*, speech *(vac)*, or body *(kāya)*, necessarily exerts an effect upon the future arising of consciousness. It is probably in this connection that *cetana* (will) is said to be the fifth aspect of *nāma*. This would also explain why *saṁkhāra* (formation), implying previous *karma*, is included in most versions of *paṭiccasamuppāda* as a condition of *viññāṇa* in addition to the mutual conditioning of *viññāṇa* and *nāma-rūpa*.

Intentionally, the term *saṁkhāra* has been left unexplained in the foregoing discussion because, as used in Buddhist psychology, it represents a concept unfamiliar to the Western mind. The difficulty of translating and explaining the term adequately has been emphasized repeatedly in modern scholarship. This difficulty arises because *saṁkhāra*, as a psychological term, refers to a characteristic of consciousness rather than to an aspect or a function of consciousness. This characteristic is the tendency to accumulate or "build up". "Building up" or "formation" is close to a literal translation of *saṁkhāra*, which is derived from the verb √*kṛ* "to make" and the prefix *saṁs-* "well or completely". In the short term, this building up constitutes ideation. In the long term it constitutes memory. Most importantly, *saṁkhāra* is held responsible for the moral fruition of past actions *(karma*, Pāli: *kamma)*.

In the context of ancient Buddhism, this tendency of consciousness requires some explanation. After all, the Buddha analyzed consciousness into several interacting levels or aspects, all of which are held to manifest their impermanence moment by moment.

> This, brethren, that we call thought *(citta)*, that we call mind *(manas)*, that we call consciousness *(viññāṇa)*, that arises as one thing, ceases as another, whether by night or by day.
>
> S2: 94 (PTS)

In the early *sutta* literature, there is no overt theory of moments of consciousness as found in the *Adhidhamma* and commentarial literature and made much of in the later logic of the Vijñānavādins. There is, however, an unmistakable tendency to view change infinitesimally as a rapid succession of arising and ceasing. Consciousness in particular is said to arise and cease continuously, if not momentarily.

> He fares along contemplating origination-things in the mind, or he fares along contemplating dissolution-things in the mind, or he fares along contemplating origination-dissolution-things in the mind.
>
> M1: 60 (PTS)

The perpetual, observable changing of consciousness, in the Buddhist context, is regarded as repeated arising and cessation. Having ceased, however, consciousness tends to arise again in a form similar to what it was previously. This observation requires explanation with regard to the Buddhist doctrine of impermanence. Moreover, again with regard to the doctrine of impermanence, the fruition of *karma* requires explanation. In the context of the above interpretation of the fundamental theoretical concepts of early Buddhist psychology, *saṁkhāra* provides both the explanations required.

Other than its psychological occurrence as the fifth aggregate and as the second link in the twelvefold *paṭiccasamuppāda* formula, *saṁkhāra* occurs primarily as a moral term in early Buddhist literature. In the moral sense of the term, the three types of *saṁkhāra*, mental *(citta* or *manas)*, verbal *(vaci)*, and bodily *(kāya)* correspond to the three types of *kamma* or *karma*. As in the case of *saṁkhāra*, the mental aspect of *kamma* is the most significant.

> Monks, I say that will *(cetanā)* is action *(kamma)*. Having willed, one performs an action by body, speech or mind *(manas)*.
>
> A3: 415

Cetanā, it will be remembered, is the fifth aspect of *nāma* as defined in the early *Nikāya* literature. In the "Cūlavedalla Sutta", *citta-saṁkhāra* is defined as being comprised of *vedanā* and *saññā*.[83]

83. M1: 301.

In terms of the integrated interpretation offered above this would mean that the "recycling" of *vedanā* and *saññā* into *viññāṇa* occurs through the karmic mechanism of *saṁkhāra*, in particular *citta-saṁkhāra*. The present interpretation suggests too that it is in this specific sense that *saṁkhāra* as the second link in the twelvefold enumeration of *paṭiccasamuppāda* is to be understood. Thus the effects of *karma*, in the Buddhist context are not conceived of as some kind of punitive blight hovering about and waiting to strike. Instead, karmic effects are actualized by the psychological tendency of consciousness to recycle into itself and arise again similar to and on the basis of what it was in the past.

The foregoing interpretation of *saṁkhāra* suggests that the term as used in early Buddhism denotes not an aspect of consciousness as the terms *vedanā* and *saññā* do, but rather a tendency observed in the reciprocal interaction between consciousness and its objects, namely, the tendency to "build up" or "construct" on the basis of previous interactions. This interpretation has the particular virtue of clarifying to a great extent the conceptual basis underlying the use of the term *saṁkhāra* in apparently widely varying contexts in early Buddhist literature. There are essentially three such contexts: 1) *saṁkhāra* as a psychological term, as in *paṭiccasamuppāda* or the five aggregates; 2) *saṁkhāra* denoting all things made or constructed of parts, as in the common phrase "all *saṁkhāras* are impermanent".[84] and 3) *saṁkhāra* as *karma* of three kinds, by mind, speech or body. According to the present interpretation, the first two contexts amount to the same thing, since the constructed objects *(rūpa)* of the world are what they are only by virtue of how they appear in the conceptual construction *(nāma)* of consciousness. In other words, the appearance of an orderly, "constructed" world depends upon the tendency of consciousness to recycle into itself and arise again on the basis of what it was in the past.

This tendency, it was argued above, also accounts for the basic mechanism of *karma*, the third context of the term *saṁkhāra*. Fundamentally *karma* is volition *(cetanā)*, and volition is an aspect

---

84. Dhp. #277-78.

of the conceptual content *(nāma)* of consciousness. Thus, consciousness, having arisen and lapsed, arises again conditioned by *saṁkhāra*, its previous, overall conceptual construction. Having arisen, its present conceptual construction will tend to reappear in its next arising. *Saṁkhāra* is, then, not an operative aspect of consciousness, but merely the recurrent configuration of the operative aspects, both "objective" and "subjective" of consciousness. Karmicly speaking, some aspects of this recurrent configuration may be insignificant. They may involve nothing more than the perceptual continuity in the repetitive, interdependent arising of *viññāṇa* and *nāma-rūpa*, for example, the conceptual content "pleasant, red, round, apple". On the other hand, more firmly established aspects of the recurrent configuration of consciousness may account for moral and psychopathological phenomena such as greed, hatred and delusion *(lobha-dosa-moha)*, the roots of moral un-skill *(akusala-mūlāni)*. The Buddhist theory of moral retribution and psychopathology is a broad and complex subject. It is not claimed that the foregoing observations account in full for the mechanism of *karma*. These observations are, however, basic to a correct understanding of the Buddhist doctrine of *karma* and its retributive effects. In the absence of a divine judge, these effects must occur entirely within the realm of a given stream of consciousness in mutually dependent interaction with its objects. Many passages in early Buddhist literature make use of a popularly accessible, and somewhat quaint concept of the effects of *karma* as the universal counterpart of human justice. The essential Buddhist theory of *karma*, however, is based upon rational observation of the nature of human consciousness.

The fundamentals of Buddhist moral theory and psychopathology are outlined in the second part of the *paṭiccasamuppāda* formula, beginning with "feeling *(vedanā)* conditions desire *(taṇhā)*". Though this subject will not be dealt with here in detail, a few general remarks, for the sake of completeness, will serve to integrate the present psychological interpretation with the remaining members of the chain. It will be noted that *vedanā* acts as a condition of both *saññā* and *viññāṇa* in the self-contained cycle of consciousness described above. In the formula of *paṭiccasamuppāda* it is also said to be the condition of *taṇhā*, desire, the second noble truth, the cause of suffering. It is no doubt due to this fundamental position of desire in the Buddhist system of thought that a quaint and entirely variant version of conditioned arising, based on *taṇhā*, is enumerated in the "Mahānidana Sutta". This variant causal sequence runs as follows:

> Thus, Ānanda, feeling *(vedanā)* conditions desire *(taṇhā);* desire conditions pursuit; pursuit conditions acquisition; acquisition conditions lust and greed; lust and greed condition attachment; attachment conditions possession; possession conditions avarice; avarice conditions jealousy, and jealousy is the basis of many evil, unskilled things (such as) resorting to blows and weapons, strife, disputation, quarrelling, confrontation, slander and lies.
>
> D2: 58-59

This situation has the effect of emphasizing the distinction between the first part of *paṭiccasamuppāda* as a psychological theory and the second part, beginning with *taṇhā,* as a moral teaching. It is undeniable that the most fundamental conditioned arising in Buddhism is the arising of suffering *(dukkha)* because of desire *(taṇhā).* In the standard *paṭiccasamuppāda* formula, however, several causal links are interposed between *taṇhā* and the arising of *dukkha,* indicated by the stock phrase "thus is the arising of this entire mass of suffering". These are: grasping *(upādāna)* conditioned by desire *(taṇhā),* existence *(bhava)* conditioned by grasping, birth *(jāti)* conditioned by existence, and decay and death *(jarāmaraṇa)* conditioned by birth. The composite nature of this list of interposed links is fairly obvious. Birth, decay and death are the most pervasive and obvious aspect of suffering. Not only biological birth, decay and death, however, is meant, but also the inherent necessity in all arisen things to pass away. "Decay and death" includes both impermanence *(aniccatā)* and its subjective counterpart soullessness *(anattatā).* These last two links and the stock ending of the *paṭiccasamuppāda* formula are thus an elaboration upon the fundamental insight of Buddhism, the first noble truth.

The conditioning of birth by existence *(bhava),* however, is somewhat artificial. In the Buddhist context, birth and death, continual arising and ceasing, in themselves constitute existence. Existence may in no sense be construed as an independent, abstract ground of being within which, on the basis of which or in relation to which arising and ceasing occur. It makes little difference if we substitute for "existence" the word "becoming" as a translation. The fact remains that *bhava* is the continual process of arising and ceasing, birth and death. The relationship of *bhava* to *taṇhā,* by contrast, is obvious, in that *taṇhā* is most commonly said to be of three kinds: sensual desire *(kāma-taṇhā),* desire for existence *(bhava-taṇhā)* and desire for non-existence *(vibhava-taṇhā).* The interposition of grasping *(upādāna)* between these two is also reasonably clear, partly because grasping is the actualization of desire. *Upādāna* is also an important term in early Buddhism by virtue of its frequent association with the five aggregates. These are often called *upādāna-khanda* "aggregates involving grasping", aggregates which, in other words, grasp and are grasped at.

> These five grasping-aggregates are themselves grasping. There is no grasping apart from the five grasping-aggregates. Whatever is lust and greed in (relation to) the five grasping aggregates, friend Visākha, that as such is grasping.
>
> M1: 299-300

The present interpretation urges that the five aggregates are not to be construed as merely an analysis of the individual as a mind based on a body. This simple dichotomy is indicated by the terms *citta,* or *viññāṇa,* and *kāya.* The five aggregates, instead, are an analysis of the experience which arises when all of the interdependent conditions upon which the occurrence of consciousness depends are fulfilled. These components of experience, the five aggregates, though entirely interdependent and thus essenceless, may mistakenly be construed as a soul *(atta),* or as permanent *(nicca).* Thus, when it is said that one may misconstrue form *(rūpa)* as a soul or self, more is meant than that one might simply think of the body *(kāya)* as the essence of one's existence. Instead, it is implied that one may grasp at any apparently external material form — for example money, house, clothes — as a definition of self. Objectively or subjectively, with regard to the essenceless, interdependent arising of consciousness and its objects, there may occur the desire *(taṇhā)* "let me or it exist *(bhava)* or not exist *(vibhava)*". Existence is thereby misconstrued as a permanent state instead of a rapid succession of arising and ceasing, birth and death. The object of this desire as well as the desiring subject will be confined to one or a combination of the five "aggregates of grasping" *(upādāna-khanda)*. According to the nature of the grasping and its object, consciousness will arise in one of the three *bhavas, kāma-bhava, rūpa-bhava,* or *arūpa-bhava.* Though these three "realms of existence" are often construed cosmologically, they are all at least theoretically accessible to any human being by means of the *rūpa* and *arūpa jhānas.* Existence *(bhava)* in any realm is of the same essential nature, characterized by birth *(jāti),* decay, and death *(jarāmaraṇa),* or infinitesimally, by the continual arising and ceasing of consciousness and its objects, whether gross or sublime.

This examination of the close-knit interrelationship among early Buddhist technical terms could and should be greatly expanded. For the purposes of the present study, however, it is sufficient to note that, contrary to what many scholars have said, the two fundamental theoretical complexes of Buddhist psychology, *paṭiccasamuppāda* and the five aggregates, are intended as an analysis of both the individual and the world. They are not merely an explanation of the functioning of the individual within a real, external, independent universe, as assumed by Jain or Ājīvika doctrines. There may or may not be such a universe, but early Buddhism does not concern itself with such ontological speculations. Early Buddhism is not, as it is often characterized, a type of realism, nor is it a pluralistic system in the sense of posing a speculative enumeration of irreducible interacting elements *(dhamma)* of matter and consciousness.[85] Instead, early Buddhism incorporates, in a fundamentally rational theoretical system, the basic insight of the Upaniṣadic synthesis of Vedic and yogic thought, namely that the human being is the supreme being and that all of the mysteries of the universe are generated and resolved within the human mind.

---

85. See Nyanaponika, *Abhidhamma Studies,* pp. 39-43.

In orthodox Hinduism, the Upaniṣadic insight into the inseparability of human consciousness and the universe was cast in a mold based on the evocative concepts of an ancient mythological cosmogony. Starting with this same, essentially humanistic insight, the historical Buddha, in a remarkably far-sighted way, dispensed with the speculative, mythological elements of religion during his age. He sought to focus the ultimately transforming religious emotion upon the human shortcoming of ignorance *(avijja)*. As the ultimate term in the formula of conditioned arising *avijja* is analogous to the Upaniṣadic *ātman-brahman* in the role of source and mainstay of this fundamentally unsatisfactory universe. *Avijja* unlike *ātman-brahman*, is not a cosmological or metaphysical principle as such. It is not the material and motive source of the universe which was sought in the *Upaniṣads*. Nevertheless, according to the *paṭiccasamuppāda* formula, the cessation of ignorance entails the cessation of each of the other links in the formula. This cessation, as demonstrated above, has profound cosmological implications, in that the cessation of *nāma-rūpa* implies, in the Pāli *suttas* as in the *Upaniṣads*, the cessation of the manifold universe of appearances. The early Buddhist *suttas* do not concern themselves with the metaphysical speculations implicit in such a concept. In a later age, however, Buddhism in India found itself in a position of challenging and being challenged by the ponderous machinery of systematic Hindu philosophy. At this time it was this very concept — the interdependence of perceiver, perception and perceived — which formed the basis of both Mādhyamaka and Vijñānavāda Buddhist philosophy.

In the *Abhidhamma* and commentarial traditions of Theravāda Buddhism, this concept was largely ignored in favor of a theory of "reals" *(dhamma)* which actually has little or no basis in the Pāli *suttas*. If, as is often the case, the Theravādin *Abhidhamma* and commentarial traditions are taken as the definitive basis for interpretation of the Pāli *suttas*, then either the so-called second and third turnings of the wheel of *Dharma* appear to be Buddhist heresies. Otherwise, depending on one's bias, the Pāli *suttas* appear to be an intentionally corrupted edition of the teachings of the Buddha.

The present work attempts to resolve a significant part of this problem by interpreting early Buddhist psychology on the basis of antecedent and contemporary rather than subsequent psychological speculations. Fundamental, deep-level similarities exist between the basic insights of Upaniṣadic and early Buddhist psychological speculations. Most notably, these are a layered model of consciousness and a theory of interdependence between the subject and the objects of consciousness.

The latter consideration is of particular significance in any attempt to formulate a coherent historical development within Buddhism. The mutual interdependence of consciousness and its objects precludes valid knowledge of any independent reality, whether objective or subjective. This point is the basis of Mādhyamika dialectic, according to which there can be no self-existent knower, no self-existent thing known, and no self existent act of knowing. Section three of Nāgārjuna's *Mādhyamika-kārikā* is dedicated to establishing this proposition.

> 1. Vision, hearing, smelling, tasting, touching and thought are the six sense faculties. The area of their concern is that which is seen [heard, smelled] and so forth. ...
> 4. When no vision occurs, nothing whatsoever is being seen. How, then, is it possible to say: Vision sees?
> 5. Therefore vision does not see, and "no-vision" does not see. Nevertheless, it is explained that also the "seer" is to be known only by his vision.
> 6. There is no "seer" with vision or without vision; Therefore, if there is no "seer" how can there be vision and the object seen? ...
> 9. [Likewise] hearing, smelling, tasting, touching and thought are explained as vision. Indeed, one should not apprehend the "hearer", "what is heard", etc., [as self-existing entities].[86]

The interdependence of consciousness and its objects is also crucial in the Vijñānavāda school of Buddhism. As classically formulated by Dharmakīrti, Vijñānavāda metaphysics does not depend upon refutation of objective reality. It depends rather upon the inability of any opponent to establish such a reality, and upon Dharmakīrti's ability to proceed without reference to any objective reality. In

86. Tsl. by F.J. Streng, *Emptiness,* Abingdon, New York, 1967, pp. 186-87.

highlighting the necessary subjective component in any experience of an object, the Pāli *Nikāyas* pave the way for discarding the objective referent of consciousness altogether.

Though archaic in terminology and less than rigorous in empirical basis and deduction, the *Nikāya* treatment of consciousness and its objects is in some ways more contemporary in outlook than either the Mādhyamika or Vijñānavāda systems which superseded it in India. Rather than advancing an anti-empirical metaphysical theory as such, the Pāli *suttas* are merely critical of common sense epistemology. They do not affirm or deny an independent, objective reality. They merely illustrate that the way in which reality is perceived is determined largely by subjective factors. This implicit critique of the possibility of objective knowledge, simultaneously recognizing the potency of objective reality, is in harmony with much contemporary philosophy. This same critique, couched as it is in psychological terms, also anticipates the fundamental tenet of modern psychotherapy: that the way in which reality is perceived is determined largely by subjective factors, and therefore can be altered.

The integrated interpretation of early Buddhist psychology offered above is somewhat at odds with the traditional Theravāda interpretation. Doubtlessly this will be viewed by some as a disadvantage. To be sure, the present interpretation goes somewhat beyond what is explicitly stated in the ancient *suttas* themselves. It does not, however, go as far beyond the original Pāli *suttas* as the *Abhidhamma* and commentarial literature go. The present interpretation, moreover, offers the following significant advantages. 1) It renders the psychological content of the Pāli *suttas* more coherent. 2) It locates this content within the context of antecedent and contemporary psychological speculation in India. 3) It makes possible a more satisfactory explanation of the development of Buddhism in India. 4) Finally, the present interpretation enhances the contemporary relevance of the original teachings of the founder of one of the world's great religious traditions.

Conclusion

This inquiry into the origins and development of theoretical psychology in ancient India has covered a time-span of over a millennium. Because of scarcity of directly relevant material during the Vedic age, because of the difficulty of accurately dating Upaniṣadic passages, and because of the absence of material representing pre-Buddhist yogic traditions, many of the conclusions reached have been tentative. Many of these conclusions are at variance with traditional accounts of the origins, development and interrelations between Hinduism and Buddhism. These traditional accounts, of course, are often at variance with one another and are often advanced with little or no textual or historical evidence. Most of the conclusions herein fit in fairly well with contemporary scholarly accounts of the development of religion and philosophy in ancient India, though there is still plenty of room for controversy.

At any rate, the present study has been an attempt to research and elucidate a crucial facet of ancient Indian thought without uncritical recourse to any account of its development, whether ancient or modern. This study has relied exclusively on texts verifiably representing the several periods of the era in question. It has insisted that these texts speak for themselves. Some speculation has been necessary in order to fill in the gaps in the account that emerges from analysis of the ancient texts themselves.

Whether or not the speculative content of this study will stand up to critical scrutiny remains to be seen. The evidence considered herein, however, is virtually exhaustive of the relevant textual material of the age in question. The footnotes, though tedious, should be particularly useful for further research, as they contain almost every psychologically relevant reference in the *Ṛg Veda* and the thirteen principal *Upaniṣads*. Because of the abundance and relative consistency of the Buddhist material, I have not attempted to note all relevant passages individually. I believe, however, that representatives of all of the various types of passages — and thereby any internal inconsistencies in the Pāli *suttas* themselves — have been noted.

Much work remains to be done in this and related areas of ancient Indian thought. At present, there are few who are in a position to pursue the research needed. For those fortunate enough to be in such a position, the best of luck.

Select Bibliography

Books:

Agrawala, Vasudeva S., *Vision in long Darkness*, Vedāraṇyaka Ashram, Varanasi, 1963.

Barua, Benimadhab, *A History of Pre-Buddhistic Philosophy*, Motilal Banarsidass, Delhi, 1921, reprint 1970.

Basham, Arthur Lewellyn, *History and Doctrine of the Ājīvikas*, Luzac, London, 1951.

Belvalkar, S.K. and R.D. Ranade, *History of Indian Philosophy*, Bilvakuñja Publishing House, Poona, 1927.

Bergaigne, Abel, *La Religion vedique*, 4 vols., F. Vieweg, Paris, 1887-97.

Blair, Chauncy, *Heat in the Ṛg Veda and the Atharva Veda*, American Oriental Society, New Haven, 1961.

Bloomfield, *Religion of the Veda*, G.P. Putnam's Sons, New York, 1908.

Conze, Edward, *Buddhism: Its Essence and Development*, Harper & Row, New York, 1959.

— *Buddhist Thought in India*, George Allen & Unwin, London, 1962, reprints by University of Michigan Press, Ann Arbor, 1967, 1973.

— *Thirty Years of Buddhist Studies*, Cassirer, Oxford, 1967.

Dasgupta, Surendranath, *A History of Indian Philosophy*, 5 vols., Combridge University Press, London, 1922, reprint by Motilal Banarsidass, Delhi, 1975.

— *Indian Idealism*, Cambridge University Press, London, 1922.

— *Yoga as Philosophy and Religion*, London, 1924, reprint by Motilal Banarsidass, Delhi, 1973.

— *Yoga Philosophy*, Motilal Banarsidass, Delhi, 1930, reprint 1974.

Deussen, Paul, *The Philosophy of the Upanishads*, translated by A.S. Geden, T. & T. Clark, 1906, reprint by Dover, New York, 1966.

— *The System of Vedānta*, translated by Charles Johnston, Chicago, 1912, reprint by Motilal Banarsidass, Delhi, 1972.

Eliade, Mircea, *Yoga Immortality and Freedom*, 2nd ed., Princeton University Press, 1969.

Gambhirananda, Swami, *Brahma Sūtra Bhāṣya of Śaṅkarācārya*, 2nd ed., Advaita Ashrama, Calcutta, 1972.

— *Eight Upaniṣads*, 2 vols. Advaita Ashrama, Calcutta, 1972.

Gonda, Jan, *The Vision of the Vedic Poets*, Mouton & Co., The Hague, 1963.

Govinda, Lama Anagarika, *The Psychological Attitude of Early Buddhist Philosophy*, 2nd ed., Rider, London, 1969.

Griffith, Ralph Th., *The Hymns of the Ṛg Veda*, revised ed., Motilal Banarsidass, Delhi, 1973.

Guenon, René, *Man and His Becoming According to the Vedānta*, Noonday, New York, 1958.

Guenther, Hevert V., *Philosophy and Psychology in the Abhidharma*, 2nd ed., Motilal Banarsidass, Delhi, 1974.

Hare, E.M., *The Book of the Gradual Sayings*, vols. 3 & 4, Pāli Text Society, London, 1934, 1935.

Hiriyana, M., *Outlines of Indian Philosophy*, George Allen & Unwin, London, 1932, 8th reprint 1970.

Horner, I.B., *The Collection of the Middle Length Sayings*, Pāli Text Society, London, 3 vols.: 1954, 1957, 1959.

Hume, Robert Ernest, *The Thirteen Principal Upanishads*, 2nd ed., Oxford University Press, London, 1977.

Jayasuriya, W.F., *The Psychology and Philosophy of Buddhism*, YMBA Press, Colombo, 1963.

Jayatilleke, K.N., *Early Buddhist Theory of Knowledge*, George Allen & Unwin, London, 1963.

Johansson, Rune, *The Psychology of Nirvāṇa*, George Allen & Unwin, London 1969.

— *The Dynamic Psychology of Early Buddhism*, Humanities Press, Atlantic Highlands, New York, 1979.

Karunadasa, Y., *Buddhist Analysis of Matter*, Department of Cultural Affairs, Colombo, 1967.

Keith, Arthur Berriedale, *Buddhist Philosophy in India and Ceylon*, Oxford University Press, London, 1923.

— *The Religion and Philosophy of the Veda and Upanishads*, 2 vols., Harvard University Press, 1925, reprint by Motilal Banarsidass, Delhi, 1976.

Knipe, David, *In the Image of Fire*, Motilal Banarsidass, Delhi, 1975.

Larson, Gerald James, *Classical Sāṁkhya*, Motilal Banarsidass, Delhi, 1969.

Law, B.C., *A Designation of Human Types*, Pāli Text Society, London, 1922, reprint 1979.

Limaye, V.P. and R.D. Vadekar, *Eighteen Principal Upaniṣads*, Vaidika Samsodana Mandala, Poona, 1958.

Mādhavānanda, Swami, *The Bṛhadāraṇyaka Upaniṣad with the Commentary of Śaṅkarācārya*, 5th ed., Advaita Ashrama, Calcutta, 1975.

Mahadevan, T.M.P., *The Philosophy of Advaita*, Ganesh & Co., Madras, 1957.

Mainkar, T.G., *Sāṁkhyakārikā of Īśvarakṛṣṇa*, 2nd ed., Oriental Book Agency, Poona, 1972.

Metha, Mohan Lal, *Jaina Philosophy*, P.V. Research Institute, Varanasi, 1971.

Monier-Williams, Monier, *Sanskrit-English Dictionary*, Oxford University Press, London, 1899, 4th reprint 1970.

Muir, John, *Original Sanskrit Texts*, 5 vols., Oriental Press, Amsterdam, 1967.

Ñāṇamoli, *The Path of Purification*, 3rd ed., Buddhist Publication Society, Kandy, 1975.

Ñāṇananda, *The Magic of the Mind*, Buddhist Publication Society, Kandy, 1974.

— *Concept and Reality in Early Buddhist Thought*, Buddhist Publication Society, Kandy, 1976.

Nārada, *The Dhammapada*, Mahā Bodhi Society, Calcutta, 1970.

Nikhilananda, Swami, *The Māṇḍukyopaniṣad*, 6th ed., Sri Ramakrishna Ashrama, Mysore, 1974.

Nyanaponika, *Abhidhamma Studies*, Buddhist Publication Society, Kandy, 1965.

— *The Heart of Buddhist Meditation*, Samuel Weiser, New York, 1973.

Oldenberg, Hermann, *Buddha: His Life, His Doctrine, His Order*, translated by W. Hoey, Williams and Norgate, London, 1882.

Organ, Troy Wilson, *The Self in Indian Philosophy*, Mouton & Co., The Hague, 1964.

Pande, Govind Chandra, *Studies in the Origins of Buddhism*, 2nd ed., Motilal Banarsidass, Delhi, 1974.

Panikkar, Raimundo, *The Vedic Experience*, University of California Press, Berkeley, 1977.

Piyadassi, *The Psychological Aspect of Buddhism*, Buddhist Publication Society, Kandy, 1972.

Poussin, L. de la Vallée, *Théorie des douze causes*, Luzac London, 1913.

Radhakrishnan, Sarvapali, *The Principal Upaniṣads*, George Allen & Unwin, London, 1953, reprint 1969.

Raghavachar, S.S., *Śrī Rāmānuja on the Upaniṣads*, Prof. M. Rangacharya Memorial Trust, Madras, 1972.

Rahula, Walpola, *What the Buddha Taught*, revised ed., Gordon Frazier, Bedford, 1978.

— *Zen and the Taming of the Bull*, Gordon Frazier, London, 1978.

Rhys Davids, C.A.F., *The Birth of Indian Psychology and its Development in Buddhism*, Luzac, London, 1936.

— *A Buddhist Manual of Psychological Ethics*, Pāli Text Society, London, 1900.

— *Buddhist Psychology*, Luzac, London, 1924.

— *Early Buddhism*, Constable & Co., London, 1914.

— and William Stede, *Pāli-English Dictionary*, Pāli Text Society, London, 1921-25.

Sarathchandra, E.R., *Buddhist Psychology of Perception*, University of Ceylon Press, Colombo, 1958.

Sinha, Jadunath, *Indian Psychology*, 2 vols., Sinha Publishing House, Calcutta, 1958.

Smart, Ninian, *Doctrine and Argument in Indian Philosophy*, George Allen & Unwin, London, 1964, reprint, 1969.

Sontakke, N.S. and C.G. Kashikar, eds. *Ṛgveda Saṁhitā with the Commentary of Sāyanācarya*, 5 vols., Vaidika Saṁśodana Maṇḍala, Poona, 1941-51.

Stcherbatsky, Th., *The Central Conception of Buddhism*, Royal Asiatic Society, London, 1923, reprint by Motilal Banarsidass, Delhi, 1970, 1974.

— *Buddhist Logic*, 2 vols., Dover, New York, 1962. (First published by the Akademy of Science of the U.S.S.R., Leningrad, c. 1930.)

Swāhānanda, Swami, *The Chāndogya Upaniṣad,* Sri Ramakrishna Math, Madras, 1956.

Thomas, Edward J., *The History of Buddhist Thought,* 2nd ed., Routledge & Kegan Paul, London, 1951, reprint 1971.

Vajirañāṇa, Paravahera, *Buddhist Meditation in Theory and Practice,* 2nd ed., Buddhist Missionary Society, Kuala Lumpur, 1975.

Velankar, H.D., *Ṛksūktaśatī,* Bharatiya Vidya Bhavan, Bombay, 1972.

Woods, James Haughton, *The Yoga System of Patañjali,* Harvard University Press, Cambridge (U.S.A.), 1914, reprint by Motilal Banarsidass, Delhi, 1972.

Zimmer, Heinrich, *Philosophies of India,* Princeton University Press, 1951, reprint 1974.

Articles:

Bondopadhyaya, S.P., "The Theory of *Mokṣa* in Jainism", *Jain Journal,* vol. 11, July, 1976, pp. 13-20.

Bothra, Pashpa, "An Examination of the *Jaina* Theory of Perception", *Jain Journal,* vol. 7, Oct. 1972, pp. 95-97.

Filliozat, Jean, "The Psychological Discoveries of Buddhism", *University of Ceylon Review,* vol. 13, nos. 2 & 3, April-July, 1955, pp. 69-82.

Jacobi, Hermann, "The Original Traits of Jainism", *Jain Journal,* vol. 2, Oct. 1967, pp. 67-93. (Partial reprint of "The Metaphysics and Ethics of the *Jainas*", *Transactions of the Third International Congress of the History of Religions,* vol. 2.).

Jain, Prem Chand, "Moksa in Jainism", *Jain Journal*, vol. 9, April, 1975, pp. 113-119.

Jayatilleke, K.N., "Some Problems of Interpretation and Translation (I)", *University of Ceylon Review*, vol. 7, no. 3, July 1949, pp. 208-224.

— "Some Problems of Interpretation and Translation (II)", *University of Ceylon Review*, vol. 8, no. 1, Jan., 1950, pp. 45-55.

Johansson, Rune, *"Citta, Mano* and *Viññāṇna:* A Psychosemantic Investigation", *University of Ceylon Review*, vol. 23, nos. 1 & 2, April-Oct., 1965, pp. 165-216.

Kalupahana, D.J., "The Philosophy of Relations in Buddhism (part I)", *University of Ceylon Review*, vol. 20, no. 1, April 1962, pp. 19-54.

— "The Philosophy of Relations in Buddhism (part II)", University of Ceylon Review, vol. 20, no. 2, Oct. 1962, pp. 188-208.

Kalupahana, D.J., *"Sarvāstivāda* and the Theory of *Sarvam Asti"*, *University of Ceylon Review*, vol. 24, nos. 1 & 2, April-Oct., 1966, pp. 94-105.

Murti, T.R.V., "The Two Traditions in Indian Philosophy", *University of Ceylon Review*, vol. 10, no. 3, July, 1952, pp. 221-42.

Rhys Davids, C.A.F., "The Soul Theory in Buddhism", *Journal of the Royal Asiatic Society*, 1903, pp. 587-91.

— "Santana", *Journal of the Royal Asiatic Society*, 1904, pp. 370-71.

— "The Vedalla Sutta as Illustrating the Psychological Basis of Buddhist Ethics", *Journal of the Royal Asiatic Society*, 1894, pp. 321-33.

Sarathchandra, E.R., "*Abhidhamma* Psychology of Perception and the Yogācāra Theory of Mind", *University of Ceylon Review*, vol. 4, no. 1, pp. 49-57.

— "Bhavāṇga and the Buddhist Psychology of Perception", *University of Ceylon Review*, vol. 1, no. 1, April 1943, pp. 94-102.

Werner, Karl, "The Vedic Concept of the Human Personality", Unpublished paper delivered at the XIIIth Congress of the International Association for the History of Religions, University of Lancaster, England, July 1975.

Wijesekera, O.H. de A., "The Concept of *Viññāṇa* in Theravāda Buddhism", *Journal of the American Oriental Society*, vol. 84, July-Sept. 1964, pp. 254-59.

— "Vedic *Gandharva* and Pāli *Gandhabba*", *University of Ceylon Review*, vol. 3, no. 1, April 1945, pp. 73-107.

— "Upaniṣadic Terms for Sense Functions", *University of Ceylon Review*, vol. 2, no. 1, nov. 1944, pp. 14-24.

— "Pāli *'Vado Vadeyyo'* and Upaniṣadic *'Avāka-Anadāraḥ'*", *University of Ceylon Review*, vol. 3, no. 2, Nov. 1945, pp. 89-94.

— "Vitalism and Becoming", *University of Ceylon Review*, vol. 1, no. 1, April 1943, pp. 49-58.

Abbreviations and Original Texts Cited

A *Aṅguttara Nikāya*, followed by vol. no., colon, and page no. in PTS Pāli ed.

A.B. *Aitareya Brāhmaṇa*, R.A. Śāstri, ed., University of Travancore, Trivandrum, 1942. Translated by A.B. Keith, *Rigveda Brāhmaṇas*, Harvard Univ. Press, Cambridge, 1920.

A.U. *Aitareya Upaniṣad*, text and translation in (R).

A.V. *Atharva Veda*, translated by W.D. Whitney, Harvard Univ. Press, Cambridge, 1905.

B.S. *Brahma Sūtra*, attributed to Bādrayāṇa, with a commentary by Śaṅkara, Translated by Gambhirananda. Advaita Ashrama, Calcutta, 1972.

B.U. *Bṛhadāraṇyaka Upaniṣad*, text and translation in (R).

C.U. *Chāndogya Upaniṣad*, text and translation in (R).

D *Dīgha Nikāya*, followed by vol. no., colon, and page no. in PTS Pāli ed., or by # and the no. of the *sutta*.

Dhp. *Dhammapada*, followed by verse no. Text and translation in Nārada, *The Dhammapada*, Mahā Bodhi Society, Calcutta, 1970.

ERE *Encyclopaedia of Religion and Ethics*, James Hastings, ed., Scribner's, New York, 1913-22.

(G) Griffith, *The Hymns of the Ṛg Veda*, revised ed., Motilal Banarsidass, Delhi, 1973, (indicates his translation).

(H) Hume, R.E., *The Thirteen Principal Upanishads*, 2nd ed., Oxford Univ. Press, London, 1977 (indicates his translation).

J.U.B. *Jaiminīya Upaniṣad Brāhmaṇa*.

K.U. *Kaṭha Upaniṣad*, text and translation in (R).

Ks.B. *Kauṣītakī Brāhmaṇa*, translated by Keith, *Rigveda Brāhmaṇas*, Harvard Univ. Press, Cambridge, 1920.

Ks.U. *Kauṣītakī Upaniṣad*, text and translation in (R).

M *Majjhima Nikāya*, followed by vol. no., colon, and page no. in PTS Pāli ed., or by # and the no. of the *sutta*.

(M) Muir, *Original Sanskrit Texts*, Oriental Press, Amsterdam, 1967, (indicates his translation).

Ma.U. *Māṇḍūkya Upaniṣad*, text and translation in (R).

— *Mīmāṁsādarśana*, attributed to Jaimini, with commentary by Śābara. Translated by G. Jha, *Śābara Bhaṣya*, Oriental Institute, Baroda, 1933.

Mt.U. *Maitrī Upaniṣad*, text and translation in (R).

Mu.U. *Muṇḍaka Upaniṣad*, text and translation in (R).

— *Nirukta*, attributed to Yāska, Ānandāśrama, 2 vols., 1921 & 1926.

— *Nyāya Bindu*, by Dharmakīrti, Chowkamba Sanskrit Series, Varanasi, 1954. Translated by Stcherbatsky, *Buddhist Logic*, vol. 2, Dover, New York, 1962.

PTS Pali Text Society, (following a quoted passage, in parentheses, indicates PTS translation).

P.U. *Praśna Upaniṣad*, text and translation in (R).

(R) Radhakrishnan, *The Principal Upanisads*, Unwin, London, 1953, (indicates his translation).

Ṛg *Ṛg Veda*, with Sāyana's commentary, Vaidika Saṁśodhana Mandala, Poona. With the commentaries of Skandasvāmin, Udgītha, Venkaṭa and Mudgala, Vishvesvaranand Vedic Research Institute, Hoshiarpur.

S *Saṁyutta Nikāya*, followed by vol. no., colon, and page no. of PTS Pāli ed.

S.B. *Śatapatha Brāhmaṇa*, Chowkhamba ed. by A. Weber, 1964. Translated by J. Eggeling in SBE.

SBB *Sacred Books of the Buddhists*, F. Max Müller, ed., (following a quoted passage, in parentheses, indicates SBB translation).

SBE *Sacred Books of the East*, F. Max Müller, ed., (following a quoted passage, in parentheses, indicates SBE translation).

S.K. *Sāṁkhya-kārikā*, attributed to Īśvarakṛṣṇa. Translated by T.G. Mainkar and G.J. Larson, Oriental Book Agency, Poona, 1972.

Sn. *Sutta-nipāta*, followed by verse no. in PTS Pāli ed. Translated by Fausböll in SBE, vol. 10.

S.U. *Śvetāśvatara Upanisad*, text and translation in (R).

T.B. *Taittirīya Brāhmaṇa*.

T.S. *Taittirīya Saṁhitā*. Translated by A.B. Keith, *The Veda of the Black Yajus School*, Harvard Univ. Press, Cambridge, 1914.

T.U. *Taittirīya Upaniṣad*, text and translation in (R).

— *Udāna*, followed by page no. in PTS Pāli ed.

Vbh. *Vibhaṅga*, followed by page no. in PTS Pāli ed.

Vsm. *Visuddhimagga*, followed by chapter and section of PTS Pāli ed. Translated by Ñāṇamoli, *The Path of Purification*, Buddhist Publication Society, Kandy, 1975.

GLOSSARIAL INDEX

Abhidhamma 129, 240, 242, 244, 310, 326, 327, 329

Aditi 11, 15, 20, 29, 34, 66, 176, 197, 198, 217, 268

afterlife (see rebirth, ancestors, heaven, hell, paradise) 8, 25-28, 30, 35, 38, 42, 44-46, 51, 56, 63, 64, 68, 83, 90, 94, 95, 144, 145, 154-157, 159, 162, 164, 172, 183, 283, 286

—**heavenly in Vedas** 38-56

—**hereditary in Vedas** 27, 31-38, 66-69, 145, 158

aggregates (five in Buddhism) 303, 308-310, 321, 292, 294, 295, 302-304, 308-310, 312, 313, 316, 322, 325, 326

Agni (god of fire) 11-14, 29, 31, 33, 41-43, 46, 49-51, 55, 59, 64, 76, 77, 79, 83, 85, 87, 94, 101, 102, 105, 106, 110, 117, 125, 127, 128, 134, 137, 138, 159, 202, 206

ahaṁ-kāra ("I-maker", ego) 231, 253, 256, 257, 280

Aitareya Upaniṣad 35, 44-46, 156-57, 166, 190, 213, 215, 217, 224, 239-241, 246, 248, 249

Ājīvikas 2, 3, 6, 8, 16, 149, 152-53, 166, 182-185, 272, 279, 283, 285, 289-90, 298, 302, 326

√an (to breathe) 91

ānanda (bliss, q.v.) 263-266, 270, 271, 274, 286, 293

anātman (non-soul) 9, 182-84, 273-76, 281-98

anatta (Skt. anātman, q.v.)

ancestors (pitṛ, q.v.) 26, 29, 33-35, 37, 38, 43, 48, 53, 55, 68, 83, 90, 156, 158-160, 162, 263, 286

annihilationism (uccheda-vāda) 146, 285, 286

antar-ākasa (subjective, "internal space", see heart) 238-39, 243

Āraṇyakas 4, 5

asaṅkhata (uncompounded element, see nirvāṇa) 272, 273

Aśoka 5

asu (vitality, q.v.) 41, 55, 80, 82-84, 86, 87, 89, 95, 145, 240

asura (Titan) 11, 12, 37, 83, 97, 204

Asya-vāmīya Hymn 13-16, 50, 60-62

Atharva Veda 3, 5, 46, 148

ātman (soul, q.v.) 8-9, 18, 23, 25, 31, 39, 43, 49, 59, 64, 65, 78-81, 84, 91-96, 110, 116, 145, 155, 157, 165, 170, 173, 177, 180, 182, 186, 187, 190-192, 196, 197, 200, 201, 204-206, 210, 224, 230, 234, 238, 241, 245, 249, 250, 252, 256, 258, 259, 261, 265-267, 269, 271, 272, 274, 277, 279, 286, 289, 290, 302, 327

atta (soul, Skt. ātman) 286, 290, 291, 325

avidya (ignorance) 274

āyu (life span) 36, 42, 49, 54, 59, 80-82, 84-91, 94, 95, 145, 206, 268, 299-301

bindu (semen, q.v.) 61, 242

bliss (ānanda, q.v.) 62, 119, 219, 225, 235, 249, 250, 263-266, 269-271, 274, 287, 293

Brahmā 11, 157, 167-169, 171, 237, 263, 287

Brahmajāla Sutta 285, 286, 290, 291

Brahman (universal principal, see ātman) 9, 14, 17, 18, 23, 30, 31, 72, 78, 91, 110, 156, 158, 163, 173, 175, 180, 187, 188, 196, 198, 202, 210, 218, 232, 236, 239, 245, 246, 249, 250, 264, 266-271, 274, 276, 327

Brāhmaṇas 4, 5, 35, 43, 48, 53-54, 56 61, 121-22, 138, 139, 148, 156, 158, 176, 190, 204, 283

breath (prāṇa) 16, 39, 41, 50, 59, 79, 80, 82, 87, 91-94, 145, 147, 155, 161, 177, 186-193, 196-214, 216-218, 220-225, 228, 230, 233, 234, 236, 237, 240-242, 245, 249, 250, 252, 257, 267-269, 271, 295, 299, 302

Bṛhadāraṇyaka Upaniṣad 11, 17, 23, 30, 32, 33, 41, 42, 47, 48, 56, 72, 73, 78, 95, 110, 111, 155, 156, 158-168, 170-177, 179, 186-189, 191-196, 198, 199, 202, 204, 205, 209-216, 221, 222, 223, 224, 226-228, 230, 234-35, 237-246, 248-251, 260-264, 268, 276, 277, 279-281, 287, 294, 295, 302, 305

Buddha 4, 5, 22, 182-184, 266, 271-275, 281, 282, 283, 285-294, 297, 298, 300, 302, 303, 305-307, 314, 320, 327

buddhi (awareness, intellect) 189, 214, 231, 233, 247, 253, 254, 256-260, 269, 270, 278, 280

buddhi-indriya (faculties of perception, see indriya) 189, 214

Buddhism 1-9, 22, 23, 27, 57, 59, 61-63, 74, 78- 79, 96, 99, 100-101, 107, 111, 115, 118, 143, 146, 149, 154, 165-66, 168, 178, 182-84, 223, 232, 234-236, 240, 242-44, 248, 251, 253, 271-275, 279, 282-99, 301-306, 310, 315-330
cakras 242
Carvakas (materialists) 146, 183
catuṣ-koṭi (tetralemma) 266
cetana (volition) 102, 255, 296, 304, 317, 320-322
cetas (thought, see citta) 99, 103, 251
Chāndogya Upaniṣad 51, 78, 89, 90, 95, 111, 159, 161, 162, 164, 166-168, 172, 173, 176, 177, 180, 186-188, 190, 194, 198-202, 204, 205, 209, 210, 212-216, 218, 219, 224, 226, 228, 234, 236-239, 241, 243, 244, 248, 249, 252, 256, 260-263, 276, 281, 294, 305
chariot 47, 48, 104, 106, 111, 112, 114, 125, 227, 257-259, 269, 276-278, 294
— **as symbol** 47-48, 104, 106, 111-14, 125
— **simile of consciousness** 227, 257-59, 269, 276-78, 294
— **wheel as symbol** 235
√cit (to think, see citta) 80, 97-108, 115, 123, 131, 132, 140-142, 251, 253, 254
citta (thought, mind, q.v.) 96, 98, 99, 101-108, 118, 119, 132, 141, 233, 242, 251-254, 257, 291, 296, 297, 302, 304, 313, 320-322, 325
conditioned arising (see paṭiccasamuppāda)
creation
— **as a dream or projection** 170-80, 226-38
— **reversal of** 173-180, 234-38
— **in Ṛg Veda** 9-24
— **in Upaniṣads** 169-84, 231-38
Cūlavedalla Sutta 301, 321
death 16, 17, 25-27, 32-38, 40, 43, 45, 46, 49, 50, 53-57, 58, 59, 61, 64, 66-68, 79-84, 86, 87, 145, 150, 153, 155-159, 162, 163, 165, 168, 169, 171, 172, 192, 197, 200-202, 205, 206, 217, 223, 234, 237, 238, 241, 244, 251, 261, 273, 286, 290, 299, 300, 302, 324-326
deep sleep (see dream) 170-172, 237, 249, 251, 262, 264, 265, 301
deva-loka (world of the gods, see heaven) 159, 167
deva-yāna (path of the gods, i.e. to heaven) 48, 159, 167
Dharmakīrti 328

√dhī (to have a vision) 99-100, 102, 107, 112, 114, 129, 131-32
dhī (a vision) 80, 98-100, 102, 106-108, 112-114, 118, 120, 123, 124, 129-135, 138, 139, 141, 142, 225, 231, 246
dhīti (see dhī) 129, 130, 134, 137, 138
digestion and vitality 161, 163, 198, 199, 201, 203, 209, 213, 215, 242, 301
Dīrghatamas 13-16, 50, 60-62
dream (see deep sleep) 116, 119, 170, 172, 193, 202, 210, 226, 227, 234, 237, 249, 264, 265
duḥkha (suffering, see dukkha) 22, 220, 221, 224, 248
dukkha (Skt. duḥkha) 273, 302, 313, 324
Eliade, Mircea 58, 148
Family Books (of Ṛg Veda) 6, 9, 13, 14
fire
— **digestive** 198-203
— **five fires** 159-63
— **universal** 197-98
five aggregates (see aggregates) 292, 294, 295, 302, 304, 309, 310, 313, 316, 322, 325, 326
five fires (see fire) 159-63
funeral 26, 35, 38, 39, 41, 47, 83, 167
— **hymns in Ṛg Veda** 39-43, 47, 49
gandharva 116, 117, 171, 263
Gonda 101, 108, 113, 123, 125, 127-131, 133-139, 141, 231
Griffith, Ralph Th. 19, 21, 34, 39-44, 46, 49-52, 55, 56, 60, 65, 67, 68, 70, 83, 87, 88, 92, 101, 105, 116, 121, 126
hadaya vatthu ("heart basis" in Abhidhamma) 242
heart 22, 84, 88, 96, 97, 103, 104, 107-109, 112, 115, 119-129, 132, 140-142, 170, 173, 180, 210, 217, 231, 233, 237-243, 250, 260, 266, 267, 295, 297
— **space within** (see antar-ākaśa) 238-39, 243
heaven (see paradise, pitṛ-loka, deva-loka) 10-12, 16, 19, 25, 27, 32-45, 47, 48, 53, 54, 58-60, 64, 66, 67, 77, 80, 82-84, 112, 113, 116, 118, 122, 127, 136, 138, 147, 155-158, 160, 165, 167-169, 192, 206, 238, 263, 267, 287
Hiraṇyagarbha 16

hṛd (heart, q.v.) 80, 84, 88, 96-98, 104, 107-109, 112, 114, 115, 117, 119, 120, 121-129, 132, 139-142, 217, 231, 237-239, 242, 260
hṛdaya (heart, q.v.) 237, 240
immortality 19, 32, 35-37, 49, 53, 54, 58, 77, 85, 125, 144, 147, 148, 157, 168, 206, 219
Indra 10, 12, 13, 18, 30, 31, 44, 54, 60, 71, 72, 76, 77, 79, 85, 88, 105, 112, 123, 127-129, 135, 136, 138, 192, 262
indriya (faculties, see buddhi-, karma- and jñāna-indriya) 189, 214-216, 220, 230, 248, 257, 258
Īśa Upaniṣad 155, 167, 205, 276
Jainism 2, 3, 6, 8, 21, 149-53, 162, 166-69, 182-85, 188, 272, 279, 283, 285, 289-92, 298, 326
jhāna (meditative absorption) 146, 286, 293, 299, 312
jīva (soul, life) 36, 80-85, 145, 200, 201, 277, 300
jīvātman (vital, individual soul, see paramātman) 15, 277, 180, 289
√jñā (to be conscious, to know) 99-100, 108, 247-51
jñāna (knowledge, consciousness, perception, see √jñā) 189, 214, 248, 259
jñāna-indriya (faculties of perception, see indriya) 189, 214, 248
Kaṭha Upaniṣad 46, 47,72, 114, 156, 167, 168, 181, 186, 188, 205, 214, 216, 227, 228, 238, 239, 241, 243, 247, 248, 249, 255, 257-60, 277-279, 281, 294
kamma (volitional action, Skt. karma) 320, 321
karma (action) 15, 151, 155, 157, 165, 166, 187-189, 196, 214, 215, 219, 220, 222, 228, 244, 276, 281, 288, 290, 292, 300, 320-323
karma-indriya 189, 215
Kauṣītakī Upaniṣad 4, 87, 157-159, 167-169, 172, 178, 187, 191, 204, 205, 211, 216, 220, 221, 224-226, 230, 234-37, 239, 241, 243, 249, 252, 276, 277, 297, 4, 157, 168, 178, 220, 234-237, 249
kāya (body, see śarīra) 111, 288, 291, 299, 301, 304, 309, 311, 318, 320, 321, 325
Kena Upaniṣad 167, 168, 188
Keśin ("long-haired" ascetic in Ṛg Veda) 69, 74, 146, 148
kratu (will) 80, 84, 88, 90, 96-98, 107, 108, 114, 115, 124, 126, 132, 134, 135-142, 188, 231, 240, 244, 245, 296
kṣetrajña ("field-knower", i.e. soul) 181, 187, 246, 255, 256

liṅga-śarīra (subtle, transmigrating body, see subtle body) 277, 279, 280, 289, 291, 180
Lokayata (materialist) 183
Madhupiṇḍika Sutta 307, 314
Madhva 281
Mādhyamika 327, 328, 329
magic, mechanism in Ṛg Veda 65-67, 72-73
Mahā Hatthipadopama Sutta 308-310
Mahākaccana 314
Mahānidāna Sutta 312
Mahāparinibbāṇa Sutta 300
Mahā Vedalla Sutta 301
Mahāyāna Buddhism 4, 5
Maitrī Upanishad 4, 20, 186-188, 210, 213, 214, 216, 224, 227, 228, 230-33, 236-38, 241, 242, 245-250, 252-257, 259, 260, 264-267, 275-279, 281, 288, 291, 307
√man (to think) 97-100, 107, 108, 112, 115, 120, 123, 124
manas (mind, q.v.) 41, 60, 64, 79, 80, 82, 84, 88, 89, 96-100, 104, 106-120, 122, 123, 124, 126, 127, 129, 131, 132, 139-142, 151, 175-177, 186, 188, 191, 204, 207, 209-213, 216, 217, 220, 222, 225, 227, 230, 231, 233, 234, 236, 238-241, 243-247, 249-254, 256-261, 264, 269, 278, 280, 284, 289, 291, 294-296, 302, 307, 308, 312, 316, 317, 319, 320, 321
— **creative in Ṛg Veda** 110-112
— **swiftness** 117-18
manasikāra (attention) 304, 317
Māṇḍukya Upanishad 172, 187, 188, 202, 228, 248-250, 264, 265, 280
mano-maya-kāya (miraculous "mind-made-body") 211, 288
māyā (illusion) 53, 72, 97
Mīmāṁsā 195

mind (see manas, citta) 18, 21-23, 34, 41, 59, 61-63, 79, 82, 84, 88-90, 96, 97, 99, 103, 104, 106, 107, 108-124, 128-133, 135, 139-141, 151, 155, 167, 175-178, 186, 188, 191-194, 196, 197, 199-205, 207-213, 215, 217, 219, 220, 221, 223, 225-228, 230, 232-234, 237, 239, 240, 245-247, 250, 258-260, 264, 269, 271, 278, 280, 281, 283, 285-288, 291, 297, 298, 302, 304, 307, 317, 320-322, 325, 326

Mitra 12, 13, 28, 44, 71, 101

mokṣa (spiritual release) 8, 25, 31, 48, 56

monism 8, 9, 13, 16, 17, 21, 23, 24, 25, 30, 95, 144, 172, 173, 179, 186, 188, 197, 207, 208, 257, 274, 276, 278, 280, 281, 284, 285, 287, 290, 297

Muir, John 19, 26, 39-42, 44, 49, 55, 83

Müller, Max 10, 83

Muṇḍaka Upaniṣad 78, 158, 164, 165, 167, 179, 186-188, 202, 214, 237-241, 248, 249, 252, 276, 277, 306

Naciketas 46, 156

Nāgārjuna 328

nāma (name, see nāma-rūpa) 61, 73-79, 174-176, 179, 187, 192-194, 196, 212, 220, 222, 303-306, 310-312, 316-318, 320-323, 327

nāma-rūpa (name-and-form, see nāma) 174-176, 179, 192, 61, 74, 78, 79, 303-306, 310-312, 316, 318, 320, 323, 327

name-and-form (see nāma-rūpa)

Nāsadīya Sukta 18, 21, 24, 109, 110, 124, 207, 232

nibbāṇa (Skt. nirvāṇa, q.v.) 287, 293, 302

nirvāṇa 8, 9, 168, 182, 183, 271-275, 285, 287, 303

Pāli Suttas 2, 5, 248, 282-331

paradise (see heaven, deva-loka, pitṛ-loka) 26, 56

paramātman (supreme soul, see jīvāman) 15, 180, 277, 289

√paś (to see) 97, 115, 116

paṭiccasamuppāda (conditioned arising) 184, 275, 292, 295, 304, 305, 307, 310, 311, 313-316, 318-324, 326, 327

phassa (sensual contact) 304, 305, 307, 308, 311, 312, 314-318

— **adhivacana** (verbal/conceptual) 311-313, 315-317

— **paṭigha** (sensual) 311, 312, 315, 316

pitṛ (ancestors) 26, 34, 35, 37, 68, 83, 159, 160, 197, 244

pitṛ-loka (world of the ancestors, i.e. paradise) 159, 160, 244

pitṛ-yāna (path of theancestors, i.e. rebirth) 48, 159

prajñā (wisdom, knowledge, consciousness) 188, 221, 225, 234, 235, 241, 248-251, 256, 265, 277, 301
prajñā-ātman (intelligent soul, cp. jīvātman, paramātman) 204, 234, 241, 249, 250, 277
prakṛti (matter, nature) 181, 199, 254-257, 259, 279, 280
prāṇa (vital force, breath, q.v.) 41, 47, 80-82, 87, 91-93, 96, 161, 170, 173, 175, 177, 186-189, 191, 203-206, 209, 210, 213, 214, 216, 217, 219, 220, 221, 222, 234-236, 240, 241, 245, 249, 250, 252, 257, 267, 268, 280, 295, 299, 302
— **digestive** 198, 201-203
— **prāṇa-saṁvāda** (dispute among the breath faculties) 204-205, 230
— **superiority to mind** 191-207,
Praśna Upaniṣad 227, 228, 78, 159, 167, 172, 181, 186, 187, 198, 204, 205, 211, 214, 215, 227, 228, 238, 241, 249, 250, 256, 257, 277, 279
punar-mṛtyu (re-death, see rebirth) 156, 158, 163, 36
Puruṣa (deity) 18-24, 29, 34, 42, 176, 242
puruṣa (person, soul, q.v.) 41, 42, 58, 78, 79, 111, 145, 155, 159, 161, 170, 180-182, 186, 187, 238-240, 245, 246, 248, 250, 255, 256, 258, 259, 261, 265, 267, 276, 289, 290, 295, 302
Puruṣa Sukta 18-21, 58, 79
Radhakrishnan, Sarvapali 4, 28, 50, 52, 201, 234, 237, 239, 240, 259, 268, 279, 280
Rāmānuja 281
rebirth 2, 7, 8, 9, 25, 27, 28, 30-34, 36-38, 44-46, 48-53, 56, 57, 94, 144-71, 179, 180-185, 188, 205, 236, 237, 241, 244, 254, 260, 276-92, 297, 301-305
— **absense in Ṛg Veda** 28-57
— **Ājīvika theory** 152-53
— **archaic Jain theory** 150-51, 188
— **Buddhist denail** 273-76, 281-98
— **classic Upaniṣadic theory** 271-81
— **cyclical** 159-64, 167
— **development in Upaniṣads** 154-66
— **linear** 164-66
re-death (punar-mṛtyu, q.v.) 156, 53-56

ṛta (cosmic order) 104, 105, 123
rūpa (form, see nāma-rūpa) 38, 61, 70-75, 78, 79, 116, 141, 174-179, 186, 187, 192, 193, 196, 210, 212, 220, 240, 295, 303-312, 314-318, 320, 322, 323, 325-327
salāyatana (six sense spheres) 311, 318
Sāma Veda 195
Sāmaññaphala Sutta 285
saṁjñā (perception) 231, 248, 249, 260, 261
saṁkalpa (intention) 210, 233, 240, 243-246, 257
saṁkhāra (mental formations) 296, 300, 301, 303, 304, 308, 313, 320-323
Sāṁkhya 180-184, 199, 227, 228, 235, 246, 254-257, 259, 260, 270, 279, 280, 290-292
saṁsāra (realm of rebirth) 15, 22, 46, 48, 151, 152, 165, 233, 254, 255, 258, 271, 272, 292
Śaṅkara 30-32, 45, 46, 168, 181, 182, 186, 196, 201, 237, 239, 268, 270, 271, 280
saññā (perception, Skt. saṁjñā) 248, 286, 300, 303, 304, 308, 312-317, 319, 321-323
śarīra (body, see kāya) 38, 40, 69, 70, 77, 180, 218, 240, 269, 277, 279, 280, 289, 291
sassatavāda (eternalism) 285
Śatapatha Brāhmaṇa 43, 44, 53, 56, 95, 138, 139, 177, 194, 204, 211, 212, 242
sat-cit-ānanda (being-consciousness-bliss, definition of brahman) 264
Satipaṭṭhana Sutta 313
Sāyana 15, 18, 20, 29, 31, 32, 37, 39, 40, 42, 44, 46, 48, 50-52, 56, 64, 69, 83, 86, 89, 90, 92, 121
semen (as vital force) 33, 68, 155, 161, 190, 204, 207, 217, 221, 240, 242
senses (see indriya, salāyatana) 95, 147, 151, 171, 172, 190, 211-34, 247-249, 260, 261, 269, 284, 286, 289, 294-296, 305, 307-309, 312, 316, 317
sensus communis (mind as integrating "common sense") 222, 225, 226, 231, 243, 245, 259, 289, 294, 296, 317
shamanism 145-48

Soma (Vedic deity) 41, 46, 66, 73, 74, 76, 85, 93, 102, 126, 133, 160, 161
soma (hallucinogenic drug) 17, 18, 41, 46, 55, 58, 88, 93, 113, 125-127, 138, 145-47, 160, 161
soul (see ātman, jīva, puruṣa) 2, 7, 8, 9, 15, 25, 36, 43, 50, 57, 64, 65, 91, 110, 111, 144-146, 150-154, 156, 157, 159, 162, 164, 166-174, 179, 180, 181-183, 185-191, 193, 196-198, 201, 203-210, 216, 224, 227, 230, 231, 232, 236, 238, 241-247, 249-253, 255-272, 275, 276, 277-281, 283-286, 288-302, 325
— **absense in Ṛg Veda** 25-57
— **ātman, q.v.**
— **chariot simile** 257-59
— **denial in Buddhism** 182-84, 281, 288-98
— **five kośas (layers)** 285-86, 265-71
— **jīva, q.v.**
— **jīvātman, q.v.**
— **kṣetrajñā, q.v.**
— **liṅga-śarīra, q.v.**
— **paramātman, q.v.**
— **prajñā-ātman, q.v.**
— **puruṣa, q.v.**
— **relation to wind in Ṛg Veda** 92-95
— **subtle body, q.v.**
— **sukṣma-śarīra, q.v.**
— **two soul theory** 188-89, 271-81, 289-92
— **in Upaniṣads** 166-85, 254-81
subtle body (see sūkṣma-śarīra, liṅga-śarīra) 41, 42, 65, 277, 280
sūkṣma-śarīra 277
śunyatā (emptiness) 242
svarga (heaven, q.v.) 167
Śvetaketu 48, 173, 200
Śvetāśvatara Upaniṣad 51, 166, 167, 180, 181, 186, 188, 239, 243, 249, 255-257, 275, 277
Taittirīya Upaniṣad 20, 110, 111, 156, 177, 188, 204, 210, 213-16, 219, 224, 238, 239, 248, 250, 262-71, 275, 280, 285, 294, 301
√tan (to spin, weave, see tanū) 67, 68
taṇhā (thirst, desire, Skt. tṛṣṇā) 272, 311, 316, 319, 323-326

tanū (form, body, see √tan) 37-39, 41-43, 63-72, 75, 76, 79, 80, 83, 84, 86, 87, 90, 93-95, 145, 155, 156, 186, 197, 198
tapas (mystic heat) 17, 22, 26, 145-148, 198, 199, 207, 270
Theravāda Buddhism 5, 242, 327, 329
thig-le (semen, q.v.) 242
transmigration (see rebirth) 150-153, 162, 179, 181, 183, 244, 280, 292
turīya (state beyond deep sleep) 264, 265
uccheda-vāda (annihilationism, q.v.) 285
universe (see creation)
— **as dream or projection** 170-180, 226-32, 234-38, 326
— **as a person** 17-21, 150-51, 174-75
— **reabsorption of** 173-80, 234-38
upādāna (grasping) 308, 309, 316, 324-326
upādāna-khanda (grasping aggregates, see aggregates) 309, 325, 326
Vak (Goddess of speech, see vak) 86, 102, 142
vak (speech) 176, 191
Varuṇa 10-13, 44, 47, 66, 71, 92, 101, 104, 105, 135, 141, 270
vāta (wind, vital breath) 92, 299
vayas (food, vital force) 80, 84, 87-90, 197
vāyu (wind, compared to breath) 39, 59, 79, 80, 92, 191, 205, 206, 219, 236, 299
vedanā (feelings) 99, 100, 303, 304, 308, 311-319, 321-324
Vedānta 14-15, 20-21, 30, 72, 93-94, 180-184, 232, 279, 280
Veṅkaṭa 15, 48
√vid (to know) 99, 100, 108, 248
vijñāna (consciousness, see viññāṇa) 99, 100, 170, 188, 231, 238-240, 245, 248-251, 254, 256, 259, 261, 265, 266, 269, 280, 289, 291, 295, 296, 301, 302
Vijñānavāda Buddhism 320, 327-329
viññāṇa (consciousness, Skt. vijñāna) 291, 295, 296, 300-316, 318-320, 322, 323, 325
vitality (see digestion and breath) 36, 38, 41, 43, 80-84, 86, 90, 95, 96, 128, 197, 200, 201, 206, 207, 209, 218, 230, 242, 266, 268, 269
— **in Buddhism** 299-301
— **in Ṛg Veda** 79-96
— **in Upaniṣads** 191-207

wind (compared to breath) 39, 58, 59, 71, 79, 80, 92-94, 102, 111, 116, 117, 141, 145, 188, 190, 191, 204-206, 217-219, 236, 245, 267, 299, 306

Yajñāvalkya 155, 156, 163, 170, 174, 222, 223, 227, 228, 235, 237, 241, 250, 260, 261

Yajur Veda 195

Yama (God of death) 14, 41, 43, 48, 49, 54, 83, 156

Yāska 7, 15, 20, 121

yoga 2, 8, 25, 58, 112, 144-146, 148-150, 156, 179-181, 208, 219, 233, 242, 255, 266, 270, 279, 287, 288, 297

— **archaic** 149-53

— **and Buddhism** 1-5

— **and Shamanism** 145-49

— **in Upaniṣads** 144-84

Yogācāra Buddhism 234, 236, 253

Zimmer, Heinrich 1, 2, 21, 56, 145, 149